FORGOTTEN CONTINENT

FORGOTTEN CONTINENT

THE BATTLE FOR LATIN AMERICA'S SOUL

MICHAEL REID

YALE UNIVERSITY PRESS

NEW HAVEN AND LONDON

For information about this and other Yale University Press publications please contact:
U.S. Office: sales.press@yale.edu   yalebooks.com
Europe Office: sales@yaleup.co.uk   www.yalebooks.co.uk

Set in Minion and Gill Sans by Carnegie Book Production, Lancaster

Printed in the United States of America by Sheridan Books

Library of Congress Cataloging-in-Publication Data

Reid, Michael
    Forgotten continent: the battle for Latin America's soul / Michael Reid.
        p. cm.
    Includes bibliographical references and index.
    ISBN 978-0-300-11616-8 (alk. paper)
    1. Latin America—Politics and government—1980- 2. Latin America—Economic conditions—1982- 3. Democracy—Latin America—History. I. Title.
    F1414.3.R35 2007
    980.03'8—dc22

                                                                    2007013492

A catalogue record for this book is available from the British Library.

10 9 8 7 6 5 4 3

To Emma, and in memory of Patricia Reid

'First, we must cure ourselves of the intoxication of simplistic and simplifying ideologies'

Octavio Paz

'The democratic will is vulgar; its laws, imperfect. I admit all this. But if it is true that soon there will be no middle way between the empire of democracy and the yoke of one man, ought we not try rather for the former than submit voluntarily to the latter?'

Alexis de Tocqueville

'It is not by chance that reforms are so difficult'

Fernando Henrique Cardoso

CONTENTS

ILLUSTRATIONS

CHARTS AND TABLES

Charts

Tables

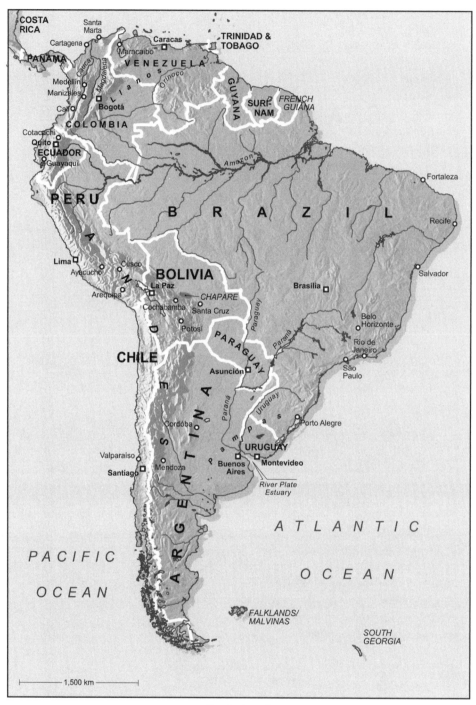

South America

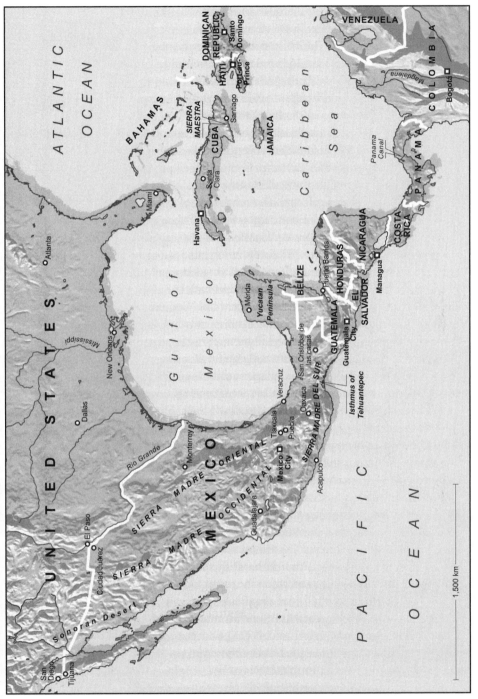

Mexico, Central America and the Caribbean

PREFACE

I began to think about writing this book in 1999, shortly after Brazil's government was forced into a devaluation it had tried, at great financial cost, to prevent. The devaluation prompted much commentary abroad that Brazil was reverting to type, that it was doomed by fecklessness and misgovernment. I had been living in São Paulo for the previous three years as *The Economist* bureau chief and had a different view. I was convinced that Brazil was undergoing a deeper process of economic reform, democratisation and progressive social change that, for all its imperfections and difficulties, would survive the devaluation. Shortly afterwards, I returned to London to take up my current job of editing The Americas section of *The Economist*. The press of events in Latin America forced me to put the book on one side for several years. Those events, especially the collapse of Ecuador's economy in 1999–2000 and of Argentina's in 2001–2, prompted wider comment to the effect that the economic reforms known as the Washington Consensus had failed Latin America. The gloom spilled over to the region's democracies, which were held variously to be under widespread threat and to be corrupt and elitist shams unworthy of the name. The setbacks in Ecuador and Argentina were indeed real and severe, and involved policy mistakes. But I did not believe that they proved the general case that economic reform or democracy had failed, nor that Latin America was in the throes of generalised revolt as was widely asserted. It was a desire to revindicate (to use a good Spanglish term) the notion of underlying democratic progress in Latin America that prompted me to start writing this book in 2004. Since then, of course, the outlook for democracy and development has improved considerably in many countries, though not in others.

The narrative that follows is based on my own observation and experience of Latin America. I first visited the region in 1980 and returned to live in Lima from 1982 to 1990, working mainly for the *Guardian* and the BBC. When I arrived, the 'old model' of protectionist, state-led development was still available for inspection, even if it was in its death-throes. The dictators were departing, though Chile would remain firmly in Pinochet's grip for several more years. I lived through hyperinflation and the terrorist insurgency of *Sendero Luminoso* in Peru, made frequent visits to Bolivia as it tried to reform its economy and to Colombia as it was opening up its political system even as it suffered the murderous assaults of drug traffickers, guerrillas and paramilitaries. In 1990 I moved to Mexico City, becoming *The Economist*'s correspondent. I spent the next three and a half years observing Carlos Salinas's ultimately flawed effort to modernise Mexico and its authoritarian political system, the winding down of the wars in Central America, the impact of the collapse of the Soviet Union on Cuba and of low oil prices on Venezuela. After an interlude in London, the three years covering Brazil and the southern cone offered *inter alia* an insight into the complexities of economic reform in democracy, the deceptive glitter of Menem's Argentina, the potential (as yet unfulfilled) of the Mercosur trade block and Chile's attempts to throw off the shadow of Pinochet. During all these years I enjoyed the journalist's enormous privilege of being able to watch history unfold at close quarters and to ask questions of many of its protagonists. I benefited from the time, opinions and wisdom of many hundreds of Latin Americans, from presidents to peasant farmers, as well as of professional observers of the region. And having married a Peruvian and acquired a Peruvian daughter, I was constantly exposed at home and through friends to Latin American perspectives on life.

I wanted to try to make sense of what I had learned in a more systematic way. What follows draws upon those conversations and upon my reporting, especially for *The Economist* over the past 17 years (and occasionally on that of colleagues at the magazine). But this book is not a collection of articles. Indeed, it is not a typical journalist's book. In trying to explain why things are as they are in Latin America, I have occasionally trespassed on academic territory. Like all trespassers, I have done so in a spirit of defiance of prohibition and in expectation of a clip round the ear from the proprieters of the territory infringed. Conversely, I hope that my step has been sufficiently light not to arouse boredom in other readers.

It was my original intention that the book's narrative would begin around 1980. But it quickly became apparent to me that I would have to start much further back. That decision was in the spirit of the conversations I had each time I ventured into a country new to me in Latin America. A seemingly simple question about some aspect of contemporary politics would lead within a few minutes to an exposition of the peculiarities of that country's nineteenth-century history; I soon came to know that this was the signal for a fascinating discussion, often lasting several hours. Since history and historical figures are being daily invoked by Latin American politicians, I make no apology for having decided to start the story around 1810, when most Latin American countries began their struggle for independence. The three historical chapters are preceded by two introductory chapters, which set out what is at stake in the region and discuss prevailing explanations for its relative difficulty in establishing prosperous democracies. The later chapters start with an assessment of the record of economic reform in the region since 1982. The next two chapters look in detail at what has emerged as the central argument in today's Latin America, between what I have called populist autocracy, as personified by Hugo Chávez and others, and democratic reformism, exemplified here in contrasting ways by Chile, Brazil and Mexico. It is my contention that at issue in this debate are differing views of the region's history as well as sharply different political and economic choices, and in that sense it is 'a battle for Latin America's soul'.[1] Further chapters sketch in more of the background to that debate, looking at social change and the unfinished tasks of state reform in the region, and assessing the overall record of democracy. The last chapter looks at Latin America's place in the world and sums up the argument of the book: largely overlooked by the outside world, most of the 'forgotten continent' is moving forward on a path of democratic reformism, even if that is contested in some places.

There are several obvious pitfalls in this kind of book. The first is that almost any generalisation about such a large and diverse region as Latin America invites instant rebuttal by means of citing one or more countries where it doesn't hold. Yet the book would become unmanageable in length and unbearably tedious if it did not make some effort at synthesis. So I have tried to pay due obeisance to diversity without neutering the explanatory potency of generalisation. Another problem is selection. I have deliberately concentrated on the larger countries. In neglecting some of the smaller ones, I can only plead that the manuscript was already long enough to test the patience of the average reader. The same reasoning led me to drop chapters that I had originally planned on the environment and natural resources and on business and finance. I have tried to incorporate some of these points elsewhere. There are many other topics that might have warranted sections or chapters that receive only cursory treatment, such as the Central American wars or transitional justice (the issue of holding past dictatorships to account for their crimes). My justification was that much has been written about such matters elsewhere. What interested me for the purposes of the book was to focus on the history, experience, problems and possibilities of democracy and of economic reform and development in Latin America. Last, history teaches that anyone who has the temerity to express cautious optimism about Latin America's prospects risks being swiftly exposed by events as being ingenuous. So be it.

I have already referred to the debt I owe to many Latin Americans, and to other observers of the region. Sadly, only a few of those concerned are mentioned in the text. Though it is invidious to do so, of many others, I must single out Maritza Alva, who has been generous in her friendship and in sharing with me over many years her extraordinary knowledge of San Juan de Lurigancho and its people.

Thanks are due to several other groups of people. James Dunkerley, Charlie Foreman and Brooke Unger gave me valuable comments on the whole manuscript from differing perspectives and were eagle-eyed in spotting mistakes; Malcolm Deas saved me from numerous errors of nineteenth-century history; Gino Costa, Joe Foweraker, Phil Gunson, Michael Shifter and Peter West made helpful observations on individual chapters. The usual disclaimers apply.

I am also indebted to colleagues at *The Economist*, which has provided me with a uniquely civilised, collegial and stimulating environment in which to work. I am especially grateful to Peter David, Bill Emmott and John Micklethwait for indulging my obsession with Latin America, encouraging me in the writing of this book and enabling me to do so while continuing with my day job. My debt to them is all the greater because the opinions that follow are strictly my own, not those of *The Economist*; some of them would not necessarily be shared by some, even many, of my colleagues. Thanks are due also to all of *The Economist* correspondents in Latin America of recent years, whose knowledge and insights I have been fortunate to be able to share; to Sophie Bradford and Celina Dunlop for generous assistance in finding the pictures; to Carol Howard for help with charts; and to Phil Kenny for drawing the maps. I am indebted to Bill Emmott for putting me in contact with Arthur Goodhart, my agent, who saw a book where many might not have done and then nursed it into life with a skill and dedication that surely went far beyond duty. Thanks are also due to Robert Baldock for his enthusiastic support of the project and to Hannah Godfrey and the rest of the team at Yale for efficient production work.

Lastly, I am deeply grateful to three women. Patricia Reid bore with great stoicism her younger son's prolonged sojourns on the other side of the world. It is a matter of great sadness that she did not live to see the publication of this book about which she was so enthusiastic. Roxani, my daughter, was similarly understanding during the years of writing. Lastly Emma Raffo, my wife, has shared with me over many years her deep insight into all things Latin American; she has read every page with critical attention and occasionally with passionate disagreement. In a very real sense, it is her book too.

Michael Reid
London, June 2007

CHAPTER I

THE FORGOTTEN CONTINENT

Scarcely a month goes by without some political leader or ageing rock star urging the citizens of the world's richer countries to do something to aid Africa. With similar frequency, as yet another statistic of economic advance comes out of Asia, we are assured that the world's future lies in China and India. Meanwhile, the terrorist attacks of 11 September 2001 and those thereafter in Madrid, London and elsewhere meant that for the United States and Europe, the Middle East and the broader Islamic world became of overwhelming strategic interest.

But what of Latin America, the other great region of the developing world? 'Latin America doesn't matter ... People don't give one damn about Latin America now,' Richard Nixon told a young Donald Rumsfeld in 1971 when advising the future American Defence Secretary which part of the world to avoid if he wanted a brilliant career.[1] With the exception of the Central American wars of the 1980s, Nixon's judgement has largely held true. To be sure, the sickening collapse of Argentina's economy in 2001–2 attracted horrified glances, as well as scaring some foreign investors away from Latin America altogether. Colombia's drug lords and guerrilla violence sometimes made headlines. Fidel Castro remained a curiosity, stubbornly ensconced in his communist island well into old age, having seen off nine American presidents. Then, suddenly, the veil of oblivion thrown over Latin America by much of the media in Europe and the United States parted. Presidential elections in a dozen countries in the thirteen months from November 2005 aroused a flurry of outside interest. This mainly focussed on the notion that Latin America was moving irrevocably to the left and out from under the thumb of the United States, where it was asserted to have forever languished. Much of the interest was catalysed by Hugo Chávez, Venezuela's voluble populist president, and by his search for disciples in the region. He aroused fears in many quarters (and hopes in others) that he might be another Castro – but one armed with oil. Seemingly in his wake stood Evo Morales, a cocagrowers' leader and socialist with a pudding-basin haircut and a stripy jumper, who became the first Bolivian of Andean Indian descent to be elected to his country's presidency. In Chile, Michelle Bachelet, whose father died after being tortured by General Pinochet's secret police and who was herself briefly a political prisoner, became the first woman to be elected president in Latin America who did not owe this distinction to marriage to a famous husband (she was a separated mother of three children). In Brazil, Luiz Inácio Lula da Silva, a bearded former trade union leader born in poverty, had been elected in 2002; he shook off a corruption scandal involving his Partido dos Trabalhadores (Workers' Party) to win a second term. Daniel Ortega, a leader of the Sandinista revolution of 1979 and an old foe of the United States, was elected in Nicaragua. In Ecuador, Rafael Correa, who described himself as being of the 'Christian left', was elected. Elsewhere, two other figures seen as leftists, Ollanta Humala, a nationalist former army officer in Peru, and Andrés Manuel López Obrador, a charismatic former mayor of Mexico City, were only narrowly defeated.

Something, it seemed, was stirring in Latin America. But this flurry of interest only served to underline the region's status as a largely forgotten continent. It is neither poor enough to attract pity and aid, nor dangerous enough to excite strategic calculation, nor until recently has it grown fast enough economically to quicken boardroom pulses. It is only culturally that Latin America makes itself felt in the world. Its music, dance, films, novels and painting have edged into the cultural mainstream in both the United States and Europe. Spanish is firmly established as the second international language of the Western world. Taking into account use as both a first and second language, Spanish is spoken by 417 million people, making it the fourth most-spoken tongue after Mandarin, English and Hindi, according to a report commissioned by the British Council. Portuguese is in seventh place, with 191 million speakers, behind Russian and Bengali but ahead of German and French.[2] Brazil is enjoying a surge of popularity that extends far beyond the football field. 'Everyone wants a Brazilian!' proclaimed London's *Observer* newspaper in 2003. 'Everyone loves Brazil,' echoed *Newsweek* the following year, noting the global reach of the country's fashion models, bikinis, capoeira and music. Tango, the jerkily melodramatic dance of Argentina, is in global vogue. So, too, is the dancehall music of pre-revolutionary Cuba, revived in the Buena Vista Social Club. Exhibitions of Mexico's cultural treasures, from the Aztecs to Frida Kahlo, have drawn massive crowds to museums across Europe. Flourishing contemporary art in both Brazil and Mexico is receiving international attention. The Latin American travels two centuries ago of Alexander Von Humboldt, a distinguished natural scientist and writer, provided the subject for Germany's best-selling novel of the past two decades, published in 2005. 'I wanted to write a Latin American novel,' said Daniel Kahlmann, its young and previously unknown author. 'I've written a Latin American novel about Germans and German classicism.'[3] At the other end of the cultural spectrum, Latin American *telenovelas* challenge American soaps for domination of much of the world's television screens, claiming an audience of some 2 billion people. Romantic melodramas from Mexico and Venezuela and grittier social dramas from Brazil have captivated viewers from Russia to Indonesia to the Middle East.[4]

Some Latin Americans have long claimed a superiority in cultural production over their materially more successful northern neighbours. Yet, paradoxically, the region's enhanced cultural prominence stems in part from the increasingly audible and dynamic presence of 41 million *Latinos* in the United States. It also reflects globalisation and one of its consequences, the rise in tourism to Latin America. That has exposed more and more people to the region's awe-inspiringly dramatic geography, the magnificent artefacts left by the ancient civilisations of the Aztecs, Mayas and Incas, and the personal warmth and relaxed approach to life that characterise the average Latin American.

There are, in fact, other reasons apart from culture and language why Latin America, a region of 550 million people, matters to the rest of the world. It is not just a source of migrants and illegal drugs – though it is that. It boasts some of the world's most ecologically important, biodiverse and endangered natural environments, from the Amazon rainforest to the Andean glaciers and the Galapagos Islands. Brazil has more 'environmental capital' than any other country in the world: it has the most biodiversity and its river systems contain more fresh water than those of any other country (almost three times more than those of the United States).[5] Latin America has the world's largest reserves of arable land, and is a storehouse of many important commodities, from oil to metals and foodstuffs. If rich countries were ever to make a serious effort to dismantle agricultural protectionism, Latin America could supply much of the world's food, as well as its industrial raw materials. In 2004, the region had 8.5 per cent of the world's proven oil reserves. Venezuela's government claims that if the extra-heavy oil from the tar sands of the Orinoco is included, its reserves total 235 billion barrels – similar to those of Saudi Arabia.[6] In 2004, Latin America accounted for almost a third of oil imports by the United States. The US Department of Energy expected that percentage to rise over the next two decades.

Demand for Latin American commodities from China, in particular, has helped to fuel a renewal of economic growth in the region. Between 2004 and 2006 the region's economies, taken as a whole, grew at an average of around 5 per cent a year. This was the best performance for more than two decades, though it still lagged that of many other developing countries. Growth remained relatively disappointing in Brazil and Mexico, the two largest economies in the region. But the potential, as always, is beguiling. In 2003 Goldman Sachs, an investment bank, published a report in which it highlighted the growing importance for the world economy of 'the BRICs', a new acronym in which Brazil took its place alongside Russia, India and China. Brazil is the world's fifth-largest country in area and population and its fourth-largest democracy. Its economy was only the eleventh biggest, when measured at market exchange rates in 2005, or the ninth in purchasing-power parity terms. But the Goldman Sachs report argued that Brazil's economy could become larger than that of France by 2031.[7] Brazil is increasingly seen as a country of global significance in other respects, such as in world trade negotiations. It also has aspirations to become a permanent member of the United Nations Security Council.

The relative neglect of Latin America by the outside world is in part benign. No news is good news, after all. Most Latin American countries are no longer home to dictators or death squads and, Argentina and a few others apart, they pay their debts. Yet what is at stake in Latin America in this first decade of the twenty-first century is of much wider importance. Along with Europe and North America, Latin America can claim to form the world's third great group of democracies (with Cuba the lone exception). But Latin America has another, less attractive, distinction: it has the most unequal distribution of income in the world. At the start of the new century, the richest 10 per cent took between 34 and 47 per cent of the pie depending on the country, while the poorest 20 per cent got just 2 to 5 per cent. By contrast, in the United States the richest 10 per cent got 31 per cent and the poorest 20 per cent got 5 per cent, while in Italy the figures were 27 and 6 per cent respectively.[8] That is why, even though most Latin American countries are officially classed as 'middle income', almost two-fifths of Latin Americans – or some 205 million people – lived below their country's national poverty line.[9] So Latin America's attempts to make democracy work, and to use it to create fairer and more prosperous societies, carry wider significance. The region has become one of the world's most important and testing laboratories for the viability of democratic capitalism as a global project.

This book is a progress report from this laboratory of democracy, on Latin America's quest to achieve the twin goals of effective and equitable political systems on the one hand, and sustained economic growth and development on the other. It is first and foremost a reporting job, drawing on a quarter of a century of observation of the region. But it is also an attempt to convey the complex realities that are so often missed by the sweeping generalisations and superficial misrepresentations that are all that Latin America merits in many media outlets in Europe and the United States. Both left and right have tended to treat the region with the utmost condescension. Rich-world leftists, while enjoying the freedoms and prosperity of capitalist democracy, worshipped vicariously Castro's defiance of the United States – increasingly mimicked by Chávez – and presumed that benevolent socialist strongmen were a worthy solution for what they saw as the corruption and poverty of capitalism in the rest of Latin America. Many NGOs, often with the best of intentions and claiming to speak for Latin American counterparts who were dependent upon them for funds, were too ready to preach anti-capitalism while offering no plausible alternative path to development for people who urgently needed it. (Such are the biases of academia that while the activities of multinational companies have received exhaustive study, the interventions of rich-world NGOs in Latin America have attracted scarcely any analysis.) On the other hand, some 'neoliberals' assumed that free markets and free trade were in themselves all that was needed to deliver a promised land. Conservatives often seemed to believe that Latin Americans were a poor, disorganised and hot-headed lot, too immature for democracy and in need of the smack of firm government from a capitalist strongman. All the evidence is that most Latin Americans, for their part, want what most people elsewhere want: freedom, security, clean and effective government, social provision and a vigorous capitalism that creates jobs, opportunities and prosperity. It is the purpose of this book to show why this deceptively simple combination has proved so elusive in the region – but also why for many Latin American countries it is within closer reach today than at any time in their history.

From hope to disappointment

In 1994, Bill Clinton, then newly elected to the presidency of the United States, invited 33 other heads of government from the Americas (all of them except Castro) to a summit in Miami. Remarkably, it was the first such meeting ever held. It had a celebratory ring to it. In the dying years of the Cold War, Latin America had undergone a historic transformation, with the seemingly definitive establishment of democratic government. In 1978, outside the Caribbean, only three countries in the region were democracies; by 1994, all except Cuba and Mexico were (and Mexico was well on the way to becoming one).[10] This democratic wave swept away some of the bloodiest and nastiest dictatorships the Latin American countries had seen in their long – though far from continuous or generalised – history of authoritarian rule. It went hand in hand with a surge of free-market economic reform after half a century of statist protectionism. This prompted much optimism that Latin

America had finally embarked on a path of sustained growth and development. At Miami, it appeared, too, that the two halves of the Americas, for so long locked in tensions and misunderstandings, had embraced diplomatic – as well as political and economic – convergence. The North American Free Trade Agreement (NAFTA), linking Mexico with the United States and Canada, had come into effect in January 1994. At the specific request of the Latin Americans, the assembled leaders pledged to work for a hemisphere-wide Free Trade Area of the Americas.

Halfway through the first decade of the twenty-first century, some of those eager expectations have turned out to be over-optimistic. Indeed, within months of the Miami summit, Mexico suffered a chaotic collapse in its currency, which dashed the previous assumption among many investors that the region would make a swift and seamless journey to development. A dozen years on from Miami, Latin America, as so often in the past, seemed to be poised uncertainly between progress and disappointment. Democracy has held up, more or less. Yet in some countries it is under strain. Carlos Mesa in Bolivia, in June 2005, became the eighth Latin American president since 1999 to have been forced from office before the end of his term.[11] Only three relatively small countries – Costa Rica, Uruguay and, less emphatically, Chile – can claim to be 'consolidated' democracies according to the strictest conceptual yardsticks of political science.[12] Elsewhere, regular and generally clean elections and a far greater respect for human rights than in the past have not been sufficient to ensure the universal application of the rule of law or good governance. Justice is too often slow, venal, arbitrary or simply non-existent. In those circumstances, equality before the law remains a distant prospect: the powerful can usually find ways to protect themselves; the poor often cannot. In many countries, the central institutions of democracy – Congress, political parties, the courts – are viewed with contempt rather than respect. Politicians are derided as corrupt and self-serving – and all too often they are. As traditional parties have declined, politics has fragmented. It has become the norm for presidents in the region to lack a reliable majority in Congress, giving rise to fears about 'governability'.

The spread of democracy across Latin America was accompanied by the widespread adoption of free-market reforms, under the aegis of the 'Washington Consensus', or if you prefer, 'neoliberalism'.[13] Yet the initial fruits of reform were disappointing. Inflation, so long a Latin bugbear, was tamed. Growth picked up at first. But it was checked, and in several countries reversed, as it became clear in a string of wrenching financial crises that capital could leave as fast as it had arrived. Between 1998 and 2002, the region suffered what the UN Economic Commission for Latin America and the Caribbean (better know as CEPAL, from its initials in Spanish) called 'a lost half-decade' of economic stagnation.[14] The upshot was that in the two decades after 1982, the gap between average incomes in Latin America and those in the rich countries widened, while in many parts of Asia it narrowed. This disappointing record meant that the free-market reforms fell into widespread, albeit often unjust, disrepute. Privatisation was particularly abhorred, partly because it was associated in a few cases with corruption or the substitution of public monopolies for private ones. Moreover, the policies of the 'Washington Consensus' were widely – if mistakenly – blamed for Argentina's economic and financial collapse. Though growth has returned, in many countries it has not yet delivered rapid reductions in poverty. Only Chile is a clear economic success. Taken together with the shortcomings of democracy, lack of economic growth and the failure to create sufficient jobs brought a palpable sense of disappointment to the region. The United Nations Development Programme, in a gloomy and influential report published in 2004, concluded that Latin America has failed to develop 'a democracy of citizens'.[15] In the same year, Mario Vargas Llosa, a Peruvian novelist and one of the region's leading liberal thinkers, worried that 'disaffection' with democracy 'may at any time turn into hostility to a system which more and more people consider less capable of resolving the urgent needs of citizens: work, security, education, health and opportunities for progress'. In all these matters, with the exception of Chile, he went on, 'All the Latin American countries are now worse than a quarter of a century ago.'[16]

Perhaps the clearest indicator of the region's relative failure was that some of the brightest Latin Americans were voting with their feet. A century ago, millions of migrants from Europe made new lives in Latin America, especially in the countries of the River Plate region and Brazil. Now, more than 25 million Latin Americans are thought to live outside their own country. The flow of illegal migrants across the southern border of the United States has again become a heated political issue. People have become an important export for some Latin American countries: remittances totalled some $62 billion in 2006, according to an estimate by the Inter-American Development Bank. This figure was a third more than in 2004 and, for the fourth year running, it exceeded the combined flows of foreign direct investment and official development aid to the region.[17] That statistic reflects above all the failure of Latin American societies to provide jobs, opportunities and security for their citizens.

Between progress and the populist temptation

Undeniable though these disappointments and problems were, they told only half the story. In the past few decades, most Latin American countries can

point to steady progress in human development (*see* Chart 1). That is despite
– or perhaps because of – three overlapping sets of wrenching changes in the
region. The first is that of democracy itself, which could draw on a long, if
truncated, tradition of constitutionalism, but had to grapple with ingrained
undemocratic habits and practices. It has also introduced new uncertainty
into economic policy – even if in the long term it can endow policy-making
with far greater predictability and legitimacy. Second, in the half-century since
1950, the region has gone from being predominantly rural to mainly urban
– a transformation that was much more gradual in Europe. That spontaneous
exodus went hand in hand with advances in public health that were prompting
rapid population growth. Average life expectancy in the region rose from 55
years in the 1950s to 71 in the 1990s, while fertility rates at first rose (they began
to fall sharply from the 1960s onwards).[18] The result of these two trends was
the explosive growth of cities: the population of greater São Paulo leapt from
69,000 in 1890 to 12 million in 1976 and some 19 million today. Similarly, the

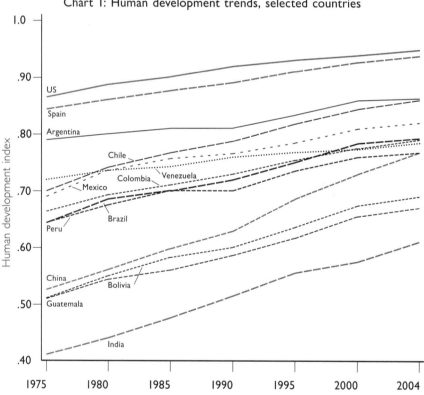

Chart 1: Human development trends, selected countries

Source: Human Development Report 2007, UNDP

population of Lima grew almost eightfold in the four decades to 1981.[19] Not surprisingly, urban growth on this dramatic scale overwhelmed governments, and public services failed to keep pace. So Latin American cities typically reflect in concrete and cardboard the injustices of the wider society: they are marked by large pockets of poverty as well as ostentatious wealth. Much of the urban population lives in self-built dwellings lacking clear legal title: in Peru, for example, more than half do, while in Haiti the figure rises to 68 per cent.[20] But over time, most of these settlements acquire many of the comforts of urban life: electricity, water, sewerage, paved roads and parks.

Third, in the past two decades, Latin American economies have shed a dense cocoon of protection and statist regulation which incubated massive and costly distortions. The most visible of these was inflation, in which the region was long a world leader. Inflation involved a transfer of income from the poor to the better-off and to the state. It led Brazilian families to invest in enormous fridges so that they could do a month's shopping before their wages lost their value. It meant that the profitability of businesses depended not on the quality and efficiency of their product or service but on the nimbleness of their finance director. But taming inflation usually involved costs before it brought benefits, and was followed by fresh challenges. The adoption of the Washington Consensus coincided with – and in some ways was made possible by – the onset of a new period of globalisation. But some Latin American countries are still trying to consolidate the nation-state – a nineteenth-century task in Europe and English-speaking North America. Suddenly, they had to combine this task with the twenty-first-century one of competing in a globalised world. Costly mistakes were made, especially the abrupt lifting of controls on capital movement combined with inadequate supervision of banks. Reforms were often left incomplete. Insufficient attention was paid to promoting competition, and to ensuring that public monopolies were not replaced by private ones. But many of the defects – poverty, inequality, job insecurity – commonly attributed to the Washington Consensus in Latin America long pre-dated it. This book will argue that the central failure was not that of the economic reforms themselves, but of what was left largely unreformed: the state and public institutions. More effective states, and better public policies, are the key to reducing inequality and to enabling Latin Americans to compete more effectively in the world.

The main argument of this book is that for the first time in Latin America's history, genuine and durable mass democracies have emerged across much of the region. In both its breadth and depth, this process is new. It has far-reaching consequences. In some countries, the process is turbulent and chaotic, and democracy is still capable of being reversed. But in many other countries, in my view, democracy is within striking distance of becoming consolidated. That said, Latin American democracy will always have some characteristics that are its own, just as French or Italian democracy differs from that in Britain or the United States. But it will be democracy. This new political reality means that most Latin American countries are less likely once again to turn their back on integration with the world economy, as they did in the period following the Second World War. However disillusioned they may be with particular reforms, Latin Americans, on the whole, want the benefits of globalisation. The Washington Consensus is indeed an irrevocably 'damaged brand' as Moises Naím, a former Venezuelan trade minister, has noted. But even as it is routinely denounced by newly elected presidents, so its central tenets – of macroeconomic stability and open, market economies – have become an enduring part of the scenery in many countries in the region. That this is not more widely perceived owes much to the baleful influence of a meaningless term: 'neoliberalism'. If this means anything, it is the polices of monetarism and a minimum state espoused by Ronald Reagan and Margaret Thatcher and better described as 'neo-conservatism' – if that term had not itself acquired a different meaning in the field of American foreign policy in recent years. In Latin America, these policies were adopted only by the 'Chicago Boys' who ran Chile's economy in the early years of General Pinochet's dictatorship in the 1970s, though they were echoed, in a different context, in Carlos Menem's Argentina in the 1990s. But 'neoliberalism' is widely used by its critics either simply to describe an open capitalist economy, or as a term of abuse.

In reality, the reform process was far more variegated and pragmatic than its many critics claim.[21] This pragmatic character has become more pronounced since the financial crises of 1998–2002. The region has emerged from these with a new, if tacit, policy consensus. In macroeconomic management, this involves floating exchange rates, combined with more or less responsible fiscal policies and inflation targets policed by more or less independent central banks. (Two countries, Ecuador and El Salvador, chose to adopt the American dollar as their currency.) The new consensus puts far more importance, rhetorically at least, on the role of the state and social policies in tackling poverty and inequality. Many of the 'left-wing' presidents elected in recent months subscribe to it. In that sense, what has happened is a 'shift to the centre', as Oscar Arias, Costa Rica's social-democratic leader put it after winning his country's presidential election in 2006:

> The governments of most South American and all Central American nations are strikingly moderate, a radical change from the ideological polarisation I encountered when I was first elected president 20 years ago. We may believe in the state's responsibility to alleviate the crushing

poverty that afflicts 40% of Latin America's population, but most of us also affirm that there is no better cure for poverty than a stronger, more globally integrated economy.[22]

Leonel Fernández, who was elected president of the Dominican Republic for a second time in 2004, is another man of the centre-left who expresses himself in strikingly similar terms:

> ... what shouldn't be done is to ideologise economic policy. What matters is what works and what doesn't. A fiscal deficit is neither of the right nor the left, it's a problem of management. First, you have to opt for a system which creates a law-bound and trustworthy democratic state. In the economic part, try to guarantee growth of more than 6% and understand that growth is not an end in itself: you have to invest in education and health to tackle poverty and social inequity.[23]

Both men echo Ricardo Lagos, Chile's president from 2000 to 2006, who persistently argued for a combination of macroeconomic stability, an open, investor-friendly economy and robust social policy:

> It's not enough to have good behaviour in macro-economic policies if you don't have social policy going in the right direction ... Europeans are discussing what social network they can keep to remain competitive. Our discussion is what social network we can build to remain competitive and to maintain social cohesion.[24]

Months before his election in 2002, Brazil's Lula became a convert to this consensus, though in some ways an ambivalent one. In an interview with *The Economist* in March 2006, he said 'we're moving along two tracks at once: a solid fiscal policy and a solid social policy'. The Brazil of the future, he said, 'will be built on strong investment in education and training, on tax relief to encourage new [private] investment; it comes from big investments in science and technology and, certainly, the result of all this will be economic growth and distribution of income.'[25]

Cuba apart, the most prominent dissenters from this consensus were Hugo Chávez, Evo Morales in Bolivia and (much less so) Néstor Kirchner in Argentina. (Correa in Ecuador seemed likely to join them.) Chávez claimed to be implementing 'twenty-first-century socialism'. His diagnosis was that Latin America must free itself from what he saw as American imperialism and 'savage capitalism'. To do so, he advocated a return to many of the policies of the past: a strong economic role for the state and the formation of an anti-American regional block based on government-arranged trade. Largely because of Venezuela's huge windfall from high oil prices, Chávez was popular; he was able to win a new six-year term in an election in December 2006, and to propagate this vision around the region. For the first time since the end of the Cold War, liberal democracy was thus facing a seemingly powerful alternative in Latin America. It was one that has aroused the support of some on the left in Europe and the United States. Ken Livingstone, the mayor of London, who invited Chávez to Britain in 2006, described him as 'the best news out of Latin America in many years ... Venezuela was like a lot of those old Latin American countries – a small elite of super-rich families who basically stole the national resources. He's now driven a new economic order through, you've got for the first time healthcare for poor people, illiteracy has been eradicated.'[26]

Nearly all of those statements are false, misleading or questionable.[27] Strip away the verbiage, and Chávez looks a lot like a typical military *caudillo* and his project an updating of populism, a political phenomenon with a long history in Latin America. Like 'neoliberalism', 'populism' has become a loaded, normative term, rather than an analytical one.[28] So here is a definition. By 'populism' I mean two things: first, a brand of politics in which a strong, charismatic leader purports to be a saviour, blurring the distinction between leader, government, party and state, and ignoring the need for the restraint of executive power through checks and balances. Second, populism has often involved redistribution of income and/or wealth in an unsustainable fashion. Populism is mistakenly assumed by some commentators to be synonymous with the left. That is not so. Thus, had the financiers of Wall Street correctly identified that Brazil's Lula was a social-democrat, not a populist, they might not have panicked at the thought of his election in 2002. The classic populist leaders included Juan Perón in Argentina and his second wife, Eva Duarte, Getúlio Vargas in Brazil, and José Maria Velasco in Ecuador. In some of its past manifestations, Latin American populism was a creative political response to inequality and the dominance of powerful conservative groups. In others, it was a vehicle for authoritarianism. In many cases, it left countries, and especially the poor whom it claims to champion, worse off, in economic terms at least.

Why is populism nevertheless so attractive to Latin American voters? Because, as Luis Rubio, a Mexican political scientist, points out, 'people remember the years of economic growth, not the years of paying the bill.'[29] In the same vein, Argentina's Juan Perón became a symbol of 'the only period in which the worker was happy', according to John William Cooke, a leader of the Peronist left in the 1960s.[30] Having appeared to fade away in the 1960s, populism's return owes much to the persistence of Latin America's extreme inequalities of income and wealth. This reduces the appeal of incremental reform and increases that of messianic leaders who promise a new world. A second driver of populism has been Latin America's wealth of natural resources, from gold to oil. Many Latin Americans are taught at school that their countries are rich, whereas in truth they are not. If it were natural resources rather than hard work and effective institutions that made countries wealthy, Singapore and Switzerland would be destitute. Populists blame poverty on convenient scapegoats: corruption, 'the oligarchy', American 'imperialism' or multinational oil or mining companies. Third, as the politics of class has faded, it has been partly replaced by a new politics of identity. Not all populists are Amerindian or *mestizo* (of mixed European and Amerindian race); conversely, Alejandro Toledo, Peru's president from 2001 to 2006, was of Andean Indian descent but was not a populist and neither are some of the leaders of Ecuador's indigenous movement. Nevertheless, the appeal of the populists, of men like Chávez, Morales and Humala, is partly one of ethnic identification, a sense among poorer and darker-skinned Latin Americans that they are 'one of us'.

Reform, not revolution

This populist challenge to liberal democracy is thus part of the high price that Latin America continues to pay for its failure to overturn at an earlier point in its independent history the two great structural causes of its socio-economic inequality, which were closely linked: on the one hand, the colonial legacy of unequal land distribution (in many countries never reversed), and on the other hand, slavery (finally abolished only in 1886 in Cuba and 1888 in Brazil) and discrimination against the indigenous Amerindian population. In Latin America, unlike in the United States or apartheid South Africa, racial mixing has long been the norm. The *conquistadores* were overwhelmingly male, and so were the colonists who followed them, at least until independence. Most Latin Americans are now *mestizo* or *mulato* (of mixed black and European race). But the poor still tend to be of darker skin than the rich. Creating a democratic society, in which equality of opportunity and equality before the law are the norm, is a task that has only just begun in many countries. Latin American societies remain palpably unjust.

But the chances remain good that in many countries liberal democracy will withstand the populist challenge. On the one hand, the populists start from a misdiagnosis of the causes of Latin America's relative failure of development. And in few other countries do would-be populist leaders dispose of the easily appropriable stream of revenue that Venezuela's state-owned oil industry offers to Chávez. On the other hand, there are plenty of signs that democracy, financial stability and economic reform are at last starting to bear fruit. That is one reason for Latin America's return to economic growth in the twenty-first century. It is also part of the explanation for the failure of the populists to carry all before them in the 2006 elections. In Mexico (narrowly) and Colombia, voters rewarded conservative candidates. In Peru Alan García, a notoriously unsuccessful populist in a first term from 1985 to 1990, reinvented himself as a candidate of moderate change. He profited, too, from Chávez's clumsy sponsorship of his defeated opponent, Ollanta Humala.

The findings of Latinobarómetro, an opinion poll taken since 1995 and now covering 18 countries, provide some support for cautious optimism regarding Latin American democracy. In its 2006 poll, 58 per cent of respondents agreed that democracy was the best system of government, up by five percentage points on the previous year. That was still five points down on the peak in 1997, but it followed three years in which the figure had stayed stubbornly static. Only in Guatemala (35 per cent), Paraguay (30 per cent), the Dominican Republic and Ecuador (both 21 per cent), and Peru (20 per cent) did more than a fifth of respondents indicate that in some circumstances an authoritarian government might be preferable. Only 38 per cent of respondents said they were satisfied with the way their democracies worked in practice, but that was a seven-point increase compared with the 2005 poll.[31] These results reflected three years of reasonable economic growth, as well as the political excitements of the electoral marathon. They underlined that creating effective democracies in Latin America is a work in progress.

The task facing the region's democratic politicians is to create greater political and socio-economic equity without endangering the conditions for profitable private investment and thus for sustainable economic growth. Fortunately, there are reasons to believe that the choice between growth and equity is a false one. Many policies can promote both. A huge effort is needed to improve the coverage and (especially) the quality of education in Latin America. A more educated workforce is essential to make Latin American businesses more competitive. More and better education is also the single most important tool in creating equality of opportunity. Similarly, effective and well-targeted anti-poverty programmes are now an essential condition for political survival in today's Latin America, but by expanding consumption they can also help growth, as the World Bank argued in a report released in 2006.[32] Not all the reforms still needed are politically popular. While Latin America has largely achieved macroeconomic stability, microeconomic reform has languished. The region's economies lag in the world league tables of competitiveness, innovation and friendliness to business. As well as a poorly educated workforce, creaking or non-existent infrastructures, piles of pointless red tape, over-regulated labour markets and over-cosseted monopolies, private and public, are all to blame. Success in both economic and social policy means not just subscribing to the new centrist consensus but putting its tenets into practice.

That points to the need for a new, more practical, brand of politics. Democracy means that technocrats, however enlightened, are unlikely to enjoy the kind of freedom to impose modernising economic policies that they enjoyed under Porfirio Díaz, Mexico's dictator of a century ago, or again, in many countries (including Mexico) for much of the 1980s and 1990s. Reforms will have to be negotiated, and coalitions painstakingly built to support them. Again, this process is wholly new for the region. Latin America has seen too many 'revolutions', most of them ersatz, and not enough reform. The rewards of successful consensual reform are potentially great. As Richard Webb, a former governor of Peru's Central Bank and an economic historian, points out, the key to explaining periods of high growth in Latin America involves political arrangements that provided local investors with security. In the past, that usually involved cosy deals between authoritarian governments and big business, with a trickle-down effect on small businesses.[33] The task now is to substitute for cosy deals broad political consensuses on the overall principles of economic and tax policy, shielding business from unpleasant surprises and allowing long-term investment to take place safely. Such a consensus exists in Chile. It was why Chile was the only country in the region where investment consistently accounted for more than 24 per cent of GDP, the rate required to sustain growth of over 6 per cent according to a calculation by CEPAL.[34]

To the extent that outsiders have a view of Latin America, it is one that is heavily influenced by the region's inequalities and injustices, and of romanticised struggles against them. This mental picture is peopled by guerrillas, obscure and quixotic revolutions, military leaders and political machismo, set against a colourful background of imposing geography, quaint costume, grasping foreigners and grinding poverty. Like all cliches, this picture contains a grain of truth. Yet it is anachronistic. In many countries, though not everywhere, Latin American realities have changed substantially. Nowadays, the typical Latin American, if such a person exists, lives in a city and has access to basic services and to much more information about the world than his or her parents. Despite many wants and problems, she or he can aspire to material progress, can vote freely and through a host of 'civil society' groups can influence public policy.

Much can still go wrong. Latin America's history since independence is by turns one of hope and despair, progress and reaction, stability and disorder, dictatorship and freedom. When Stefan Zweig, an expatriate Austrian author who had fled Nazism for Brazil, declared in delight that his new home was 'the country of the future' it was not long before popular humour added the bitter rider 'and it always will be'.[35] Even in the most hopeful view, several countries are likely to remain trapped in a vicious circle of low growth, populism and instability. Latin American history is marked by short bursts of remarkable synchronisation among the region's various countries, interspersed with periods of greater diversity. The spread of democracy and economic reform in the 1980s and 1990s was one such period of synchronised change. The coming years are likely to see greater heterogeneity, with different countries going in different directions.

One and many Latin Americas

Before proceeding, another definition is in order. What does one mean when one talks of 'Latin America'? The term itself is a relatively recent invention, and it is fraught with difficulties. It was popularised by José Maria Torres Caicedo, a Colombian writer, in 1856.[36] It was quickly taken up by French propagandists, ever conscious of Anglo-Saxon power and keen to stake out a claim for their country's influence in the 'other America' (a claim that Louis Napoleon pushed beyond prudence with a tragic attempt to install Maximilian, a Habsburg prince, as emperor of Mexico). Unfortunately, it is geographically vague. *Pace* my own misuse of the term in the title of this book, Latin America is not itself a continent. Clearly it includes South and Central America, but most of Mexico is in North America (geographers normally place the sub-continental divide at the Isthmus of Tehuantepec). And what of the Caribbean? Cuba, the Dominican Republic, and Haiti clearly qualify. But Puerto Rico has been part of the United States since the Spanish–American war of 1898. And the English-speaking Caribbean (along with Belize and Guyana), though included with Latin America in many international bodies and sharing some of its problems (e.g. the drug trade), constitutes a distinct sub-region. On the mainland, Cayenne is a *département* of France; Suriname, a former Dutch colony, is independent but separated from the other republics by language. But language is not a defining criterion either. While Spanish is the official language of 18 republics spread across Central and South America and the Caribbean, Portuguese is spoken in Brazil. As well as in Haiti, Cayenne, Guadeloupe and Martinique, French is spoken in Quebec and New Brunswick in Canada. And a number of indigenous languages remain important, each spoken by several million people. They include Quechua in the countries of the former Inca empire (Peru, Bolivia and Ecuador, where it is called Quichua); Aymara, too, is spoken widely in Bolivia and around the Peruvian shore of Lake Titicaca; Guaraní is the lingua franca of Paraguayans, spoken at home even by members of the country's elite; a score of Mayan languages are spoken in Guatemala and parts of southern Mexico.

In all, Mexico has more than fifty Indian languages in current use, including Nahuatl, the tongue of the Aztecs.

For the purposes of this book, I will use Latin America to refer to the Spanish-speaking countries and Brazil (and only occasionally to Haiti). But even in this more restricted universe, there are obvious differences. The problems of Haiti are more akin to those of Africa, whence most of its inhabitants originally came against their will, than to those of Chile, a Europeanised country whose income per head is six times as large. Brazil is a country of continental scale; El Salvador is the size of Wales or Massachusetts. Peru and Mexico are the seats of sophisticated ancient civilisations; Brazil and Argentina are 'new' countries.

Inevitably, a book which attempts to explain such a vast region of the world involves generalisation and synthesis. In an attempt to do justice to the diversity of Latin America, let us start with a rapid explanatory tour – the equivalent in reverse of the kind of package tour of Europe that middle-class Latin Americans hope to make at least once in their lifetime. Its purpose is to review briefly some of the differences in culture, history and outlook among the region's constituent countries.

Start with Brazil. It has a strong sense of its own separateness, a result not just of its vast size and different language but also of history and geography. Portuguese colonialism was a looser affair than its Spanish counterpart: while the Spaniards sought treasure and the domination of new lands, the Portuguese were predominantly traders. Uniquely in Latin America, Brazil was a constitutional monarchy for the first seven decades after independence. Until recently, Brazilians have felt self-contained by the vastness of their territory, separated from their neighbours by the Amazon rainforest, the swamps of the Pantanal, and the mighty Paraná river. Brazil's Indian tribes were mainly nomadic, and had erected no great civilisations at the time of their conquest. But the import of African slaves had a far more profound influence on Brazil than on anywhere else in the region except Cuba and the island of Hispaniola. Of the 8 million or so Africans who survived the passage to the Americas, at least 3.65 million and perhaps more were shipped to Brazil in the four centuries to 1850 – considerably more than the number taken to the United States.[37] Along with Cuba, Brazil was the last American country to abolish slavery, in 1888 (a decision that brought down the monarchy). Despite the huge impact of slavery, Sérgio Buarque de Holanda, one of Brazil's most distinguished essayists, noted 'the practically complete absence among (the Portuguese) of any racial pride', the result he said of their prior mixing with North Africans.[38] Brazil's long-standing claim to be a 'racial democracy' is now widely viewed as exaggerated. But if racism is not absent from contemporary Brazil, it is far more subtle than in many other countries. Walk through Parque Ibirapuera, São Paulo's equivalent to London's Hyde Park, and you see Brazilians of all colours playing football or volleyball together. In Brazil, unlike the United States or South Africa, racism never implied racial segregation.

Unlike Mexico, Brazil has long felt confident about absorbing cultural influences from Europe and the United States and melding them into something uniquely Brazilian. Oswald de Andrade, a modernist writer and critic, called this *antropofagia*, or cultural cannibalism. During a fertile period in the mid twentieth century, Brazil forged a self-image as a self-consciously modern nation. That period began with the Modern Art Week, held in São Paulo in 1917, which influenced the country's architecture in particular, bringing the ideas of Le Corbusier to South America. It climaxed with the whispery, cool jazz music of *bossa nova* and the building of Brasília, the new capital, where the modernist palaces of Oscar Niemeyer added grace to an otherwise Orwellian project. 'Le Corbusier took the right angle while I was concerned with the creation of curves,' Niemeyer explained, in an example of architectural *antropofagia*. That was because curves are found in 'the mountains of my country, in the sinuousness of its rivers, in the waves of the ocean, and on the body of the beloved woman'.[39] Like Australians, Brazilians live their culture out of doors, in the street and on the beach, in carnival, football and the weekly *churrasco* or barbecue at which friends and family gather.

Brazilian officials dislike the idea that their country is part of Latin America. Especially since Mexico signed NAFTA, throwing in its lot with the United States, Brazil prefers to talk of the unity of South America as a counterweight. In 2000, President Fernando Henrique Cardoso called the first of what have become regular South American summits. They began by promoting better transport links across the continent. In November 2004, at a meeting in Cusco, the former Inca capital in Peru, Brazil's vision of South American unity took a further step forward when all 11 South American countries (including Guyana and Suriname) proclaimed a South American Community of Nations, with the eventual aim of a common passport and common currency. As always with such schemes in Latin America, proclamation and rhetoric come more naturally than the hard slog of integration.[40]

In Brazil itself, change has tended to be peaceful and evolutionary. The country lacks the tradition of political violence of some of its Spanish-speaking neighbours. After a difficult transition from military rule in the 1980s, democracy has recently seemed more robust as two contrasting reformers, Cardoso, an urbane sociologist, and Lula, a former lathe operator and trade union leader, succeeded each other in the presidency. But Brazil continued to grapple with relatively slow economic growth, a bloated state, social injustice, violent crime and political corruption.

In some ways, Mexico, the region's other giant, could hardly be more different. It is intensely proud of being an ancient society, the site of several Indian civilisations dating back millennia. For most of the colonial period, after the decline of the Potosí silver mine in what is today Bolivia, it was Spain's richest and most populous possession. In comparison, the United States seems a brash *parvenu*. The conservative bedrock of Mexican society is the heavily Indian centre and south, where communalism and the Catholic Church were powerful influences. Change has tended to come from the free-wheeling north, a frontier society of more individualist farmers and ranchers. Mexico's revolution of 1910–17 (some argue it lasted until 1940) forged a distinct political system, under which the official Institutional Revolutionary Party (PRI) ruled continuously until 2000. It also spawned an official culture of *indigenismo*, aimed at promoting (or at least proclaiming) the country's racial integration. One of the early ideologues of the post-revolutionary period, José Vasconcelos, the education minister in the 1920s, argued that Latin America was in essence *mestizo* (a 'cosmic race', he called it, referring to its claimed spirituality). Having lost half its territory to the United States in a war of 1846–8, and living cheek by jowl with the twentieth century's superpower, Mexico developed a defensive, almost xenophobic nationalism. 'Poor Mexico – so far from God and so close to the United States,' Porfirio Díaz famously said of his country. As a result, official Mexico felt it could not afford to be as easygoing about its culture as Brazil was. And while Brazilians live in the street, Mexicans, or at least the better-off among them, live behind the high walls of houses vaguely modelled on the colonial *hacienda*. Those defensive walls are also metaphorical. 'The Mexican,' wrote Octavio Paz, the country's Nobel-prize-winning poet and essayist, 'builds a wall of indifference and remoteness between reality and himself.'[41] Mexico's political culture remains relatively opaque. Its transition to democracy was slow and late, culminating with Vicente Fox's historic defeat of the PRI in 2000. Until then, never in the history of Mexico had power passed peacefully to an opposition party as the result of a democratic election. As Enrique Krauze, a historian, has pointed out, the norm in Mexico has been the concentration of power in a single person: the Aztec *tlatoani* (meaning 'he who speaks'), the colonial viceroy, the nineteenth-century *caudillos*, the revolutionary chiefs, and the PRI's omnipotent presidents.[42] The absence of even a truncated democratic tradition long distinguished Mexico from South America. That made the narrowness of the mandate won by Felipe Calderón, a conservative from Fox's party, in the 2006 presidential election, a potential problem.

Argentina, Uruguay and Chile – South America's southern cone – are yet another story. Sparsely populated in the colonial era, they were the great success stories of the first era of sustained economic growth in Latin America, from 1870 until World War One. They were blessed with fertile land – extraordinarily so in the case of the vast, flat grasslands of the Pampas – and, for the most part, temperate climate. Argentina and Uruguay (along with southern Brazil) attracted large numbers of European migrants.

Argentina offers 'one of the most puzzling stories in the annals of modern economic history', according to a recent account.[43] A century ago, it had become the first 'developed' country in Latin America. In 1913, income per head in Argentina was slightly higher than in France and Germany, and far ahead of that in Italy or Spain. It lagged only the United States, the United Kingdom and three British colonies – which Argentina resembled in some ways – Australia, Canada and New Zealand. That followed three decades of growth averaging 5 per cent a year, driven by exports from the Pampas, foreign (mainly British) investment, especially in railways, and immigration (mainly from Spain and Italy).[44] Growth then slowed, but on the eve of the Second World War, Argentina remained a relatively rich country. It has been pretty much downhill ever since. Argentina is thus not a 'developing country'. Uniquely, development slipped from its grasp. That is a haunting condition: it may explain why psychoanalysis and the nostalgia-ridden tango are so popular in Argentina. It is reflected, mockingly, in the fading *belle époque* splendour of Buenos Aires. In 1913, Argentina's capital had more sewerage connections per head than Paris. It was the second-largest city in the Americas, after New York; the second to boast an underground railway; the only city outside London to boast a branch of Harrods (it closed in 1995 and the building remained empty in 2006). Argentina's long decline reached rock bottom in the financial and economic collapse of 2001–2. This saw tens of thousands of young Argentines migrating to Spain and Italy in search of work, repeating in reverse the journey made by their grandparents. Despite a vigorous economic recovery, the scars from the collapse have not entirely healed. In the rustbelt suburbs, a generation of young adults has grown up in mass unemployment. No longer an offshoot of Europe in the Americas, Argentina has become a Latin American country.

Across the broad silt-brown estuary of the River Plate lies Uruguay, a small, compact country of temperate climate. It prospered by exporting beef and wool to Britain from the port of Montevideo. It became urbanised early, with European migrants setting up manufacturing industries. Uniquely in Latin America, Uruguay established a European-style welfare state – before most of Europe. Two loose parties, the Colorados ('Reds', or Liberals) and Blancos ('Whites', or Conservatives, also known as the National Party), had dominated politics in the nineteenth century, a system which evolved into democracy in the early years of the twentieth century. With its middle-class society, economic stability and use of referendums, Uruguay liked to consider itself the 'Switzerland of South America'. Argentines and Brazilians traditionally holidayed on its beaches and kept their money in its banks. This reputation was first strained by economic stagnation and a period of dictatorship (1973–84) that saw many younger Uruguayans seek opportunities abroad. More recently, Uruguay has suffered the knock-on impact of Argentina's economic collapse. But its response was markedly different. Unlike its neighbour, it did not default on its debts, and it actively sought foreign investment. These policies were maintained when the left-wing Frente Amplio ('Broad Front') took power in 2005. They achieved an economic recovery that was at least as fast as Argentina's.

Paraguay could hardly be more different to Uruguay. The Gran Chaco, a parched, empty, sweltering scrubland, makes up half of its territory. Paraguay is poor, Indian, and has a powerful authoritarian tradition. Its destiny was shaped by being landlocked, its trade on the River Paraguay a potential hostage to Argentine interference. That led its first dictator, the implacable Gaspar Rodríguez de Francia (1816–40), known by his subjects as *el Supremo* (the supreme one), to close Paraguay to the world and pursue autarky. To neuter potential rivals, he expropriated many landowners, and turned the Guaraní peasantry into tenants of the state. His authoritarian egalitarianism would be hailed by left-wing writers more than a century later. Yet out of this paranoid dictatorship developed a militarism which led to disaster. Francia's successor, Carlos Solano López, built up a massive and well-equipped standing army of 50,000 troops. Its alarmed neighbours saw in Paraguay a South American Prussia. In 1865, Solano's son, Francisco, allowed himself to be trapped into war with a Triple Alliance of Argentina, Brazil and Uruguay. After five years of fighting, largely against Brazilian armies, Paraguay was destroyed. Its pre-war population of 1.2 million was said to have been reduced to 300,000, of whom very few were males (recent scholars suggest that these casualty figures are exaggerated). In the 1930s Paraguay would fight another war, this time with success, wresting part of the Chaco from Bolivia. It long remained an enclave of dictatorship and smuggling, culminating in the kleptocratic rule of Alfredo Stroessner (1954–89). Yet it is perhaps the national football team, with its almost unbeatably stubborn defence, which expresses the essence of Paraguayan identity.

Chile represents a sharp contrast to Argentina, its trans-Andean neighbour to the east. Its compact geography – or at least that of its populated central third – and relative ethnic homogeneity helped it to become a cohesive nation-state long before many others in the region. Simón Bolívar, South America's independence hero, spotted Chile's potential early: 'If any American republic is to endure,' he wrote in 1815, 'I am inclined to believe it will be Chile ... Its territory is limited; it will always be free of contagion from other peoples; it will not alter its laws, its customs, or its habits; it will preserve its uniformity in political and religious ideas; in a word, Chile can be free.'[45] Chile achieved political stability by the 1830s. But it suffered national trauma in the early 1970s. First Salvador Allende tried to use a narrow electoral mandate to impose socialism on a deeply polarised country. Then General Augusto Pinochet ended more than a century of almost uninterrupted civilian rule, installing a dictatorship that cruelly repressed Allende's supporters. Despite that trauma – some would say because of it – Chile has subsequently become the big success story of contemporary Latin America. Since 1990 the country has been governed by a stable centre-left coalition that has retained the free-market economic policies imposed by the dictatorship. Economic growth has gone hand in hand with an increasingly solid democracy. Chileans worry that, in the terminology of an estate agent, they are 'a good house in a bad neighbourhood', as a senior official put it.[46]

Further north, what are commonly referred to as the Andean countries are culturally very different from the southern cone. While Bolivia and Ecuador retain large Indian populations, Colombia is mainly *mestizo*; Peru is somewhere in between. Venezuela, like Brazil and Cuba, has a large black and *mulato* population. All the Andean countries suffer from difficult geography. In Bolivia's case, that was aggravated by the War of the Pacific of 1879–83, which led to Chilean annexation of its mineral-rich coastline, leaving the country landlocked, isolated from most of its neighbours by the Andean cordillera, Amazon rainforest and endless tropical savannahs. Nowadays, a socio-economic divide has emerged between the poor, Indian Altiplano – the bleak 4,000-metre-high inter-montane plain – and the eastern tropical lowlands, the centre of commercial farming and the oil and gas industry. Peru and Ecuador also suffer a sharp geographical divide: coastal lowlands are the centre of commercial farming; subsistence farming by indigenous communities is predominant in the valleys and mountainsides of the Andean cordillera; while to the east lies the Amazon jungle, where indigenous tribes have clashed with oil companies. In recent decades the trade in cocaine, whose production is centred in Colombia, Peru and Bolivia, has hindered democracy and provided a ready source of finance for illegal armies: it is no accident that the only Latin American guerrilla groups to have outlived dictatorship and the ending of the Cold War are in Colombia and Peru.

Peru was both the seat of the most sophisticated of the pre-Columbian states, the Inca empire (which stretched as far as southern Colombia and northern Argentina), and the administrative centre of Spanish South America.

As a republic, it has dealt with its geographical challenge by excessive centralisation of economic and political power in Lima, with consequent regional rebellions. Even more so than the Latin American norm, the army has been a powerful force in Peruvian political history. It took the military dictatorship of Juan Velasco (1968–74), a left-leaning nationalist much admired by Hugo Chávez, to break the power of the landlord oligarchy, something achieved earlier by revolution or civilian politics in many other countries. But Velasco left a socio-political vacuum, especially in the Peruvian Andes. That was exploited by *Sendero Luminoso* (Shining Path), a fundamentalist Maoist group. After passing through the traumas of hyperinflation, the murderous insurgency of *Sendero* and its heavy-handed repression, which between them left 70,000 dead between 1980 and the mid-1990s, and the increasingly corrupt and authoritarian rule of Alberto Fujimori, Peru is trying to rebuild democracy amid promising economic growth but continuing socio-political fragility. Peru's cultural richness is expressed in music, literature and handcrafts such as weavings and pottery. Thanks to its varied microclimates and the rich fisheries of the cold Humboldt current, coastal Peru boasts South America's richest cuisine, involving a fusion of Andean, African, Spanish, Italian and Japanese elements.

Bolivia and Ecuador are the most volatile polities in the Andean region. The poorest South American republic, Bolivia (or Upper Peru as it was then known) was for a few decades Spain's most valuable colony, thanks to the fabulous silver mountain at Potosí. Discovered in 1545, the Cerro Rico (literally 'rich hill') provided the main source of treasure for Spain's European wars for more than a century. Tens of thousands of Indians, forced to labour in the deep and narrow mine shafts, perished in extracting the silver. At its zenith, Potosí, a bitterly cold place 4,070 metres (13,380 feet) above sea level on the Altiplano, was the largest city in the Americas. Its population of 160,000 was similar to London's at the time. City and country then sank back into obscurity. Potosí is today a quiet place of too many colonial churches, where a few thousand miners, working informally and in dangerous conditions, pick over the dregs of the mineral ore. Between 1825 and 1980 Bolivia suffered almost 200 coups, although a nationalist revolution in 1952 began to lay the basis of a modern state and started to address the exclusion of the Andean Indian majority from political and economic power. For two decades until 2003, Bolivia was an unexpected success story for democracy and economic reform. Then two presidents were toppled in as many years by mass demonstrations led by radical left-wingers. Economic stagnation, the discredit of traditional political parties, resentment at the US-backed 'war on drugs', demands for greater political participation by indigenous Bolivians and regional tensions all combined to produce a seeming political deadlock. It was not clear whether the election, in December 2005, of Evo Morales, a socialist of indigenous extraction who pledged to 'refound the nation', would resolve this.

Ecuador has failed to resolve the geographical tension between coast and sierra which has dominated its history. That has resulted in political fragmentation and extreme instability: since it became an independent republic in 1830, the average life of Ecuador's constitutions has been just ten years. Since the 1930s, the average president has survived in office no more than two years. Between 1997 and 2005, Ecuador had six different presidents, with none of the three elected in that period lasting longer than 27 months. Since the 1970s, oil has provided booty for the politicians to contest and reduced the incentives for economic reform. In recent years, Ecuador has seen the emergence of Latin America's most powerful indigenous movement.

Both Colombia and Venezuela resisted dictatorship in the 1970s, but both have had more than their share of problems since. Colombia is cursed with a geography that by one count is the world's third-most adverse for economic development.[47] The Andes break into three chains, separated by deep valleys; much of the country's two coasts are backed by jungles, swamps or semi-desert. Colombia's population of 44 million is the third largest in Latin America; it is also the most dispersed. These factors combined to make Colombia inward-looking but difficult to govern and to police. That impeded authoritarian government. With one brief interlude, Colombia has been ruled since the mid-nineteenth century by only two parties, the Liberals and Conservatives. Party loyalty was fierce, passed on within villages and families. This arrangement generated periodic civil wars but also a certain stability: Colombia was unusual in the region in avoiding populism; for half a century until 1995 its economy grew at an annual average rate of almost 5 per cent, avoiding both recession and debt default. Colombians long prided themselves on their country's cultural prowess: their cities teem with bookshops and public libraries, and the country is the largest exporter of books in Latin America. In Gabriel García Márquez and Fernando Botero Colombia boasts the region's best-known living novelist and painter respectively.

The past three decades have been difficult for Colombia. Weak government allowed the drug trade to flourish. Drug income helped to fuel the rise of three illegal armies: the leftist Revolutionary Armed Forces of Colombia (FARC) and National Liberation Army (ELN) and their foes, the right-wing paramilitaries of the United Self-Defence Forces of Colombia (AUC). Colombia's violent conflicts gave it the worst human-rights record in the hemisphere in the 1990s. At its peak, the conflict claimed the lives of some 7,000 people a year, while another 3,500 or so were kidnapped. A total of perhaps 2 million were 'internally displaced' – refugees forced to flee from their homes in the countryside, often at gunpoint. In response, Colombian governments have forged a strategic alliance with the United States. 'Plan Colombia' was controversial, but in some ways it has been effective. It will not end the illegal drug trade (only legalisation in the consumer countries could do that) but it gave Colombia's armed forces the mobility needed to regain the strategic initiative against the guerrillas. Colombians themselves have recognised that without greater security their country cannot prosper, and they have given strong backing to Álvaro Uribe, their tough conservative president since 2002. Violence declined steadily from its peak in the late 1990s and economic growth resumed.

Like Argentina, Venezuela once glimpsed prosperity. In the 1970s, it was the richest country in Latin America, thanks to oil. The oil money transformed what had been a sleepy agricultural country. It also helped to make Venezuela the most 'Americanised' country in South America, the only one where baseball is more popular than football. Venezuela's political tradition was in marked contrast to Colombia's. Dictators and strongmen were the norm until 1958, when a democracy based on two seemingly strong parties was installed. Oil financed a welfare state, but also a spoils system and much corruption. By the 1990s, as the population grew while the price of oil languished, oil revenue per head had declined steeply from its peak of two decades earlier. But attempts to reform a bloated state met fierce popular resistance – not least because corruption robbed many Venezuelan politicians of the moral authority required to impose austerity. In desperation, Venezuelans turned to Hugo Chávez, who had been jailed (and then amnestied) for leading a coup attempt against a democratic government. A charismatic *mestizo*, Chávez has attracted almost religious devotion among many poorer and darker-skinned Venezuelans. But in many ways, his Bolivarian Revolution is a repeat of the policies of unsustainable redistribution of oil revenues pursued by his predecessors – but with one party in power rather than the previous, alternating, two. Partly in response to a short-lived coup in 2002, and an attempt by the opposition to unseat him through a recall referendum in August 2004, Chávez's rule has become increasingly authoritarian and his revolution has moved in the direction of military socialism. Democracy is in greater danger in Venezuela than anywhere else among the larger countries of Latin America. As long as oil prices remain high, Chávez seems likely to continue in power. But when they fall, Venezuela faces a reckoning.

For most of their independent history, the small countries of the Central American isthmus were an obscure backwater. Costa Rica apart, they were marked by repressive dictatorships. Following the Sandinista revolution of 1979 in Nicaragua, they were suddenly thrust into the spotlight as a theatre of the Cold War. As well as Nicaragua, Guatemala and El Salvador suffered civil wars, as left-wing guerrillas backed by Castro's Cuba battled dictatorships supported, with varying degrees of enthusiasm, by the United States. After the fall of the Berlin Wall, the administration of George H W Bush wisely decided that democracy was the only solution for Central America's conflicts. Central America is once again a backwater. It has close ties with the United States, partly through migration. American-style youth gangs are among the less desirable imports from the north. All the countries of the isthmus are grappling without much success with the twin problems of crime and youth unemployment. But even within Central America there are differences. Relatively equitable landholding, European migration and a strong democratic tradition mark Costa Rica out from the others. Guatemala, with a large Indian population, suffers from a racist and backward political elite and an over-mighty army, but is showing timid signs of democratic progress. In El Salvador, the right has held a monopoly on power since democracy was established in the early 1990s. That applied to Nicaragua until Daniel Ortega profited from a split in the Liberal Party to win the 2006 election. Honduras is poor but politically stable.

Like Central America, the Dominican Republic has seen much interference from the United States. Culturally, Dominicans (or at least the better-off among them) have largely defined themselves in racial terms, in being *mulatos* or *mestizos* but not black and therefore not like the impoverished French-speaking Haitians next door. Under Leonel Fernández, a pragmatic social-democrat who was president from 1996 to 2000 and again from 2004, the Dominican Republic has enjoyed bursts of rapid economic growth based principally on tourism and *maquiladoras* (export assembly plants).

Cuba is the largest island in the Caribbean. Like Haiti, it was marked by its history as a sugar colony. In both places, African slaves were imported on a large scale to work in the plantations. While the countries on the mainland gained their independence in the 1820s, Cuba's island status allowed Spain to hang on there until the Spanish–American war of 1898 (in which Spain lost Puerto Rico and the Philippines as well). The United States opted to keep Puerto Rico, because of its strategic position close to the entrance of the Caribbean. Cuba was forced to swap colonial status for that of an American neo-colony: under the notorious Platt Amendment, the United States reserved the right to intervene in the government of the island at will. This was unilaterally abrogated by a Cuban government in 1933. But Americans controlled much of the island's economy. Fidel Castro's revolution was first and foremost a nationalist one. By adopting communism and placing Cuba under the Soviet Union's protection, Castro forged the only alliance certain to keep the United States at bay and ensure his own exercise of total power for an indefinite period. Just as it delayed independence, Cuba's island status delayed the fall of communism – long enough for Castro to find a new external sponsor in Hugo Chávez's Venezuela. As successive waves of richer Cubans fled to Florida, the population of Castro's island – though not the leadership of the communist government – became darker skinned.

In August 2006, on the eve of his eightieth birthday, Castro underwent serious intestinal surgery: he transferred power to Raúl, his brother, the defence minister and his designated successor. Raúl Castro was himself aged 75 in 2006. He lacked Fidel's charisma and mythical aura. For the immediate future, Cuba was likely to be governed by a collective leadership in which the armed forces would play a central role. Looking further ahead, a transition to capitalism and democracy (perhaps in that order) looked inevitable. What was not clear was how long this might take, whether it would happen peacefully, what the roles of the United States and Venezuela would be, and whether the two Cubas – the richer, whiter one in Florida, and the poorer, blacker one on the island – would reach reconciliation, or would fight over property and power.

Finally, there is now another Latin America – in the United States. Some 41 million *Latinos* live there, of whom some 26 million are of Mexican descent, 2 million are from Puerto Rico, 1.6 million from Cuba, 1.3 million from El Salvador and 1.2 million from the Dominican Republic.[48] *Latinos* are now not only the largest minority in the US, making up 14 per cent of the total population, but also the fastest-growing demographic group.[49] The *Latino* population is highly varied. Some two-thirds were born in the United States – they are hyphenated Latino-Americans. There are differences according to national origin, by generation, between migrants and those born in the United States, and among the former, between those with legal residence and illegals. What is indisputable is that Latinos are having an impact on the United States, on its politics as well as on its economy and culture. Although only 47 per cent of *Latinos* voted in the 2004 presidential election, compared with 60 per cent of blacks, they split their vote more evenly between the two parties, making them more sought after. Although many are trapped in low-wage jobs, their remittances are having a similarly important impact on Latin America itself. What is less clear is whether their presence will effect significant changes in relations between the United States and Latin America. Certainly, George W Bush's rhetorical interest in Latin America would appear to owe much to the *Latino* presence. At the same time, the increasingly bitter debate about immigration control in the United States has the potential to complicate relations with Mexico and Central America.

Common materials

Such diversity defeats some casual generalisations. Latin America is far from being a monolith. But it is built from many common materials. The former Spanish and Portuguese colonies of Latin America share more than the same corner of the world. They have a shared experience of Iberian colonialism, of Catholicism, similar languages and, with many variations, similar ethnic identities. As already noted, that legacy has involved a further shared characteristic: deep inequality in the distribution of income, wealth and (until recently, at least) political influence. Many, but not all, of the larger countries suffer from challenging geography. Indeed, one of the most striking differences in Latin America is between coastal and mountain peoples, irrespective of country. As elsewhere in the world, the coast tends to be more outward-looking, commercially minded and racially *mulato*, while people of the mountains are more conservative and more Indian. This similarity has led Sergio Ramírez, a Nicaraguan writer and politician, to describe Brazil as a 'Caribbean country' despite its purely Atlantic seaboard.[50]

But all Latin Americans share to a greater or lesser extent some social attitudes and a common culture. Many of those who can afford to do so work to live rather than live to work. Many of Octavio Paz's observations regarding the central place of the fiesta in Mexican life apply to the region as a whole, and along with the fiesta goes the importance of music and dance.[51] Despite their prowess at football, a team sport, Latin Americans are torn between gregarious and anarchic impulses. Across the region, the family functions as both a powerful bulwark of social stability and an economic network. Until recently, there was a striking absence in the region of the kind of voluntary civic groups that Alexis de Tocqueville so admired in the United States.

Brazilian pop music and Mexican *rancheras*, along with *telenovelas* from both countries, are popular throughout the region. So are the novels of Gabriel García Márquez (a Colombian who lives mainly in Mexico and Cuba), and Mario Vargas Llosa (a Peruvian who lives mainly in Europe). The love poems of Chile's Pablo Neruda have been recited by several generations of adolescents across Latin America. There have been other shared ways of thinking as well. From the Jesuits and scholasticism, to liberalism and positivism, corporatism and Marxism – and liberalism again – Latin American countries have drawn from the same European political philosophies and often adapted them to the conditions of the New World in similar ways.[52] Broadly speaking, their economic and political histories since independence have been similar. It is not coincidental that events have sometimes been strikingly synchronised across the region. Thus, Cuba and the Dominican Republic apart, all the Latin American countries gained independence between 1810 and 1830. Once independent, the Latin American republics have often copied from each other. Thus, as Bushnell and Macaulay have pointed out, six South American republics completed the abolition of slavery between 1851 and 1854, while five expelled the Jesuits between 1848 and 1859.[53] There have been several waves towards and away from authoritarianism. In the wake of the Wall Street crash of 1929, and the resulting world economic depression, no less than 16 countries suffered military coups or authoritarian takeovers of other kinds. That democratisation and liberal economic reform in the 1980s and 1990s took the form of a regionwide wave was thus far from coincidental.

Indeed, some writers have argued that so great are the similarities among the Latin American countries, and so great their differences with other parts of the world, that the region constitutes a distinct civilisation. Samuel Huntington, a conservative American political scientist, is the most prominent proponent of this view. 'Latin America has a distinct identity which differentiates it from the West ... it has a corporatist, authoritarian culture,' he argues.[54] However, most Latin Americans would see themselves as part of the 'Western world'. Their cultures are a unique mix of European, indigenous and African elements. But there is nothing in the historical record to suggest that Latin America is intrinsically incapable of following Europe and the United States down the path of democracy and capitalism – even if both will be of a distinct, Latin American kind. Alain Rouquié, a French political scientist and former diplomat, seems near the mark when he describes Latin America as the 'far west'[55] – the west's most challenging frontier of democracy and development.

CHAPTER 2

THE LATIN AMERICAN CONUNDRUM

Until at least the middle of the eighteenth century, the southern part of the Americas was on most counts far more developed than the English-speaking colonies of the north.[1] By 1551, universities had been founded in Peru, the Dominican Republic and Mexico, almost a century before Harvard. Though the economies of the Spanish colonies were dominated by plantation agriculture, subsistence farming and mining, they also boasted handcraft workshops. Some of these, especially for textiles, qualified as rudimentary factories. But in the second half of the eighteenth century the soon-to-be United States experienced incipient industrialisation and rapid economic growth. Some scholars reckon that by 1800 its income per head was twice that of Latin America, while others say that it was broadly similar, though income and wealth was much more unevenly shared out in Iberian America, which lacked the puritan egalitarianism of New England. Either way, there is consensus that at that point Latin America was the richest region of what is now called the 'developing world'.[2] It retained that status until fairly recently. At various times, its economic prospects have inspired the kind of excitement now reserved for China and other Asian countries. An observation typical in its tone, and in its self-interest, was that of Thomas Ashe, a Briton who in a work published in 1812 saw Latin America as 'embracing the finest country of the same magnitude in the world, peopled by 40,000,000 of inhabitants, abounding in riches, and wanting only our manufactures to possess every comfort of life.'[3] On the eve of the First World War, a similar enthusiasm was again widespread, and not just about booming Argentina. As recently as the 1960s Latin America seemed to be 'catching up' with the developed world. Yet development has proved a tantalising mirage – more so, even, than the quest for democracy. The diverging fortune of the two halves of the Americas has generated a deep and abiding sense of failure.

Chart 2: Growth of per capita GDP, 1820–1998

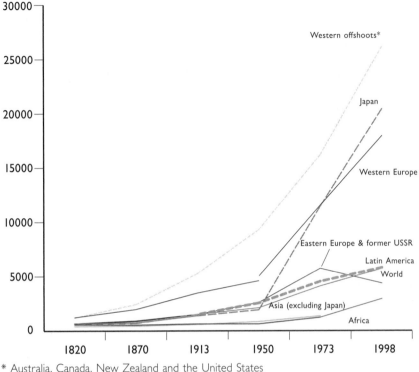

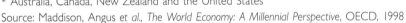

* Australia, Canada, New Zealand and the United States
Source: Maddison, Angus et al., The World Economy: A Millennial Perspective, OECD, 1998

That failure has been relative. According to calculations by Angus Maddison, an econometrician, income per head in Latin America in 1820 was roughly half that of the United States and Western Europe, similar to that of Eastern Europe and somewhat larger than the average in Asia. By 1998, he calculates, Western Europe was three times as rich as Latin America, and the United States more than four times. But income per head in Latin America was still higher than in Eastern Europe and Asia, if Japan is excluded[4] (see Chart 2). On most social indicators – but not education – Latin America also does better than other parts of the developing world (see Table 1).

Importantly, economic performance in Latin America has been far from uniformly unimpressive: it has varied sharply in different periods and between different countries. Much of the *widening* of the gap between Latin America and the rich countries derives from two periods in which the region as a whole fared badly: the first half-century after independence, when political turmoil and internal warfare caused economic havoc, and the years since the

Table 1: Comparative socio-economic indicators by region

	Life expectancy at birth, 2005 (years)	Infant mortality rate per 1,000 live births, 2005	Proportion of people living on less than $2 a day, 2004 (%)	Proportion of people with access to improved water source, 2004 (%)
East Asia & Pacific	71	26	36.6	79
Europe & Central Asia*	69	27	9.8	92
Latin America & Caribbean	72	26	22.2	91
Middle East & N Africa	70	43	19.7	89
South Asia	63	62	77.7	84
Sub-Saharan Africa	47	96	72.0	56

* Low- and middle-income countries only
Source: World Bank, World Development Indicators 2007

Table 2: Growth of per capita GDP by region, 1820–1998, annual average (%)

	1820–70	1870–1913	1913–50	1950–73	1973–98
Western Europe	0.95	1.32	0.76	4.08	1.78
Western offshoots	1.42	1.81	1.55	2.44	1.94
Japan	0.19	1.48	0.89	8.05	2.34
Asia (excluding Japan)	−0.11	0.38	−0.02	2.92	3.54
Latin America	0.10	1.81	1.42	2.52	0.99
Eastern Europe & former USSR	0.64	1.15	1.50	3.49	−1.10
Africa	0.12	0.64	1.02	2.07	0.01
World	0.53	1.30	0.91	2.93	1.33

Source: Maddison, Angus et al., The World Economy: A Millennial Perspective, OECD, 1998

debt crisis of 1982 (*see* Table 2). Maddison finds that between 1820 and 1870, income per head in Latin America grew by just 0.1 per cent a year. During the same period, the equivalent figure for the United States, Canada and Australia – other 'offshoots' of Western Europe – was 1.42 per cent. Between 1870 and the end of the Second World War, the eight biggest Latin American economies grew faster than the average of the rich countries that would make up the Organisation for Economic Co-operation and Development (OECD). Thereafter, growth remained respectable until 1982, but lagged that of the rich world. It was disappointingly weak after that, until 2004–6. In other words, Latin America fell behind in the first two-thirds of the nineteenth century, then held its own but failed to converge – as economic theory suggests it should – with countries which did achieve developed status. It then fell behind again for two decades after 1982.

Most accounts of Latin American economic history from 1870 to 1982 divide the period into two. Until 1930 the region sought export-led growth. The industrial revolution in Europe and the United States and its technological application to transport, combined with the development of capital markets, led to unprecedented growth in world trade and a first period of what would later be called globalisation.[5] Demand boomed for Latin America's minerals, from Chilean nitrates to Bolivian tin and Mexican and Peruvian silver; and for many of its food products, from Brazilian and Colombian coffee to Central American bananas, Cuban sugar and Argentine beef and wheat. From 1930, it is argued, many of the larger countries pursued *desarrollo para adentro* (inward-looking development), with greater tariff protection and state intervention. Though the Wall Street crash and the depression which followed had an important impact on Latin America, much recent research finds that 1930 was less of an economic turning point than previously thought: industrialisation and more interventionist policies go back before the First World War, while some smaller countries continued to pursue export growth after 1930. Maddison's figures suggest that growth performance was respectable in both periods. However, there are two important caveats which point to the costs of *desarrollo para adentro*. In contrast to the earlier period, between 1950 and 1973 growth in income per head lagged the world average. And secondly, the attempt to sustain inward-looking policies involved huge costs and distortions – notably inflation and foreign indebtedness.

Some countries in the region did worse than others in different periods. Victor Bulmer-Thomas, an economic historian, uses slightly different criteria than Maddison. Since income per head in the United States grew at 1.5 per cent a year in the nineteenth century, and population in Latin America expanded by 1.5 per cent a year in this period, to narrow the gap the region's economies would have to grow by more than 3 per cent a year. He calculates that this would require export growth of at least 4.5 per cent a year. For the period from 1850 to 1912, only Argentina and Chile managed this (Peru and Mexico did for shorter periods). Uruguay may have met the target because of the strength of its non-export economy.[6] During the second period, from 1928 to 1980, income per head in the United States grew at a faster annual average rate of 2 per cent. Bulmer-Thomas finds that in this period, Brazil, Costa Rica, Cuba, Mexico, Peru, Puerto Rico and Venezuela all narrowed the gap by achieving growth in income per head of more than 2 per cent per year (and Colombia exactly that).[7] The successful countries of the first phase performed poorly. In other words, some Latin American countries have managed to grow fast, but they have found it hard to sustain this for long enough to converge with the rich world. What is galling for Latin Americans is that many countries in Asia and southern and eastern Europe have pulled ahead over the past two generations. In 1966, Mexico was richer than Portugal and Brazil richer than South Korea. In 2002, income per head in Portugal and South Korea was roughly double that of Mexico and Brazil respectively. More broadly, in 1950 average income per head in Latin America was 25 per cent of that in the United States while the equivalent figure for Asia was only 10 per cent; by 2000, the Latin American figure had fallen to 20 per cent while that for Asia had risen to 25 per cent.[8]

A similar sense of thwarted possibility applies to Latin American democracy. Unlike Asia or Africa, Latin America has a history of liberal constitutionalism spanning almost two centuries. It is a troubled history, in which constitutionalism has often been truncated or merely served as a mask for tyranny. Nevertheless, it should not be lightly dismissed. A century ago, most of the main Latin American countries had achieved civilian constitutional rule under the auspices of limited or 'oligarchical democracy', to use a helpful oxymoron.[9] The franchise and participation were limited, but these incipient democracies were broadly comparable to those of much of Europe in the same period. Yet after 1930 nearly all countries in the region suffered repeated military interventions in politics. Dictatorship and brief periods of civilian rule alternated in pendulum swings; by the 1970s the generals were in charge nearly everywhere. More recently Latin America's restored democracies have struggled against institutional failings, poverty and economic instability. By contrast, new European democracies, such as Spain, Portugal or Greece, appear much more solid than many in Latin America. Relative though it may be, Latin America's development failure and its difficulty in consolidating democracy have given rise to a large and almost obsessive literature. There are four main schools of thought: dependency theory, cultural explanations, policy mistakes and institutional weaknesses. Let us examine them one by one.

Dependency: a theory in search of facts

The dependency school, composed mainly of left-wingers, blames United States intervention and Latin America's 'subordinate' role in the world economy as an exporter of raw materials for both its failure to achieve development and its history of political authoritarianism. Dependency theory grew out of a marriage between Marxist sociology and an economic doctrine known as structuralism, associated in Latin America with CEPAL. Structuralism was formulated in the late 1940s by a group of economists led by CEPAL's first secretary general, Raúl Prebisch, an Argentine. Prebisch's basic argument was that Latin America suffered from a structural decline in its terms of trade: its exports of primary products got ever cheaper because a surplus of labour held down wages, while its imports of manufactures from rich countries became more expensive because productivity gains were pocketed by increasingly monopolistic industrial firms rather than passed on as lower prices.[10] It followed from this that free trade would not enable Latin America to accumulate the surplus capital required to industrialise. Instead, governments should intervene to do the job, promoting industrialisation through protective tariffs, subsidised credit and a host of other incentives, and with the state itself setting up basic industries where private initiative could not or would not. This was the rationalisation for the policies of *desarrollo para adentro*.

Structuralism was soon taken up by sociologists and turned into a broader theory of 'dependent development'. Their central argument was expressed by Fernando Henrique Cardoso, a Brazilian, and Enzo Falletto, a Chilean, in *Dependencia y Desarrollo* ('Dependency and Development'), a slim volume first published in 1969. Between developed economies (which they called 'central' or 'metropolitan') and their underdeveloped ('peripheral') counterparts, they wrote, 'There is not just a simple difference of stage (of development) or of state of the productive system, but also of function or position within a single international economic structure of production and distribution. This presupposes, on the other hand, a defined structure of relations of domination.' In other words, poor countries are poor because others are rich, rather than because they have failed, for whatever other reason, to develop.[11] Dependency applied, too, they argued, to social and political systems. In an economy dominated by industrial monopolies, mainly foreign owned, the masses were excluded from employment ('development ... is done by intensifying social exclusion'[12]). The result was 'urbanisation without industrialisation'. At the same time, in return for investment, foreign capitalists demanded of the state action to discipline the wage demands of the workers. That, it was held, led inevitably to military dictatorships.

The argument of Cardoso and Falletto contained some nuances. They accepted that there were important differences between foreign investment in industry and earlier foreign 'enclaves' in mines and plantations. 'Peripheral industrial economies' could achieve a considerable degree of development and autonomy in relation to 'the centre', they conceded. In a memoir published in 2006, Cardoso, who would serve as Brazil's president from 1995 to 2002, argued that 'the primary message of "Dependency and Development" was that the people of Latin America had control over their own fate ... The problem faced by Latin America was political in nature rather than economic. Our backwardness was our own fault, not anybody else's.'[13] But that was not the way it was interpreted at the time, as Cardoso concedes. In other hands, there was no place for such nuances in dependency theory. It quickly became a dogma – heavily influenced by Marxist class analysis – according to which capitalism, foreigners and their local allies were directly responsible for Latin America's poverty and failure.[14]

Dependency theory was – and still is – enormously influential. At the beginning it seemed to chime with its times. In the 1960s American multi-nationals set up shop in many Latin American countries – sometimes displacing local firms that were unable to compete. The cities were swelling with rural migrants, who gathered in squalid shantytowns at the gates of the elegant residential districts of the better-off. During the Cold War, the United States preferred reactionary military dictatorships to reformist democrats. To varying extents it backed military coups, from Guatemala to Argentina. The emergence of military dictatorships in some of the most developed countries in the region appeared to contradict standard modernisation theory.[15] This holds that as countries industrialise and become richer, they become more socially varied, with a middle class that pushes for mass education and political pluralism, gradually but inevitably creating the conditions for democracy.

Students and academics, part of a rapidly expanding middle class, seized upon dependency theory as an explanation for Latin America's relative backwardness – and as a justification for revolution. This movement found its evangelist in Eduardo Galeano, a Uruguayan Marxist journalist. As its subtitle makes clear, his popular economic history, *Open Veins of Latin America: Five Centuries of the Pillage of a Continent*, is a scorching denunciation of foreign exploitation. First published in 1971 by Siglo XXI, a Mexican publisher, in 2004 it reached its seventy-sixth edition in Spanish – as well as having been liberally pirated across the region and widely translated. The book begins by stating: 'to each area has been assigned a function, always for the benefit of the foreign metropolis of the moment.'[16] Its basic, oft-repeated, theme is that 'underdevelopment in Latin America is a consequence of development elsewhere, that we Latin Americans are poor because the ground we tread is rich, and that places privileged by nature have been cursed by history. In this world of ours, a world of powerful centres and subjugated outposts, there is no wealth that must not be held in some suspicion.'[17] He brackets as identical 'agents of plunder' both 'the caravelled conquistadors and the jet-propelled technocrats; Hernan Cortés and the [US] Marines; the agents of the Spanish Crown and the International Monetary Fund missions; the dividends from the slave trade and the profits from General Motors'.[18]

Galeano is a writer of brilliance and passion. But his history is that of the propagandist, a potent mix of selective truths, exaggeration and falsehood, caricature and conspiracy theory.[19] Fundamentally, his message is one of anti-capitalism as well as anti-imperialism. He seems to reject all possibility of reform; local capitalists are dismissed as mere sepoys in the service of foreign masters. Latin America, because of its mineral and agricultural wealth, is rich. If most of its people are poor, it follows that someone must be stealing the wealth. These messages still echo across Latin America today, especially in the mouths of the leaders of radical social movements and populist politicians. The notion that Venezuela and Argentina are rich countries impoverished by foreigners, capitalism and corruption lies at the root of the peculiarly powerful appeal of populist politicians in both these countries – Perón and Peronism in Argentina, and Hugo Chávez in Venezuela. In addition, such beliefs lie behind much of the recent opposition to foreign investment in mining and oil and gas in countries such as Bolivia and Peru. Paradoxically, given structuralism's disdain for commodity exports, dependency theory has served to sustain in Latin America what economists call 'the natural-resource myth' – the view that what makes countries rich is what lies below their soil rather than the work and productivity of their inhabitants. It is a myth to which the *conquistadores* subscribed, so its currency across Latin America today is perhaps unsurprising. It is summed up in a common saying in Peru, falsely attributed to Antonio Raimondi, a nineteenth-century geologist, that the country is 'a beggar seated on a golden bench'. In Brazil, as Roberto Campos, an economic liberal and former planning minister, once pointed out, such illusions are encouraged even by the national anthem. It lauds the country as *gigante pela propia naturaleza, deitado eternamente em berço esplendido* ('a giant of nature itself, lying eternally in a splendid crib'). Dependency theory has also nourished a view of trade as a zero-sum game, rather than a source of mutual profit. This is strikingly similar to eighteenth-century mercantilism. As a result, many Bolivians would rather their country's natural gas remain in the ground than be exploited by foreigners or exported to their Chilean foes. Burned on their collective memory was the fabulous wealth extracted by foreigners from the Potosí silver mine and how little of it has been left behind.

The view of foreign investment in Latin America as malign is widely propagated. It is given credence in a second book which, along with Galeano's, has had a fundamental role in fixing the mental picture of the region's history carried by Latin Americans and outsiders alike. In the climactic scene of *One Hundred Years of Solitude*, Gabriel García Márquez describes a massacre of striking workers by troops acting at the behest of an American banana company whose plantations are held to have replaced a prosperous Eden with an oppressive monoculture. In the novel, more than 3,000 workers, women and children are cut down by army machine guns; their bodies are loaded onto a train and thrown into the sea, as the government silences news of the outrage. These scenes are loosely based on a strike in 1928 against the United Fruit Company in Magdalena department, on Colombia's Caribbean coast. But the actual events were very different. Historians estimate that no more than 75 people were killed (an appalling enough figure in any event). The massacre was widely denounced on the radio by opposition politicians, and it contributed to the election of a Liberal government which successfully pressed the company to concede many of the workers' demands.[20] Before the United Fruit Company's arrival, Magdalena had been one of the poorest and most backward departments of Colombia. The banana industry paid above-average wages, and attracted thousands of migrants.[21] Of course, the massacre was reprehensible, as was much else in the record of the United Fruit Company elsewhere in Latin America.[22] But by exaggerating its scale, García Márquez distorted its historical import. As Eduardo Posada Carbó, a Colombian historian, has pointed out, the discrepancy in the casualty figures was acknowledged by García Márquez himself. When he realised that 'the number of deaths must have been very small', the novelist recalled, 'This was a big problem, because when I found out that it wasn't really a spectacular massacre in a novel where everything was extraordinary ... where I wanted to fill a whole train with dead bodies, I couldn't stick to historical reality.'[23] Since the novel's publication in 1967, the figure of 3,000 dead has taken on a life of its own. In his memoirs, García Márquez notes with satisfaction that 'not long ago, on one of the anniversaries of the tragedy, a speaker in (Colombia's) Senate asked for a minute's silence in the name of the 3,000 anonymous martyrs slaughtered by the security forces'.[24] Unlike Galeano, García Márquez has the good excuse that he is a novelist. Nevertheless, many writers of the magical realism school have played a full part in burnishing the mythology of dependency theory.

Albeit in more scholarly form, dependency theory remains the dominant prism through which Latin American studies are taught in the United States. Take one of the standard introductory texts to the region: Thomas Skidmore and Peter Smith admit to borrowing all but one of the concepts that underpin their book from the dependency school (though they acknowledge 'limits to the utility of this approach').[25] Certainly, the dependency school can point to a few basic historical truths: the exploitation of Indian serfs and black slaves; the asymmetry of power between rich and poor countries and between the United States and Latin America. Foreign firms have sometimes behaved abusively; the United States has often bullied Latin American countries, from its 1846–8 war of annexation with Mexico to its encouragement of coups to its contemporary 'drug war'. Latin American economies have often found themselves vulnerable to sudden changes in a world economy over which they have little or no control.

But, for several reasons, dependency does not stack up as an explanatory theory – especially as an economic one. For a start, it is unable to explain what is without doubt the most significant development in the world economy of the past thirty years: the journey towards development through the medium of capitalism and international trade of many Asian countries. That explanatory failure is hardly surprising. Dependency theory rests on flimsy foundations, as Stephen Haber, a historian at Stanford University, has pointed out.[26] It employed ad hoc reasoning, such as the notion that foreign investment decapitalised Latin America because the value of repatriated profits over time might exceed the value of the original investment. This confused a stock and a flow, and failed to take into account the creation of value in the host country in the form of jobs, demand for inputs, and transfer of technology (and tax revenues).

The main tenets of dependency theory have been disproved by later empirical research. For example, contrary to Prebisch's assertion, recent econometric work shows that commodity prices and Latin America's terms of trade have not suffered secular declines, but rather have shown cyclical swings and no clear overall trend. There is much evidence that local capitalists were powerful, independent and innovative, and that governments often regulated foreign capital to serve the interest of national development.[27] This research 'has led to the virtual redundancy of the concept of the enclave economy', in which it was held that foreign investment in export products brought little benefit to the rest of the economy.[28] Of course, there were exceptional cases, such as Peru's International Petroleum Company, an affiliate of Standard Oil. From 1916 to 1934, just 16 per cent of the value of its total sales (most of which were exports) stayed in Peru in the form of wages, taxes and payments to local suppliers (of which there appear to have been none).[29] But such cases should not automatically be taken as the norm. For example, it is now recognised that foreign investment in railways was crucial in the development of local production and markets, not just for exports. Similarly, recent research has demolished the notion that Latin American economies were 'underdeveloped' by free trade. In fact, the region has been the most protected in the world for most of its history. Even as they paid lip-service to free trade in the nineteenth century, governments levied tariffs on imports because foreign trade was the handiest source of revenue, and the wars and internal strife of 1810–70 needed to be paid for. In a recent study, John Coatsworth and Jeffrey Williamson overturned much conventional wisdom on this subject.[30] They found that in a sample of 11 of the main Latin American countries, customs revenues averaged 57.8 per cent of total government revenues between 1820 and 1890. But even after internal peace was achieved, in the years preceding the First World War, governments raised import tariffs, switching from revenue-maximising protectionism to explicit industrial protectionism. That was partly to compensate local producers for the impact of lower shipping rates on the price of imports. And it was partly because the agro-export 'oligarchy' had less political clout or was less committed to free trade than is often asserted. Pre-First World War Latin American landowners were never as powerful as the European aristocracy and, anyway, they often invested in manufacturing too. Urban artisans and workers gained increasing political influence as the cities grew. Coatsworth and Williamson conclude that Latin America had very high tariffs for a century before the 1930s – and contrary to the arguments of protectionists, those countries with the highest tariffs grew slowest while those with the lowest tariffs grew fastest.

Overall, it is fair to conclude with Haber that 'in retrospect, dependency thinking about foreign capital and national sovereignty might have had a good deal of accuracy in regard to the smaller countries of Latin America, such as Honduras, Guatemala or Cuba, but held limited explanatory power for the larger countries of the region'.[31] The same goes for politics. The smaller countries of the Caribbean rim suffered repeated American intervention. The larger countries of South America, and Mexico, have generally gone their own way. True, the United States encouraged coups, especially during the Cold War. But in nearly all cases those coups were internally generated, and external support, while sometimes important, was not decisive.[32] Apart from being wrong, dependency theory had the unfortunate consequence of encouraging Latin Americans to blame all their woes on outsiders, rather than taking a closer look at themselves. (Conversely, many American academics and pundits appear to suffer from a guilt complex that leads them to exaggerate the scale and impact of US intervention in the region as a whole.) As David Landes, an economic historian at Harvard who is by no means a slave to neo-classical economics, noted: 'Cynics might even say that dependency doctrines have been Latin America's most successful export ... They are bad for effort and morale. By fostering a morbid propensity to find fault with everyone but oneself, they promote economic impotence. *Even if they were true, it would be better to stow them.*'[33]

A reactionary culture – but what if it changes?

Dependency theory has been mirrored among some conservative commentators by an alternative explanation for Latin America's woes, one which is very different in content but is similar both in inducing impotence and in being based on assertion more than empirical testing. This school holds that Latin America has been doomed by its culture, and in particular an Iberian, Catholic tradition of social organisation and political thought which, it is argued, is both anti-capitalist and inimical to democracy. The most elegant and erudite expression of this viewpoint is to be found in the writings of Claudio Véliz, a Chilean historian. In *The New World of the Gothic Fox*, he adapted an ancient Greek metaphor previously employed by Isaiah Berlin, an Anglo-Russian liberal philosopher, to distinguish between two groups of Western thinkers. In the metaphor the hedgehog is said to know one big thing while the fox knows many small things. Berlin called 'hedgehogs' those thinkers, such as Plato and Marx, 'who relate everything to a single, central vision', as against 'foxes', such as Aristotle, Erasmus, Shakespeare or Goethe, whose 'thought is scattered and diffused, moving on many levels'.[34] In other words, the hedgehog way of thinking carries the seeds of authoritarianism and totalitarianism, while that of the foxes embodies liberal pluralism. Véliz argues that Latin American culture is like a 'hedgehog': he sees it as marked by a monolithic, ordering vision composed of centralisation, civil law, Baroque classicism, and a notion of society as a hierarchical, organic whole, in which each person has his or her place. For Véliz, English-speaking North Americans, by contrast, are 'foxes'. Their culture has featured decentralisation, the common law, romanticism and the Gothic. Another hedgehog-like characteristic of the Ibero-American peoples, he notes, is their capacity to resist change, and especially the transformations associated with the Industrial Revolution in the Anglo-Saxon world. The reward for this stubborn Catholic conservatism is that values of family and community have been better preserved than in the Anglo-Saxon world.

The architects of this Iberian cultural edifice were the theologians of the Counter-Reformation, 'the greatest and most enduring achievement of (Spain's) impressive imperial moment', according to Véliz.[35] Its driving spirit was provided by the teachings of St Thomas Aquinas, which became entrenched at the University of Salamanca. Aquinas held that human society was an organic hierarchy governed by natural (i.e. divine) law. This view of the world was inimical to individualism, pluralism or the clash of competitive interest groups; the only restraint on absolute power was the duty of *noblesse oblige*, not that of man-made constitutions.[36] The mania for central control generated a habit of obsessive regulation which began with Philip II, the austere monarch at the zenith of Spanish power, who sat for long hours in his forbidding monastery-palace of El Escorial, in the hills outside Madrid, penning detailed ordinances to his viceroys across the ocean with only his impressive collection of Titian nudes for relief.

The 'culturalists' hold that this mindset still governs Latin America. Thus, Véliz says of the Counter-Reformation: 'the stability of its uncompromising symmetries largely dominates, even to this day, the lives of the Spanish-speaking peoples almost as convincingly and pervasively as the dynamic asymmetries of the Industrial Revolution preside over the English-speaking world.'[37] Sometimes the rejection of capitalism and industrialisation has indeed been turned into an explicit virtue by Latin American thinkers. In *Ariel*, a hugely influential book published in 1900, José Enrique Rodó, a Uruguayan journalist and man of letters, argued that Latin America, inspired by Hispanic Christianity and classical antiquity, should pursue the ideals of beauty and truth. He admired the vigorous prosperity of the United States, but saw that country as the source of a vulgar utilitarianism. Like some of today's critics of globalisation, he feared that the United States wanted to impose its ideas on everybody else. Rodó accepted democracy as inevitable, but called for its 'regeneration' by an aristocratic intellectual elite.[38] Rodó was writing in the aftermath of Spain's comprehensive military defeat by the United States in the Spanish–American war of 1898. This entailed the loss of Cuba and Puerto Rico (as well as the Philippines) and thus the end of the empire begun by Columbus. Paradoxically, after a century in which many of Latin America's leaders had imbibed and propagated a *leyenda negra* (black legend) which attributed all of their countries' ills to the colonial power, Spain's defeat in 1898 prompted an outpouring of sympathy in its former territories. *Arielismo* gave rise both to a conservative and almost racist Hispanicism and, on the left, to a new Latin American nationalism, which included a pronounced anti-*Yanqui* element. It would not be the last time that leftists and conservatives found common inspiration in an anti-liberal agenda, and one that seemed to justify the conditioning of democracy to other, allegedly higher, values.

Those writers who stress the influence of Iberian culture argue that when Latin American leaders have seemed to embrace change and democracy, it has been, as with the Sicilian aristocrat of Lampedusa's novel *The Leopard*, in order that everything should remain the same. Latin American democracy has always been more formal than real, they say. Absent, the argument goes, was the tradition of Anglo-Saxon liberal democracy, associated in particular with John Locke, who stressed the importance of the rights of the citizen and checks on an over-mighty executive. Rather, the notion of democracy that has prevailed in Latin America, it is said, has been one derived from French political philosophy, and especially that of Jean Jacques Rousseau, who argued that the ruler would be legitimated by interpreting the 'general will'.[39] This is at once both a defence of popular sovereignty and the perpetual excuse of the tyrant. Similarly, when Latin America appeared to embrace capitalism and democracy, during what Véliz has called 'the liberal pause' from 1870 to 1930, in several important countries it did so under the auspices of positivism. Not only was this another French doctrine, but it was one which essentially justified enlightened despotism or top-down reforms, separating economic freedom from political freedom. In this view, Latin America's industrial bourgeoisie, far from challenging an aristocratic, authoritarian state as their European counterparts did, allied with it. In this unflattering portrait, Latin American capitalists were rent-seekers rather than entrepreneurs, soliciting the comforts of protection, subsidies and privileges from the state, rather than risk the bracing challenge of unfettered competition. The result, it is argued, is a prevailing corporatist culture, in which Latin Americans see success as deriving not from individual merit but from patronage and personal contact – know-who rather than know-how. Behind a façade of constitutionalism and democracy, hierarchical domination and corporatist anti-individualism are held to thrive.

There is some truth in this explanation of the failure of capitalist democracy to flourish in Latin America. In particular, it is not hard to see in the Iberian legacy the origins of the mania for regulation and red tape that burdens business in the region. It is undeniably true that corporatism has been influential in Latin America, and with it the comfortable monopolies granted to many businesses or trade union confederations. It is true, too, that politics in Latin America has long been marked by undemocratic practices, such as 'patrimonialism' and 'clientelism'. The former refers in essence to the hijacking of the government, or bits of it, by powerful private interests. The latter term defines a pattern of politics in which local or national notables or political bosses extract votes and political loyalty from groups of poorer and less powerful followers in return for offering a degree of protection and access to state resources.[40]

But ultimately, the 'cultural explanation' fails to convince as an overarching theory. First, it cannot account for the diversity of outcome within the region. Why have some countries been so much more successful than others at different periods? Given a presumed cultural heritage in common, why is Chile so different from Argentina, Colombia from Venezuela, or Mexico from Peru? Second, it is simply nonsense to claim that the influence of French political philosophy is self-evidently inimical to democracy per se. Thus, Mario Vargas Llosa, a Latin American liberal democrat *par excellence*, professes himself a passionate admirer of French culture. From it, he says, he has learned above all 'to love liberty over all other things and to fight everything that threatens and contradicts it'. This 'insubordinate, libertarian, rebellious tradition and its universal vocation' is 'the most fertile and remains the most current' among 'the various tributaries of the great river of French culture', he said when accepting an honorary doctorate from the Sorbonne in 2005.[41] Third, in the two centuries since independence, Latin America has been shaped and enriched not just by its indigenous peoples and the Iberian legacy but by migration from other parts of Europe and from Asia, as well as from Africa. Some of those migrants have adhered to authoritarianism, just as many Iberians have been democrats. As Alain Rouquié, a distinguished scholar of Latin American militarism, asked mischievously: 'How much do generals Stroessner, Geisel, Medici, Leigh and Pinochet owe to Castile?'[42]

Above all, the 'cultural explanation' cannot explain recent, dramatic change in Spain itself. For much of the past two centuries, Spain was notorious for political instability and authoritarianism and for economic backwardness. Since the end of the Napoleonic invasion, Spain saw six constitutions, seven military *pronunciamientos*, two monarchical dynasties (and four abdications), two dictatorships, four civil wars and then the 36-year dictatorship of General Francisco Franco. 'Thus, Spain in the early 1970s stood in sharp contrast to the rest of Western Europe, except for neighbouring Portugal. While democratic systems had been fully entrenched for decades nearly everywhere else, Spain lacked a tradition of stable democratic governance throughout its history,' as a recent study put it.[43] Yet thirty years later, Spain has become a consolidated democracy and the world's ninth-largest economy, its success a marked counterpart to the travails of Italy. If culture was the problem, clearly the culture has changed. And if it can change in Spain, then it can change in Latin America. The Spanish transition was still fresh in the mind when the democratic wave swept over Latin America in the 1980s. Behind much of the recent disillusion in Latin America would appear to lurk the contrast with Spain's successful democratic consolidation. It is only fair to note that Spain enjoyed two big advantages as it embarked on its transition to democracy. First, its income per head was considerably higher than the average that prevailed in Latin America when it followed suit. That greater wealth was the result of more than 15 years of rapid economic growth, starting when Franco, at the urging of technocrats from Opus Dei, a Catholic group, opened Spain's economy to foreign trade and investment in the late 1950s. Second, the prospect of entry to the European Economic Community (as it then was) was a powerful incentive to adopt the rule of law. And while poverty and inequality in Spain were high by West European standards, they were nowhere near the levels in Latin America. The underlying point remains: culture is not the main obstacle to either democracy or development.

Of policies and institutions

So what is? Take economic development first. Economic theory says that growth comes from the accumulation of physical and human capital (in other words, investment and education), from applying technological innovation and from the efficiency with which all these are combined (i.e. productivity). Why has Latin America been relatively poor at doing these things? Some economists focus on policy mistakes. Thus, they looked at the rapid growth of some East Asian economies from the 1950s onwards, and argued that Latin America's choice of *desarrollo para adentro* and state intervention were catastrophic mistakes. Latin America opted to close its economies, limiting its access to new technology, just when world trade was about to enter a period of unprecedented growth. Yet countries such as Brazil and Mexico remained open to foreign investment in manufacturing in this period. And there is much debate about which combination of factors lay behind the Asian miracle: while promotion of exports was crucial (and lacking in Latin America), some observers also pointed to superior educational performance and prior land reform in Japan and South Korea, and to their protection of infant industries. Even so, neo-conservative writers imagined that merely to dismantle the mistaken policies of state intervention and protectionism would propel Latin America along a seamless path of development. The free play of market forces and openness to trade and investment, it was thought, would raise the rate of growth. This would cut poverty and expand the middle class, and thus create a sound basis for democracy as well as economic development. This belief echoed the arguments of some Latin American leaders in the immediate aftermath of independence that free trade and the encouragement of European migration would be enough to achieve European levels of development. Some of the enthusiasts for the Washington Consensus appeared to share a similar faith in the unalloyed power of open markets and open trade.

Yet setbacks in the 1990s quickly showed that Latin American development remains an obstacle course. Argument rages as to whether the 'lost half-decade' of 1998–2003 was caused by the policy reforms themselves or because these had not gone far enough. Some economists say that the abrupt lifting of barriers to trade and capital movement ('shock therapy') made Latin America more vulnerable to financial crises originating in the outside world. Others argue that the problem was not the opening in itself, but the failure to deal with its consequences. These included increased flows of short-term foreign capital and overvalued currencies. In economies that were only partly reformed, these changes eventually triggered financial crises because of weaknesses in local banking systems. But the wider point, on which many agree, is that getting macroeconomic policies right is a necessary but not sufficient condition for sustained high growth. Among the reformers themselves, by the mid-1990s it had come to be recognised that 'Institutions Matter', to cite the title of a World Bank report on Latin America.[44] Its authors noted that while the policies of the Washington Consensus had brought macroeconomic stability and raised growth rates (from the anaemic levels of the 1980s), they had not had the anticipated impact on poverty, inequality or job creation. To achieve these goals, and to raise the rate of growth, the report stressed the importance of microeconomic reforms (sometimes known as 'second-generation' reforms), of such institutions as labour markets, banking systems, legal systems and machinery for the enforcement of contracts, the state bureaucracy and regulatory bodies.

The dividing lines between culture and institutions and between institutions and policy are blurred. 'Culture' refers to the prevailing sets of customs, values and beliefs of a society. Institutions may express such habits, values and beliefs. But another way of looking at institutions is to see them as the result of policy choices: 'We can view institutions as the cumulative outcome of past policy actions.'[45] In recent decades, many economists have come to see institutions as fundamental to explaining how economies work. The 'new institutional economics', as it is called, does not reject orthodox neo-classical economics, but attempts to build into it more realistic assumptions about the way that markets operate. Institutions – meaning rules, though these are normally expressed in or applied by organisations – serve to reduce uncertainties and transaction costs in human exchange.[46] What matters is that decisions by the state should be predictable – the rule of law, rather than of arbitrary, dictatorial whim, or the opaque bending of justice according to private interest. Crucially, even where sound macroeconomic policies are in place, poor regulation and ill-defined or poorly enforced property rights can serve to restrict rather than stimulate economic activity, encouraging rent-seeking rather than rising productivity.

This argument was powerfully expressed by Hernando de Soto, a Peruvian economist, in *El Otro Sendero* ('The Other Path'), published in 1986. De Soto applied the new institutional economics to the vast 'informal' sector of unregistered businesses that had grown up in Lima and other Latin American capitals. His research institute, the Instituto Libertad y Democrácia (ILD), calculated that the informal sector accounted for 39 per cent of Peru's GDP and employed 48 per cent of the workforce. In Lima, some 440,000 people – more than a tenth of the capital's population at the time – worked as street vendors or in 'informal' commerce. Informal businesses also ran nearly all of the city's buses. More than 40 per cent of the houses in Lima were self-built.[47] Traditional conservatives saw the informals as unfair, tax-evading competitors, while the left, following the tenets of dependency theory, saw the informals as marginalised by an economic order of 'urbanisation without industrialisation'.[48] De Soto, by contrast, saw the informal sector as an 'insurrection' against the legal institutions of a corporatist state: 'access to private enterprise is difficult or impossible for the popular classes, legal norms are excessive and vexatious, public and private bureaucracies are enormous, redistributive coalitions have powerful influence in the formulation of law and the intervention of the state is patent in all activities.'[49] Informality, he argued, has 'turned a large number of people into entrepreneurs'.[50] The ILD found that the obstacles to setting up a legal business were gigantic. To prove the point, it set up a small tailoring shop; registering this required 11 different permits, which took ten months and cost $194 (or five times the minimum wage in Peru at the time). Far from being an unfair advantage, informality was a crushing handicap: the ILD found that informal businesses paid 10 to 15 per cent of their gross revenues in bribes. They were restricted to buying and selling among family and trusted friends, unable to develop economies of scale or get access to bank loans. De Soto, a brilliant marketer of ideas, subsequently developed this work into a broader theory of why capitalism has struggled in developing countries.[51] The poor have plenty of assets, he argued, but because they are not documented by the formal legal system they cannot be mobilised as capital. Instead, the poor have developed extra-legal arrangements, based on a mixture of custom and informal consensuses. The challenge for governments is to merge these two legal systems.

The value of de Soto's campaign lies in highlighting the way in which law, property rights and enforceable contracts underpin economic development, and that the weakness of these institutions in many Latin American countries raises the costs of transactions and stunts growth, affecting informal and formal businesses alike. This approach has spawned a host of more or less successful government efforts to cut red tape. Yet useful though it is, it does not add up to a complete theory of underdevelopment. The problem with de Soto's argument is that gaining legal title for their assets doesn't necessarily allow the poor to turn them into investment capital. For most poor people in Latin America, their self-built house is too important to risk losing by offering it as guarantee for a loan. Take the example of Felipe Copaja, a stocky 45-year old of Aymara descent who owns a small workshop in a side-street in the city of El Alto in Bolivia. He set up his own business making pumps and parts for wells and greenhouses. On the wall of his living room, in his simple but comfortable three-room house in a corner of the workshop yard, hangs a framed certificate that shows that his business is legally registered. But his situation is still precarious. He works with his brother and nephew, taking on outside labour only when business is good and then only temporarily. His legal title means that he could get credit to expand the business, but he has not done so. 'The banks will lend against title, but at 18 per cent in dollars. I prefer not to risk losing my home so that I can sleep easily.'[52] Not only does the house provide the family with shelter but it can also be a source of income, by renting out a room or two. A study in Buenos Aires found that titling did lead residents to spend more on improving their homes, but had no significant effect on their access to credit.[53] But perhaps the most powerful evidence comes from Peru itself, where under de Soto's influence over 1.2 million property titles were issued to urban households between 1995 and 2003. Research has found that those with titles were no more likely to obtain a loan from a commercial bank than those who lacked one – perhaps because banks fear that the courts will recoil from exercising the loan guarantee by seizing the homes of the poor.[54] However, urban squatter families who lack property titles have to devote more time to protecting their homes. Titling does lead to a substantial increase in hours worked outside the home by adults, and a reduction in child labour.[55] While some informals are indeed entrepreneurs, many choose to work for themselves because they lack the skills to obtain decent employment. Poverty, lack of education and good healthcare are formidable barriers that better legal institutions alone will not change.

That said, there can be no doubt that good legal institutions do indeed matter a lot for economic growth. One recent large cross-country econometric study, by Dani Rodrik, an economist at Harvard University, and two colleagues, found that institutional quality – measured by the perceptions of investors regarding the effectiveness of contract enforcement and protection of property rights – has a big impact on the income level of a country.[56] This study also looked at the influence of geography and the intensity of trade on development. It found little evidence that either by themselves *cause* countries to be richer or poorer (though richer countries tend to trade more). However, geography does appear to have an indirect impact on income by influencing the quality of institutions – on which more in a moment. Deficient legal institutions do much to explain the shape of Latin American businesses, in which the family-owned diversified conglomerate has long been the dominant force and Anglo-Saxon-style equity capitalism has struggled to take off. Research by a group of economists from the universities of Harvard and Chicago suggests that the French civil-law tradition of the *Code Napoléon* adopted by Latin America on independence provides markedly less protection for outside minority shareholders than either Anglo-American common law or the civil-law systems of Germany and Scandinavia.[57] Yet sceptics might object that the *Code Napoléon* has not stopped France from becoming one of the world's richest economies.

The price of inequality

It is a mistake to seek a single, overarching explanation for Latin America's relative failure, as the dependency theorists, the advocates of cultural explanations and de Soto all do in their differing ways. Much of the answer to the Latin American conundrum surely lies in the interplay between several sets of factors. History (the circumstances in which Latin America was colonised, became independent and related to the world economy), geography (climate, obstacles to transport, the presence of a large indigenous population), political institutions and policies have combined to mould the region's fate. A recent study by Rosemary Thorp and others stresses this interplay between institutions, geography and natural resource endowments.[58] It also notes that institution-building – the development of markets and a modern state – was crucial in determining the Latin American economies' 'capacity to change'. By that they mean both the capacity to absorb new technologies and to innovate and to respond to shifting external conditions.

As an increasingly rich and lively academic debate on Latin American economic history unfolds, inequality – of wealth and of political power – is moving to the heart of the story. Two American economists, Stanley Engerman and Kenneth Sokoloff, argue that geography in the form of different 'factor endowments' (meaning climatic suitability for particular crops, natural resources, and the relative abundance of labour) has played a crucial role in the different way in which institutions were structured in the two halves of the Americas, and that this in turn had an effect on growth.[59] Thus, in Brazil and the Caribbean, the soils and climate favoured sugar, cotton and coffee, which were all of high value and attracted economies of scale. These crops stimulated the formation of large plantations and estates, and the import of slaves to work them. In Mexico and Peru, wealth came from exploiting mines and the initially large population of sedentary Indians. Again, large landholdings were the rule. In both cases, extreme inequalities of wealth and power were the norm. The institutions of colonial Latin America served to protect those inequalities. By contrast, in Canada and the northern British colonies (not the pre-Civil War South, whose economy was similar in many ways to those of Latin America), climatic conditions favoured mixed farming of grains and livestock, with no economies of scale. So small family farms became the norm, there was less demand for slaves, and a more equal society emerged. 'It seems unlikely to have been coincidental that those colonies with more homogenous populations ... evolved a set of institutions that were more oriented towards the economic aspirations of the bulk of the adult male population,' Engerman and Sokoloff argue.[60] These arrangements tended to persist because factor endowments were difficult to change. Although they concede that the relationship between equality and economic growth is complex, the authors argue that the more egalitarian society of the United States encouraged early industrialisation by providing a market and by making technical innovation easier. In Mexico and Brazil, by contrast, access to patents was in practice restricted, by costs and regulations, to the wealthy or influential. In addition, in Latin America the close correlation between economic status and race may have served to make inequality harder to break down.

Others argue that inequality restricted growth not because it begot poor institutions but because it generated economically costly political conflicts. Coatsworth argues that extreme concentration of land, wealth and power in Latin America did not date from the colonial period, but from the second half of the nineteenth century when the region's economies began to grow as a result of being drawn into the world economy in a first period of globalisation.[61] But inequality, he notes, did not impede growth: governments cut deals with local and foreign investors in a kind of 'crony capitalism'.

Yet those political arrangements condemned Latin America to a series of vicious circles. Perhaps the most important example concerns the labour market. In Latin America, as in the United States, land was abundant and labour was scarce. That should have lead to higher wages and labour-saving innovations to increase productivity. This is what happened in farming in the United States. In Latin America, on the whole it did not (Argentina was a partial exception). Perhaps because of the prevalence of slavery and forced Indian labour during the colonial period, Latin American landowners were reluctant to pay higher wages, preferring continued coercion. There was a profusion of different forms of servitude associated with the *haciendas* or large estates. Indeed, the desire to gain control of labour, rather than the accumulation of land itself, was probably the main factor driving the expansion of *haciendas* at the expense of communal landholdings in the nineteenth century. These patterns in land and labour markets discouraged both innovation and the growth of the domestic market, and thus were an important factor delaying industrialisation.[62] In Europe and the United States, the benefits of economic growth were eventually spread wide because, as productivity increased, trade unions secured higher wages and democratic governments established welfare states. That did not happen to the same degree in Latin America. Import-substitution industrialisation served to reduce competition and to maximise the gains and privileges of the politically well-connected. Inequality remained high and poverty widespread. The beneficiaries of the established order blocked the adoption of the reforms – of landholding, trade, taxes, credit and education – which might have promoted greater equity. Yet such arrangements became harder and harder to sustain, leading to an increase in political instability and populist attempts to remedy inequality by expropriations of land or businesses (or the rhetorical threat of them). There is evidence that such political instability undermined economic growth, and served to make it more volatile.[63] Such political conflicts also help to explain why for so long Latin America seemed to defy modernisation theory.

The burden of history is great in Latin America, but it is not absolute. The diversity of experiences across the region is a caution against the notion of inevitability. To take just one example, Colombia's coffee boom rested in large part on family farmers: in 1932, 60 per cent of the country's production of coffee beans came from farms smaller than 12 hectares.[64] The broader point is that the advent of increasingly established and durable mass democracies in the region provides grounds for optimism. True, democracy involves particular problems of collective action. But at least in theory, it holds out the possibility of the peaceful resolution of conflicts, of lasting political stability, of swift problem-solving, and the speedy copying of successful models within the region. It thus offers Latin America an unprecedented opportunity to combine faster growth with greater equity. And in a globalised world in which rich countries have become post-industrial, there are many new opportunities as well as problems. Rather than being culturally or externally determined, it is more fruitful to see Latin American history as a contest, between modernisers and reactionaries, between democrats and authoritarians, between the privileged and the excluded. That contest is the subject of the next three chapters.

CHAPTER 3

THE SEED OF DEMOCRACY IN THE LAND OF THE *CAUDILLO*

'Weapons have given you independence. Laws will give you freedom.' This pledge to his fellow countrymen from Francisco Paula de Santander, a Colombian independence leader, is inscribed above the doorway of the Palace of Justice in Bogotá's Plaza Bolívar, its paved main square. The inscription has an unintentionally ironic ring to it – and not only because freedom and the rule of law long proved elusive, in Colombia and throughout Latin America. The current version of the palace, of blond stone blocks, dates only from the 1990s. The previous building was destroyed by fire after guerrillas from the nationalist M-19 movement seized it in 1985, taking the Supreme Court hostage. The army, deploying armoured cars, retook the palace after hours of fighting; 95 people, including 11 Supreme Court justices, died in the confrontation.[1] Not far away from the palace are other reminders of the violence that has intermittently dogged Colombia. Near the Congress building on the Carrera Septima, the city's main artery, a plaque marks the spot where General Rafael Uribe, a Liberal leader of the civil war of 1899 to 1902 – chronicled in García Márquez's *One Hundred Years of Solitude* – was assassinated a decade after he had made peace with a Conservative government. Half a dozen blocks to the north along the same avenue a similar plaque marks a still more controversial assassination: Jorge Eliécer Gaitán, a crowd-pulling populist Liberal who seemed assured of victory in Colombia's 1950 presidential election, was shot at point-blank range by a lone assassin as he left his lawyer's office. His murder on 9 April 1948 triggered a yet bloodier civil war, known simply as *la violencia*, which claimed perhaps 180,000 lives. It is still debated today in Colombia whether the killer acted alone or at the behest of the Conservative opposition.

Though falling short of the abysmal standard set by many other parts of the world, notably Europe, political violence has been all too commonplace in

Latin America over the past two centuries. In that regard, Colombia occupies a prominent role, though it is unusual partly because armed conflict has continued into the twenty-first century even as it has died away everywhere else in the region over the past decade. Paradoxically, Colombia has another claim to exceptionalism – one for which Santander and his followers can take much credit. The country has an unusually long democratic tradition: with only one brief exception, it has elected civilian governments since the 1830s with suffrage arrangements that compared favourably with much of Europe. That statement requires one or two caveats. There were periodic civil wars, mainly between the Liberals and the Conservatives. The murder of Gaitán plunged the country not just into *la violencia* but also into a short military dictatorship. Civilian rule was restored under a power-sharing pact between the two main parties. This lasted from 1958 to 1974; it brought stability but restricted political competition. And the writ of government has never extended over the whole of a huge and fragmented territory with poor internal communications. Even so, Colombia, along with Costa Rica and Uruguay, stands out from the rest of Latin America: in all three countries, authoritarian dictatorships have been brief and rare. In much of the rest of the region, periods of civilian rule alternated with dictatorship; in some countries authoritarian rule was the norm at least until the 1980s.

As Santander's injunction makes plain, some of Latin America's independence leaders of the 1820s wanted to lay the foundations of democratic government. So why has democracy fared so poorly? This chapter will explore that question by surveying the region's history for the first century or so after independence. History still hangs heavy in Latin America: it is the stuff of contemporary politics, constantly invoked by Hugo Chávez or Mexico's Zapatista movement or by Argentina's Peronists, recalled in street names and statues. As Enrique Krauze, a Mexican historian, has said of his country, 'the weight of the past has sometimes been more present than the present itself. And a repetition of the past has sometimes seemed to be the only foreseeable future.'[2] That is especially true in Mexico, but it also applies in many other Latin American countries. It is hard to analyse the prospects for consolidating democracy without regard to this history, to the lessons that Latin Americans draw from it, and the institutions, political traditions and economic practices which it has bequeathed to the region.

Independence at a price

The revolt of the 13 British colonies against King George III firmly planted democracy and enlightenment republicanism in the western hemisphere. Along with the writings of the French *philosophes* and British economic liberalism, the political example set by the founding fathers of the United States exercised a strong intellectual appeal for many of the independence leaders in Latin America. It would not be until the end of the nineteenth century, the age of *Arielismo*, that 'anti-Americanism' would take a firm hold in the region. Yet several things would hold the newly independent Latin American nations back, and impede them from following the United States on its path of democracy and development. These included the nature of the independence struggle itself, the socio-economic order bequeathed by Iberia, geographical factors and consequent economic fragility.

By comparison with the war of American Independence of 1776–82, the fight for independence in Spanish America was longer, bloodier and more destructive. It differed, too, in being triggered by events on the other side of the Atlantic. Napoleon Bonaparte's invasion of Iberia in 1807–8 and his overthrow of the Spanish Bourbon monarchy created a power vacuum at the heart of the empire. In 1808, as news of these developments reached first Caracas, and then Buenos Aires and other colonial centres, *juntas* were formed to exercise power. They proclaimed a nominal loyalty to Fernando VII, who was a captive in a French chateau. But discontent among the *criollos*, as American-born whites were known, had been building for at least a generation. At the start of the nineteenth century, *criollos* made up some 3.3 million of Spanish America's total population of 16.9 million.[3] They were outnumbered by 7.5 million Indians, 5.3 million *mestizos* and 776,000 blacks. Many *criollos* formed part of an incipient middle class of managers, lawyers and other professionals. Others formed part of the economic aristocracy of Spanish America, the owners of the great *haciendas* and the mines and the merchants and traders. But all of them were excluded from political power.

During his reign from 1759 to 1788, Carlos III, Fernando's grandfather, had made a vigorous effort to halt his country's long decline, and to reform its system of colonial rule. These 'Bourbon reforms' were in part the result of new ways of thinking. The rationalism of the French enlightenment had an important influence in Iberia. It challenged – albeit moderately at first – the Catholic conservatism that had held Spain and its colonies in its thrall since the Counter-Reformation. In Spanish America, the reforms involved more open trade (but only between ports within the empire, not with other countries), the weakening of the power of the Church (the Jesuits were expelled, for example), and a modest opening to new ideas. Above all, the reforms involved more efficient administration. But that meant a tightening of the control of Madrid over local affairs – a 'new imperialism' as John Lynch, a historian of the independence era, puts it.[4] In particular, the Bourbons restored a near-monopoly of political office in the Americas to Spanish-born *peninsulares* (who numbered no more than 40,000 in the empire as a whole around 1800). This applied not just to the viceroys and other senior officials but to membership of the *audiencias* or high courts: of 266 appointments to *audiencias* from 1751 to 1808, only 62 were of *criollos*.[5]

These reforms had two unintended effects. First, they helped to divide the rich and powerful in both Spain and its colonies into liberal and conservative camps – a division that would last in both places until at least the early twentieth century. In Spain itself, liberalism first showed its hand when opponents of Napoleon convened in Cádiz in 1810 a parliament or *Cortes* – an institution with medieval origins but which had been snuffed out by centuries of absolutism. A majority of the members of the *Cortes* were reformers: they called themselves Liberals, the first time anywhere that the word was used as a political identity.[6] The *Cortes* proceeded to declare itself sovereign and issue a constitution which called for a parliamentary monarchy and widespread male suffrage. Second, in Spanish America, the reforms rammed home to the *criollos* that they lacked the political power to defend their economic privilege. That gave rise to grievance, over the trade monopoly and taxes, for example. It also bred disquiet: some *criollos* came to see Spanish weakness as being as big a threat to their interests as Spanish power. They worried that a power vacuum at the top would threaten social order and private property.

They were haunted by a two-headed spectre of popular rebellion. In 1791, inspired by the principles of the French Revolution, the black slaves of the sugar island of Saint-Domingue, France's richest colony, revolted. 'It was a terrifying revelation of the explosive force of stifled savage hatred,' as one account puts it.[7] In the first two months, 2,000 whites (or one in five) were killed, 180 sugar plantations and 900 coffee and indigo farms were destroyed and 10,000 slaves died in fighting, repression or famine. After a dozen years of violence and warfare, in which they successively defeated armies sent by Republican France, Spain, Britain and Napoleon, the former slaves triumphed, and in 1804 Saint-Domingue became Haiti – the second independent nation in the western hemisphere. But such was the destruction and the infighting among the patriots that the victory was a Pyrrhic one.[8]

Ten years prior to Haiti's slave revolt, in the mountains south of Cusco, the former Inca capital, an Andean Indian *cacique* (local boss) called José Gabriel Condorcanqui had rebelled against the viceroy in Lima. He took the name of Tupac Amaru II, after the last Inca. His demands were a vague mixture of opposition to the Bourbon reforms, Inca revivalism and independence. After six months, he was captured and, along with his wife Micaela Bastides, was executed with great cruelty in Cusco's main square. His rebellion had extended over much of the southern half of the viceroyalty of Peru, as far as northern Argentina. Some 100,000 people died, and there was much destruction of property.[9] Although Condorcanqui himself had stressed that his movement was a multi-ethnic one, many of his Indian supporters had been quick to turn their ire on the whites.

The memory of these events meant that many *criollos*, especially in Peru and Mexico with their large Indian populations, did not at first favour cutting the link with Spain. Even Simón Bolívar, the great Liberator of northern South America, worried about the sheer numbers of the slaves and the mixed-blood *pardos* in his native Venezuela, stating: 'A great volcano lies at our feet. Who shall restrain the oppressed classes?'[10] Many historians have thus seen independence not as a progressive revolution in the mould of that of Washington and Jefferson, but rather as a conservative reaction. It was that – but it was more than that. Motives and interests within Spanish America varied, but the desire for the removal of colonial restraints was strong. It expressed itself first in Venezuela and the River Plate region, in part because they were the first to hear the tumultuous news from Spain and in part because as trading colonies they had been hit hardest by the Bourbon reforms. In both places, the *criollos*, invoking a Spanish tradition of communalism with strong medieval roots, called a *cabildo* (town meeting), deposed the colonial authorities and proclaimed a governing *junta*. In Caracas, independence was declared in 1811; in the United Provinces of the River Plate, from which would emerge Argentina, the declaration came five years later. In Mexico alone the cry for independence came from below, from Miguel Hidalgo, a parish priest in the central Bajío region, who raised an Indian horde.

The struggle was almost everywhere protracted and convoluted, taking on the character of a civil war. The patriots were often divided, by local interest as much as by ideology. Social disorder, or the fear of it, caused many *criollos* to hesitate before breaking the bonds with Spain. The defeat of Napoleon saw Fernando restored to the Spanish throne in 1814, able to despatch reinforcements to America. An expedition of 10,000 seasoned troops reached Venezuela in 1815, the darkest period for the patriot cause across the region. These were partly offset by the arrival of 6,000 mainly British and Irish volunteers who fought as mercenaries with Bolívar's armies. This force apart, Latin America lacked the kind of external support that France had offered to Washington in the United States.

Two things combined finally to prise South America from Spain's grasp. The first was better strategy and organisation on the patriot side. In southern South America, José de San Martín, an Argentine who had served for two decades as a regular officer in the Spanish army before joining the patriot cause, pulled off a bold strategic move. He organised and led a force of 5,000 troops across the Andes to Chile, through snowy 4,000-metre-high passes, and surprised the Spanish forces there. Having secured Chile, he embarked in the ships of Thomas Cochrane, a swashbuckling British admiral who served the patriot cause as a mercenary, and landed his army in Peru. He (temporarily) freed Lima, which until the Bourbon reforms had been the capital of the whole of Spanish South America and remained a royalist bastion. San Martín's forces joined up with those of Simón Bolívar. Bolívar himself had recovered from a rout in his native Venezuela in 1812. By allying with the *llaneros* (cowboys) of the Venezuelan plains, and through indefatigable generalship, including a march up and over the Andes to Bogotá even more demanding than that of San Martín, he had freed northern South America. Spain's last redoubt in Peru was surrounded and would fall to a multinational army under Bolívar. In 1826, the last remaining Spanish troops surrendered to his forces in Upper Peru (soon to become Bolivia).

The second factor was the twists and turns of peninsular politics, as power in Spain's restored monarchy oscillated between incipient parliamentary liberalism and absolutist reaction. Spanish strategy was misguided as well as confused. The liberals failed to seek compromises, such as home rule, until it was far too late. Royalist repression was often self-defeating. The Spanish forces sequestered the property of their opponents and, in Colombia for example, executed a number of patriots. On the other hand, the advent of a liberal government in Spain after 1820 prompted the conservative *criollos* of Mexico to opt for independence. The disorderly Indian armies led by Hidalgo and another radical priest, José Miguel Morelos, had rampaged across half the country to the alarm of the *criollos*, before being defeated and their leaders killed. In 1821, Agustín Iturbide, a *criollo* general who had fought for Spain, made common cause with the remaining rebel leaders, proclaimed independence and ruled briefly as emperor of Mexico.

Only in Brazil was independence a less-than-traumatic affair. When Napoleon invaded Iberia, Britain arranged to ship the Portuguese monarch and his court across the Atlantic to Rio de Janeiro. It was the only occasion in the history of European empire in which a colony became the metropolis. The result was that it was the Portuguese monarchy that provided Brazil with 'almost all of the founding institutions, usually the task of a postcolonial government: a centralised administration and bureaucracy; superior law courts; a public library and an academy of fine arts; a school of medicine and law; a national press and national bank; and a military academy.'[11] After hostilities ceased in Europe, King João VI returned, with some tardiness, to Lisbon. As the *Cortes* in Portugal attempted to reassert colonial control, João's eldest son, left behind as regent, quickly realised that the price of maintaining monarchy in Brazil was independence. He declared it in 1822 and ruled as Dom Pedro I. Though war with Portugal followed, it was brief and mainly settled at sea by the skill of Cochrane.[12]

The armies involved in the independence wars were not large: Bolívar never led more than 10,000 men into battle. But in some places almost two decades of near-continuous fighting wreaked a heavy toll. Mines had been flooded, farms looted and bridges destroyed. In 1821, the coin produced by the mint in Mexico City from the country's silver mines totalled just 6 million pesos, down from 26 million pesos a year before the wars.[13] Recovery would take decades. With elegance but perhaps some exaggeration, Felipe Fernández-Armesto, an Anglo-Spanish historian, has recently summarised the comparative impact:

> the independence wars were, in short, the making of the United States and the ruin of much of the rest of the Americas ... To fight the wars, all the affected (Spanish-American) states had to sacrifice liberties to *caudillismo* and civil values to militarism ... People in the Americas often speak of the chaotic politics, democratic immaturity, and economic torpor of Latin American tradition as if they were an atavistic curse, a genetic defect, a Latin legacy. Really, like everything else in history, they are products of circumstance, and of the circumstances, in particular, in which independence was won.[14]

The colonial inheritance

Apart from its costly birth, the second handicap faced by newly independent Latin America was the legacy of the Iberian colonial order, which made it ill equipped for democracy and development. Colonial Latin America differed radically from New England or Canada (though less so from the more southerly of Britain's American colonies). In the sixteenth century, the *conquistadores* had brought with them a kind of militarised feudalism. This had been honed in the *reconquista*, the seven centuries of intermittent war that had driven the Moors from Spain. In 1492, in one of history's more striking coincidences of date, Columbus made his first landfall in the 'new world' just as the Muslim emirate of Granada, the last Moorish foothold in Iberia, was overrun, completing the *reconquista*. The Spanish took two other sixteenth-century philosophies across the Atlantic. One was a militant, intolerant Catholicism, derived partly from the *reconquista* but given more force by the Counter-Reformation with its Inquisition and apparatus of censorship. The Spanish crown tried to control who settled in the Americas – indeed it went so far as to obtain a papal bull to uphold its authority to do so. In sharp contrast with English-speaking North America, no heretics, dissidents or freethinkers needed to apply. The second guiding philosophy was mercantilism. This doctrine held that gold and silver bullion was the ultimate source of wealth – and not merely another commodity – and that trade was a zero-sum game. So Spain imposed a rigid monopoly of trade with its colonies, and discouraged the production of items that might compete with its own farmers and artisans. The backbone of the colonial economy became the *hacienda* (the large landed estate with resident serfs), the plantation and the mine. The crown had swiftly imposed central authority on the *conquistadores*. The principal institution of government was the *audiencia*, a judicial body but one which was presided over by the king's representative – the viceroy or captain general – whom it also advised. Though there were also *cabildos* (town councils) their responsibilities were minor. The crown issued a constant flow of decrees – over 400,000 by 1635, though they were later codified into 6,400.[15] Almost from the start, the crown relied on the sale of offices to raise revenue. Several familiar characteristics of Latin American government thus date from the colonial period: centralisation and the blurring of executive and judicial authority.[16] To this list one might add a regulatory mania. Legislation in Latin America often embodies an ideal world, impossible to carry out in practice. That gave rise to a famous response among colonial officials: *obedezco pero no cumplo* (I obey but I do not comply). The result was less the rule of law than the realm of discretion, giving rise to corruption and politically influenced justice.[17]

Unlike the Pilgrim Fathers (and the Portuguese in Brazil), the Spaniards conquered territories with large populations of native Americans. In Mexico's central plateau, in Guatemala and in Peru, these had formed sophisticated and wealthy societies based on sedentary farming. At the time of their respective European conquests, Latin America may have contained some 20 million people, compared with some 3 million spread across what would become Canada and the United States. Millions of native Americans died, above all from disease but also from forced labour and conquest itself. But one of the enduring differences between the two Americas is that many more Indians survived in Latin America. The Spaniards quickly realised that they needed Indian labour. Colonial Spanish America became a caste society: a small group of large landowners, officials and clergy ruled over a much larger population of Indians. Spanish absolutism recognised some rights (known as *fueros*) for its subjects, but these were exercised by groups, not individuals. The Church, the army and militia, some professions and the Indians had their own *fueros*. Indeed, the Spaniards found it convenient to administer the Indian population through *curacas* or *caciques*, local Indian leaders, many of whose privileges were left intact (this arrangement came to be known as the *República de Indios*). Many of their charges suffered servitude in mines and *haciendas*. Others continued to live in traditional communities, whose lands were given some legal protection. But they paid tribute to their new overlords.

This arrangement was basically stable. Pre-conquest Indian societies were themselves rigidly hierarchical: the Indians thus swapped a local master for a European one – although the Incas, in particular, had been more paternalist rulers than the Spaniards. The conquest had involved the brutal imposition of a new ideological order as well as a political and economic one. In Mexico City recent excavation has revealed how the Spaniards built their cathedral on top of part of the Aztec *Templo Mayor*; in Cusco, a Dominican monastery stands on top of the *Koricancha* (the temple of the sun), the holiest shrine of the Inca empire. The Indian gods had failed, and those of the *conquistadores* had triumphed. No wonder that the Indians would embrace the Catholic religion while seeking to infuse it with their own practices, beliefs and images (such as Mexico's Virgin of Guadalupe). No wonder, too, that some of Latin America's Indian peoples to this day remain suspicious of change and modernisation. Their history since the conquest has been one of enforced submission, followed by more or less successful adaptation punctuated by occasional outbursts of rebellion, often of great violence. In places where the Indian population was wiped out (Cuba, Hispaniola), or where Indians were relatively few, nomadic and difficult to subjugate (Brazil), the colonists turned to the mass import of African slaves instead.

Inequality was a fundamental and integral aspect of colonial societies, whether they were based on serfdom or slavery or both. 'Perhaps nowhere is inequality more shocking,' noted Alexander von Humboldt, an aristocratic German scientist and traveller, in his essay on New Spain (Mexico) published in 1811. 'The architecture of public and private buildings, the women's elegant wardrobes, the high society atmosphere: all testify to an extreme social polish which is in extraordinary contrast to the nakedness, ignorance and coarseness of the population.'[18] Spanish colonial theory did not entertain the idea of racial integration. It envisaged racial separation, partly in order to protect the Indian population from the *criollos*. Spaniards, *criollos* and Indians lived under separate laws. Yet over the centuries much racial mixing occurred. Men always greatly outnumbered women among Iberian colonists, and overwhelmingly so at the start. Miscegenation resulted in a large number of *mestizos* and *mulatos*, *pardos* and *zambos*. In that sense, Spanish colonial society was more fluid than that of British North America (and Portuguese Brazil even more so). The colonial period saw 'the incomplete development of a heterogeneous hispanic-indigenous-*mestizo-criollo* society, which to this day exists in ferment', in the words of Jorge Basadre, Peru's greatest historian.[19] This was even more the case in Mexico.

Even so, the underlying socio-economic divides, broadly speaking, ran along racial lines. The fears, resentments and ignorance which racial difference generated made that divide all the harder to break down. At the heart of the history of Latin America since independence has been the tension between the beneficiaries of that divide and the gathering forces of socio-political *mestizaje.*

The challenge of geography

While Brazil remained intact, by 1830 mainland Spanish America had fragmented into 15 separate countries.[20] Given its size, this was inevitable. The new republics extended over an area stretching from the borders of Oregon and Oklahoma to the stony desert of Patagonia. But while some of the new countries, such as those in Central America, looked too small to be viable, others were too big and unwieldy quickly to become coherent nation-states. The most obvious example was Mexico. It would lose half its original territory, as first Texas declared itself independent and then the United States waged a successful war of conquest (1846–8), seizing northern Mexico in the name of its 'manifest destiny' to occupy the North American continent.[21] Meanwhile, Yucatán was for practical purposes all but independent during the first half of the nineteenth century. In 1849, it asked to be annexed by the United States, but was turned down. It had no road or rail link with Mexico City until as late as the 1950s. Until then, its ties with New Orleans and Havana, via steamer services, were closer than those with the Mexican capital.

Geography placed huge obstacles in the way of development. Distances are vast: Brazil is as large in area as the continental United States, while Argentina (with 37 million people today) is almost as big as India (with 1 billion). The Andes are a formidable barrier to communication, as is the Amazon basin. Most of the more populated parts of Latin America lack navigable rivers. There are no significant ones on the Pacific Coast at all. In South America, three mighty river systems – the Amazon, the Paraná and the Orinoco – traverse the continent from the Andean watershed to the Atlantic. Only in the past decade have the Paraná-Paraguay and stretches of the Amazon been turned into reliable waterways for the transport of bulk cargoes.[22] In the high altitudes of the Andes, life is harsh.[23] To survive, farmers must exploit microclimates at varying altitudes as well as grappling with erratic rainfall. To do so demands a high degree of collective organisation – a world away from the family homestead of bucolic New England. Tropical lowlands pose a different set of challenges, including disease, flooding and hurricanes. While some parts of Latin America get little or no rain, others get far too much: some 70 per cent of Mexico's total annual average rainfall lands on the state of Tabasco, for example. To cap it all, earthquakes are relatively common along the region's western mountain spine, and so are volcanic eruptions. Mexico, Central America and the Caribbean suffer frequent hurricanes.

Yet Latin America also possesses geographical advantages. These include abundant natural resources, and much good land. The Pampas of Argentina, Uruguay and southern Brazil form some of the world's most fertile farmland, blessed with a temperate climate. For much of the nineteenth century, land was abundant in relation to population (which is variously estimated to have totalled only 15 to 20 million at independence). But transport difficulties only began to be eased by the coming of railways in the second half of the nineteenth century, and later by air transport, which flourished as early as the 1920s in countries such as Brazil and Colombia. Contrary to nationalist myth, the railways did much to develop the domestic economy, as well as exports. In southern Brazil, for example, railways gave a big boost to commercial farming aimed at supplying the growing cities.[24] Even so, in the larger countries communications between the capital and outlying areas often remained poor until the mid-twentieth century. This stimulated regional political movements and engendered persistent localism as well as impeding internal trade. 'Its own extent is the evil from which the Argentine Republic suffers ... wastes containing no human dwelling, are, generally speaking, the unmistakeable boundaries between its several provinces,' complained Domingo Faustino Sarmiento, later president of Argentina, in *Facundo*, his mid-nineteenth-century tract against the evils of *caudillismo*.[25]

Caudillos and modernisers

Spain's monopoly of trade and high political office during the colonial period meant that the new republics had no experience of self-government, as Bolívar bitterly complained. It would take many of them half a century or more to achieve a degree of stability. Intermittent internal conflict added to the damage inflicted by the independence war. When they were not merely struggles for local or national power, these battles were over how the new republics should be governed – and by and for whom. Early efforts to establish a degree of popular sovereignty failed almost everywhere. Most of the new republics lapsed into three decades or more of rule by *caudillos* or strongmen, most of them army officers of the independence campaigns. Some were enlightened; many were not.

For different reasons, many writers on Latin America of both left and right have stressed the continuities rather than changes associated with independence. Rule by a small 'white' elite and the basic inequalities of colonial society were preserved. In some ways they were aggravated: the liberal commitment to private property weakened some of the legal protections for Indian communal land. In many countries, that would allow some degree of land-grabbing by *hacendados* throughout the rest of the nineteenth century.

Together with mineowners and large-scale traders, the landowners would form an oligarchy, holding political as well as economic power. Yet to stop there is misleading. The removal of the Spanish monopolies on political office, trade and the economy did usher in a new order, but they did so gradually and by no means smoothly. Overall, 'Latin America was a far more egalitarian place after independence than before. Indians and *mestizos* rose to positions of power all over Spanish America,' in the words of David Bushnell and Neill Macaulay, two historians of the nineteenth century in the region.[26] The newly independent countries all adopted constitutions based, broadly speaking, on liberal principles. This in itself was notable, given that most of Europe was still in the sway of absolutism. The constitutions were heavily influenced by that of the United States, by its Bill of Rights and the Declaration of the Rights of Man of the French revolution. Though suffrage was limited by property qualifications, usually to only a small percentage of adult males, so it was in Britain and the United States in this period.

In Brazil, Dom Pedro I established a liberal constitutional monarchy which included elements of representative parliamentary government. This involved indirect elections – deputies were picked by provincial electors, and senators chosen by the emperor. Suffrage was relatively wide for the times, with some 11 per cent of the total population able to vote for the provincial electors in 1872.[27] According to a recent study by Bolívar Lamounier, a Brazilian political scientist, the grafting of this representative element onto the remnants of Portuguese absolutism was essential to maintain government control over such a large country, riven with bloody local rebellions in the first thirty years after independence.[28] Under the first emperor's long-reigning and Brazilian-born son, Dom Pedro II (1831–89), this incipient parliamentary system worked well for several decades. In the view of Thomas Skidmore, a scholar of Brazil, it offered a political environment comparable to that of Victorian Britain in a much poorer and less developed country.[29] The emperor was a fair and honest ruler, an urbane and learned man who took the trouble to learn Guaraní, the most widely spoken indigenous language. But the last two decades of his rule, following war with Paraguay which he pursued implacably, were marked by political stagnation. In 1868 Dom Pedro dismissed a Liberal administration, replacing it with a Conservative one. Thereafter, the emperor increasingly became a hostage to advisers who were bent on delaying change – and the abolition of slavery in particular – for as long as possible. This doomed Latin America's only experiment with monarchy. But the Brazilian empire's notable achievements had been to keep the vast country united – it was potentially as fissiparous as Spanish America – and to implant a representative tradition.

In the new Spanish-speaking republics, as in Brazil, the basic political split was between liberals, like Santander, who wanted to move swiftly to dismantle the colonial order, and conservatives, such as Bolívar became, who were worried about instability and disorder ('governability', one might say). Across the region, the role of the Church became a battleground. It was seen by liberals as a reactionary bastion and as an obstacle to new ways of thinking and by conservatives as a powerful force for social order. Another divide was over federalism: liberals tended to favour decentralisation, though not always. Argentina was an exception: there federalism was seen as a way of recognising regional differences, and of neutralising the overweening economic power of Buenos Aires, home of liberalism and jealous monopoliser of lucrative customs revenues. Looked at through another optic, liberals were standard-bearers of modernisation and of French and British enlightenment thought, while conservatives defended a paternalist social order derived from Church and colony. Such divisions cut across class: artisans and Indians were as likely to support conservatives as liberals, partly because liberals tended to oppose communal ownership of land and to favour lower tariffs on imports. This division is an enduring one. It is reflected in part in two archetypal figures in Latin American politics: the *caudillo* and what one might call the modernising technocrat. The modernisers were not always liberals, though they often were, while the *caudillos* were characteristically, but not necessarily, conservatives, and some (though by no means all) were social paternalists.

Many elements of both these archetypal figures were awkwardly united in the person of Simón Bolívar. He was 'an exceptionally complex man, a liberator who scorned liberalism, a soldier who disparaged militarism, a republican who admired monarchy,' as John Lynch put it in a recent biography.[30] Bolívar was a cultivated man. He had spent several years in Europe – he famously (and perhaps apocryphally) swore to liberate South America while visiting Rome with his tutor and friend, Simón Rodríguez. While on campaign, his aides lugged around a large trunk of books: Voltaire and Montesquieu were among his favourite reading, but the trunk also included Locke and Bentham.[31] He was a great correspondent, and wrote with clarity and vigour. He admired the systems of government of both the United States and Britain, the most democratic of the day. He found slavery abhorrent. He argued passionately for co-operation among the new republics, and is rightly invoked today as a precursor of Latin American integration. He attempted to maintain Venezuela, Nueva Granada (present-day Colombia) and Ecuador united as a single country, Gran Colombia. And yet his chief political legacy is a yearning for strong government and paternalist authoritarianism. He was insistent that without a strong central authority the new republics would fall apart. Though he subscribed to Montesquieu's doctrine of the separation of powers, what he most liked about the French philosopher was his insistence that laws and institutions should be adapted to a country's geography and culture. From

Rousseau he took the idea that it is the role of the leader to interpret and represent 'the general will'. In other words, strong and effective leadership is self-legitimating and when necessary should override institutions that guarantee individual liberty. Thus, much as Bolívar admired the United States, he once said that he would rather see the Latin American republics adopt the Koran than US federalism, which was 'too perfect'. In South America 'events ... have demonstrated that perfectly representative institutions are not appropriate to our character, our customs, and our current level of knowledge and experience', he wrote in 1815.[32]

The definitive statement of Bolívar's political thought came a decade later, when he was asked to write a constitution for a new republic which had taken his name: Bolivia. This document had some features of liberal democracy: nominally at least, the executive, legislature and judiciary were to be separated, and were to be complemented by a fourth 'moral' power, a 'chamber of censors' with a scrutinising function. But Bolívar also included a hereditary senate and a president for life, who would have far-reaching emergency powers and the right to name his successor. This is constitutional monarchy in all but name. This document was swiftly discarded by Bolivia. In 1828, Bolívar assumed the dictatorship of Gran Colombia. He proceeded to undo some of the liberal reforms introduced during his long absence campaigning in Peru by Santander, his vice-president from whom he had become estranged. Bolívar restored the Indian tribute and the privileges of the Church and banned the works of Bentham. Despite his own views on the matter, he never tried to force through a ban on slavery. After Gran Colombia split into its three constituent parts in 1830, Santander, a pragmatic liberal, was elected as president of Colombia and is the founder of its democratic tradition. But he is long forgotten outside his own country. It is the great Liberator who still casts a shadow today.

Bolívar was not himself a *caudillo*: he always sought to institutionalise authority.[33] But his name has long been invoked and misused by authoritarian rulers of far less noble qualities, and far less sense. Venezuelan dictators, starting in the late nineteenth century, found it expedient to establish an official cult of Bolívar. His remains were repatriated in 1842, and in 1876 placed in a giant casket which rests in the national Pantheon, a former church a few blocks up the hill from his birthplace in the centre of Caracas. The latest exponent of the cult is Hugo Chávez, who claims to be implementing a 'Bolivarian Revolution' in Venezuela. Chávez included some elements from the Bolivian constitution (such as the 'moral power') in Venezuela's charter of 2001. He shows a Bolivarian disregard for checks on executive power. Although he has not dispensed with elections, Chávez shows every sign of wanting to be president for life.[34] But there is no reason to believe that Bolívar, the patrician aristocrat, the instinctive liberal turned pragmatic conservative who admired British parliamentary monarchy, the man who tried to sell his mines to British investors, would have felt represented by Chávez's militarist populism. This, Lynch observes tartly, is a 'modern perversion of the cult' which distorts Bolívar's ideas; at least past dictators 'more or less respected the basic thought of the Liberator, even when they misrepresented its meaning.'[35]

Where Bolívar was arguably too deferential to what he saw as Latin American weaknesses, the modernising technocrats paid insufficient heed to local realities. They wanted to make the new republics in the image of Europe or the United States. One of the first to try to do so was Bernardino Rivadavia in the province of Buenos Aires, the most important of the (still dis-)United Provinces of the Rio de la Plata, the forerunner of Argentina. Rivadavia, a merchant and lawyer, was an admirer of Jeremy Bentham's utilitarianism. He dominated Argentine politics for much of the 1820s, first as chief minister and then as president of Buenos Aires province. He and his supporters founded the University of Buenos Aires and other educational establishments, endowing them with a scientific bias absent from Spain's scholastic educational tradition. He promoted the theatre and other cultural enterprises. Rivadavia abolished the ecclesiastical and military *fueros*, restricted Church landholdings, transferred some Church welfare activities to a state-sponsored body, established freedom of worship, and cut the size of the army. He signed a trade treaty with Great Britain. In a debate that echoes to this day, his critics then and since blamed the problems of the textile and wine producers of the interior on Rivadavia's commitment to free trade. But the problems of these incipient local industries had more to do with inefficiency and distance from markets than with imports. When Juan Manuel de Rosas, a dictator, increased tariffs in 1835 the response of local industries was 'slow and feeble'.[36] From 1870 onwards, policies of Rivadavian inspiration aimed at promoting trade, foreign investment and European immigration would eventually see Argentina become one of the richest countries in the world. Less happily, Rivadavia's government contracted a loan from Britain, spent it on war with Brazil over Uruguay, and quickly defaulted. His liberalism was tinged with elitism. He tried to control wages, rather than leaving them to the market. And he handed out the best lands of the Pampas on long leases which in practice became grants. Intended to create a middle class of farmers, the measure had the opposite effect: by 1830, just 538 beneficiaries had received a total of 20 million acres of some of the world's best farmland. Rivadavia drew up a constitution that would have given Argentina a strong central government – something that conservative federalists in Buenos Aires province, and especially beyond it, were not prepared to accept. In 1827, he headed into exile – like so many subsequent would-be reformers.

Liberal achievements and frustrations

The Rivadavians failed partly because they had little understanding of the difficulties of the Argentine interior, and partly because they were simply ahead of their time. Across many of the Spanish-speaking republics, the Liberals' day would not dawn again until after the 1848 revolution in Europe, which had almost as great an impact in Latin America as in the old continent. In the following three decades, the Liberals – and by now they called themselves thus – would return to power in many countries and carry through much of the unfinished business of independence. They laid the basis for republics based on civilian democratic politics and popular sovereignty, even if much of the population was still excluded. In many countries, slavery and the Indian tribute were finally abolished along with the *fueros* of the Church and the army. Elected civilian presidents began to replace the *caudillos*, although the vote was generally restricted to adult men and subject to property and literacy qualifications.[37]

This new flowering of liberalism in the third quarter of the nineteenth century was generally pragmatic and reformist. It coincided with, and was strengthened by, the emergence of Latin America from its post-independence economic torpor. Innovations in transport and communications begat a first age of globalisation, in which the region enjoyed sustained export-led growth as a supplier of commodities to the industrial world. Coffee transformed the economies of Brazil, Colombia, Venezuela and Central America; grain, meat and wool did the same for Argentina and Uruguay; oil for Mexico and Venezuela; mining for Chile, Peru, Bolivia and Mexico; and sugar for Cuba, Mexico and Peru. A new urban middle class, of merchants, lawyers and doctors, arose, which though still numerically small was socially significant.

In Mexico, where the mark of church and colony went deeper than almost anywhere else, the Liberal triumph was heavily contested. In the wake of military defeat by the United States in the war of 1846–8, Benito Juárez, a Zapotec Indian from Oaxaca, beat Bolivia's Evo Morales to the title of Latin America's first elected president of indigenous descent by more than 150 years. Juárez's Liberals abolished the military and Church *fueros*, and banned the Church from owning property. Their Conservative opponents made the fatal mistake of appealing for outside help: France's Louis Napoleon responded by installing Maximilian, a Habsburg prince and his distant relative, as emperor. The Liberals won the resulting civil war, and the hapless Habsburg perished by firing squad.

Even in Peru, where military men had been politically dominant, in 1872 Manuel Pardo, a young businessman, was elected as the country's first-ever civilian president, at the head of a promising Civil Party. His election marked the triumph of a new generation of Liberals, exemplified by Francisco Laso, a painter and writer. In a country that had preserved much of the caste society of the colonial period, Laso challenged racial exclusion. His painting *The Three Races or Equality before the Law*, which today hangs in Lima's Museum of Art, shows a rich young white boy playing cards with two girls, one black, the other Indian. The girls are presumably servants. Cards in hand, they watch with quiet resignation. But the message of the picture is that they are all equal players of the game. Pardo cut the military down to size, reformed taxes and began to give Peru the rudiments of a modern state. But much of this progress was undone when Chile declared war on Peru and Bolivia in a scramble for the nitrates of the Atacama. Chile won partly because it had British support but mainly because it was a better-organised state. That achievement was the legacy of Diego Portales, a conservative who, like Bolívar, favoured strong government. Portales was a minister, but never sought the presidency: he believed in the rule of law rather than of individuals. In the 1830s he laid the foundations of a stable political system. In Chile, too, the Liberals gained the ascendant by the 1870s.

The Liberals did not hold sway everywhere. In Colombia, Conservative governments held power from 1885 until 1930. Venezuela and several Central American countries remained in the grip of dictators, although several of these claimed allegiance to liberalism. In many countries, *caudillos* survived as local strongmen. Much as some Liberals regretted this, they could not be wished away. The *caudillos* embodied 'the will of the popular masses, the choice of the people'; they were the 'natural representatives' of the 'pastoral classes', according to Juan Bautista Alberdi, the pragmatic architect of Argentina's 1853 constitution (which remains largely in force today).[38] Although this constitution gave the federal government the power to intervene in the affairs of the provinces in exceptional circumstances, the long-term price of Argentine unity and internal peace was to allow the *caudillos* to preserve their fiefdoms in the poorer provinces of the interior. That price would prove to be a heavy one. Much the same went for several other countries.

The Liberal era lasted, broadly speaking, from the mid-nineteenth century until 1930. For all its limitations, the Liberal order represented important progress. In many countries, relatively enlightened civilian governments made efforts to tackle Latin America's huge deficit in education and transport infrastructure. Even so, in 1900 three-quarters of the 70 million Latin Americans still lived in the countryside, three-quarters were illiterate and average life expectancy was only forty years.[39] Shaky as they were, from these foundations there was certainly a chance that Latin America might have gone on to create genuine democracies and sustained development. Yet three things were to conspire to frustrate that chance. First, before it could consolidate its triumph, Latin American liberalism mutated into a new and more authoritarian political philosophy: positivism. Second, Latin America's underlying inequalities meant that the benefits of economic growth did not reach much of the population. And third, from the outbreak of the First World War, the world economy entered upon three decades of turbulence, while economic development and inicipient industrialisation in the Latin American countries brought new social tensions.

Order and progress

In the history of political ideas in Europe, positivism is little more than a footnote. In parts of Latin America, it looms large. It is derived chiefly from Auguste Comte, a French social theorist of the early nineteenth century. He saw the key to progress as lying in order and 'scientific development', to be implemented by an enlightened intellectual elite. This would be echoed in Rodó's elitist 'regeneration'. And it suited the privileged groups of Latin America admirably, seeming as it did to justify restrictions on popular sovereignty. Positivism did promote industrial development, foreign investment, and reforms, for example, of education. But like Bolívar's thinking, it was another version of enlightened despotism and provided a new justification for authoritarianism. Not for the last time in Latin America, economic and political liberalism were divorced, as modernising technocrats were happy to serve Conservative dictators who gave them a free rein in economic policy. Like General Augusto Pinochet, Chile's dictator, or Alberto Fujimori, Peru's ruler from 1990 to 2000, the positivists championed economic freedom but not political freedom.

When linked to the social Darwinism of Herbert Spencer, positivism seemed to provide a scientific justification for inequality – and indeed for racism.[40] In the late nineteenth century, conventional wisdom among educated Latin Americans was that the region's Indian and black peoples were a brake on progress. One consequence was the promotion of immigration from Europe, though there were other, more powerful motives for that: South America in particular was sparsely populated. Between 1880 and 1915, Argentina received 4.2 million immigrants (chiefly from Spain and Italy) and Brazil 2.9 million (mainly from Italy and Eastern Europe). Though this represented only 23 per cent of the 31 million migrants who crossed the Atlantic in this period (70 per cent went to the United States), it was a significant number for the receiving countries. In 1914, around 30 per cent of Argentina's population was foreign-born, a much higher percentage than in the United States.[41]

Positivism was especially influential in the two largest countries in Latin America. In Mexico it buttressed ideologically the long dictatorship of Porfirio Díaz (1884–1914), who had first been elected in 1876 as a liberal. A tough and shrewd *mestizo*, from Oaxaca like Juárez for whom he had fought against the French, Díaz gave Mexico its first period of stability since the viceroyalty. During the 'Porfiriato', a team of modernising technocrats known as the *científicos* (scientists) proceeded to lay the foundations of a modern economy and railway system. Díaz respected constitutional forms, duly having himself elected president every four years. But in the words of a contemporary observer, he had 'demolished the apparatus of government and concentrated all the subdivided power into his own hands'. Another contemporary, Justo Sierra, an educationalist, gave Díaz a friendly warning: 'There are no institutions in the Republic of Mexico – there is a man.'[42] Díaz visited terrible repression on Indians, in the far north-west and the south-east, who stood in the way of progress. Social conditions remained grim: in 1900 one child in two died in the first year of life, while 84 per cent of Mexicans were illiterate.[43]

In Brazil, positivism inspired the very creation of the republic. As Dom Pedro II clung to his coterie of conservative landholding advisers, agitation against slavery increasingly took on republican tones under the aegis of a group of positivist lawyers and writers. Their leader, Benjamin Constant, lectured in the military academy, and influenced a generation of army officers.[44] When Dom Pedro finally yielded and agreed to abolition in 1888, it was too late. His action alienated conservatives from the monarchy while coming far too late to satisfy liberal elements in the growing cities. Within months, a bloodless military coup ushered in a republic. Brazil adopted a new flag emblazoned with the positivist slogan 'Order and Progress'. Though the new republic was nominally a civilian democracy, it was a disappointingly elitist affair, dominated by the newly rich coffee barons of the two most prosperous states, São Paulo and Minas Gerais. Though voting became direct, suffrage was more restricted than under the empire. At local level, postivists dispensed with many of the trappings of democracy. State governors gave unconditional support to the federal president; in return, their local Republican parties were given a free hand. Two positivists, Júlio de Castilhos and his disciple, Antônio Augusto Borges de Medeiros, ran the southern state of Rio Grande do Sul from 1893 to 1928. They left as their monument in the state capital, Porto Alegre, a fine collection of public buildings in the French *belle époque* style – a provincial version of the architectural splendour of Porfirian Mexico City and oligarchical Buenos Aires. These buildings were doubtless intended to persuade the *gaúchos*, as the local inhabitants call themselves, that they were well on the way to creating a new Paris in the Pampas. But positivist certainties were to suffer a bruising encounter with social realities in Brazil.

In 1899, a revolt by an obscure millenarian preacher, Antônio Conselheiro, at Canudos, in the parched interior of Bahia state, mushroomed into a tragic confrontation between modernising technocracy and the traditionalism of the neglected poor. Conselheiro's makeshift army of cowherds and peasants defeated three military expeditions, including a column of a thousand crack federal troops backed by field artillery. Canudos was finally quelled only after a four-month siege and weeks of house-to-house fighting involving half the Brazilian army. This episode left 15,000 dead, including some prisoners garrotted after they had surrendered.[45] From this tragic clash, some members of Brazil's political elite drew the conclusion that their country's common people were too 'backward' to benefit from democracy. But others recognised the need to spread the benefits of economic growth.

Argentina was less influenced by positivism. It had embarked on a golden age of economic growth and civilian rule. In 1862 the country had finally achieved internal unity. It quickly acquired the rudiments of a nation state: a national legal system, a bureaucracy, a tax system, a national electoral law, a new national army and two national newspapers.[46] From 1890, Argentina advanced steadily towards democracy: in 1916, Hipólito Yrigoyen, a Radical representing a growing middle class, became the first president to be elected under universal male suffrage (though the many foreigners were not allowed to vote). Yet Argentine democracy was being erected on somewhat shaky foundations. The Pampas, whose development was the source of the country's headlong economic growth, had been fully settled by the First World War. Between them, Buenos Aires and the Pampas accounted for more than 90 per cent of Argentina's cars and telephones in the early 1920s, two-fifths of Latin America's railways, half of the region's foreign trade and three-quarters of its educational spending.[47] The rest of Argentina's vast territory was less prosperous. Liberals from Rivadavia to Alberdi and Sarmiento had supported American-style homesteading policies, but had been unable to impose them in the face of oligarchical opposition. The Pampas had been divided up very unequally: according to the 1914 census, the largest 584 farms occupied almost a fifth of the total area, and those of over 1,000 hectares (2,470 acres) more than 60 per cent. The mean average landholding in Argentina was 890 acres, compared with 175 acres in New South Wales and 130 acres in the United States.[48]

Across the Rio de la Plata in Uruguay, the rise of Montevideo as a port serving parts of Argentina and Brazil similarly spawned a vigorous middle class, reinforced by European migration. Through the medium of the Colorado party, leaders of this social group struck a political alliance with the sheep farmers of the interior. Under José Batlle y Ordóñez (president, 1903–7 and 1911–15), Uruguay established the foundations of a modern democracy and one of the world's first welfare states. The death penalty was banned and divorce legalised. Legislation imposed the eight-hour working day, social insurance and free secondary education. In a foretaste of policies that would be adopted more widely in the region two decades later, state monopolies were created to run services from the port to electricity generation and insurance. Thanks to this social contract forged by *Batllismo*, as it was called, Uruguay, the smallest country in South America, has also long been the most egalitarian. Elsewhere, things were very different.

Land but not liberty: a revolution creates a corporate state

In September 1910, delegations from across the world came to Mexico City to celebrate the centenary of Mexican independence – and a quarter-century of 'peace, order and progress' under Porfirio Díaz. Within months, the appearance of stability was shattered. After Díaz had claimed to a North American journalist that he would 'bless' an opposition, Francisco Madero, the austere scion of a wealthy northern business family, stood for the presidency against the dictator under the banner of 'effective suffrage, no re-election'. After mobilising support in rallies across the country, he was arrested. Bailed, he escaped to the United States, and re-entered Mexico in February 1911 at the head of 130 armed men. Other rebels launched local risings, many of them unconnected. By May, Madero's troops captured Ciudad Juárez, the most important customs post on the border with the United States. Faced with a national rebellion that he could not defeat, Díaz finally resigned.

Madero was a liberal democrat, an eccentric Spiritualist and medium who believed himself chosen to redeem Mexico, and a man of great personal integrity and decency.[49] But he was politically inept. He disbanded his own troops while allowing supporters of the dictatorship to cling to positions of power. He failed to reach agreement with Emiliano Zapata, an Indian peasant leader who had launched his own localised revolution in Morelos, a small central state whose modernised sugar mills had made voracious encroachments on peasant land. In 1913, Madero was overthrown and murdered in a coup led by Victoriano Huerta, an army commander backed by the Porfirians and by Henry Lane Wilson, President William Howard Taft's meddling ambassador in Mexico City. This coup served only to intensify discontent. In 1915, Huerta would in turn be defeated by revolutionary armies sweeping down from the north. They were led by Francisco Villa, a bandit turned follower of Madero, and Álvaro Obregón, a farmer from Sonora, an important centre of commercial agriculture in the north-west, who emerged as the revolution's most gifted and ruthless military commander. Venustiano Carranza, another northerner, a pre-revolutionary state governor but an admirer of Juárez, became president.

The revolution had long since acquired its own momentum: it had become a confused and prolonged series of local and national struggles over power and land. Zapata had raised the ancestral Indian demand for land restitution, under the banner (borrowed via a Mexican anarchist intellectual from Alexander Herzen, a Russian liberal) of *Tierra y Libertad* ('Land and Freedom'). But Zapata lacked interest in forging national alliances, or in venturing far beyond the villages of Morelos. He would be betrayed, and shot by federal troops working for Carranza's government. In 1916, Carranza convoked a constituent assembly in Querétaro, north of Mexico City, to draw up a new constitution. The resulting document remains in force, though much amended. It was a compromise between Carranza, a liberal in the nineteenth-century tradition but an authoritarian one who believed in a strong executive, and radical social reformers, some of whom had advised Zapata and who had the backing of Obregón. Notably, the constitution declared both land and the sub-soil to be the property of the nation – provisions which sounded socialist but were also a throwback to the colonial period when they were vested in the crown.[50]

It would be another two decades before local rebellions and violent power struggles among the commanders of the victorious revolutionary armies died away. What eventually emerged was a more broadly based nation-state, but one in which power was ruthlessly centralised – not the liberal democracy of which Madero had dreamed. The post-revolutionary state was largely the creation of three men: two Sonorans, Obregón and Plutarco Elías Calles, a conservative former teacher and local police chief; and Lázaro Cárdenas, the last of the revolutionary generals to become president and a reformer with socialist leanings. The great achievement of the post-revolutionary system was to bring lasting stability by institutionalising political conflict and allowing for regular political renewal. Thus, almost uniquely in Latin America, in Mexico the army was politically neutralised. In 1928, Calles created an official hegemonic political party, known (after 1946) as the Institutional Revolutionary Party (PRI). The PRI system was a civilian one. It gave the president the powers of an absolute monarch – but only for six years. Though he was allowed to choose his successor, once out of office the president was a political nobody. He could not be re-elected. The constitution was nominally federal. During his presidency (1934–40), Cárdenas suppressed the remnants of the separation of powers: he purged the Congress and the state governors, and scrapped Carranza's idea of appointing judges for life. After Cárdenas, the president had all the levers of power. Congress and governors did his bidding, but they did form channels through which grievances could be funnelled upwards to the president. All this was carefully legitimated through elections. The PRI ruled by consent and co-option when possible, and by electoral fraud and violence only when necessary. The system paid more than lip-service to the myths of the revolution. Its rule was less elitist than the Porfiriato. Its main characteristics were a corporate state, social reform and nationalism.

Cárdenas re-organised the ruling party, as a mass organisation on functional lines, with sections for peasants and workers (and later for middle-class professionals). He put into practice many of the social aspirations of the radicals in the Querétaro assembly. He distributed 18.4 million hectares of land among 1 million peasants in the form of *ejidos*, a term which dated from pre-Hispanic communal landholdings. But the land was not owned directly by the communities and individual farmers, as Zapata had wanted. Under Cárdenas's system, while the community enjoyed the use of *ejido* land, the state remained its owner. The peasants were tied into the PRI system. They were demobilised, not empowered. They had won land but not freedom.[51] Nor did many of them escape poverty. Cárdenas also set up a national trade union confederation. The PRI guaranteed to private industrialists and other capitalists political stability, subsidised credit and an expanded and protected domestic market – provided they played the rules of the political game. The Church, too, was subordinated to the state: the 1916 constitution echoed the fierce anti-clerical laws of Juárez, though these were applied with decreasing severity after the 1920s.

If the PRI had an ideology, it was nationalism – the party even adopted the national flag and colours as its own emblems and Mexico came to define itself in rhetorical opposition to the United States. During the revolution, the United States twice sent troops to Mexico: in 1914 President Woodrow Wilson sent marines to Veracruz, to prevent arms from reaching Huerta; when in March 1916 Villa, resentful at American recognition of the Carranza government, briefly raided the border town of Columbus, New Mexico, Wilson dispatched a futile 'punitive expedition' under General John Pershing (who the following year commanded a much more significant force in France). Even so, in the view of Alan Knight, a historian of the revolution, 'at no point can it be said that US policy ... was primarily responsible for making or breaking a regime south of the border. Still less could Standard Oil, or any other corporation, make a similar claim.'[52] But the generous concessions made by the Díaz regime to foreign capital, especially in mining and oil, angered the revolutionaries. They argued that the oil companies, both Standard Oil and the British-owned El Aguila, operated as states within a state, and evaded taxes. In 1938, Cárdenas acted: he nationalised the oil industry, declaring *el petróleo es nuestro* ('the oil is ours!'), though he paid compensation. A state company, Petróleos de Mexico (Pemex), was given a monopoly over the industry. Post-revolutionary ideology also embraced *indigenismo* – an intellectual current that called for the integration of the Indian into the mainstream of society.

At several junctures, Mexico might have taken the more democratic road espoused by Madero. In the early 1920s, a Liberal Constitutionalist

Party pushed for municipal autonomy and the separation of powers. Such sentiments inspired some of the backers of a failed rebellion in 1923. In 1929, José Vasconcelos, who as Obregón's education minister had been a patron to Diego Rivera and his fellow muralists, stood for the presidency on a platform of *maderista* democracy. But he was defeated by Calles's machine, which employed the electoral fraud and strong-arm tactics which would become the PRI system's less attractive trademarks.[53] In the event, under the PRI Mexico adopted many elements of corporatism, the ideology championed and discredited by Southern European fascism in Mussolini's Italy, Franco's Spain and Salazar's Portugal. But the PRI was not grossly repressive, and it was essentially pragmatic, not revolutionary. Some of its presidents, like Cárdenas, veered left. Others were right-wing: Miguel Alemán (1940–6) forged a wartime alliance with the United States and was friendly to private business. The PRI co-opted the left – especially writers, artists and academics – but it was also anti-communist. The PRI's rule gave Mexico stability, and laid the basis of a modern nation-state and an industrialised economy. From 1930 until at least 1968 it was highly successful. The economy grew at an annual average rate of 4 per cent from 1929 to 1950, accelerating to 6.4 per cent from 1950 to 1980.[54] On the whole, there was social peace. The PRI system mimicked the outward forms of liberal democracy. But in reality it was 'the perfect dictatorship', as Vargas Llosa, the Peruvian novelist, said in 1990. The system had huge defects: corruption, lack of political and media freedom, massive waste and inefficiency, all of which became more important as time went by.

Building the Popular Nation

The Mexican revolution and its aftermath had a singular political influence in much of Spanish-speaking America. Other countries faced the same challenges as Mexico, of consolidating a modern nation-state, of industrialisation, the growth of cities, the emergence of an organised working class; they, too, saw the rise of new political currents, such as nationalism, socialism and corporatism. One early admirer was Victor Raúl Haya de la Torre, an exiled Peruvian student leader. He founded the Alianza Popular Revolucionaria Américana (APRA) as a continental movement in Mexico City in 1924, and then as a political party in Peru in 1930. APRA's founding 'international maximum programme' called for action against Yankee imperialism, the political unity of 'Indo-America' (as Haya called Latin America in deference to its indigenous peoples), the nationalisation of lands and industries, the internationalisation of the Panama Canal, and international solidarity.[55] This smacked of radical socialism, but Haya favoured a broad non-communist front, in which the middle class would take the lead along with workers and indigenous peasants. In his long life – he died in 1979 while president of a Constituent Assembly preparing the return of democracy to Peru – his ideas went through various evolutions. 'Since its creation, APRA has been a study in contradictions,' as Julio Cotler, a Peruvian sociologist, has put it.[56] In Peru, APRA would at first flirt with revolutionary violence, and always retained a conspiratorial flavour. But Haya's preference, if allowed, was to compete for power through elections. He said that APRA would respect democratic liberties. Haya became increasingly conservative, but many in his party yearned for a Mexican-style corporate state and nationalisation of American mining companies in Peru.[57] The army repeatedly intervened to prevent APRA winning power; it would take office only in 1985, under the inept leadership of Alan García. Even so, Haya was a hugely influential figure in his country's politics and beyond. He supported the campaign in Nicaragua of Augusto Sandino, a dissident liberal general, against a government backed by American marines.[58] APRA became the transmission belt for the ideas of the Mexican revolution to South America.

The Liberal order had lasted for two decades longer in South America than in Mexico. Its death knell was sounded by the Wall Street crash of October 1929 – as it was in Europe. If the Great Depression did not amount to a decisive turning point in Latin America's economic history, it certainly marked a sharp political rupture. The impact of the depression on employment and living standards was severe. Ten countries in the region saw the value of their exports fall by more than half between 1928 and 1932. No other country in the Western world was as badly affected by the crash as Chile, whose trade fell by 83 per cent between 1929 and 1932. In Chile and Cuba income per head fell by a third.[59] Many governments defaulted on their foreign debts for the first time since the mid-nineteenth century. Across the region, the depression prompted discontent and agitation by fledgling labour unions, many of anarcho-syndicalist persuasion, and small left-wing political parties. In El Salvador, an attempt at an insurrection by the small Communist Party was crushed in a bloodbath. In Peru, risings by APRA and the Communists were repressed. In Chile, a brief socialist republic was declared by Marmaduque Grove, an air-force officer and uncle of Salvador Allende. Cuba saw a short-lived revolution by radical students and army sergeants.

Conservatives felt threatened by mass demonstrations and the new left-wing parties. Some looked to military rule to save them from the masses. Some were attracted by fascism, especially in its Mediterranean form of corporatism. Many on the left, too, would be attracted by corporatism. In Latin America, Mussolini and Franco were more influential than Marx and Lenin. Within two years of the Wall Street crash, army officers had sought or taken power in Argentina, Brazil, Chile, Peru and three Central American countries

(Guatemala, El Salvador and Honduras).[60] In 1933, the army took power in Cuba. In Argentina, the crash ended fifty years of broadly stable civilian rule. It found the second administration of Hipólito Yrigoyen, the elderly leader of the Radical Party, fiscally exposed: his efforts to cut a vast budget deficit undermined his political support. In September 1930, a military *junta* took power. It was not particularly repressive, and it presaged a decade of civilian-military rule. But in deciding that it would accept as legal the *junta*'s edict, the Supreme Court elaborated a dangerous doctrine of *revolución triunfante* – or might is right.[61] For half a century after 1930, that doctrine brought Argentina instability and the subordination of civilian politics to the armed forces. In Chile, the lasting impact was in reverse: a wave of protest and anti-militarism swept away Carlos Ibañez, a moderate conservative military dictator. Two brief military interventions followed. But exceptionally, democratic and constitutional rule was strengthened, lasting until the overthrow of Salvador Allende in 1973. Exceptional, too, was Colombia: in an election in 1930, the Liberals ended fifty years of Conservative rule, helped by the impact of the crash and their opponents' divisions. A period of vigorous social reform followed. Many of the Latin American economies recovered fairly swiftly from the depression, thanks both to renewed export growth and Keynesian measures of state intervention and import-substitution industrialisation. But politics had changed for ever. Only in a few smaller countries did 'oligarchical' liberalism survive the crash.

Mexico was unique in institutionalising corporatist nationalism. But its revolution was strongly echoed four decades later in Bolivia. In 1951, the National Revolutionary Movement (MNR), a mainly middle-class party but with support among miners, workers and peasant farmers, won an election. Robbed of power by a military coup, in 1952 it staged a popular rising. For three days, the MNR's urban militias fought army conscripts in La Paz. The battle was turned in the MNR's favour by the arrival of a contingent of armed miners, and by splits in the security forces. Some 500 people died, but the old order had been toppled.[62] The MNR's leader, Victor Paz Estenssoro, a university teacher of economics, was installed as president. His government enacted universal suffrage, nationalised the tin mines which provided the main export, and broke up most of the *haciendas* on the Altiplano, handing over the land as family plots to the Indian resident serfs. A serious effort was made to provide universal education, at least at primary level. And for the first time Indians were allowed to enter the Plaza Murillo, La Paz's main square and the site of the cathedral, the presidential palace and the Congress. The MNR would be the dominant political force in Bolivia for the next half-century, but it neither achieved the supremacy of the PRI nor tamed the armed forces.

Elsewhere, corporatism tended to be articulated by charismatic nation-builders – old-fashioned *caudillos* in a new, more powerful incarnation. In this form, political scientists have often preferred to label corporatism as populism. The most prominent populists included Brazil's Getúlio Vargas, who as governor of Rio Grande do Sul was heir to that state's positivist tradition, and who became president through a civilian-military coup in 1930. Vargas ruled as a dictator from 1937 to 1945, and then was elected president again in 1950. In Argentina, Juan Perón, an army colonel, ruled from 1945 to 1955; the movement he founded has remained the dominant political force in Argentina to this day. But Perón did not hold a monopoly on Argentine populism: Yrigoyen's Radicals also had strong populist streaks. In Venezuela, Acción Democratica (AD), with which Peru's APRA had especially close links, evolved from populism to social democracy. AD dominated Venezuelan politics for much of the period between the 1940s until the rise of Hugo Chávez. There were some differences between these movements. For example, Perón's government of 1945–55 was the closest Latin America came to a fascist regime. It gave refuge to at least 180 Nazis and their collaborators, including such notorious figures as Adolf Eichmann, Eduard Roschmann, Joseph Mengele (who was later in Brazil) and Klaus Barbie (who moved on to Bolivia).[63] During the dictatorship of the *Estado Novo* ('New State'), Vargas also flirted with fascism. Haya de la Torre was, at least for parts of his career, closer to democratic socialism though APRA was organised on corporatist lines. Of the larger countries, only Colombia and Chile remained relatively aloof from populism.

In Latin America, unlike in Russia and the United States, populism was an overwhelmingly urban movement and ideology.[64] It was above all a political response to urbanisation, and to what was seen as the elitist and exclusionary politics of the pre-1930 'oligarchical' republics. It reflected what Jorge Castañeda, a Mexican writer and politician, has called the 'unfulfilled Latin American dream of painless modernity'.[65] The original populist movements flourished from the mid-1920s to the mid-1960s – though populism has enjoyed an unanticipated recent revival in the region. They promoted industrialisation, a policy on which local industrialists, the middle class and organised labour could all agree. Populist movements were multi-class electoral coalitions. Their leaders deliberately talked of *el pueblo* (the people) rather than, say, *la clase obrera* (the working class). As well as nationalism, they injected the concept of *lo popular* into Latin American political vocabulary (meaning for and by the people), as in their claim to lead 'popular' governments. Their programme involved protection and subsidies for local industry, and political representation and welfare provision for the urban masses. This in turn involved an expansion of the role of the state in the economy and society, which generated new jobs for the middle classes. Populist movements opposed foreign domination and the power of what they called the agro-export 'oligarchy'. Although they often proclaimed themselves to be 'revolutionary', these movements were reformist – unlike parties of the Marxist left, they aimed to mitigate class conflict rather than stimulate it. Even so, populist movements were often seen as a threat by conservative agro-exporting interests (and by the United States). In a way they were: they sought to redistribute resources from farming to the cities. The result was that populists were often the target of repression. Another distinguishing characteristic of populist movements was their reliance on charismatic leadership. The populist leaders were often great orators or, if you prefer, demagogues. Ecuador's most emblematic populist leader, José Maria Velasco, famously said: 'Give me a balcony and I will become president.' This was no idle boast: his campaigning skills saw him elected president five times – though his lack of governing skills, and the fierce opposition he generated among conservatives, saw him ousted four times by the army. Such leadership exalted an almost mystical bond between leader and masses. This sometimes involved the use of religious imagery or techniques, as with Haya de la Torre.

For better or for worse, populism was the political vehicle through which many Latin American countries entered the modern era of mass politics and bigger government. Its achievements included a boost to industrialisation, and an improvement in social conditions for favoured sectors of the urban workforce. Workers received tangible benefits, such as paid holidays, pensions and health provision. Those benefits were sufficient to encourage remarkably durable loyalty among the beneficiaries, as the longevity of the PRI and Peronism in particular illustrate. Perón's social reforms deprived Argentina's small Socialist and Communist parties of working-class support; they were never to regain it. Whereas liberals and positivists had often looked abroad for inspiration, populists promoted a 'national culture', rescuing indigenous people and their cultural artefacts from official neglect.

In these respects, populism played an analogous role to social democracy in Europe. But there were important differences. Overall, populism had a negative impact on Latin American democracy and development. Four defects stand out. First, although it employed electoral means, populism was in many ways less than democratic. As Paul Drake puts it, populist leaders 'were devoted to expanding popular participation but not necessarily through formal, Western democratic mechanisms'.[66] Perón, Vargas, and Haya 'repeatedly exhibited dictatorial propensities toward their followers and opponents. They apparently favoured controlled, paternalistic mobilisation of the masses more than uninhibited, pluralistic, democratic competition.'[67] In fairness, their conservative opponents, too, were often less than democratic. In Argentina, even a liberal such as Jorge Luis Borges, the writer, came to believe that Peronism showed that his country was not 'ready' for democracy.

He argued at one point that military dictatorship was a necessary evil to prevent Peronism from remaining in power. A second, linked failing was the reliance on charismatic leadership. Max Weber, the German sociologist, defined charismatic authority as being exercised by an individual who is 'set apart from ordinary men and treated as endowed with supernatural, superhuman, or at least specifically exceptional qualities'.[68] Weber contrasted it with two other forms of authority, traditional and rational-legal. As Weber's definition makes clear, charismatic leadership is inimical to the rule of law – or indeed the separation of powers and the construction of democratic institutions. Populist leaders relied on a direct bond between themselves and the masses: not for nothing did they emerge simultaneously with the radio and the cinema. Eva Perón had worked as an actress in radio soaps; like FDR, Getúlio Vargas made regular radio broadcasts to Brazilians. They established political clienteles, rather than creating citizenship. Benefits came from loyalty, not as a matter of right. The reliance on charisma was one reason why populism was inherently unstable.

Third, perhaps the most disappointing feature of populism was its failure to make a serious attack on inequality. In contrast to Mexico and Bolivia, where revolutions broke the political power of the traditional *hacendados*, other populist leaders usually excluded the poorest sections of the masses – the peasantry – from their coalitions. Populist governments made no attempt to extend the franchise to illiterates, nor to implement land reform. And in attempting to transfer resources from agriculture to industry, such as by controlling food prices, they were impoverishing peasant as well as landlord. Their reliance on inflation, rather than thoroughgoing tax reforms, to finance government hurt the poor disproportionately too. This was but one aspect of a fourth defect of populism: its economic policy. Populist governments were not alone in pursuing statist protectionism: by the 1960s many military dictatorships did too. But the constant tension in populist governments between industrialisation and welfarism (as Drake puts it) led them to rely on over-expansionary macroeconomic policies and made them prey to extreme economic volatility. While claiming to champion the creation of a modern state, the clientelist approach to politics adopted by many populist leaders led them to create inefficient public bureaucracies stuffed with their supporters.

Some of these weaknesses, combined with the opposition that populists aroused among some powerful conservative groups, meant that from the 1930s on, Latin America's incipient democracies were subject to chronic instability, and to what came to be known as the pendulum effect, as civilian governments alternated with dictatorships. In the aftermath of the Second World War, an external conflict would intensify these political battles in Latin America, to tragic effect.

CHAPTER 4

COLD WAR AND REVOLUTION: THE UNITED STATES AND THE LEFT REJECT DEMOCRACY

Guatemala is the saddest country in Latin America. The beauty of its verdant highlands dotted with whitewashed colonial towns, its shimmering lakes overlooked by soaring volcanoes and its Mayan ruins half buried in rainforest cannot conceal the ancestral oppression of its indigenous majority. It has had an elected civilian government since 1986. But a guerrilla war lasting almost three decades was settled only in 1996. It cost some 200,000 lives; most of the victims were Mayan Indians killed by the army.[1] The war continues to cast a dark shadow. Guatemala's democrats must struggle against what some have called *poderes fácticos* – shadowy networks linking corrupt former army officers and organised criminal gangs of drug traffickers and money launderers. In many ways, these networks are the real power in the country. They appeared to flourish under Alfonso Portillo, the country's president from 2000 to 2005, who fled to Mexico on leaving office and faced charges of stealing $16 million of public money. Under Óscar Berger, a reforming liberal elected in 2004, a new effort began to cut Guatemala's army down to size and to liberate democracy from military tutelage.

The CIA snuffs out the Guatemalan spring

And yet Guatemala might have developed into a far more robust democracy much earlier. That it did not do so is in large part the fault of the United States: more than anywhere else in Latin America, Guatemala is a victim of American intervention. In 1954, the Eisenhower administration organised a coup to topple the democratic, reformist government of Jacobo Arbenz, which the American president alleged to be a possible 'communist outpost on this continent'.[2] Though the enterprise was initially hailed as a success by its authors, in the words of one historian sympathetic to them 'in light of subsequent events it might reasonably be considered little short of disaster'.[3] Not only did Guatemala itself pay a high price for the American intervention: the lessons drawn by the United States and by Latin Americans of both left and right had tragic consequences in other countries, handicapping democracy in the region for a generation or more. How was it that Guatemala came to be the first battle in the Cold War in Latin America?

Central America was an underdeveloped backwater throughout the nineteenth century. After independence in 1824, the United Provinces of Central America soon fragmented into five separate countries of which Guatemala, the seat of the colonial captain-generalcy, was the largest. Except in Costa Rica, an unenlightened despotism was the norm in the isthmus.[4] In Guatemala, a long line of brutal dictators went through the motions of legitimating their rule through elections, but these were farcical affairs in which opposition was rarely registered. An oligarchy of coffee planters dominated the republic; they assured themselves of a seasonal Indian workforce through debt peonage.

When the Second World War drew to a close, democratic eddies washed across Latin America. Several dictatorships in the region fell, to be replaced by governments elected on a reasonably broad franchise. Labour unions expanded, and flexed their muscles in a strike wave. Communist parties grew rapidly, from a total membership of less then 100,000 in 1939 to 500,000 by 1947.[5] In Latin America, as elsewhere in the world, there were expectations that a new era of democracy was beginning. According to one account, this opened up an opportunity for Latin American countries to move towards social democracy – as much of Western Europe would do in the aftermath of war – through an alliance between industrialists and the emerging middle and organised working classes.[6] But the opportunity proved tantalisingly brief. In Latin America, the rural landlords had not been hurt by war, and they still exercised a powerful political grip, while the trade unions were still weak. By 1948, in most countries, the progress towards democracy had been rolled back, and Communist parties had been banned. By then, the Cold War had begun. It did not create anti-communism in Latin America. This had been espoused by conservatives and the Catholic Church since the formation by Lenin in 1919 of the Third Communist International (Comintern) with its brief of world revolution. So most Latin American governments were happy to line up with the United States in the Cold War. For Washington, it began to matter more that those governments should be reliably anti-communist rather than democratic.

In Guatemala the post-war democratic spring lasted longer. In 1944, protests by students, teachers and other members of an incipient middle class prompted Jorge Ubico, a dictator even more repressive than his predecessors, to step down. Three months later, junior army officers rebelled against his chosen successor. This 'October revolution' was carried out not in the name of Bolshevism but of 'constitution and democracy'. Both were quickly achieved. Juan José Arévalo, a mild-mannered teacher of philosophy who had returned from years of exile in Argentina, was elected president in the freest vote Guatemala had seen. Arévalo claimed inspiration from Franklin Roosevelt's New Deal and from the Four Freedoms – of speech, religion and from want and fear – for which the American president had fought the war. A new constitution extended the franchise to all except illiterate women, created elected local authorities, made racial discrimination a crime and banned military men from standing for office. Arévalo's government gave rights to trade unions, established a social security system, central bank and statistical office, and built hundreds of new schools. It brooked no restrictions on political or press freedom, despite suffering frequent plots from conservatives.

In 1950, Jacobo Arbenz, a leader of the 'October revolution', was elected to succeed Arévalo, with 65 per cent of the vote. While Arévalo had established democratic freedoms, Arbenz promised 'to convert Guatemala from a backward country with a predominantly feudal economy into a modern capitalist state'.[7] His plans to do this centred on agrarian reform and public infrastructure projects, several of which had been proposed by the president of the World Bank. On both counts, that meant a confrontation with the United Fruit Company, an American firm based in Boston. Known to Central Americans as *el pulpo* ('the octopus') because of its all-encompassing tentacles, in 1899 United Fruit had obtained a 99-year concession over a vast tract of jungle from Guatemala's then dictator and with it, the right to finish and operate a railway to the Caribbean coast. The company thus obtained a monopoly over much of Guatemala's trade: its port at Puerto Barrios was the country's only Atlantic port, and its railway the only means of transport to and from the port. In return, it paid only a small tax on banana exports.[8] Arbenz proposed to build a public port next to Puerto Barrios and a highway to it; United Fruit, which had already seen a rise in trade union organising, became the main target of his land reform.

Even by Latin American standards, land distribution in Guatemala was highly unequal: 2 per cent of landowners held three-quarters of all cultivatable land, while more than half of all farmland was made up of large plantations (above 1,100 acres). Much of this land was left fallow. Arbenz's reform affected farms larger than 670 acres whose land was not fully worked, or those above 223 acres where a third of the land was uncultivated. Compensation was paid in interest-bearing bonds according to the land's declared taxable value. In two years a million acres – a third of this from German-owned farms nationalised at American insistence during the war – were distributed to 100,000 families. Arbenz ordered the expropriation of 380,000 acres of United Fruit land – a substantial chunk of its holdings, of which 85 per cent were left fallow, supposedly in case of banana diseases. The government offered compensation of $1.1 million; the company claimed the land was worth $16 million, thus revealing the scale of its tax evasion. Its claim was backed by the US Department of State.

By then, the Eisenhower administration was bent on overthrowing Arbenz, whom it accused of presiding over a communist takeover. With support from Nicaragua's notorious dictator, Anastasio Somoza, and his counterpart in Honduras, the CIA trained and armed a force of 170 men, and assembled a dozen planes. Their 'invasion' was a halting affair. But bombing and strafing from the air, combined with disinformation broadcasts suggesting a force of thousands, caused the army high command to oblige Arbenz to resign. Through a mixture of threats and manipulation, the Americans quickly secured the appointment as president of Carlos Castillo Armas, the undistinguished retired colonel they had chosen to lead the 'invasion'. Guatemala's ten-year democratic spring was over.

Ever since, controversy has raged over the American action. Was the coup an enterprise of crude economic imperialism, in which the Eisenhower administration was acting as enforcer for United Fruit? Since the days of Arévalo, the company had conducted an effective propaganda campaign in the United States, painting Guatemala as being in the grip of communists. The family of John Foster Dulles, the secretary of state, and his brother Allen, the CIA director, were shareholders in the banana company; both brothers had worked for Sullivan & Cromwell, a New York law firm which had represented United Fruit's rail subsidiary. Several of the company's officials had close contacts with the administration. But J F Dulles insisted: 'If the United Fruit matter were settled, if they gave a gold piece for every banana, the problem would remain as it is today as far as the presence of communist infiltration in Guatemala is concerned.'[9] Just five days after Arbenz was toppled, the US Justice Department began an anti-monopoly action against United Fruit; as a result, the company eventually agreed to hand over some of its land in Guatemala to local firms and sold the railway. In 1972, it sold its remaining interests in Guatemala to Del Monte. (United Fruit changed its name to Chiquita in 1989; the company filed for bankruptcy protection in 2001).

In recent years, as official archives have been opened, historians have come to accept Dulles's contention. But many question his verdict on Arbenz. Not for the last time in Latin America, the critics argue, the United States failed to distinguish between a nationalist reformer and a communist. The

Guatemalan Labour Party, as the communist party was called, was tiny; it never had more than 2,000 activists. Though an enthusiastic backer of Arbenz and the land reform, it was the smallest of the four parties in the governing coalition. It won only four of the 56 seats in Congress in an election in 1953, had no Cabinet members, and fewer than ten senior government jobs. Guatemala had no diplomatic relations with the Soviet Union and the eastern bloc. Until the late 1950s, the Soviet Union had only three embassies in the whole of Latin America, a region which Stalin had dimissed as 'the obedient army of the United States'.[10] Dulles made great play of an arms shipment from Czechoslovakia received a month before the coup. But the United States had imposed an arms embargo on Guatemala since 1948, and the Czech arms were of limited use. Arbenz's coalition was fractious, the army restless and the middle class became disillusioned as tensions with the United States rose. The president did come to depend on the communists, who alone could mobilise popular support for the government. His wife is alleged to have been a communist sympathiser. The CIA feared that land reform would create a base for the communists in the countryside. Even so, it is hard to see the army or the civilian politicians acquiescing in a communist takeover.

In the event, the US crushed democracy not communism in Guatemala. Castillo Armas swiftly reversed the agrarian reform, reached agreement with United Fruit, and restored the old order of corrupt dictatorship. In 1960, junior army officers would rebel in the name of nationalism, angry that Guatemala was being used by the CIA to train anti-Castro Cuban exiles. The rebellion failed, but two of its leaders went on to found Guatemala's first guerrilla group. This was crushed after right-wing death squads murdered thousands of civilians, many of whom had no connection to the guerrillas. In the mid-1970s, new Marxist guerrilla groups established a presence among the Mayan Indian communities of Guatemala's western highlands. That prompted the army to undertake a scorched-earth campaign that saw scores of Indian villages wiped out, their inhabitants butchered and the survivors forcibly relocated and conscripted into army-backed auxiliary forces called 'civil patrols'. Of all the counter-insurgency campaigns in Latin America during the Cold War, only that in Guatemala merits the much-abused term of genocide. Repression by dictatorships in Chile and Argentina, where most of the victims were middle class, attracted far more outside attention. But in the deliberate infliction of mass terror, the massacres of Mayan Indians in the Guatemalan highlands in the late 1970s and early 1980s had no parallel in the region. Those excesses caused Jimmy Carter to cancel the United States' previous aid to the army. Another Democratic president, Bill Clinton, made a formal apology for that aid on a visit to Guatemala in 1999. But by then the Cold War was long over.

The ease with which Arbenz was overthrown would lead policy-makers in Washington to adopt 'regime change' as their standard response to perceived communist threats in Latin America. A few years later, another such attempt on a much larger scale would end in disaster at the Bay of Pigs in Cuba. Thwarted, President John F Kennedy would launch the Alliance for Progress in an attempt to stall the spread of communism in Latin America by encouraging democratic reform. 'Those who make peaceful change impossible make violent change inevitable,' Kennedy declared. Indeed, had Arbenz's agrarian reform taken place a decade later – or a decade earlier when FDR was preaching freedom from want – it might well have drawn applause from Washington.

The Latin American left, too, drew lessons from Guatemala. A young Argentine doctor, Ernesto Guevara, had arrived there on New Year's Eve 1953 and witnessed the fall of Arbenz. By the time he was given safe conduct from the Argentine Embassy to Mexico, he had acquired the nickname *Che*, bestowed by leftist exiled Cubans he met in Guatemala.[11] According to one of his most perceptive biographers, Guatemala was Che Guevara's 'political rite of passage'. Guevara thought the coup showed that the United States 'was *a priori* ruthlessly opposed to any attempt at social and economic reform in Latin America'. So he inferred that the left should be prepared to fight US interference rather than try to avoid or neutralise it.[12] He also thought that Arbenz had allowed his enemies too much freedom, especially in the press, and had erred in not purging the army. This is confirmed by Hilda Gadea, Guevara's first wife, who wrote: 'it was Guatemala which convinced him of the necessity for armed struggle and for taking the initiative against imperialism'.[13]

From the Monroe Doctrine to the corollary of intervention

The overthrow of Arbenz was far from the first intervention by the United States in Latin America. Yet Guevara's analysis was flawed: intervention was by no means constant, and it was almost wholly confined to the Caribbean basin. The policy of the United States towards its neighbours went through several contrasting phases. In the century following George Washington's presidency, his successors had two main foreign policy priorities. One was to prevent European involvement in the Americas. The second was to expand their own territory across North America. The first aim was formulated by President James Monroe in 1823, when he warned the European powers: 'We should consider any attempt on their part to extend their system to any portion of this hemisphere as dangerous to our peace and safety.'[14] The Monroe Doctrine, as it came to be called, was defensive in inspiration. It also envisioned a commonality of liberal economic principles and civil, political and religious freedom across the republics of the Americas.[15] Thus President Harry Truman would say in 1947: 'There has been a Marshall Plan for the Western hemisphere for a century and a half. [It is] known as the Monroe Doctrine.'[16] In any event, the United States long lacked the power to enforce it; throughout the nineteenth century, European powers would occasionally intervene in Latin America, pursuing trade or protecting the lives and investments of their citizens.

The second aim came to be known as the pursuit of the United States' 'manifest destiny' to occupy North America from the Atlantic to the Pacific seaboard.[17] The process began with the purchase of Louisiana and Florida. It continued with the admission to the union of Texas, which had declared its independence from Mexico in 1836. This was followed swiftly by an expansionary war with Mexico from 1846 to 1848. To the victor went the present-day states of Arizona, California, Colorado, Nevada, New Mexico and Utah in return for a payment of $15 million. Cuba, still under Spanish rule, was also the object of American covetousness. As early as 1823, John Quincy Adams, the secretary of state, argued that 'Cuba, forcibly disjointed from its own unnatural connection with Spain, and incapable of self-support, can gravitate only toward the North American Union, which by the same law of nature cannot cast her off from its bosom.'[18]

Together with Central America, Cuba would be the focus of the next phase of American expansionism, from the 1890s to 1930. In this period, successive presidents – not just Theodore Roosevelt, the rough-riding Republican, but also Woodrow Wilson, the idealistic Democrat – concluded that control of the Caribbean basin was of crucial strategic importance for the defence of the homeland and its commerce. This control was challenged by Germany and, to a lesser extent, Britain. Kaiser Wilhelm II believed that Germany should be the 'paramount power' in Latin America, and that Cuba should be a 'European state'. Germany sought a naval base in the Caribbean. Against the background of 'a scramble for Africa' among the European powers, many influential Americans reckoned that the United States had to assert a policing role in its 'sphere of interest' in the Caribbean and Central American region – or risk seeing another power do so.[19] The chaotic misrule afflicting many of the small countries in the area provided ready pretexts for intervention in the name of stability. In 1904, Theodore Roosevelt summed up the new policy thus:

> Chronic wrongdoing, or an impotence which results in a general loosening of the ties of civilized society, may in America, as elsewhere, ultimately require intervention by some civilized nation, and in the Western Hemisphere the adherence of the United States to the Monroe Doctrine

may force the United States, however reluctantly, in flagrant cases of such wrongdoing or impotence, to the exercise of an international police power.[20]

This became known as the 'Roosevelt corollary' to the Monroe Doctrine. It was an ex-post justification for American intervention in Cuba.

Since the 1850s, American policy-makers had made it clear that Cuba's transfer to any other European power would be unacceptable. By 1898, Spanish control over its 'ever-faithful isle' was tenuous. When the USS *Maine*, an American battleship on a visit to Havana, exploded, killing 266, a clamour for American intervention followed. (That the explosion was almost certainly an accident, caused by a fire in a coal bunker that ignited the forward magazines, was ignored.) The four-month war that followed shattered the remnants of Spanish empire and signalled the advent of the United States as a world power; it annexed Puerto Rico, the Philippines (for which it paid $20 million) and the Pacific island of Guam. It had gone to war in support of *Cuba Libre* (Free Cuba), but opted to make the island a protectorate. Roosevelt turned a minor role as a cavalry officer in the expeditionary force in Cuba into a national legend that swept him to the White House. Two years later, he created a new country in Central America. The United States had negotiated a treaty with Colombia allowing it to build a trans-isthmian canal at Panama. When Colombia's Senate was slow to ratify this (partly because of the Thousand Days' War), Roosevelt organised and financed a revolution for Panamanian independence. Panama, like Cuba, became a de facto American protectorate. 'I took the isthmus,' Roosevelt would subsequently boast.[21]

Under Woodrow Wilson, American imperialism took on a more idealistic tinge, influenced by the Progressive reform movement. The man who joined the First World War 'to make the world safe for democracy' claimed a similar motive closer to home. 'We are the friends of constitutional government in America; we are more than its friends, we are its champions,' he said.[22] Yet American views of the neighbourhood were coloured by a racism akin to that of the positivists in Latin America in that period. The countries of the Caribbean Basin, many assumed, were not ready for democracy. Wilson despatched the marines for what turned into lengthy sojourns in the Dominican Republic (1916–24) and Haiti (1915–34), where they built roads and health clinics as well as imposing order. In Nicaragua, the marines stayed from 1912 to 1933 (apart from a brief interval in 1925–7). But instead of building nations, they built *gendarmeries*. It would be a recipe for trouble. In Nicaragua, the marines trained a National Guard, which suppressed Sandino's low-level guerrilla campaign. After Sandino made peace with the government, he was murdered on the orders of Anastasio Somoza, the guard's commander. Somoza went on to seize power in 1936, inaugurating a kleptocratic family dynasty that would last until 1979 when it was overthrown by leftist revolutionaries who claimed inspiration from the memory of Sandino. In the Dominican Republic, Rafael Leónidas Trujillo would use his command of the American-created army to impose a personal tyranny from 1930 until he was murdered in 1961, by which time this tropical *generalísimo* had become an embarrassment to his former sponsors.

From the First World War onwards the United States began to displace Britain and Europe as the main source of trade and investment in the northern part of the region, though not in Argentina or some other South American countries. In the 1920s, intervention went hand in hand with commercial aggrandisement and 'dollar diplomacy' as American banks lent to eager but cash-strapped governments. This often-inglorious period in the United States' relations with Latin America was caustically summed up by General Smedley Darlington Butler, who was said to be embittered at having been passed over for the job of commandant of the US Marine Corps:

> I spent thirty-three years ... being a high-class muscle man for Big Business, for Wall Street and the bankers. In short, I was a racketeer for capitalism ... I helped purify Nicaragua for the international banking house of Brown Brothers in 1909–12. I helped make Mexico and especially Tampico safe for American oil interests in 1916. I helped make Haiti and Cuba a decent place for the National City [Bank] boys to collect revenue in. I helped in the rape of half a dozen Central American republics for the benefit of Wall Street.[23]

In all, between 1898 and 1934 there were some 30 separate military interventions by the United States in nine countries of the Americas – all of them in the Caribbean Basin. Most of these exercises were self-serving, even if they were driven, too, by a high-minded sense of the United States' improving mission in the world – a mixture of motives that is once again familiar today. On the other hand, interventionism was restrained both by a desire to avoid foreign entanglements and by the moral rejection of imperialism on the part of a former colonial people. The result, in the balanced judgement of one historian, was 'a kind of ambivalent imperialism continually modified by guilt, domestic politics and the lack of a true colonial drive.'[24]

These interventions impregnated the popular view in both halves of the hemisphere of US policy towards Latin America. They provided fuel for dependency theorists, especially when they were repeated in Central America in the 1980s. Yet they applied to only a small part of the region. And intervention is only one motif in the pattern of hemispheric relations.

Another is a search for peaceful co-operation. At the first Pan-American Conference, held in Washington in 1889, James G Blaine, the US Secretary of State, proposed a hemispheric customs union and arbitration mechanisms to settle disputes between nations. These ideas were not adopted, because of opposition led by Argentina and Chile. But they set the stage for increasingly busy hemispheric diplomacy – and would find an echo in the Miami summit of 1994. A similar approach would be followed by Franklin Roosevelt. On taking office in 1933, he proclaimed his administration's intention to be a 'good neighbour'. Roosevelt read Spanish; he had visited both Central and South America, and gave the region great importance in foreign policy (until the Japanese attack on Pearl Harbour in 1941 imposed other priorities). The United States committed itself not to intervene in the affairs of other countries. But that also meant it made no effort to promote democracy. Haya de la Torre, the leader of Peru's APRA, noted pointedly that Roosevelt was 'the good neighbour of tyrants'.[25] However, the famous comment attributed to FDR concerning Somoza ('He's a son of a bitch but at least he's our son of a bitch') was probably apocryphal. With the advent of the Second World War, the administration's main concern was to ensure access to Latin America's raw materials. The 'good neighbour' began to dispense economic aid, such as a cheap loan to enable Brazil's government to build a large, integrated steel mill at Volta Redonda.

The interventions of the first three decades of the twentieth century generated anti-Yankee feeling in Latin America. This had not previously been the norm. When the Monroe Doctrine was first enunciated, some in Latin America, such as Santander, saw it as a useful commitment by the United States to buttress still-fragile independence against Spanish and European covetousness. But Bolívar, for all his admiration of the United States, was wary. (Instead, he wanted an alliance with Britain.) To this day, Latin American leaders remain torn between these two impulses. Brazil, for example, enjoyed a special relationship with the United States, which lasted until the 1970s. The Baron of Rio Branco, whose career as Brazil's premier diplomat spanned the empire and the early republic, argued: 'Latin America has nothing to fear from Anglo-Saxon America ... Nothing, absolutely nothing, in the policies of the United States would be able to cause uneasiness to the national sensitivity of the other American countries. Just the opposite, these nations find in the preponderance of the first nation of the continent support for their causes and aspirations.'[26] But some other countries, especially Argentina – whose special relationship with Britain endured until the Second World War – saw Pan-Americanism as limiting their options. As more confident nation-states emerged in Latin America, they began to elaborate diplomatic defences. In the last decades of the nineteenth century, an Argentine diplomat, Carlos

Calvo, had argued for a strict version of national sovereignty. He rejected the notion that foreign governments had the right to intervene to protect the lives and property of their citizens abroad, as both the European powers and the United States frequently did in Latin America. The 'Calvo Doctrine' held that foreigners, including investors, should be treated exactly the same as nationals, with no right of appeal to foreign governments even if host nations unilaterally changed the rules under which investments had been made.[27] This principle was adopted by Carranza in Mexico's 1917 constitution, and found adherents elsewhere in the region – including Néstor Kirchner, Argentina's current president, in his handling of foreign investors in his country's privatised utilities. A second principle, known as the Drago Doctrine after another Argentine, held that debts owed by one nation to another should not be collected by force. Again, its target was mainly European powers.

By the end of the Second World War, Latin America's mighty northern neighbour had become a superpower, while Europe, immersed in its own reconstruction, was temporarily disabled and permanently weakened. As the United States embarked on the Cold War, it dusted off the Monroe Doctrine and applied it to the Soviet Union's efforts to spread communism around the world (cautious though these were in the Americas). That was one inspiration behind what came to be called the Inter-American system, comprising the Rio Treaty of mutual defence and, in 1948, the establishment of the Organisation of American States (OAS). In deference to Calvo, the OAS Charter emphasised the principle of non-intervention. Nevertheless, to obtain diplomatic cover for the Guatemalan coup, J F Dulles spent a fortnight personally arm-twisting his Latin American counterparts at an OAS Assembly in Caracas in 1954. Only with great reluctance did they accept Dulles's proposition that 'the domination or control of the political institutions of any American state by the international communist movement' would constitute a threat to the Americas as a whole and would require 'appropriate action'. This would be the guiding principle of American foreign policy in the western hemisphere until the fall of the Berlin Wall. At first Latin America was a minor theatre in the global rivalry between the United States and the Soviet Union. That would soon change.

The 'sugar prison' changes jailers

Like the island of Hispaniola and Brazil's north-east, Cuba was shaped and distorted by sugar. The cane plantations and sugar mills depended on slave labour. Between 1820 and 1865, up to 500,000 African slaves were imported; by 1841, they made up 43.5 per cent of the population.[28] Such was Spain's desire to maintain Cuba's sugar wealth that it hung on to the island through the nineteenth century by means of an implacable dictatorship. In the words of Hugh Thomas, a British historian, Cuba was 'a sugar prison rather than a sugar palace'.[29] A prolonged guerrilla war from 1868 to 1878 failed to dislodge Spanish rule. After the abolition of slavery in 1886, a more powerful independence movement emerged. Its leader was José Martí, a writer and political activist who founded the Cuban Revolutionary Party (PRC). Martí had spent fifteen years living in New York. He was just one among many Cubans, both white and black, who had migrated to the United States. They were the forerunners of a large Cuban-American community that has endured to this day while undergoing many changes. Martí admired the United States' democracy, but was a critic of some aspects of its capitalism, and deeply mistrustful of its intentions towards Cuba. In his last letter, written in 1895 after he had landed on the island as part of a liberating expedition and two days before he was killed, Martí declared:

> I am now every day in danger of giving my life for my country and for my duty ... to be in time to prevent with the independence of Cuba that the United States extends itself through the Antilles and falls, with that great force, upon our lands in America. Everything I have done hitherto, and will do, is for that purpose ... I lived inside the monster and I know its entrails: and my sling is that of David.[30]

Martí's fears were soon justified by the aftermath of the Spanish–American war. The rebel army (many of whose members were black) which had fought the Spaniards to a standstill in 1895-8 was disdained by the Americans. After four years of American military rule, Cuba emerged independent in name, but a protectorate and economic colony of the United States in practice. Into Cuba's constitution were inserted restrictions known as the Platt Amendment (to the Army Appropriations Act of 1901). These limited the Cuban government's freedom to contract debt and make military alliances; required it to grant bases to the United States (one was promptly set up at Guantánamo Bay, which has recently become notorious); and allowed the US the right to intervene in Cuba to ensure 'the maintenance of a stable government adequately protecting life, property and individual liberty'.[31] Although abrogated in 1934, the Platt Amendment served merely to inflame Cuba's frustrated search for nationhood. During the first thirty years of the new republic, government was generally corrupt and elections rigged; the losers would rise in arms and appeal for American intervention, which was often forthcoming. Political gangsterism was common.[32] Gyrations in the world price of sugar served to consolidate the control of deeper-pocketed American companies over the economy. Some 60 per cent of rural properties came to be owned by Americans. Cuban society was less racist than that of the southern United States, but power lay firmly with the whites.

The Great Depression hit Cuba very hard, prompting a collapse of sugar prices – the value of the island's sugar crop plunged from $199 million in 1929 to $42 million in 1932.[33] The resulting hardship and discontent brought down the repressive regime of Gerardo Machado, an elected dictator (dubbed a 'tropical Mussolini' by one of his opponents). An attempt by Sumner Welles, the American ambassador, to select a new government was thwarted by a rebellion of army NCOs led by Sergeant Fulgencio Batista, a handsome *mulato* stenographer. Batista allied with students and university professors who formed a revolutionary government of socialist and radical-liberal inspiration. It decreed the nationalisation of the American-owned electric company and of several sugar properties. But Welles withheld recognition of the government, and Batista withdrew his support. Subsequent democratic governments were marred by corruption, and the chance of reform was lost. Batista would remain the dominant figure in Cuba for the next quarter of a century, ruling as an elected president in 1940–4 and returning as a dictator in 1952. Within a year, his dictatorship was challenged by Fidel Castro, a young lawyer, former student leader and member of the radical Ortodoxo Party (which claimed descent from Martí's PRC). Acting in the Cuban tradition of violent risings, he organised an attack on the Moncada army barracks in Santiago, Cuba's second city. It failed, but Castro survived. He was sentenced to 15 years' imprisonment, but was soon released under a general amnesty. Having made his way to Mexico, in December 1956 he tried again, landing with 82 guerrillas (including his younger brother, Raúl, and Che Guevara) in Oriente province, many of whose people were black and poor. Against all odds, the guerrilla force established itself in the mountains of the Sierra Maestra. The rest is history – but history wrapped in many myths.

There is, of course, a vast literature on the Cuban revolution. The main question that need concern us here is why Castro and his fellow-revolutionaries did not restore democracy but opted instead to extinguish capitalism. After all, less than a year before Castro marched into Havana, across the Caribbean in Venezuela an alliance of civilians and dissident army officers had ousted another dictator, Marcos Pérez Jiménez, but had established a democracy under a pact which excluded the Communist Party from power. The answer has much to do with Castro himself and with Cuban history, in which his revolution was grounded. As a student leader at Havana University, Fidel claims to have read Marx and to have become a 'utopian communist'.[34] Never an ideologue, he has always been a man of action, a political and military strategist, a man who wants and understands power above all else. As a young lawyer, he was a rising star of the Ortodoxo Party; he would almost certainly have been elected as a deputy in the 1952 election had this not been cancelled by Batista's coup. Even before the coup, disillusioned by what he saw as the betrayals of the democratic governments of the 1940s, he had decided that Cuba needed a revolution and that he would lead it. But what sort of revolution? The manifesto of Castro's 26th of July Movement (named for the date of the assault on the Moncada barracks) issued at the outset of the guerrilla war was couched in moderate terms: it called for the restoration of the 1940 constitution, agrarian reform, and nationalisation of public utilities. Several of Fidel's inner circle were communist sympathisers. Raúl Castro had been a member of the Communist Youth while Che Guevara was a self-taught Marxist and fellow-traveller of communism, though not a party member. According to Tad Szulc, a well-informed biographer of Fidel, 'the historical [*sic*] decision that the revolution should lead to the establishment of socialism and then communism in Cuba was reached by Castro alone in the late spring of 1958 – probably during the series of crucial political meetings held in the Sierra during May and June'.[35]

That decision was carefully concealed. As Batista fled Havana on New Year's Eve 1958, Castro named Manuel Urrutia, a provincial judge, as president; the cabinet was drawn mainly from the moderate, non-communist, wing of the 26th of July Movement. But power lay with Fidel, who made himself commander-in-chief of the armed forces and established what Szulc calls a 'parallel' government, based on the new National Agrarian Reform Institute. He and Guevara applied the lessons they had learned from Guatemala: Batista's army was destroyed; an alliance with the Popular Socialist Party (as the old Communist Party called itself) was struck but concealed for two years until Castro had full political control and had established the security apparatus of a police state.[36] The Eisenhower administration saw through the democratic facade: although Castro would not nationalise all American businesses in Cuba until October 1960 and would not declare himself to be a communist until December 1961, as early as March 1959 the National Security Council began to review how 'to bring another government to power in Cuba'.[37] The CIA began sabotage operations; in March 1960, it blew up a Belgian freighter unloading a shipment of rifles in Havana harbour, killing a hundred people. When an invasion force of 1,500 Cuban exiles organised by the CIA landed at the Bay of Pigs in April 1961, Castro, the master strategist, was ready as Arbenz had not been. The invasion was crushed on the beach by Castro's militias, partly because Kennedy refused to commit American air power. In October 1959, just nine months after entering Havana, Castro had already begun the contacts with the Soviet Union that would lead to a full-scale military and economic alliance. In 1962, the Soviet Union's decision to station missiles on Cuban soil brought the world closer to nuclear war than it had ever been.

Kennedy and Khruschev negotiated the withdrawal of the missiles in return for a guarantee that the United States would not again invade Cuba. Castro, who had wanted a military pact with the Soviet Union but not the missiles, was furious at being excluded from the negotiations, and at what he saw as Khruschev's climbdown.[38]

The evidence suggests that those who have argued that Castro was somehow pushed into the arms of the Soviet Union and communism by the American trade embargo decreed in November 1960 are mistaken. The Cuban government's decisions were of its own volition.[39] It is safe to say that two, linked, political impulses drove Fidel Castro: one was anti-Americanism[40] and the other was to render permanent his revolution and his personal control over his country. Communism provided the tools to satisfy both impulses, rather than being an end in itself. Fidel has always claimed primary inspiration from Martí – the nationalist, anti-imperialist Martí, rather than the democrat – not Marx. 'The intellectual author of this revolution is José Martí, the apostle of our independence,' he said at the Moncada trial in 1953.[41] It may not be coincidental that in both Cuba and Mexico revolutions whose aims included the consolidation of the nation-state in the face of what was perceived to be a threat from the United States led to the establishment of one-party regimes. Yet democracy is far from incompatible with national self-determination, as many other countries have demonstrated. Castro drew on Cuba's traditions of guerrilla warfare and revolutionary violence, and its long struggle for nationhood and racial and social justice. The extent to which he came to embody that struggle explained the affection and respect many Cubans held for him despite their privations. But Fidel was also a Latin American *caudillo*, who militarised Cuban society as never before. The American trade embargo, and the countless failed assassination attempts against Castro by the CIA, served only to aggravate this. They allowed Castro to claim that Cuba was in a permanent war with American imperialism.

The left turns against democracy

As well as awakening outside interest in Latin America, the Cuban revolution inspired a generation of young Latin American radicals. Ultimately, it would have much less influence on the region than the Mexican revolution, but that would not be for want of trying. Its appeal to the Latin American left was enormous – and tragic. Before the Cuban revolution, the left in Latin America was in most places fairly weak. Its three main components were anarcho-syndicalists, many of them European immigrants; Communist parties, formed in most places in the 1920s and subservient to the Comintern in Moscow; and third, the more radical supporters of populist leaders. In some countries, the

Communists had achieved a small but significant following, especially in trade unions. In Brazil, they had some support among army officers and conscripts. In 1935, the party attempted a coup against Getúlio Vargas, with a rising at three army bases. It was crushed, and gave Vargas a pretext to declare the *Estado Novo*, a quasi-fascist dictatorship.[42] Everywhere, the Communists faced a structural problem: how to make a revolution where its main presumed protagonist, the urban working class, was small and its trade unions weak. It was for this reason that populists – with their appeal to a broader, multi-class coalition – rather than social-democrats, were the midwives of mass politics in Latin America. (The main exception was Chile, whose mining industry, isolated in the distant Atacama desert, generated a powerful union movement, and Socialist and Communist parties.) The Communists' answer would eventually be a cautious one: that they should first ally with the 'national bourgeoisie' against the 'feudal' agrarian oligarchy and 'imperialism' in order to create a 'bourgeois-democratic' (i.e. capitalist) revolution. Only then would socialism be on the agenda.

A dissenting response came from José Carlos Mariátegui, a journalist and essayist who founded what would become Peru's Communist Party. His thought combined Marxism and *indigenismo* which, inspired by the Mexican example, took powerful root among Peruvian writers and painters alike in the 1920s.[43] Mariátegui argued that in Peru, at least, the source of revolution would be the peasantry in alliance with the workers. This was because Peru's history was very different from that of Europe. He saw in the Andean Indian peasant community 'elements of practical socialism' and of 'agrarian communism'. At the same time, the prevalence of the *latifundio* (a large landholding with indentured serfs) militated against capitalist development. 'Democratic and liberal institutions cannot flourish or function in a semi-feudal economy,' he wrote.[44] Only socialism could bring development to Peru, he argued; achieving it was a long-term task and would require a mass movement from which would emerge a revolutionary party.

Mariátegui was opposed from two sides. In Peru, it was Haya de la Torre and APRA, not the socialists, who led the opposition to the modernising dictatorship of Augusto Leguía of 1919–30. Abroad, at the first Latin American Communist Conference, held in Buenos Aires in 1929, unimaginative bureaucrats from the Comintern imposed orthodoxy.[45] Months later, Mariátegui, long an invalid, died at the age of 35 from a bone disease. He seemed to have lost the argument. Yet his thought is reflected in several of the traits that came to distinguish the Latin American left, such as the importance given to nationalism, popular religiosity and social movements. It was not surprising that in Peru, unlike the rest of Latin America, Maoism, which also gave a pre-eminent role to the peasantry, should find adherents. The fundamentalist Maoist guerrillas who terrorised Peru from 1980 to 1993, claimed inspiration from Mariátegui: their full name was the *Partido Comunista del Perú – Por el Sendero Luminoso de José Carlos Mariátegui* (Peruvian Communist Party – by the Shining Path of José Carlos Mariátegui). Unlike the Shining Path's founder, Abimael Guzmán, Mariátegui was an undogmatic Marxist, not a terrorist. But like so many other Latin American leftists he was a disciple of Georges Sorel, a French theorist of anarcho-syndicalism, and he did believe in revolutionary violence. Mariátegui's vision of an indigenous Andean utopia, menaced by capitalism and imperialism, is today echoed by radical leaders such as Bolivia's Evo Morales. It is based on myth. Mariátegui had little knowledge of the Andean world; his illness prevented him making more than one visit to the Peruvian sierra, and not a single peasant was among the founders of his party. 'He had constructed the image of an egalitarian and conflict-free [indigenous peasant] community which had never existed and still less at that time,' admitted Alberto Flores Galindo, a Peruvian historian sympathetic to Mariátegui.[46]

Thirty years later, the Cuban revolution seemed to many on the left to offer the solution to their frustrated quest – a 'revolution in the revolution', as Régis Debray, a French theorist, put it. In the view of Che Guevara – whose writings on the Cuban campaign in which he fought achieved wide circulation – the only thing that had been missing previously was the courage of revolutionaries. In *Guerrilla Warfare*, a slim but enormously influential volume published in 1961, he stated:

> We consider that the Cuban Revolution contributed three fundamental lessons to the conduct of revolutionary movements in America. They are:
>
> 1 Popular forces can win a war against the army.
>
> 2 It is not necessary to wait until all the conditions for making revolution exist; the insurrection can create them.
>
> 3 In underdeveloped America the countryside is the basic area for armed fighting.[47]

This seemed to make sense. There were, after all, tens of millions of poor peasants in Latin America, and Mao Zedong's revolution in China had successfully based itself on the peasantry and rural warfare. Yet Guevara's message found its most receptive audience among the middle-class youth of Latin America, a group which was expanding rapidly as a result of economic growth and urbanisation. Many of these middle-class students were acutely conscious of the injustices in their societies, and saw in the Cuban revolution an effective way to tackle them. At the same time, the Catholic Church – which had blessed injustice in Latin America since the moment a Dominican friar had taken a full part in the capture and murder of Atahualpa, the Inca – had an attack of conscience. Stimulated partly by the reforms of the Second Vatican Council and Pope John XXIII, a new current emerged, which preached that the Latin American Church should concern itself primarily with helping the poor. The main impact of liberation theology, as it was called, was to form a network of grassroots 'base communities' which agitated for change. But some of its proponents flirted with Marxism and violence. Nearly a thousand priests submitted a manifesto to a conference of Latin American bishops, held at Medellín in Colombia in 1968, in which they differentiated between the 'unjust violence of the oppressors' and 'the just violence of the oppressed'.[48] That stance would create many martyrs, among both priests and nuns and their followers. As Cardinal Oscar Andrés Rodríguez Maradiaga, a Honduran archbishop, put it recently: 'there were many priests in Central America who supported violent change ... There was a big temptation to try and change things through violence, and what did we get? Only dead people.'[49]

For the best part of three decades after 1959, across Latin America a radicalised left committed itself to revolution. Rural guerrilla *focos* soon appeared in more than half a dozen countries, including Guatemala, Colombia, Venezuela and Peru. Yet Guevara's prescription for the *foco* – the Spanish word means 'focus' or 'centre', but also 'light-bulb' – had two fatal flaws. The first was that, like Mariátegui's vision, it involved a mythologised rewriting of history. Recent research has underlined that Fidel Castro's rebel army did not make the Cuban revolution alone. It depended for its survival, and for its eventual victory, on a broad range of alliances with groups of middle-class professionals, the churches, labour unions, and various revolutionary organisations. Strikes, agitation and sabotage were important in wearing down the will to fight of Batista's army, allowing the guerrillas to triumph.[50] The second flaw in Guevara's argument was even more serious. There was a world of difference between an armed rising against a corrupt and brutal dictatorship in an American neo-colony, such as Cuba, and attempting guerrilla warfare against the more powerful armies of the larger, independent nations of South America. That was especially so where governments enjoyed legitimacy and had carried out significant, if inadequate, social reforms. Guevara himself half-recognised this. In *Guerrilla Warfare* he had written: 'Where a government has come into power through some form of popular vote, fraudulent or not, and maintains at least an appearance of constitutional legality, the guerrilla outbreak cannot be promoted, since the possibilities of peaceful struggle have not yet been exhausted.'[51] But in practice, he would ignore this rider. His central message was that 'it is the duty of the revolutionary to make the revolution'. The voluntarism of a self-appointed revolutionary elite and a murderous militarism would thus come to substitute for any missing political conditions.

Guevara was right, however, that after the Cuban revolution, 'imperialism' (i.e. the United States) 'will not allow itself to be caught by surprise'; the same went for the 'higher bourgeoisie' in the region (i.e. Latin American governments).[52] Ever since 1959, it has been a basic tenet of the United States' policy towards Latin America to prevent a 'second Cuba'. That led successive administrations into alliances with some brutal or unsavoury dictatorships and served to stoke the fires of nationalist anti-Americanism in the region. In Washington's eyes, the first candidate for the role of another Cuba was the Dominican Republic. Following the assassination of Trujillo, an election in 1962 was won by Juan Bosch, an ineffectual social-democrat. Bosch was soon overthrown by a military coup. When a subsequent government collapsed, a 'constitutionalist' group of army officers and their civilian allies attempted to restore Bosch to power. In fighting in Santo Domingo, the capital, they drove back conservative military officers who opposed them. The administration of Lyndon Johnson feared that communists were behind Bosch. It dispatched the marines as the spearhead of a force that would total 23,000 American troops – the lesson of the Bay of Pigs was thought to be not to do such things by halves. Their ostensible mission was to protect American civilians from chaos. In an echo of the Roosevelt corollary, Johnson claimed in justification of his action that there were 'headless bodies lying in the streets of Santo Domingo'. When opponents challenged this, he is said to have called the American ambassador, enjoining him, 'For God's sake see if you can find some headless bodies.'[53] The outcome was the defeat of Bosch's supporters, and the installation in a less-than-free election of Joaquín Balaguer, a quiet and reliably anti-communist lawyer and amateur poet who had been Trujillo's amanuensis and, at the end, his frontman as president for a couple of years. He would win five more increasingly rigged elections. Though the outcome was less tragic than in Guatemala, the Dominican Republic would not become a democracy until well into the 1990s.[54]

For his part, Fidel Castro saw 'exporting the revolution' as a way to defend it on his island. Cuba trained, armed, financed and advised thousands of revolutionaries from other Latin American countries. In turn, the sudden advent of an increasingly loyal ally in the Caribbean caused the Soviet Union to take a much more active interest in Latin America. 'Cuba forced us to take a fresh look at the whole continent, which until then had traditionally occupied the last place in the Soviet leadership's system of priorities,' according to Nikolai Leonov, who was long the KGB official closest to the Castro brothers.[55] In 1961, the Soviet leadership adopted a KGB plan to 'activate … armed uprisings against pro-Western reactionary governments' around the world, placing Central America at the top of the list.[56] The bureau had a habit of overstating its powers, and the Soviet Union became increasingly cautious about provoking the United States in its 'backyard'. Internal factors were almost always more important than external factors in the conflicts which played out in Latin America after the Cuban revolution. But the recent availability of archive material from the former Soviet Union underlines that outside intervention in the region during the Cold War was not a game played only by the United States.[57]

The main outcome of the first wave of rural guerrilla movements in the 1960s was the slaughter of some of the best and brightest among a generation of idealistic middle-class youths – and of the peasants and conscripts who were unlucky enough to get in their way. Guevara himself famously practised what he preached, going first to the Congo and then to Bolivia in answer to his own call to create 'two, three ... many Vietnams'. His Bolivian venture summed up the arrogant futility of his quest. Although he had spent several weeks there on his way to Guatemala, he seemed oblivious to the fact that Bolivia's 1952 revolution had granted land and appreciable benefits to many peasants.[58] To compound his difficulties, most of Bolivia's communist leaders were unenthusiastic about Guevara's plan for a guerrilla *foco*, and steered him to barren and remote territory near Vallegrande in the south-east, far from the country's mines and their powerful trade union movement. Not a single peasant joined the guerrillas, and several passed on information to the army, so the *foco* was quickly detected. A score of Green Berets from the United States swiftly trained a new Ranger unit of the Bolivian army in counter-insurgency. Together with regular army troops, within months they annihilated the *foco*, and captured and shot Guevara.

The manner of his death, at the age of 39, would make Guevara a universal icon. He had three times risked his life to bring revolution to countries that were not his own. That quest turned him into a symbol of romantic rebellion everywhere. Thus Diego Maradona, Argentina's troubled multi-millionaire football hero, explained his tattoo of Che: 'He was a rebel. So am I.'[59] To others among his acolytes, it seemed that Guevara, an ascetic, symbolised a selfless quest for utopia – that mirage which has dazzled so many Latin Americans and those who are drawn to the region. As Jorge Castañeda points out in his biography of Guevara, the photos of the dead guerrilla portrayed him as 'the Christ of Vallegrande' whose eyes expressed 'the tender calm of an accepted sacrifice'.[60] The stubborn, dogmatic and militaristic Argentine Marxist-Leninist thus became transubstantiated into a figure akin to that of a Christian martyr. His visage not only adorns the most unlikely products of global capitalism, from bars to coffee-mugs, but it takes its place in the gallery of popular saints with whose images Latin

America's truck and bus drivers choose to adorn their vehicles to ward off the demons of the road.

Only in Nicaragua would something resembling the Cuban revolution be repeated, with the Sandinista insurrection of 1979. Not by coincidence, Nicaragua, like Cuba, had suffered American intervention, was ruled by a corrupt dictator, and its army was a US-created *gendarmerie* which lacked legitimacy. The Sandinista regime was a far from cohesive coalition of Marxists, liberation theologians, nationalists and social-democrats. The Reagan administration saw in it the nightmare of a 'second Cuba'. It moved to overthrow the Sandinistas by organising the *contra* guerrillas. The Sandinistas were determined to avoid the fate of Arbenz. With support from Cuba and the Soviet Union they created a 100,000-strong army and an increasingly militarised state – 'a Central American Sparta', as Castañeda puts it.[61] The Reagan administration was hamstrung by opposition in the United States Congress, and further embarrassed by the exposure of its illegal efforts to funnel to the *contras* the proceeds of clandestine arms sales to Iran. As a result, the *contras* were no match militarily for the Sandinista army. But the Sandinistas' economic mistakes, their arrogant treatment of the peasantry and the hardships imposed by an American trade embargo and the *contra* war engendered a growing groundswell of discontent. By then, Mikhail Gorbachev was acutely aware of the bankruptcy of the Soviet economy: after providing $1.1 billion in mainly military aid, the Soviet Union told the Sandinistas that they were on their own.[62] That encouraged the Sandinista leadership to embrace a peace plan authored by Oscar Arias, Costa Rica's president, and backed by the rest of Latin America, involving free and fair elections. Eventually this was supported by George H W Bush, who had replaced Reagan; he was eager to turn the page on Iran-Contra and involvement in Nicaragua. After electoral defeat, the Sandinistas left power voluntarily in 1990. Nicaragua became a democracy, albeit a poor and troubled one.

In neighbouring El Salvador, another small Central American country with a dire history of dictatorship, a powerful left-wing movement based on trade unions, radical priests and peasant groups emerged. In 1972, a reformist coalition was denied victory in a presidential election only by fraud in favour of the military party, whose only platform was anti-communism.[63] Thereafter, El Salvador spiralled into civil war between leftist guerrilla groups and the armed forces, some of whose leaders formed death squads. The United States pumped in military aid, while coaxing the generals towards democracy. The guerrillas of the Farabundo Martí National Liberation Front (FMLN) enjoyed considerable popular support; they fought the army to a standstill over a decade. By then, the Cold War was over. A peace agreement signed in Mexico in 1992 turned El Salvador, like Nicaragua, into a democracy. But it is one in which the right-wing Arena Party has held power continuously since 1989. That was partly because the FMLN, which turned into a political party, failed to throw up new, more moderate leaders.

As the Cold War ended, the cycle of US interventions in the Central American isthmus that had begun in Guatemala in 1954 closed with the invasion of Panama in 1989. At a cost of some 500 to 1,000 Panamanian dead, between civilians and soldiers, and the lives of 25 American troops, this overthrew Manuel Noriega, a thuggish strongman but one who was no nastier than many American allies (which he himself had been for much of his career as intelligence chief of the Panama Defence Forces).[64] Noriega had annulled an election which appeared to have been won by a large margin by the opposition candidate, Guillermo Endara, whom the American troops installed in office. He was a troublesome figure in a country to which the US was committed to turning over the Panama Canal ten years later. But in the end Noriega was overthrown because of his links with drug traffickers at a time when the 'war on drugs' was almost as all-consuming in Washington as the 'war on terror' would become a dozen years later. Noriega was arrested and jailed on charges of aiding drug traffickers.[65]

If revolution and American pressure helped in the end to democratise Central America, that was not what Guevara and Castro had fought for. Under their influence, a generation of leftists gave priority to social justice and nationalism, and disdained democracy and the rule of law.[66] Not all of the myriad 'new left' groups – of Maoist, Trotskyist and nationalist inspiration in addition to Guevarists – which sprung up across Latin America embraced violence and *la lucha armada* ('the armed struggle'). But many were equivocal on the matter; some would even welcome the arrival of dictatorships in the deluded belief that repression would arouse the masses.

Meanwhile, Cuba itself would find that national self-determination again proved elusive. It became a Soviet satellite, a producer of Caribbean sugar for the eastern block in return for some $4 billion a year in economic aid – a vast sum for an island of fewer than 10 million people. Even after the initial fervour had faded, the revolution's foreign defenders would point to its undoubted achievements in health and education. Its critics pointed to the cost – the extinction of all political and economic freedom. They also noted that back in 1959 Cuba was already one of the top five Latin American countries on a wide range of socio-economic indicators.[67] True, the distribution of income, schooling and health was highly unequal then. A third of the workforce lived in severe poverty, dependent on seasonal work on the sugar harvest; most of these Cubans were black. But in average life expectancy, Cuba in 1959 was close to the United States, and it had more doctors per head than Britain and France. Fidel Castro poured resources into health, education and biotechnology, but that could not conceal the poverty and inefficiency of the communist economy. Sympathisers blamed the American embargo, of course, and there is no doubt that this ill-conceived and self-defeating policy added to the difficulties of the Cuban people while doing nothing to weaken the regime. But the main fault lay with central planning, which has failed as a method of economic development the world over.

The collapse of the Soviet Union and the disappearance of its subsidies had an impact on Cuba comparable only to that of the Great Depression: the economy contracted by a third and discontent grew. Many believed that Castro's revolution was bound for swift extinction.[68] To save it, Castro enacted economic reforms for what he called 'the Special Period in Peacetime'. He encouraged foreign investment, especially in the tourist industry. He gave state enterprises much more autonomy over their trade and finances. He allowed the use of the American dollar, to attract remittances from Cuban-Americans (who now number more than a million). And he gave the smallest of nods to private enterprise in the form of peasant markets and small, family-run private businesses, such as restaurants and plumbing. Many in Cuba and beyond hoped that economic reform would lead to political liberalisation. Yet such concessions turned out to be strictly tactical. At the start of the twenty-first century, Castro at last found replacements for his lost Soviet sponsor in China and, especially, in Hugo Chávez's Venezuela. China provided Cuba with cheap loans for infrastructure and some consumer goods. Venezuela gave Castro all the oil he needed at a heavily subsidised price, as well as other goods. In return, some 16,000 Cuban doctors (a third of the total) worked in Venezuela for several years, and Castro provided Chávez with political advice and advisers. Thus fortified, in 2005 Castro declared the 'Special Period' over. With it went many of the reforms. The year before he had banned the use of the dollar, and re-imposed central control over state companies. Foreign investors – except for a few large ones considered vital – and small businesses faced mounting bureaucratic regulation and harassment. By mid-2005, half the 800 foreign investors had gone, while only 140,000 small businesses remained, down from 240,000 a decade earlier.[69] After more than two centuries, sugar has finally been eclipsed – by tourism and remittances – as Cuba's main source of foreign exchange, as it has been across the Caribbean. In 2002 the government decreed the closure of almost half the island's 156 sugar mills; half of the land under sugar was to be turned over to other crops, and at least a quarter of the 400,000 workers in the industry lost their jobs (officially, they were to be retrained).[70] Growing world demand for ethanol subsequently held out the possibility of a new lease of life for sugar.

In his twilight years, Fidel Castro once again enjoyed a certain political influence in Latin America. His disciples included not just Venezuela's Chávez

– with whom Castro established a relationship of mutual dependence – but also Bolivia's Evo Morales, Nicaragua's Daniel Ortega, and the leaders of some radical social movements, such as that of Ecuador's indigenous peoples and Brazil's Movimento Sem Terra of landless workers. But Venezuela, Bolivia and Nicaragua apart, no other government showed interest in a close alliance with Cuba, though they condemned the trade embargo against it. Other Latin American countries have begun to surpass Cuba's social achievements, without its sacrifice of human freedom: Argentina, Chile, Uruguay and Costa Rica all scored higher than Cuba in the United Nations Human Development Report in 2006, and Mexico was close behind.

Cubans retained residual respect for Fidel. But beneath the surface, there were many signs of widespread discontent over crumbling infrastructure, a health service weakened by medical diplomacy, the drabness and hardships of everyday life and the lack of opportunity and of freedoms. A mild relaxation of political control during the 'Special Period' was reversed too. In April 2003, while the world was distracted by the start of the war in Iraq, Castro's secret police rounded up 78 dissidents and independent journalists. In the biggest crackdown in a decade, after summary trials they received jail sentences averaging 28 years. More than two-thirds of the detainees were independent journalists and/or activists for the Varela Project, a pro-democracy group of Christian democrat inspiration. The Varela Project is based inside Cuba, not in Miami. Its leader, Oswaldo Payá, refused help from the United States and condemned the American trade embargo.[71] That made him especially dangerous for Castro's autocracy as he could not be dismissed as a 'mercenary'. At the same time, Castro launched a crackdown on pervasive corruption, sending brigades of unemployed youths, called 'social workers', to run petrol stations and getting students to stage unannounced audits of state companies.

Castro became increasingly preoccupied with arrangements for what the regime called 'the succession' to his leadership, shuffling provincial party bosses and ministers. In July 2006, the party's central committee recreated its secretariat, apparently as a transitional leadership. Shortly afterwards, it was announced that Fidel Castro had undergone abdominal surgery and had 'temporarily' turned over his powers to his brother Raúl and a collective leadership. Raúl Castro was a powerful figure in his own right as head of the armed forces, which manage much of the economy and the tourist industry. After reportedly coming close to death through peritonitis, Fidel's health appeared to improve in early 2007. As long as Fidel lives, the revolution will survive in its island fastness, just as Spain retained its 'ever-faithful' isle. After that, Cuba will head into the unknown. Raúl Castro, by all accounts an efficient administrator, is said to favour a Chinese-style opening of the economy while retaining political control. Economic change might help to gain political consent for the 'successor' regime. But Raúl, who turned 76 in June 2007, is likely to be a transitional figure.

After half a century of Fidel, ordinary Cubans both want and fear change. Nobody knows what would happen if discontent boils over and the army is called upon to fire upon the people – something it has not had to do since the revolution. Another unknown is whether the United States will seek to intervene as events unfold in Cuba, and whether or not it will restrain Cuban-American claims for the restitution of homes and business premises. A further doubt concerns the role that Venezuela will play. Left to its own devices, Cuba could evolve towards an authoritarian capitalist regime in the style of Mexico's PRI, or it could move fairly swiftly towards democracy.

CHAPTER 5

FAILED REFORMERS, DEBT-RIDDEN DICTATORS: THE RIGHT RESISTS DEMOCRACY

On the Rua do Catete, a busy commercial street that connects Rio de Janeiro's central business district with the southern beaches of Copacabana and Ipanema, stands a neo-classical mansion whose exuberant external embellishment bespeaks its tropical location. Built by a coffee baron, it served as the residence of Brazil's presidents from the foundation of the Republic until the move to Brasília in 1960. It is now a museum. On the top floor, faithfully preserved, is the bedroom where, early in the morning of 24 August 1954, Getúlio Vargas reached for his revolver and shot himself through the heart. 'I gave you my life. Now I offer my death,' he wrote in a last letter to the Brazilian people.[1] Vargas had been Brazil's nation-builder, ruling from 1930 to 1945 mainly as a dictator. He had reinvented himself as a populist democrat, and won a presidential election in 1950. He had been ground down by bruising battles with a powerful conservative opposition, first over the setting up of Petrobrás, the state oil firm, then over the minimum wage and a government-backed attempt to bring trade unionism to the *fazendas* of the countryside. When an aide, acting apparently without the president's knowledge, arranged a botched murder attempt against one of Vargas's chief tormentors, the army demanded that the president resign. In choosing suicide, Vargas, ever the political survivor, made himself a martyr and ensured that his brand of developmentalist politics would predominate in Brazil for another decade. But it would be a struggle. Across much of South America in the quarter-century after the Second World War, reformers of varying hues would try to achieve peaceful, democratic change. They had to chart a narrow and treacherous course between public expectations and entrenched landowning oligarchies, and between restless armies and radicalised left-wing movements. Many were not helped by the inflation and volatility generated by their economic policies. Few succeeded for long.

A decade after the coup in Guatemala, this contest again reached a denouement, this time in Brazil. Vargas was succeeded by Juscelino Kubitschek, a genial medical doctor and skilled political deal-maker who had been governor of the large state of Minas Gerais and mayor of its capital, Belo Horizonte. Kubitschek promised 'fifty years' progress in five', to be achieved through a combination of state and private, especially foreign, investment. Deep in the *cerrado*, Brazil's great inland savannah, he built Brasília, a previously unfulfilled mandate of the 1891 constitution – one much desired by nearby *mineiros*, not a few of whom grew rich on the building contracts for the new capital. Under his presidency, foreign firms set up from scratch what would become a fully integrated car industry. Kubitschek founded a development agency for the backward north-east and gave a decisive push to Brazil's industrialisation. The economy grew at an annual average rate of around 9 per cent from 1957 to 1961. But all this came at a price. Opponents jibed that Kubitschek had notched up 'fifty years' inflation in five', while the current account plunged deep into deficit.[2] He called in the IMF, but then refused to implement a stabilisation programme. That allowed him to pose as a champion of national independence and leave office more popular than he had entered it. Indeed, Kubitschek was the first president in Brazil's new democratic era to complete his term – and the only elected one to do so until Fernando Henrique Cardoso served two full terms from 1995 to 2002. But the economic problems he had left unresolved would defeat his successors. Jânio Quadros, an eccentric anti-corruption campaigner from São Paulo, resigned after less than seven months in office. That prompted a constitutional crisis, since the vice-president was elected separately, and Quadros's running-mate had been narrowly defeated by João Goulart, a radical populist who was Vargas's former Labour minister and political heir. Goulart, an ineffectual politician, was distrusted by the right who saw him as pro-communist. The army, then the ultimate arbiter of power in Brazil, was divided. A compromise was reached: Goulart would take office, but for two years many of his powers would be vested in Congress.

Goulart's political base lay in the unions, but he was also backed by the Communist Party and newer left-wing forces such as peasant leagues in the north-east. The Communist Party was fairly strong: it had won 10 per cent of the vote in the 1945 elections (it was banned three years later). It also had support in the armed forces, especially among the lower ranks; in addition, some twenty to thirty senior officers were party members.[3] Goulart steered a vacillating course. In just thirty months in office, he had no fewer than five different finance ministers. He twice appointed competent economic teams, but shrank from backing the stabilisation programme that Brazil clearly required if growth was to resume. In mid 1963 he veered left, egged on by his brother-in-law, Leonel Brizola, the governor of Rio Grande do Sul and an irresponsible demagogue. Facing an opposition majority in Congress, the government organised a series of mass demonstrations at which Goulart announced a programme of 'basic reforms'. These were to be carried out by decree, and included some land expropriation and the nationalisation of privately owned oil refineries. He fatally antagonised a pivotal group of moderate army commanders by supporting the unionisation of the lower ranks of the armed forces, encouraging a Communist-supervised mutinous movement of army sergeants and navy petty-officers.[4] As a result, these moderate commanders threw their decisive weight behind a rising against the president. On 1 April 1964 Goulart fled to one of his ranches in Rio Grande do Sul (whence he would seek asylum in Uruguay). Later that week, the Congress elected Humberto Castello Branco, a moderate general, as president. To legitimate itself, the new government, mainly made up of civilian technocrats from the conservative União Democrática Nacional (UDN) Party, issued an 'Institutional Act'. Its main author was Francisco Campos, who had drafted the constitution of Vargas's dictatorship, the *Estado Novo*. As in Argentina in 1930, the Act relied on the dubious juridical principle of *revolución victoriosa* – or might is right. It gave the regime the power to purge Congress.

The armed forces thus extinguished two decades of civilian democracy in Brazil. They claimed to be acting in the name of legality, and many believed them. The coup was almost bloodless. It was supported by the elected civilian governors of the three most powerful states, two of them from the UDN. Castello Branco, a moderate, said he would serve only for the rest of Quadros's original term. It was widely expected that Kubitschek would win the election due in 1965. But the armed forces were split between moderates and hardliners. They would end up staying in power for two decades. The left claimed that Brazilian democracy was overthrown because Goulart had used it to challenge, on behalf of the poor, the interests of Brazil's landowners and bankers. They also argued that the United States had helped to organise the coup. Neither claim is well founded. There is much evidence that Goulart could have survived had he heeded the pleas of the military moderates to break with the far-left and to assert rather than subvert military discipline. In the end the coup happened because Brazilian politics had become too polarised, and because of Goulart's mistakes. His opponents were convinced that the president himself was using his military and union supporters to seek dictatorial powers, in the mould of Vargas in 1937 or Perón in Argentina. In the view of Lincoln Gordon, the American ambassador to Brazil, 'it had become a choice between populist coup from the top down and preventative counter-coup from the mainstream military. The latter prevailed.'[5] The United States blessed this outcome, but did not create it. The Brazilian armed forces had a vigorous anti-communist tradition since the uprising of 1935. Elio Gaspari, a distinguished Brazilian journalist, recently concluded after an exhaustive investigation of the matter: 'not a single Brazilian, civilian or military, took part in the deposing of João Goulart because the United States desired it'.[6]

A coup in Chile

The events in Brazil acquired greater resonance as further military coups followed elsewhere. In all, there were nine between March 1962 and June 1966; all but one were against governments seen as weak in the face of communist and Cuban influence.[7] Moderately reformist governments were toppled in Bolivia in 1964, in Argentina in 1965, in Peru in 1968, and in Ecuador in 1962 and again in 1972. Even Uruguay's democracy, one of the most robust in the region, succumbed. It had been built on an unusual combination of rural *latifundia* and urban socialism.[8] The harmonious process in which farm exports paid for a paternalist state and a large public sector broke down. On the one hand, the world market for wool collapsed in the 1950s; on the other, public employment had become a tool for rewarding party loyalty and grew inexorably, with no corresponding increase in the output of public services.[9] Between 1960 and 1970, income per head barely grew, inflation rose and strikes became common. Compromise gave way to polarisation: ranchers sought to curtail the public sector, whose workers and pensioners resisted. The Tupamaros, an urban guerrilla movement of Guevarist inspiration, further inflamed matters by killing military men and policemen. In what one historian called the 'longest coup d'état', civilian presidents first decreed a state of siege, and then placed the armed forces in charge of internal security, unleashing a murderous wave of repression against the law-abiding left as well as the guerrillas.[10] Finally, in 1973, President Juan María Bordaberry dissolved Congress and ruled as the civilian face of a dictatorship. Three years later, the armed forces pushed him aside, even though they had already crushed the Tupamaros.

It was the coup in Chile in 1973 that shocked the world. Since 1932, Chile had appeared to offer a model of political stability and civilian democracy. But problems, including chronic inflation, were accumulating. With a small domestic market, the prevailing economic policy of industrialisation behind high tariff barriers produced disappointing results in Chile. Private investment was feeble; the economy was uncomfortably dependent on the export of copper. In the 1960s, Chile saw a determined attempt to remedy these problems through moderate reform. Eduardo Frei, a Christian Democrat elected in 1964, promised a 'revolution in liberty'. This was based on Catholic social doctrine. It also received enthusiastic backing from the United States, which saw Frei as an exemplar for the Alliance for Progress. Frei's government negotiated the partial nationalisation of the American copper companies. It also pushed through a radical land reform, limiting farm size to just 80 hectares, and encouraged the unionisation of rural labourers. Some 22,000 families got land, but implementation of the reform did not satisfy the exaggerated expectations it had aroused. That went for the government's overall performance. Frei's achievements were real, but they alarmed the right while failing to satisfy the left or the more radical elements in his own party. A policy of inflationary wage increases led only to an increase in strikes. The search for compromise which had traditionally marked Chilean democracy was giving way to polarisation, as in Brazil. And, as in Brazil, that process would intensify with the arrival of a left-wing government with a narrow electoral mandate.

The victory in the 1970 presidential election of Salvador Allende, a Socialist doctor of great personal charm, did not represent a big underlying swing to the left among Chileans.[11] Allende, in his fourth presidential campaign, won with just 36 per cent of the 3 million votes cast – or only 39,000 more than those received by Jorge Alessandri, a former president who stood for the right-wing National Party. Allende proposed a democratic but revolutionary government. The main aim of the programme of his six-party Popular Unity coalition was 'the search for a replacement of the present economic structure, doing away with the power of foreign and national monopoly capital and of the *latifundio* in order to initiate the construction of socialism.'[12] The government proposed to nationalise 76 companies, accounting for 44 per cent of total manufacturing sales, enact a more radical agrarian reform, redistribute income and promote 'popular participation' in the economy, politics and the administration of justice. Implementing this 'Chilean Road to Socialism' without violating the law or the constitution, as Allende proposed, would have been hard even if he had enjoyed majority support and a cohesive coalition. He had neither. The opposition had majorities in both houses of Congress. And Popular Unity was deeply divided. On the one hand, the Communists, the small Radical Party and Allende himself wanted to move cautiously and seek agreements with the Christian Democrats. On the other, a large section of the Socialist Party had become enamoured of the Cuban revolution and, at least in theory, armed struggle. At its 1967 Congress, a majority of the party declared itself Marxist-Leninist and backed the *vía insurreccional* ('the insurrectional road') to socialism. A far-left Socialist splinter group, the *guevarista* Movement of the Revolutionary Left (MIR), was outside the Popular Unity, but its commitment to direct action exercised a gravitational pull on some of the coalition's supporters. These anti-democratic elements on the left were mirrored on the far right by Patria y Libertad ('Fatherland and Freedom'), a small fascist group, by hardline elements in the National Party and a minority of military officers.

In office, Allende quickly completed the nationalisation of copper, with unanimous opposition support. Far more controversially, the government also took over 507 industrial and commercial firms; these included eighty large concerns, and nearly all of the banks. In the case of the takeover of industrial firms, it resorted to legal chicanery or to the punitive application of price controls. An obscure 1940s law allowed the government to intervene in firms facing an industrial dispute, so officials encouraged strikes in firms they wanted to nationalise.[13] Allende also drastically speeded up implementation of Frei's agrarian reform, and did nothing to discourage land seizures by peasants. By 1973, about 60 per cent of Chile's farmland had been transferred; two-thirds of these transfers happened under Allende. Taking into account the compensation paid, landowners suffered a net capital loss of up to $1.6 billion (a sum equal to 130 per cent of Chile's GDP at the time), according to one estimate.[14] The main beneficiaries were the resident labourers on the *haciendas*; there was nothing for the numerous *minifundistas* (small-scale farmers) or day labourers.

The government's macroeconomic policy was recklessly populist, designed to increase public support for Popular Unity and thus for socialist structural changes in the economy. The government granted big wage increases, cranked up public spending and public employment (which increased by almost 40 per cent in three years[15]), maintained an overvalued currency, printed money on a massive scale and imposed price controls. The result was predictable. At first, the economy grew rapidly as unused capacity was brought into play; unemployment and inflation fell. But big distortions soon appeared: the public-sector deficit was a massive 15.3 per cent of GDP in 1971, the trade account had moved from surplus to deficit and the government was forced to suspend debt payments. Predictably, too, private investment dried up, since business was scared of expropriation. State and nationalised firms were badly run, requiring huge subsidies. By 1973, Chile was in the grip of shortages, rationing and black markets. As the public-sector deficit reached a colossal 30.5 per cent of GDP, inflation climbed to 605 per cent, growth gave way to recession, and international reserves were enough to cover only three weeks of imports.[16]

The economy's initial expansion did produce an increase in support for the government. In a municipal election in April 1971, Popular Unity won 48.2 per cent of the vote. But this share then fell to 44.2 per cent in a Congressional election in March 1973. The speed and scale of the state takeovers intensified opposition, and polarised the country. Congress refused to approve tax reforms to plug the fiscal chasm, and did its best to make life difficult for the government. Bosses' strikes, such as a month-long stoppage by the truckowners, compounded the economy's problems. Professionals and small businessmen agitated against the government. Much of the press was hostile and partisan. The United States helped the opposition. The CIA had spent $425,000 on anti-communist propaganda during the 1970 election. On the other hand, it now appears that the KGB spent some $500,000 in support of Allende's presidential campaign – including $10,000 to dissuade a potential left-wing rival from standing, which might just have tipped the result.[17] After the election, President Richard Nixon authorised the CIA to spend up to $10 million to try to prevent Allende from taking office. In the hope of provoking a coup, the agency organised a bungled attempt to kidnap General René Schneider, the army commander, which ended in his murder. Nixon then told Richard Helms, the CIA director, to 'make [Chile's] economy scream'.[18] After Allende took office, the administration blocked loans to Chile by the IMF and the World Bank. Allende's refusal to pay compensation to the copper companies (alleging 'excess profits') aggravated relations. The CIA gave money to the truckowners, other opposition groups and *El Mercurio*, a conservative newspaper. The KGB countered, though probably less lavishly, giving further funds to Allende and to publications sympathetic to him, as well as its regular stipend to the Chilean Communist Party.[19]

In the end, it was not American machinations that destroyed Chilean democracy, but the economic chaos engendered by Popular Unity together with its political intransigence, as well as that of its opponents. Efforts to broker an agreement between Popular Unity and the Christian Democrats, which might have saved democracy, foundered because too many on both sides opposed a compromise. The Christian Democrats then joined the National Party in opposing Allende. But between them they lacked the two-thirds majority in Congress needed to impeach the president. Allende himself was powerless to restrain Popular Unity's left wing and the MIR, which pushed ahead with takeovers of land and of even small and medium businesses and set up parallel political structures known as *poder popular* ('popular power'). Popular Unity was fatally divided between those trying to make a socialist revolution and those attempting radical reform within democracy. Finally, on 22 August 1973 the Chamber of Deputies declared the president to have violated the constitution and, by a vote of 81 to 47, invited the armed forces to defend it.[20]

More surprising than the coup that followed three weeks later was that the armed forces had not intervened earlier. They had a long tradition of respect for the constitution and the law. In 1972–3, several military commanders served as ministers. Allende, unlike Goulart, did not intervene in military matters. The army put down at least five coup attempts between 1970 and 1973.[21] But its involvement in government dragged it into politics. The army commander Carlos Prats and the other Popular Unity supporters among the generals became increasingly isolated within the officer corps. On 23 August, Prats resigned, convinced that his replacement by his loyal deputy, Augusto Pinochet, offered the only hope of averting what seemed an imminent coup.[22] At the last minute, Pinochet joined a coup plot that was about to be unleashed by conservative members of the armed forces. On 11 September 1973, as the air force bombed La Moneda, the presidential palace, Allende committed suicide. The armed forces faced little resistance; subsequent claims by apologists for General Pinochet that Chile suffered civil war are false. The coup enjoyed the support of many Christian Democrats as well as of the National Party, the far right and, probably, a majority of Chileans. Most expected the army to restore order and call fresh elections. Most were surprised and dismayed by the scale of the violent repression that followed the coup, and at Pinochet's determination to stamp out not just Popular Unity but Chilean democracy.

Was the coup inevitable? On its eve, Allende told several of his aides that to thwart it he was planning to announce a plebiscite on his rule, which he expected to lose. But by then it was too late.[23] Today, a statue of Salvador Allende stands in the square behind La Moneda, which has been restored. The man who put it there, Ricardo Lagos, Chile's president from 2000 to 2006, has done much to reconcile his country to its past. A moderate socialist, his judgement on the Allende period in which he was a government official carries weight: 'No country can survive when dreams spill over, when polarisation exacerbates differences, and when the authority doesn't govern. Those were the mistakes. But after September 11th, 1973, came the horror.'[24]

Political failure in Argentina

If Chile had seemed a model of democratic stability, Argentina had become a pathological case of political failure. The passions surrounding Juan Perón's decade in power and his overthrow by a military coup in 1955 had produced a political stalemate. The country was divided into two, incompatible, halves – the larger one made up of Perón's supporters. The army's solution was to proscribe Peronism and exercise tutelary power over the republic. This produced only instability – between 1955 and 1973 Argentina had eight presidents, of whom only three were civilians – and, eventually, political violence on a scale not seen for a century or more. Peronism itself became factionalised. With their chief in exile, Augusto Vandor and other trade union leaders attempted to mould a Peronism without Perón. Had this project succeeded, it might have produced a moderate labourism and an accommodation with the armed forces that might have permitted a return to stable civilian rule.[25] But it did not succeed, partly because it was opposed by a growing Peronist left wing. This was drawn mainly from middle-class youths; paradoxically, in some cases their political roots lay in violent right-wing Catholic nationalism.[26] Out of this milieu would come Latin America's most powerful urban guerrilla movement, the Montoneros (founded in 1968), along with a slew of violent *grupúsculos*. Generally anti-Marxist, but not anti-Guevara (an Argentine after all), the Montoneros drew together 'radical Catholicism, nationalism and Peronism into a populistic expression of socialism' according to a historian of the organisation.[27] They received encouragement from Perón, because he saw them as a counterweight to Vandor. Perón was at heart a corporatist; he chose Franco's Madrid as his place of exile. But to keep control of the self-contradictory movement which claimed loyalty to him, he played its warring factions against each other. In 1970 he told Tomás Eloy Martínez, an Argentine writer, that when he was visited by supporters from the right or left of his movement he talked to each 'in the language they wanted to hear'.[28] It was a game which would end explosively. At first, the Montoneros concentrated on spectacular acts of 'armed propaganda' against a military dictatorship reeling from the *Cordobazo* – in 1969 two days of rioting by striking workers in the industrial city of Córdoba ended with 14 killed by the army. Three years of low-level warfare by Peronism's armed gangs delayed, but did not reverse, a retreat by the armed forces, whose commanders concluded that only Perón's return could pacify the country. Restored to office with 60 per cent of the vote in 1973, an old (aged 78) and ill Perón had no use for the Peronist left. The Montoneros and their allies began to kill 'corrupt' trade union leaders (Vandor had been murdered in 1969) and managers at businesses suffering strikes, as well as policemen and army officers. Perón and, after his death, his third wife and successor, María Estela 'Isabelita' Martínez, a former nightclub dancer, unleashed against the Montoneros the indiscriminate violence of the Argentine Anti-Communist Alliance, or Triple A, a death squad made up mainly of policemen.

Most Argentines saw the military coup that overthrew 'Isabelita' in 1976 as inevitable and many at first welcomed it.[29] The country was suffering galloping inflation, a political killing every five hours and a bomb explosion every three hours.[30] The violence of Argentina's guerrillas was far from trivial. By 1975 the Montoneros comprised some 5,000 people under arms (though many were not full-time fighters) and had extorted $60 million by kidnapping a leading businessman, Jorge Born (a figure equal to a third of Argentina's defence budget, as Born pointed out). They began to flirt both with regular warfare, with attacks on army bases, and with terrorism (a bomb in an army cinema wounded sixty among a group of retired officers and their wives).

The scale of Montonero violence goes some way to explaining, without in any way justifying, the unprecedented wave of terror unleashed by the military *junta* of 1976–83. General Jorge Videla, its head until 1981, declared: 'A terrorist is not just someone with a gun or a bomb but also someone who spreads ideas that are contrary to Western and Christian civilisation.'[31] The armed forces proceeded to institutionalise the methods of the Triple A. Victims included not just guerrilla suspects but their relatives and friends, peaceful dissidents and innocent bystanders. The methodology involved abduction, 'disappearance', lengthy and unrestrained torture, murder and then the disposal of the body at sea or in secret graves. Military installations were turned into clandestine concentration camps. An investigative committee set up by the democratic government of Raúl Alfonsín later found that at least 8,960 people had disappeared in this war – almost three times the number killed by the Pinochet regime in Chile.[32] Human-rights groups estimated the total figure killed at up to 30,000, though without proof. Within two years of the coup, the Montoneros and many of their sympathisers had been wiped out.

From *caudillos* to bureaucrats of repression

From 1930 to the early 1970s, across much of Latin America civilian governments and dictatorships interrupted each other in what came to be called the 'pendulum' effect. By the mid-1970s, dictatorship had become the norm. In 1977, more than two-thirds of Latin Americans – and eight out of ten South American republics – lived under the heel of the armed forces. Add Mexico's civilian authoritarianism, and democracy appeared to have failed completely in the region. It survived only in Costa Rica, and in Colombia and Venezuela. In the latter two countries, pacts between the main political parties allowed for varying degrees of power-sharing and fixed limits to political competition. This guaranteed stability, though at some cost to democracy itself; in both countries opponents would claim, more or less plausibly, exclusion from the democratic process as a justification for taking up arms.

The dictatorships of the 1960s and 1970s were different from those of the past. On the whole, armies were no longer vehicles through which *caudillos* could construct personal dictatorships – though Pinochet would be an exception, while in Paraguay, the lengthy tyranny of General Alfredo Stroessner (1954–89) was a throwback to an earlier era. Nor did these new regimes merely back one civilian faction against others. They were more ambitious, seeking a permanent re-ordering of society. Eliminating communism, General Pinochet declared, required ending democracy since this had shown itself 'no longer able to confront an enemy that has destroyed the state'.[33] The terror they meted out was far more intense and systematic than that to which most of South America (though not Central America) was accustomed.

What explained this new brand of dictatorship and the failure of democracy? It is as well to start with the armies themselves. Many on the left pinned the blame on the United States and the training in anti-communist soldiering it imparted to Latin American officers at places such as the School of the Americas, in Panama. Certainly, after Guatemala the United States had in effect given the green light to coups in the name of anti-communism. The Cold War was an important factor in the rise of the dictatorships, yet it is patronising as well as false to assume that Latin American armies required lessons in anti-communism – or in coups. One of the few empirical studies of such matters, of the coup which overthrew a populist government in Ecuador in 1963, found that the US-trained officers involved were no more anti-communist than the others.[34] National security doctrines, under which the armed forces saw themselves as fighting a total war against communism involving politics and the economy as well as military confrontation, were home-grown products rather than American imports.[35] And not all armies behaved in the same way. The Venezuelan army, which traditionally had close links with the United States, yielded to a democratic regime in 1958.

Other analysts attributed democratic breakdown to the contradictions of 'dependent capitalism'. Guillermo O'Donnell, an Argentine political scientist writing in the midst of the political violence and state terrorism in his country in the 1970s, described the new breed of dictatorships in Brazil and the southern cone as 'bureaucratic authoritarian' regimes, a term that gained wide currency. By that he meant that they had arisen to enforce the dominance of a 'highly oligopolised and internationalised bourgeoisie' (i.e. local business magnates and multinational firms). They did this by excluding from power 'popular sectors' (such as workers and peasants), restoring political order and stabilising the economy in ways that benefited large companies at the expense of workers.[36] There seemed to be much truth in this. The military dictatorships typically banned political parties, trade unions and other grassroots groups, often hunting down and killing or imprisoning their leaders. They sometimes handed over economic policy to conservative technocrats. Strikes were normally banned, and military governments often tried to impose wage cuts as part of efforts to stabilise the economy. A partial exception was Brazil's regime: more politically sophisticated than its peers, it purged Congress but did not shut it down, and allowed (heavily controlled) elections for state governors. But most senior government jobs went to generals or technocrats.

Yet the facts do not support the notion that the dictatorships' primary purpose was to impose 'neoliberal' economic policies. Only in Chile would the dictatorship impose comprehensive and far-reaching free-market economic policies. A telling counter-example was Peru's dictatorship of 1968–83, especially in its first phase under General Juan Velasco. Like the 'bureaucratic-authoritarian' regimes it was a government of the armed forces as an institution. Yet it enacted a radical agrarian reform, expropriated foreign oil and mining companies and the fishmeal industry. It set up a host of new state companies and co-operatives, and required private firms to grant workers a share of the profits and seats on the board. It was not particularly repressive, but it did limit freedom of expression, seizing control of the press and television. The regime declared itself 'neither capitalist nor communist'. But despite Velasco's nationalisation of American firms (for which Peru eventually paid compensation), his government did not attract outright hostility from Washington. That was partly because it signed new contracts for private foreign investment in oil and mining, and partly because it was accurately seen as staunchly anti-communist, even though it was supported by the local Communist Party and bought large quantities of military hardware from the Soviet Union. Indeed, the 'Peruvian experiment' was an attempt to prevent future social conflict, and to deter the rise of the left, by implementing much of Haya de la Torre's populist programme of the 1920s and 1930s. In 1968, Peru was perhaps the least developed of the larger Latin American countries. Even by regional standards, landholding was highly unequal: fewer than 10,500 big *haciendas* (or 1.2 per cent of the total number of farms) accounted for more than half of all farmland. Some of Velasco's reforms were overdue, but many were heavy-handed or poorly executed, and some created new problems, such as a bloated state. His government failed to create an organised base of civilian support, and the military regime was eventually undermined by debt and popular protest against consequent austerity measures.[37]

In retrospect, it is clear that some fairly straightforward factors lay behind the genesis of the 'bureaucratic-authoritarian' regimes. Depending on the country, guerrilla action, the breakdown of order, extreme political polarisation, the discontents and disorders generated by inflation and stop-start economic policies – and usually a combination of several of these things – prompted military officers to believe that the survival of the state itself was at risk. They were often encouraged to step in by civilians, and not just businessmen. Just as parts of the left turned their backs on democracy, so had many on the right (some conservatives, of course, had never embraced democracy). They feared that they would lose the game of mass politics. In Argentina, the Peronists seemed electorally unbeatable. In Brazil, the anti-Vargas UDN despaired of its inability to win the presidency democratically. Business groups feared expropriation or punitive policies by elected populist or leftist governments. Together with parts of the middle class and of the poor, they came to value order and economic stability above democracy and liberty. Politicians failed to find compromises. Above all, the economic policies of state-led industrialisation and protectionism were limping into more and more problems. It is not coincidental that these policies had been pursued with particular fervour in Brazil, Argentina, Chile and Uruguay – and that in the three countries of the Southern Cone they had produced disappointing growth rates. Political instability and breakdown were indeed a faithful reflection of economic disorder and the distributional conflicts which this generated. Since the prevailing economic policies gave such a vast role to the state, it is not surprising that the battle for control of the state became so desperate.

The rise and indebted fall of statist protectionism

After the Second World War, many Latin American governments had adopted the policy recommendations of CEPAL in an attempt to speed industrialisation. In addition to raising tariffs on imports, governments added many non-tariff barriers (such as outright prohibitions) against goods which competed with local production, and gave soft loans and subsidies to favoured industrial firms. They also used the state aggressively to promote development, through state-owned companies and regulation, and to try to spread its benefits around. This effort was partly successful: economic growth was fairly brisk; by the end of the 1960s, Brazil, Mexico and Argentina were at least semi-industrialised and Chile and Colombia not far behind.[38] But the cost was heavy. Because they were over-protected, many industrial firms were very inefficient. Some of the main beneficiaries of protection were multinationals, which set up factories behind the tariff barriers where they could often get away with using old technology. State-owned companies multiplied, partly because of the reluctance or inability of the private sector to make large industrial investments. Sometimes companies ended up in state hands when they failed as private enterprises. By the end of the 1970s, Brazil had established no fewer than 654 state firms, including 28 of the 30 largest companies in the country.[39] Only a handful were paragons of efficiency. The propietorial state in Latin America owed as much to Mussolini as to Marx. It was supported by many in private business (who saw state companies as a source of padded contracts or subsidised raw materials) and by the armed forces (which favoured it for reasons of national security) as well as by trade unions and the left.

In sharp contrast to industrialising countries in Asia, exports were neglected. Latin America deliberately turned away from the world economy just as international trade began its long post-war boom. In 1946, Latin America (with 6.5 per cent of world population) accounted for 13.5 per cent of world exports, a figure that had fallen to just 4.4 per cent by 1975.[40] But the new industries relied on imported machinery and components, so periodic balance-of-payments crises became the norm. There were clear signs from the mid-1960s that the policies needed adjusting. The *cepalistas* argued that the key to making the model work was to expand the size of the domestic market to allow manufacturing firms to operate more efficiently. To do this, they favoured structural reforms, such as agrarian reform and tax changes. Yet such reforms were fiercely opposed by the landed oligarchy and other powerful groups, and governments normally shrank from them; even where they were adopted, they had only a marginal effect. Regional free-trade schemes did provide some additional markets for manufacturers, but their implementation was patchy.

To keep the economic model going, all too often governments resorted to short-term fixes. The tools of choice for market expansion were unsustainable wage increases and printing money to cover the subsidies and losses of state-owned companies. These policies fuelled two characteristic Latin American economic vices: inflation and sickening boom–bust cycles, ending in currency devaluation (which in turn fuelled inflation). Inflation meant that workers frequently had to strike to try to stem the plummeting value of their wages. That was one reason why the CEPAL policies failed to reduce income inequality. Another was that protection from imports, and other shields against competition, granted businesses near-monopolies from which they could derive exaggerated profits (called rents by economists). The whole system rewarded businesses for their effectiveness at lobbying rather than their efficiency in production. Governments often resorted to multiple exchange rates, under which importers of goods deemed essential by the bureaucrats and planners would get artificially cheap dollars. This encouraged corruption and the misallocation of resources.

Above all, governments borrowed abroad in a desperate attempt to keep the state-led model on the road. Commercial banks in the United States, Europe and Japan, flush with petrodollars, were eager to lend. Yet they can hardly be accused of mis-selling. Governments and state firms gobbled up these loans, not least because they came without the strings attached to IMF loans. The catch was that they also carried higher, and variable, interest rates. When the Iranian revolution of 1979 triggered a second 'oil shock', the subsequent stagflation in rich countries drove up international interest rates while causing export earnings to fall in many Latin American countries. By 1981, base rates in rich countries had reached 16 per cent. With hindsight, Latin American governments should have adjusted their economic policies while external finance was still abundant – or at least they should have called an earlier halt to the debt merry-go-round by defaulting. Instead, the banks made fresh loans to cover the interest payments on previous ones. Between 1979 and 1982, Latin America's total debt rose from $184 billion to

$314 billion, while the ratio of debt payments to exports jumped from 26.6 per cent in 1975 to 59 per cent in 1982.[41] Richer and smarter Latin Americans used this expensive hiatus to get their money out before the crash. Estimates of the money that went abroad range from $50 billion to $100 billion, with Argentina, Mexico and Venezuela the most affected.[42] The tone was set by Mexico. Flush with new oil discoveries, President José López Portillo threw aside a cautious economic programme, proclaiming that Mexico's challenge was now to 'administer abundance'. A binge of spending, pharaonic investment and corruption ensued. When the oil price fell again and interest rates rose, López Portillo pledged to defend the peso 'like a dog'. A fortnight later the Bank of Mexico gave up trying to defend the exchange rate, which plunged from 26 to 45 to the dollar. Six months after that, in August 1982, the government stopped payments on Mexico's $80 billion foreign debt and suspended foreign-exchange transactions. In a last, destructive throw, López Portillo nationalised the banks. Over the next twelve months, debt defaults ricocheted across Latin America. It was by no means Latin America's first debt crisis: most countries in the region had defaulted in the 1820s and again in the 1930s (some had done so at other times, too). Just as on those previous occasions, default marked the end of an era and the start of a new one.

Neither Che nor Pinochet: the democratic wave

In 1977 all but four Latin American countries were dictatorships. By 1990 only Cuba was, while Mexico had begun to move along its slow road to democracy. Even as academic treatises were being published claiming that Latin America suffered from 'blocked societies', incapable of democratic modernisation, winds of change blew through the region. The democratic wave began in the Dominican Republic and moved quickly to Peru, Ecuador and beyond (*see* Table 3). At first, some analysts saw this as just another swing of the pendulum. Yet it soon became clear that several deeper factors were at work. The first was

Table 3: The democratic wave: a chronology

1977: only Colombia, Costa Rica and Venezuela	had democratic governments.
1978: Dominican Republic	Opposition victory in presidential election ended 12 years of rule by Joaquín Balaguer. (Subsequent elections, three of which were won by Balaguer, were marked by fraud. Since 1996, elections have been free and fair.)
Peru	Military government calls elections for a Constituent Assembly.

1979: Ecuador	Presidential election ends seven years of military rule.
1980: Peru	Presidential election ends 12 years of military rule. (In 1992 President Alberto Fujimori dissolved Congress; a Constituent Assembly was elected later that year. In 2000, Fujimori fled the country after winning an unconstitutional third term in a fraudulent election; democracy was again restored in 2001.)
1981: Honduras	Presidential election ended ten years of military rule (but government remained under military tutelage until 1984)
1982: Bolivia	Civilian government elected in 1980 but blocked by military coup takes office.
1983: Argentina	Presidential election ends seven years of military rule, following defeat in Falklands/Malvinas war.
1984: El Salvador	Presidential election ends half a century of military-dominated government. Civil war continues until 1993 peace agreement.
Uruguay	Presidential election; restoration of democracy in 1985 ends 12 years of military rule.
1985: Brazil	Congress elects a civilian president, as part of a gradual transition to democracy; the armed forces return to barracks having seized power in 1964.
Guatemala	Presidential election restores civilian government after three decades of military-dominated rule. Civil war continues until 1996 peace agreement.
1989: Chile	Election of civilian government ends General Augusto Pinochet's dictatorship (begun in 1973), following his defeat in a referendum in 1988.
Paraguay	Presidential election after General Alfredo Stroessner, dictator since 1954, ousted in a coup.
1990: Haiti	First-ever free presidential election won by Jean-Bertrand Aristide; overthrown by military in 1991; restored to power by US invasion in 1994; and resigned in 2004 following armed rebellion and US and French pressure. Free presidential election held under UN supervision in 2006.
Nicaragua	A free and fair election, held as a result of US pressure and a regional peace agreement, ends 11-year Sandinista regime, which had overthrown the dictatorship of Anastasio Somoza in 1979.
Panama	Civilian government takes office following US invasion of December 1989 which overthrew the authoritarian regime of General Manuel Antonio Noriega; free and fair election takes place in 1994.
2000: Mexico	Victory of Vicente Fox in presidential election ends seven decades of rule by the Institutional Revolutionary Party.

that the international climate was changing. The Cold War would last another decade. But in the late 1970s, Jimmy Carter had proclaimed the importance of human rights in American foreign policy, especially as regards Latin America. That led to friction between the United States and some of the dictatorships. As important, in Spain and Portugal, mortality put paid to the longstanding fascist dictatorships of Francisco Franco and António de Oliveira Salazar. The Iberian transition to democracy in the 1970s was highly influential across the Atlantic. Second, state terror and long years of exile caused the left to reflect on the folly of its conduct in the 1960s and 1970s. Many left-wingers came to accept the value of civil liberties and of democracy – without the derogatory adjectives, such as 'bourgeois' or 'formal', with which they had previously vilified it.

An analogous re-evaluation took place on the right and among businessmen. Many of them had assumed that dictatorships, free of the need to satisfy voters, would be able to take the unpopular decisions required to put in place policies that would guarantee faster economic growth in the medium to long term. Yet it had not turned out like that – and this was the third and most important factor behind the turn to democracy. Most of the dictatorships had proved as incapable of grappling with the economic challenges facing the region as their civilian predecessors had been. In fact, if not in left-wing myth, military officers around the world tend to be hostile to free-market economics.[43] In Latin America, that was partly because the armed forces themselves had a vested interest in a large state, since this provided jobs for officers and subsidies for military enterprises such as arms factories.[44] Many military governments in the 1960s and 1970s began stabilisation programmes that involved a retreat from *cepalista* policies of state-led industrialisation, but few sustained the effort. Thus, Brazil alternated between the liberal reforms of Roberto Campos, the planning minister from 1964 to 1967 (dubbed 'Bobby Fields' because of his anglophilia), and of Mário Henrique Simonsen (finance minister, 1974–9), and the expansionary populism of the Brazilian economic 'miracle', as it was called, under Antonio Delfim Neto (planning minister from 1967 to 1974 and again from 1979 to 1983). Argentina's dictatorships of 1965–73 and 1976–83 both embarked on stabilisation programmes only to abandon them. In some cases, reforms were incompetently designed. Thus, José Martínez de Hoz, Argentina's finance minister of 1976–80, used an overvalued exchange rate (i.e. a cheap dollar) to bring down inflation. To reactivate the economy, he abolished controls on capital inflows and deregulated the banks. But he did not do enough to promote exports, or to reduce the economic role of the state. The result was predictable: a balance-of-payments crisis followed by the collapse of inadequately supervised banks. The resulting unpopularity of the government caused these policies to be abandoned in favour of a return to economic populism. What these cases showed was that contrary to conventional wisdom dictatorships, lacking an electoral mandate, depended on short-term economic success for legitimacy.[45]

The exception was General Pinochet's Chile.[46] In 1975 Pinochet appointed a team of liberal economists (known as the 'Chicago Boys' after the university where many of them had imbibed the teachings of Milton Friedman as doctoral students). They carried through a drastic programme of reform. They cut tariffs from a peak of 750 per cent under Allende to a flat 10 per cent; used a strong peso to fight inflation; implemented large-scale privatisations, cut the fiscal deficit and began a compulsory private pension system. Their policies had some heterodox elements: they did not privatise the state copper company, partly because the armed forces took a share of its profits for arms purchases. They eventually adopted a gradualist approach to getting inflation down. To balance the public finances, they decreed a mildly progressive tax reform, levying a surcharge on income tax and abolishing exemptions to VAT. The drastic reform programme was put to the test after Mexico's default in 1982, when Chile suffered a catastrophic collapse of the banking system, income per head fell by 19 per cent and unemployment climbed to almost 30 per cent. After a temporary retreat in 1984, a new and more pragmatic economic team returned to many of these policies but in more gradual form. Pinochet was able to impose this free-market programme because, uniquely among his dictatorial peers, he managed to concentrate absolute power in his own hands. Chile's armed forces lacked the inter-service rivalry and politicisation of those in Argentina, Peru and elsewhere. Pinochet appointed a large and cohesive team of civilian liberal economists – partly in order to cement his own power and autonomy in relation to the armed forces.[47]

Elsewhere, when the 1982 debt crisis broke, the dictatorships buckled under the opprobium of economic failure. They had not broken decisively with the *cepalista* policies. Some had faced mass protests, such as the strikes in the São Paulo car factories that would first bring a bearded trade union leader called Luiz Inácio da Silva (or Lula) to the attention of Brazilians. The generals had found governing urbanised societies and increasingly complex economies was not simple. Rather than risk their professional cohesion, Latin America's armies sat down with the civilian politicians and negotiated a return to the barracks. The first task facing the newly established democracies was thus to deal with the economic wreckage left behind by the dictatorships. Only in Argentina did military retreat turn to rout, and that thanks to the dictators' folly in invading the Falkland Islands (Islas Malvinas) in a desperate attempt to whip up popularity. Like so many other things in Argentina over the previous decades – and over the decades to come – it reflected the delusions of grandeur of a country that was neither reconciled to, nor understood, its puzzling decline.

CHAPTER 6

THE RISE AND FALL OF THE WASHINGTON CONSENSUS

The Casa Rosada, Argentina's presidential palace, turns its back on the estuary of the Rio de la Plata and looks out over the Plaza de Mayo, the heart of Buenos Aires during the centuries of Spanish rule when it was no more than a small muddy settlement for the trading of hides. The present palace was built in the 1870s in an eclectic mixture of the Florentine and French styles, just as Argentina was beginning its rise to fleeting greatness. From its balcony, Juan and Eva Perón conducted their love affair with the *descamisados* (literally, 'shirtless ones'), the masses of industrial workers and migrants from the interior who crowded into Buenos Aires in the 1940s – a scene re-enacted by Madonna in the film *Evita*. On an overcast October day in 2001, in the southern-hemisphere spring, the Casa Rosada looked unusually gloomy, its appearance not helped by a recent official decision to paint the frontage a garish puce instead of the previous gentle pink. The mood within was scarcely more cheerful. The previous Sunday, the battered governing coalition, an alliance of the Radicals and Frepaso, a new social-democratic grouping, had suffered a swingeing defeat in a mid-term Congressional election at which almost half the electorate was so disillusioned with politicians of all stripes as to either stay away from the polls or to cast spoiled or blank ballots. In a small sitting room on the first floor of the palace, lined with smudgy scenes of the port and the Pampas by Argentine impressionists, Fernando de la Rúa, the president, did his best to sound upbeat, though that merely suggested that he was in denial. The election was 'not a vote against the government but against the political class', he explained over a cup of tea. 'The electoral results, given the (austerity) measures I've taken, are excellent.'[1]

De la Rúa, a cautious lawyer, took pride in his public image as a boring but honest administrator. He had stuck doggedly to the conservative economic policies of his predecessor, Carlos Menem. These centred on an arrangement known to economists as a currency board and to Argentines as *convertibilidad* (convertibility). This involved fixing the currency – by law, not just policy decision – at par to the dollar, abolishing all exchange and capital controls, and restricting the money supply to the stock of hard-currency reserves. The effect was that Argentina renounced both exchange-rate policy and monetary policy. The interest rate for borrowing both by the government and ordinary Argentines would, in effect, be that of the US Federal Reserve plus a risk premium (known to Argentines as *riesgo país*, or country risk). The currency board, together with an array of free-market reforms, brought rapid growth in the 1990s. But then capital suddenly stopped flowing to emerging-market economies, plunging Argentina into a recession which by October 2001 was entering its fourth year. The confidence that foreign financiers and locals had shown in the country for a decade turned to a stampede for the exit. Despite two IMF loan packages in nine months, totalling $22 billion, a run on deposits saw some $15 billion leave the banks between July and November 2001. Much of this money left the country. Under the currency board, the resulting fall in the Central Bank's reserves automatically translated into a monetary squeeze which throttled the economy: in the second half of 2001, Argentina's GDP shrank at a rate equivalent to 11 per cent a year. Every day, Argentine newspapers would report anxiously on the oscillations of *riesgo país*. By July 2001 it had climbed to 16 percentage points – a rate at which the government's debt was unpayable under any reasonable assumptions. Even so, de la Rúa rejected calls for a change in economic policies. 'There will be no [debt] default, no devaluation … We will fulfil our obligations,' he insisted.[2]

Out in the rustbelt suburbs that ring Buenos Aires to the south and west, the mood among the descendants of the *descamisados* was turning from despair to anger. At dusk in a backstreet in Mataderos, a district of shuttered cold stores that once supplied the world with chilled beef, a ragged line of several hundred people spilled out from a charity soup kitchen. They were queuing for an evening meal, a thin stew of rice with small lumps of sausage and carrot and, on this occasion, a rare handout of flour, pasta and a few oranges. Many in the queue said they had not had a job for years. In what had long been Latin America's richest country, 'Each year, there's more and more hunger and less and less hope,' said Monica Carranza, who ran the soup kitchen and a hostel for destitute young women.[3]

When the run on deposits threatened to bring down the two biggest local banks, on 1 December the government imposed restrictions on withdrawals, in effect freezing most savings. This enraged the middle class, and seemed to undermine the whole point of convertibility. It prompted the IMF to pull the plug on Argentina, halting disbursement of its loan. A fortnight later, angry mobs began to loot supermarkets, at first in the interior and then in Buenos Aires. On 19 December, de la Rúa went on television to declare a state of emergency. That night, Buenos Aires echoed with the sonorous roar of a *cacerolazo* ('mass pot-banging'), a traditional form of protest among the Latin American middle class. The next day tens of thousands of mainly unemployed protestors, many of them organised by the Peronists, converged on the Plaza de Mayo. After 29 people were killed, most when police opened fire on demonstrators, de la Rúa resigned. He was spirited away from the Casa Rosada by helicopter.

Over the next week, as power passed to the deeply divided Peronists, three provisional presidents came and went. One of them declared a default on $81 billion in foreign-currency bonds issued by the government – the biggest sovereign debt default in world history. The announcement was greeted with cheers in the Congress and shouts of 'Argentina, Argentina' as if the national team had just won a football match. Congress then installed Eduardo Duhalde, the Peronist boss of Buenos Aires province, as president. He decreed the end of the currency board. 'Argentina is bust. It's bankrupt. Business is halted, the chain of payments is broken, there is no currency to get the economy moving and we don't have a peso to pay Christmas bonuses, wages and pensions,' Duhalde declared with grim realism.[4] He devalued the peso, which quickly sank to three to the dollar.

Argentina suffered a national catastrophe in 2001–2, a collapse that was economic, financial, political and social. In the year to March 2002, the economy shrank by 15 per cent, the proportion of Argentines living below the poverty line rose from 38 per cent to 56 per cent and unemployment climbed to 21 per cent. Although a vigorous recovery followed, it would be mid-2005 before the economy regained its size of 1998. Until the 1970s, Argentina had boasted a European-style society, in which some 60 per cent considered themselves to be middle class.[5] Now, the social pyramid resembles that of the rest of Latin America.

The Washington Consensus on trial

For many in Argentina and beyond it, this collapse became the prime exhibit in the case against 'neoliberalism', the Washington Consensus and the policies pursued by the IMF in Latin America. These policies, it is variously asserted, led to an increase in poverty, inequality, unemployment and the informal economy across the region; through privatisation and free trade they enriched a few at the expense of the many; they benefited multinationals at the expense of national enterprise, especially small and medium firms; they led governments to give priority to debt payments instead of social spending; and they were imposed on Latin America in a doctrinaire 'one size fits all' manner by the IMF, the World Bank and the United States, and by Latin American presidents who employed undemocratic methods.

Because of the application of 'a perverse model that wrongly separated the economic from the social, put stability against growth and separated responsibility from justice', the 1990s in Latin America was a 'decade of despair', Lula da Silva told the UN summit on development at Monterrey, Mexico, in 2004.[6] One popular text attacking the reforms concluded: 'Although the rich have had a vintage two decades, most of the region's people are poorer and more insecure: their homes, communities, schools and hospitals are collapsing around them, and their cities, towns and villages are increasingly polluted.'[7] Such views extend a long way beyond the far left and the NGOs. Thus, an editorial in the *New York Times* in 2005 asserted that 'many governments south of the border blame the model of free trade, open markets, privatisation and fiscal austerity pushed by the United States for the vast increase in social inequality in the region'.[8] If nothing else, the Washington Consensus had clearly become a 'damaged brand', as Moisés Naím, a former Venezuelan trade minister, noted.[9]

The rest of this chapter will assess to what extent, if any, such charges – and the more nuanced criticisms of the Washington Consensus by various economists – are true. But given the severity of the Argentine collapse, it is important to explain why it happened and who or what was to blame. The first point is that convertibility was a purely Argentine invention. It was not imposed on the country by outsiders. Rather, it was a desperate home-grown remedy for Argentina's long, and accelerating, decline. Between 1976 and 1989, first under dictatorship and then democracy, income per head had shrunk by an average of 1 per cent a year. A bout of hyperinflation and two banking collapses destroyed confidence in the peso and in economic policy. In Argentina, the old model of state intervention and protectionism had led to economic distortions on a pathological scale. Government, especially at provincial level, had become a vast employment agency, incapable of delivering basic services efficiently.[10] State-owned companies were no better: between 1983 and 1988, their losses averaged 5.6 per cent of GDP per year.[11] The state railway company employed 95,000 people, but only half of its locomotives were in working order.[12] The telephone system was especially notorious: the waiting list for a line was more than six years, and businesses employed staff whose sole job was to hold a telephone handset for hours on end until a dialling tone appeared.[13]

Menem's predecessor, Raúl Alfonsín, a Radical and an exemplary democrat but a poor economic manager, had tried to tackle inflation using 'heterodox' methods, such as price controls. When these failed, discontent boiled over, with lootings of supermarkets on a larger scale than in December 2001. Alfonsín was forced to step down several months early. In 1989, the economy shrank by 6 per cent, inflation climbed to 200 per cent a *month*, the consolidated public-sector deficit had reached the incredible figure of 21 per cent of GDP, the foreign debt had not been serviced for a year and national morale was on the floor.[14] Inflation cut the value of state pensions to only $26 a month. Just as happened in 2002, an army of the destitute toured the streets picking over rubbish for items to sell. The difference was that in 1990 it was made up of pensioners, rather than the unemployed. The public administration was close to collapse: in ministries, typewriters, photocopiers and toilets were broken and unrepaired; in the economy ministry, only one of the 12 lifts worked.[15]

When campaigning for the presidency, Menem, a traditional Peronist political boss from the backward Andean province of La Rioja, criticised the free-market reforms sweeping across the region. Once in office, a second burst of hyperinflation changed his mind. In setting up the currency board, Menem's economy minister of 1991–6, Domingo Cavallo, a Harvard-trained economist, deliberately harked back to Argentina's golden age. For much of the period before 1935, the country had operated a currency board in which a body known as the *Caja de Conversión* was charged with maintaining the peso's value in gold.[16] The purpose of convertibility was to restore economic stability and confidence in the currency by making it impossible for the government to print money and debauch the peso, as it had done so often before. But linking the peso to the dollar was rash: only 15 per cent of Argentina's trade was with the United States in 2001, and the two economies did not move in tandem.

Menem also dismantled barriers to trade and privatised nearly all of the state's vast holdings, from the oil company to the railways and the post office. Capital flooded in from abroad, the economy grew fast and the number of Argentines living below the national poverty line fell from 41.4 per cent in 1990 to 21.6 per cent in 1994.[17] Mexico's disorderly devaluation of 1994–5 subjected convertibility to a first test, as financial investors temporarily yanked money from Latin America. Argentina suffered a deep, but brief, recession, several banks collapsed, and poverty rose again (to 29.8 per cent by 1998). But growth quickly returned and the arrival of more foreign banks strengthened the financial system. Convertibility had seemingly passed the test with flying colours. Officials at the IMF swallowed their previous doubts about the currency board. Few at the Wall Street investment banks had held such doubts: for foreign investors, convertibility seemed conveniently to have removed all risk of devaluation. Argentina became a poster child for free-market reform in Latin America. In a rare accolade, Menem was invited to join the host, Bill Clinton, in opening the IMF's annual meeting in Washington in October 1998.

Yet, by then, several officials at the Fund were privately expressing grave doubts about Argentina's policies.[18] They worried specifically that the government's relatively loose fiscal policy meant that public debt was rising despite rapid growth. The ratio of public debt to GDP increased from 29.2 per cent in 1993 to 41.4 per cent in 1998.[19] The government's deficits were not as large as they had been in the 1970s and 1980s. They were partly the result of a pension reform, which saw future provision pass from the state to private funds. This involved a transitional cost to the government of 2.5 per cent of GDP a year by 2000, since the state still had to pay existing pensioners but no longer received contributions. But part of the deficit came from Menem's profligacy. Instead of pressing on with further structural reforms to make the economy more efficient, Menem tried to buy political support for an unconstitutional third term. The underlying point was that to sustain convertibility, the government needed to notch up fiscal surpluses in good times so that it could safely increase spending in bad times, and it wasn't doing so.

The miracle formula becomes the perfect trap

Bad times soon came. They exposed Argentina's lack of policy flexibility. First, the devaluation of the Thai *baht* in July 1997, and then Russia's debt default of mid 1998, prompted a retreat by foreign financial investors from many emerging markets. In response Brazil – Argentina's largest market, accounting for 30 per cent of its exports – devalued in January 1999. Convertibility prevented Argentina from following suit, pricing many of its exports out of Brazil. To make matters worse, the dollar, to which Argentina was tied, was appreciating against other currencies, and world prices for the country's commodity exports were falling. Under convertibility, the only way to restore competitiveness was deflation – driving *nominal* prices and wages down, something which economists have long recognised is politically far more difficult than allowing inflation to cut the real value of wages. The only way to restore growth was to attract renewed inflows of foreign capital. But Wall Street finally woke up to Argentina's fiscal fragility. To make matters worse, de la Rúa, who had replaced Menem at an election in 1999, presided over a weak coalition government – a new experience in Argentina, where *caudillos* were the norm. De la Rúa's policies were even more orthodox than Menem's: he tried to balance the budget and to change the law to make the labour market more flexible. But his coalition fell apart after it became clear that bribes had been paid in Congress to secure passage of the labour law. And balancing the budget required ever greater spending cuts as recession cut into tax revenues. The miracle formula had become the perfect trap.

Ironically, it was Domingo Cavallo, recalled in desperation by de la
Rúa as economy minister in March 2001, who delivered the coup de grace
to convertibility. He fiddled with its rules, so that for exporters the peso
would be pegged half to the dollar and half to the euro. That was a good
idea in principle, but the timing was disastrous. By introducing the notion
of devaluation, it triggered the run on the banks. Cavallo then proceeded to
behave like a desperate gambler who clings to the hope that he can recover
his losses by borrowing to double his stake. He browbeat the IMF, against the
better judgement of many of its officials, into a second loan (of $8 billion) in
September 2001. Having laboured to establish the independence of the Central
Bank, he proceeded to oust its governor, who opposed his policies. He strong-
armed local pension funds into buying government paper and local banks into
swapping their holdings of government bonds for low-interest loans. He thus
weakened what had been seen as Latin America's strongest financial system.
He also arranged a wider bond swap whose only practical effect was to provide
$90 million in fees to a group of Wall Street banks.[20]

Right to the end, polls suggested that convertibility retained the support of
70 per cent of Argentines. Many had taken out dollar loans and mortgages. In
retrospect, it is clear that the government should have voluntarily dismantled
the currency board in the late 1990s, when it could have done so from a
position of strength. But why fix something that didn't appear broken? By 2001
the system could only be dismantled under duress, at a much higher cost. So
it seemed reasonable to many officials to try to do everything possible to save
the currency board even though, with hindsight, that had become impossible.
In retrospect, too, Argentina should have defaulted on its debt earlier. In April
2001 Charles Calomiris, a conservative economist at Columbia University in
New York, argued publicly that this was the only way to preserve Argentina's
financial system (he had pressed this case privately with Argentine officials
seven months earlier).[21]

Many Argentines blamed the IMF when it pulled the plug on convertibility
– but then quickly came to blame it for not doing so earlier. They felt let down
when the IMF did not rush to their aid after the currency board collapsed. Yet
when Néstor Kirchner, who was elected as president in 2003, called the IMF
'the promoter and vehicle of policies which provoked poverty and pain in the
Argentine people' he was guilty of a wilfully misleading exaggeration.[22] The
IMF was an accessory to the Argentine disaster, not its author. As Michael
Mussa, the Fund's chief economist from 1991 to 2001, has noted (in the jargon
of international financial diplomacy), 'policy ownership was not an issue in
Argentina … For better or worse, all the key policies were fully owned by the
Argentine authorities.'[23] The Fund's mistakes were of omission, according to
Mussa. It should have pressed the Menem government much harder to adopt

a responsible fiscal policy in the mid-1990s, and should have resisted Cavallo's demand for additional help to maintain the currency board after the failure of the first loan in 2001. One might add that the Fund was wrong to have been such an enthusiastic public cheerleader for Menem's Argentina.

A second claim of the Fund's critics is that Argentina has recovered since 2002 by ignoring the IMF's policy advice. That claim has a bit more plausibility, but is also exaggerated. Certainly, the hard line that the Kirchner government took on the debt restructuring – in defiance of the IMF and others – meant that debt repayments were not a fiscal drag on recovery. The government offered a tough take-it-or-leave-it deal to its bondholders, giving them only around 40 per cent of the face value of their bonds. Yet the recovery mainly stemmed from the success of Roberto Lavagna, appointed by Duhalde as economy minister in May 2002, in imposing relatively tight fiscal and monetary policies which brought stability to the exchange rate and choked off the threat of high inflation. Second, the devaluation did its work, as exports boomed and local industry began to substitute for imports. Under Lavagna, Argentina had the 'most orthodox macroeconomic policies of the past 50 years', according to Javier González Fraga, a former Central Bank governor and a critic of convertibility.[24] The third factor was that luck finally turned Argentina's way again. Soaring world prices for its commodity exports and strong growth in the world economy added up to the most favourable international conditions for Argentina in half a century. Lastly, a decade of free-market reform bequeathed a more competitive economy, and one whose infrastructure had been modernised by privatisation.

The IMF might have done more to speed the recovery. Lavagna did not want to borrow more money from the Fund simply to be able to offer more to the bondholders, many of whom had benefited from high interest rates or had bought cheap. In May 2002, his first action was to withdraw his predecessor's request for a $25 billion loan from the IMF. But in order to start negotiations on the debt he did want a medium-term agreement with the IMF sooner than he got one (in September 2003).[25] A senior IMF official conceded that outsiders were slow to recognise that Lavagna had put in place a coherent policy framework.[26] What delayed the agreement was chiefly an argument over fiscal policy in which the IMF was probably too cautious given the scale of Argentina's social problems. Yet in the view of many analysts, Kirchner began to store up trouble by ignoring the IMF's advice on at least two matters. One was the government's failure to reach agreements with privatised utilities, whose tariffs were converted from dollars to devalued pesos and then frozen in early 2002. In many cases, the tariffs were not adjusted for several years. Lavagna had wanted to settle this issue as early as the end of 2002, but was blocked from doing so.[27] The result was that by 2006, Argentines were paying less than half as much for energy as people in neighbouring countries and the country's natural gas reserves had been depleted from fifteen years of output to fewer than ten.[28] In mid-2007 the country began to suffer from wholly predictable energy shortages. The other problem was inflation, which reached 12 per cent by the end of 2005. The government responded by bullying supermarkets and producers into freezing prices – a recipe for shortages and higher inflation in the medium term. In early 2007, in a desperate attempt to keep the annual rate in single figures, the government began to massage the consumer price index itself.

For the first two and a half years of his presidency, Kirchner felt obliged to tolerate Lavagna at the economy ministry. Kirchner was weak: he was elected in April 2003 without a clear popular mandate when Menem disgracefully pulled out of a run-off ballot he was certain to lose. In a mid-term Congressional election in October 2005, the president finally won that mandate. He moved quickly to sack Lavagna and break free of the IMF, paying off early the $9.8 billion that Argentina owed the Fund. In essence, Kirchner was betting on faster growth now at the price, sooner or later, of higher inflation – a bet that Argentine rulers had often made, invariably to the country's cost.

What killed Argentina's economy in 2001 was not 'neoliberalism' or the free-market reforms, but a fiscal policy incompatible with the exchange-rate regime, and a lack of policy flexibility. That inflexibility meant that Argentina was worse-placed than others when the wave of financial crises hit emerging-market countries in 1997–8. Convertibility, with its emphasis on sound money at any cost, was a policy of conservative, not liberal, inspiration. Contrary to many claims, Argentina's policy mix was in direct contravention of the Washington Consensus. At least as it was conceived by John Williamson, the veteran British economist who coined the term, this called for a competitive exchange rate and sound fiscal policy.[29] Unfortunately, the debate over the Washington Consensus has been one of much heat and insufficient light, one in which the meaning of the term itself has mutated. So what exactly was it, and how did it come about?

A paradigm shift

The origins of the Washington Consensus lie in the debt crisis of 1982. Latin America had been living on borrowed money and time since the mid-1970s. Even so, Latin American policy-makers and international bankers initially saw the debt crisis as a short-term liquidity problem. So the debts were rolled over. However, it soon became clear that Mexico's default had touched off the most serious international financial crisis since 1929. In the early 1980s, the world economy was suffering from a miserable combination of high oil prices, sluggish growth, inflation, an increase in interest rates, and a fall in non-oil commodity prices. This combination helped to trigger the debt difficulties, and made recovery harder. The years of living beyond its means caught up with Latin America with a vengeance. The region was forced into a savage economic adjustment. Governments took steps to slash imports, public spending and domestic demand, and to boost exports in order to plug the payments gap and honour their rescheduled debts. The flow of money reversed: an average net *inflow* of capital of $12 billion a year between 1976 and 1981 turned into a net *outflow* averaging $26.4 billion a year over the next five years.[30] For ordinary Latin Americans, the cost was dramatic. In 1986, income per head in the region stood 0.7 per cent below its level of 1982; by 1992, it had still not recovered its level of ten years before. With reason, CEPAL spoke of a 'lost decade', though the picture varied from country to country. Some of the economic damage proved lasting. Investment, both public and private, took many years to recover.

Inflation, chronically higher in Latin America than elsewhere, took off. Devaluation increased the price of imports. Budget-cutting was offset by recession, which cut tax revenues, leading many governments to print money on an unprecedented scale. The average annual inflation rate across 19 countries in the region rose from 33 per cent in the 1970s to 437 per cent in the 1980s.[31] Several countries would suffer devastating hyperinflation. High inflation acts as a tax on the poor: the better-off normally secure some degree of protection against the declining value of money through wage indexation, buying dollars or holding assets. The poor have no income protection. Since other taxes are collected in arrears, governments gather less revenue in real terms; that leads them to still-greater reliance on printing money, in a vicious circle. In addition, inflation upsets relative prices: wages and the prices charged by state-owned companies, for example, tend to lag the general price level. High and rising inflation destroys the possibility of financial planning, or of agreeing long-term contracts. It triggers social conflicts, undermines trust in government and so tends to lead to political instability.

Some economists of the structuralist persuasion argued that inflation was being caused not by the fiscal deficit but by a combination of inertia (i.e. it was fuelling itself) and *insufficient* demand in the economy, which meant that producers were operating inefficiently. Under the influence of this thinking, so-called 'heterodox' stabilisation programmes were launched in the mid-1980s in Brazil (José Sarney's 'Cruzado Plan'), Argentina (Alfonsín's 'Austral Plan') and Peru (under Alan García). These involved an effort to break inflationary expectations through new currencies and price controls and, in Peru's case, a ceiling on foreign debt payments and measures to expand domestic demand.[32] In each case, after initial apparent success, the economy ended up worse than at the outset as inflation soared still higher – mainly because of fiscal weakness.

The failure of these 'heterodox' plans gave force to a rethink that was already under way among many Latin American economists. Some of these economists had studied as post-graduates in American universities. They were influenced by the success of Chile's market-based economic policies and by the rise of the East Asian tigers. Chile's economic reforms had been implemented, not without costly initial mistakes, under the Pinochet dictatorship. But by the late 1980s they were producing impressive economic growth and low inflation. In 1985, they were imitated by a democratic government in Bolivia. In assessing the 'East Asian model', the reformers put more stress on macroeconomic stability and export performance than on the industrial policies pursued by some of those countries. These economists concluded that Latin America required a radical change of course, abandoning the state-led protectionism of the previous half-century. In the 1980s even CEPAL, the guardian of structuralist orthodoxy, had begun to shift towards these positions. By 1992 there was 'a trend towards convergence' around the new policies, according to Enrique Iglesias, who had been CEPAL's boss from 1972 to 1985, and went on to head the Inter-American Development Bank from 1988 to 2005.[33]

It was this shift in Latin American thinking towards the economic orthodoxies of the IMF, the World Bank and the OECD countries that Williamson intended to capture in his ten-point list of policies. The list was contained in a background paper for a conference convened by the Institute of International Economics, a Washington think-tank, bringing together policy-makers from across Latin America. He called it the Washington Consensus because his intention was to demonstrate to 'official Washington' that Latin America was reforming, and deserved debt relief. As things turned out, the name 'was, I fear, a propaganda gift to the old left', as he wrote later.[34]

Williamson's ten points were as follows:

1 Budget deficits ... small enough to be financed without recourse to the inflation tax.

2 Public expenditures redirected (from subsidies) ... toward ... fields such as primary education and health, and infrastructure.

3 Tax reform ... so as to broaden the tax base and cut marginal tax rates.

4 Financial liberalisation, involving an ultimate objective of market-determined interest rates.

5 A unified exchange rate at a level sufficiently competitive to induce a rapid growth in non-traditional exports.

6 Quantitative trade restrictions to be rapidly replaced by tariffs, which would be progressively reduced until a uniform low rate in the range of 10 to 20 percent was achieved.

7 Abolition of barriers impeding the entry of foreign direct investment.

8 Privatisation of state-owned enterprises.

9 Abolition of regulations that impede the entry of new firms or restrict competition (including in the labour market).

10 The provision of secure property rights, especially to the informal sector.[35]

Williamson insists that his formulation did not endorse 'neoliberalism' if by that is meant 'monetarism, supply-side economics and minimal government' as advocated in the 1980s by some advisers to Ronald Reagan and Margaret Thatcher. That, however, is the meaning that many of its critics have given to the Washington Consensus.[36] Most of the ten points are basic principles of economic management which nowadays command wide consensus across the world. Second, the main thrust for the reforms came from within the region. In most cases, they were not imposed from outside. It is certainly true that the IMF, the World Bank and the United States' Treasury supported many of the reforms. Especially in smaller countries such as those in Central America, the IMF and the World Bank conditioned some of their loans to their adoption. But normally, such conditions were a matter of negotiation rather than of imposition – and Latin American governments had a long tradition of failing to comply with the conditions of IMF loans.

Williamson's list boiled down to three main elements. The first was the importance of achieving **macroeconomic stability** and taming inflation through the control of fiscal deficits. The second was dismantling protectionism and **opening up** to foreign trade, competition and investment. The third aspect was **reforming the role of the state** in the economy and **promoting the role of markets** in allocating resources and generating wealth. That meant getting the government out of producing goods through privatisation. The implicit idea was to focus the state's activity on regulation, social provision and poverty alleviation. But this was not made explicit.

Debt and the battle for stability

Contrary to how it is portrayed by some of its critics, the reform process varied hugely in timing, speed and extent from country to country. The most progress was made on the first point, macroeconomic stabilisation. Chile in the 1970s and Bolivia and Mexico in the 1980s were the first to tackle inflation by closing the fiscal deficit. Unlike the 'heterodox' plans, these orthodox programmes brought more lasting success, and would be imitated across the region. They usually involved a combination of tax increases and spending cuts. In most cases, income and corporate tax rates were simplified, with top rates being cut and minimum rates raised, and VAT introduced, sometimes at punishingly high rates. Usually, more of the initial burden fell on spending cuts. Privatisation helped, since many state-owned companies regularly recorded big losses. Governments moved to eliminate many across-the-board subsidies, such as those on petrol or foodstuffs, which had benefited rich and poor alike. In their place, social safety nets for the poor were set up, but often too slowly. Often, spending was cut indiscriminately, or the burden fell disproportionately on public investment. Monetary policy was reformed, too. Nearly everywhere, governments renounced printing money. Many countries moved towards giving their Central Banks legal or de facto independence. The upshot was that by the early 1990s, fiscal deficits and inflation had been brought down sharply almost everywhere.[37] Mexico moved from a primary deficit (i.e. excluding debt interest) of 8 per cent of GDP in 1981 to a surplus of 8 per cent of GDP by the end of the decade. In Argentina, Menem fired 100,000 central government employees, causing much hardship for those involved but no discernible effect on the efficiency of administration.

Stabilisation was helped, too, by a new approach to the debt problem. As debt service took an ever-larger slice of government revenues, this weakened the incentive to reform. Eventually – and later than was desirable – it came to be recognised that forgiving part of the debt was in the interest not just of debtor countries but also of creditors, who might thus get at least some of their money back. Nicholas Brady, a former Wall Street banker who was the Treasury Secretary in the administration of George H W Bush, put this idea into effect in 1989. Under the Brady Plan, countries had to show willingness to reform, and some action in that direction. The essence of the plan involved swapping the old, defaulted debt, for new bonds either of lower face value or that paid a much lower interest rate. The new bonds were guaranteed by some $30 billion of US Treasury Bonds put up as collateral by the multilateral financial institutions and Japan. The Brady Plan worked, though more favourable conditions in the world economy helped too. At the same time, the creation of a secondary market in Latin American debt had allowed governments to start buying back some of their old debt at discounted prices. The ratio of net foreign debt to exports for 17 highly indebted countries (of which 12 were in Latin America) fell from 384 per cent in 1986 to 225 per cent by 1993, while the ratio of net debt to GNP fell from 67 per cent to 42 per cent over the same period. By 1994, there had been 18 Brady deals, covering

$191 billion in debt, of which $61 billion was forgiven. Whereas Latin America had been locked out of capital markets for forty years after the defaults of the 1930s, this time capital began to flood back to the region within a decade.[38]

Tearing down barriers

The record of structural reform was more mixed. It went furthest in trade policy and financial liberalisation. Given Latin America's long history of protectionism, the trade reform was dramatic. In the mid-1980s, barriers to imports in Mexico and Central America were greater than anywhere else in the world, while those in South America were surpassed elsewhere only in Africa.[39] Since many exports, especially of manufactures, themselves included imported components, protection carried a strong anti-export bias. Tariff rates on imports varied wildly, and were backed up by a battery of non-tariff barriers, ranging from quotas to outright bans and a labyrinth of form-filling permits.

The reformers implemented a sweeping unilateral trade liberalisation. Average tariffs across the region fell from over 40 per cent in the mid-1980s to around 10 per cent (many tariffs fell much further than the average). Nearly all quotas and import prohibitions were swept away. Tariff structures were radically simplified. Many countries joined the General Agreement on Tariffs and Trade (which became the World Trade Organisation in 1996), from which Latin America had largely absented itself at its foundation in 1945. The upshot was that by the end of the 1990s, Latin America was the most open region of the developing world.[40] At the same time, free-trade agreements multiplied, and interest in regional integration schemes revived. In the past, such schemes had been an attempt to broaden the scope for import-substitution and industrial planning. Now, they had a radically different aim. The 'new regionalism', as some called it, was 'an integral part of the structural adjustment process that is designed to make the economies more market-oriented, open, outward looking, and internationally competitive in a modern democratic institutional setting'.[41] Some countries went further. Carlos Salinas, Mexico's president, who had a doctorate in economics from Harvard, led his country into the North American Free Trade Agreement of 1994 with the United States and Canada – the first such accord between a Latin American country and industrialised nations. Mexico and Chile led the way in striking bilateral free-trade agreements with the EU and Asian countries. On imports from countries with which it lacked a free-trade agreement, Chile imposed a flat tariff of only 8 per cent. Many of these trade agreements were aimed mainly at attracting foreign investment by 'locking in' the reforms by international treaty.

The aims of liberalisation were to turn trade into a motor of economic growth and to increase the efficiency and competitiveness of Latin American firms. It largely worked. It eventually helped to produce an export boom, starting in Mexico, Central America and Chile and more recently encompassing Brazil and Peru. In the 1990s alone, the total volume of Latin America's trade doubled.[42] But there were losers as well as winners. The process was made more costly than it might have been by the way in which trade liberalisation interacted with stabilisation and financial reform. Many governments tore down barriers to the movement of money as well as goods. That was partly because they saw exchange controls as ineffective and as sources of corruption, and partly because they hoped to attract foreign capital. But the resulting surge of money from abroad saw many Latin American currencies appreciate in the early 1990s. Strong currencies and cheap imports helped to get inflation down, and thus took some of the pressure off fiscal adjustment. But orthodoxy – and the Washington Consensus – holds that trade reform should start with a big real-terms devaluation. When that didn't happen, it meant that some manufacturers and farmers who were reasonably efficient went under in the face of competition from cheap imports.

The combination of trade opening and overvalued currencies resulted in ballooning current-account deficits. Some, such as Pedro Aspe, Mexico's finance minister under Salinas, argued that these did not matter. They merely mirrored the inflow of foreign investment, he argued.[43] Aspe was unperturbed even as Mexico's current-account deficit hovered around 7 per cent of GDP in 1992–4. The problem was that much of this investment was 'hot' money, placed in shares and bonds. It could leave as fast as it came. That is what happened in Mexico in 1994, an election year and one of political turmoil. The new government promptly ordered a devaluation that became a rout. This 'tequila crisis', as it became known, plunged Mexico into a deep recession (GDP shrank by 6 per cent in 1995, though recovery was swift).[44]

It was a foretaste of problems to come for Latin America. In 1998, when Russia's devaluation and default triggered what would become worldwide financial strain in emerging markets, the region's current-account deficit stood at 4.5 per cent of GDP. Just as Mexico had four years earlier, many countries suffered a 'sudden stop' in capital inflows.[45] Private capital inflow to the seven biggest Latin American economies had totalled about 5 per cent of their combined GDP in 1997 and the first half of 1998. By mid-1998, this figure had plunged to less than 1 per cent.[46] This time the impact was particularly severe in South America. It forced half a dozen countries to abandon pegged exchange rates and undergo a new round of economic adjustment. External factors – the dotcom crash of March 2001 in the United States – and turbulence within the region, including Argentina's collapse and the knock-on effects, meant that recovery did not come until 2003. CEPAL promptly dubbed this period the 'lost half-decade'.[47] Life in a world of free-flowing capital had proved to be something of a roller-coaster for Latin America.

In some cases, the ride was made choppier by flaws in banking systems. Under the old model, governments played a big role in allocating credit, both directly through state-owned development banks and indirectly by requiring commercial banks to lend to favoured sectors at subsidised interest rates. In 1986, up to 80 per cent of total credit was allocated by such non-market mechanisms in Brazil and 40 per cent in Argentina. In Brazil, government credit subsidies amounted to almost 8 per cent of GDP.[48] It was thought that these policies would raise savings and guide investment in ways that would boost growth. The effect was often the opposite. Negative real interest rates (i.e. lower than inflation) promoted capital flight and discouraged saving and bank lending. The government was often a poor judge of the most efficient investments. Except for the favoured few, credit was scarce. In the early 1980s, in most Latin American countries the ratio of money and credit to GDP was below 30 per cent; in rich countries, it was 90 to 100 per cent.[49] Commercial banks faced a battery of restrictions, but were otherwise poorly supervised: their accounts were often opaque, they made insufficient provisions for bad loans while routinely lending to companies owned by their shareholders. But governments offered an implicit guarantee that they would reimburse depositors when banks went bust.

When the reformers took charge, they freed interest rates, abolished rules on credit allocation, and sharply reduced reserve requirements. In some countries, state-owned banks were privatised or wound up. Restrictions on foreign ownership of banks were removed. In countries such as Mexico, Argentina and Peru, foreign banks came to dominate the financial system. The reformers also made efforts to improve banking supervision, but these would often prove to be belated and inadequate. Sudden stops in capital flows and interest-rate rises were followed by banking collapses in Mexico and, to a lesser extent, Argentina in 1995, and in the Andean countries three years later. These inevitably amplified recessions.

In Ecuador, political instability, flooding caused by the El Niño weather pattern, low oil prices, poor economic management and a dozen bank failures triggered a financial and economic collapse only slightly less severe than that of Argentina. As the country tottered towards hyperinflation, the government decreed that Ecuador adopt the US dollar as its currency. It had little choice in the matter: Ecuadoreans showed no desire to hold the sucre, the debauched local currency. Dollarisation brought stability. But the economy had contracted by 7 per cent in 1999. The bank collapses ended up costing the government $3.5 billion; it chose to repay depositors in full but failed to recover many of the banks' defaulted loans, partly because of pressure from politically powerful debtors. A million Ecuadoreans migrated, many to Spain and Italy. In 2000, the daily Iberia flight, a big Airbus-340, would make its outward journey from Madrid to Quito almost empty, but be overbooked for the return leg. Stability and high oil prices eventually brought growth. But Ecuador remains a largely unreformed economy, hog-tied by a fragmented political system, regional cleavages and a strong populist tradition. To make dollarisation work in the long term, further structural reforms will be required. If the political will for these remains absent, it is possible that a future Ecuadorean government could face political pressure to abandon the dollar and issue a new local currency.[50]

Even Colombia, long a paragon of effective orthodox macroeconomic management, succumbed to the credit bubble. It was the only Latin American country not to reschedule its debts in the 1980s and the proud possessor of an investment-grade credit rating. But when it opened its economy in 1990, capital inflows (including drug money) caused the peso to appreciate, and pushed up asset prices, especially those of property. In part because of the spendthrift injunctions of a new constitution, fiscal policy was uncharacteristically loose in the 1990s. In 1998, Colombia registered fiscal and current-account deficits of 5 per cent of GDP. When the money stopped flowing, property prices crashed, several banks collapsed and the country suffered its first recession since the 1930s.

Governments also moved to reform pension systems. That was partly for fiscal reasons. State-operated pay-as-you-go pension systems were generally poorly managed. They were over-generous but benefited relatively better-off workers, and some faced deficits. Many had been raided by government for other purposes. Proponents hoped that pension reform would boost national savings; they also thought it would strengthen local equity and bond markets by creating institutional investors. The move from state-run pay-as-you-go systems to compulsory saving for retirement in individual capitalised accounts managed by private funds began in Chile, and was later adopted in Argentina, Bolivia, Colombia, Mexico and Peru. The switch was not without problems. On the one hand, it achieved some of the reformers' objectives, reducing the fiscal burden on future generations and helping to develop and modernise capital markets, according to a study by the World Bank in 2004.[51] However, there were two drawbacks. One was that the transitional costs to governments were high, as in Argentina. The second problem concerned the new system itself. The private funds charged high fees, especially at the start. Typically, workers were required to contribute 10 per cent of salary, which many found too much. The result was that many failed to make contributions. Even in Chile, only about half the workforce is covered by the new system.

Elsewhere, coverage is even lower. In a partial reversal of policy, the World Bank concluded that the private schemes will have to be supplemented by a public pension safety-net.

Public vices, private passions

Cochabamba, Bolivia's third city, sits at a comfortable altitude of 2,500 metres (8,200 feet) in a broad valley where family farmers with small or medium-sized holdings provide much of the country's food. In 1980 it was a pleasant, rather sleepy place of some 200,000 people. At weekends, the *cochabambino* middle class would head for the pavement restaurants of the Prado, a broad sunny avenue then on the outskirts, to eat roast duck washed down with lager from the local brewery founded by German migrants.[52] It was shaken out of its bucolic torpor by rising demand for cocaine in the United States. The city became the jumping-off point for the coca fields of the Chapare in the tropical lowlands to the east. Swollen by migrants from the dying tin mines and the impoverished Altiplano – of whom Evo Morales was one – Cochabamba is now a disorderly metropolis of some 600,000 people. The nocturnal calm of the Prado has yielded to the thumping beat of Colombian *cumbias* blasting out from discos.

For the anti-globalisation movement Cochabamba occupies a prominent place in the mythology surrounding the Washington Consensus. The city's chaotic growth put great pressure on water supplies. The government was keen to attract private investment to the water industry. In Cochabamba, the mayor reckoned the solution was to bring water to the city from the Misicuni river, on the far side of a mountain range. This involved building a 120-metre-high dam and boring a 19.5-kilometre tunnel through the mountains. The project would provide hydroelectricity as well, but it cost $252 million. The World Bank argued that it was unnecessarily expensive. It backed a cheaper option under which no tariff increases for water would have been permitted for five years. The government, under pressure from the mayor, went ahead with the Misicuni scheme anyway, signing a contract with a consortium called Aguas del Tunari led by Bechtel, an American engineering giant, which took over Semapa, the municipal water company. To defray the cost of the Misicuni project, the consortium raised water charges by 43 per cent on average.[53] Charges doubled for a small number of very poor consumers – though of course this is the figure that is indiscriminately repeated on internet sites (try googling 'Misicuni' or 'water war'). A few people found themselves paying a third of their income on water. The new charges drew protests in January 2000 in which a 17-year old was killed by a soldier. The government of Hugo Banzer, a former military dictator turned conservative democrat, panicked.

Instead of dealing with the injustices of the new system, it tore up the contract with Aguas del Tunari. Under a better-designed contract, Aguas del Illimani, a consortium led by Suez, a French utility, was administering and expanding water and sewerage services in the capital, La Paz, and its satellite city of El Alto. But because of the Cochabamba unrest, the government refused its request to raise tariffs, even though these were lower than those of publicly owned water companies elsewhere in Bolivia. Instead, the government raised charges for new connections by the company, to $450 for water and sewerage – or six months' wages for poorer Bolivians. The mayors of El Alto and La Paz called for the contract to be rescinded. In January 2005, the weak, interim government of Carlos Mesa did just that.

These 'water wars' were hailed by the radical left, in Bolivia and beyond, as proof of the iniquities of privatisation. Certainly, water is especially sensitive. Not only is its supply a natural monopoly, but in Andean Indian culture water is a divine gift that belongs to everyone, not a commodity. The livelihoods of farmers in much of Latin America depend on water for irrigation. But the Bolivian experience was a failure of government regulation rather than of privatisation. Although Misicuni was a longstanding demand of civic leaders in Cochabamba, it should not have been approved. In La Paz and El Alto, Aguas del Illimani had a good record. It invested $63 million (though some of this came from soft loans through the government). After years in which the state water company failed to keep pace with demand, the annual rate of new sewerage and water connections rose by two-thirds in the first three years of its contract. Thanks largely to private investment, many more Bolivians, and especially poorer ones, gained access to basic services. In 1992, only 50 per cent had piped water, while in 1997 only 45 per cent had electricity. In 2004, according to the World Bank, 70 per cent had water and 60 per cent had electricity.[54]

In Cochabamba, six years after the water war, victory was hardly sweet. Semapa was under 'community control'. Half of the city's population still lacked piped water. For the other half, service was poor; some had running water only three hours a day.[55] Across Latin America, those who lack piped water normally pay more for it – sometimes up to ten times more – than those with a mains connection. The unconnected get water from tankers, usually operated by private, informal, businesses. This water is rarely clean. In some cities in Argentina, too, water was privatised in the 1990s. Suez took a controlling stake in Aguas Argentinas, which operated in Buenos Aires. By applying more efficient management, it was able to cut water tariffs while extending service to an extra 3 million poor people (though connection charges were high).[56] According to one study, water connections increased from 64 to 71 per cent in provincial areas of Argentina where water was privatised, compared with an increase from 87 to 90 per cent where it was not. The authors calculate that the faster increase in safe water supplies provided by privatisation cut child mortality rates by 5 per cent in the areas concerned.[57] In many parts of the region, there were valid reasons for water prices to rise, both to cover new investment and to discourage wastage. But the lesson from Cochabamba was that if water privatisation is to be politically viable and socially just, it should go hand in hand with targeted subsidies (in the form of cash payments) for the poorest, as happens in Chile.

More than any other policy, the Washington Consensus came to be identified in Latin America with privatisation – and controversially so as the 'water wars' exemplified. The sell-offs began in Chile in the 1970s, as the Pinochet regime handed back the companies nationalised by Allende (except Codelco, the state copper company) and then went on to imitate the sweeping privatisations of Margaret Thatcher in Britain. Privatisation spread to Mexico in the 1980s, and took off across the region in the 1990s. In Latin America as a whole, more than 2,000 enterprises were sold, ranging from steelworks to electricity companies, and banks to airlines. The state's share of production declined more in Latin America in the past twenty years than in any other region except the former communist countries in Central and Eastern Europe. In the 1990s, government receipts from privatisations in Latin America totalled $178 billion (of which $95 billion came in 1997–9), accounting for 55 per cent of the total in the developing world.[58]

The scale of privatisation was as much tribute to the multiplicity of state companies in Latin America as to reforming zeal. In Peru, for example, not only were the commanding heights of the economy largely in state hands – oil, mining, agriculture (in government-organised co-operatives), steel, fishmeal, a chunk of banking, utilities – but also the marketing of food staples and minerals, not to mention a pornographic cinema, a former asset of an insolvent banking group. Though there were islands of excellence – Venezuela's state oil company, PdVSA, for example, and the public-utility company of Medellín in Colombia – most state-owned companies were poorly run, and by the 1970s many were chronically loss-making. In Mexico, at their peak in 1982, 1,155 state-owned companies received transfers and subsidies equal to 12.7 per cent of GDP, according to Jacques Rogozinski, who as a finance official was involved in privatising many of them under Salinas.[59]

Governments privatised for a mixture of ideological and pragmatic reasons. If one aim was to promote economic efficiency, another, often equally pressing, was to plug holes in the public finances. (Too often, governments mistakenly used privatisation revenues for current spending, rather than to pay debt or for public investment.) In the first aim, privatisation was highly successful. A comprehensive analysis of the performance of privatised firms in seven countries shows that on average they increased output (by 40 per cent), and profits while shedding labour (a quarter of the workforce on average).[60] Take Brazil's steel industry, sold as six separate companies in 1991–3. In state hands in 1990, it employed 115,000 people and produced 22.6 million tonnes of steel. By 1996, it produced 25.2 million tonnes with just 65,000 workers. In most cases, privatised firms increased sales and profitability. Labour productivity thus increased sharply; in some cases, such as in Argentina, firms also made big new capital investments. Above all, performance in privatised firms improved because of better management. The firms also paid more taxes when in private hands. Wages for workers who kept their jobs rose – in Bolivia they more than doubled.[61] In many cases, privatised firms subsequently expanded. For example, since its privatisation in 1997, Brazil's Companhia Vale do Rio Doce, an iron ore and transport group, increased sales by 2.5 times and its profits by 13 times. In 2005, it employed 39,000 people, up from 14,000. It has been transformed from a conglomerate into the world's second-biggest multinational mining company.[62]

Despite the overall success of privatisation, it became very unpopular in Latin America. After the Cochabamba water war, and a similar riot in Arequipa, Peru's second city, over the proposed sale of two small electricity companies in 2002, privatisation all but stopped in the region. Its unpopularity was mainly because the benefits to consumers and taxpayers were thinly spread and often not very visible. On the other hand, the losers tended to be vocal. In some countries, workers sacked as a result of privatisation found it hard to get other jobs. In Argentina, for example, the payroll in formerly state-owned companies fell from 250,000 in 1989 to around 60,000 in 1993.[63] Many of those laid off when YPF, the oil company, was privatised were in far-flung provinces with little alternative work. They tended to be older workers, with specific skills. Many spent the next decade living on government handouts and staging frequent protests. One study of 504 workers laid off by YPF in 1991 reckoned that over the following decade their earnings declined by around a half. In 2001, 26.4 per cent of this group were jobless, when the unemployment rate in Greater Buenos Aires stood at 13.9 per cent.[64]

The relatively few failed privatisations attracted more attention than the many success stories. Privatised airlines floundered in Argentina, Mexico, and Peru but not Chile, where LAN became the region's strongest airline and expanded into Peru, Ecuador and Argentina. Salinas's privatisation of Mexico's banks turned into a costly boomerang: 12 of the 18 banks sold in 1991–2, mainly to stockbroking groups with little banking experience, had to be taken back a few years later when the peso crisis revealed the shakiness of their balance sheets. Mexico's pioneering effort to get private companies to build toll roads also stumbled. When a new motorway from Mexico City to

Acapulco opened in 1993, the tolls for the five-hour journey totalled more than $100 – higher than the cost of a flight. To attract traffic, motorway tolls had to be cut sharply. Compensating the highway companies and bailing out the banks increased Mexico's public debt from 25 to 50 per cent of GDP.[65]

Another reason for privatisation's unpopularity was that it became identified in the public mind with corruption, largely because some of the early asset sales in Chile, Mexico and Argentina were not carried out in an open manner. But the main target of public opprobrium was the higher tariffs charged by some privatised utilities. Often the increases were because services had previously been subsidised by the state. But in some cases, charges remained high because public monopolies were turned into private ones. Governments either failed to build in competition, and/or failed to establish effective and professional regulatory frameworks for natural monopolies, such as electricity, telecoms and water. Telmex, the Mexican phone company was granted a six-year monopoly for many of its services after it was sold. It continued to have a dominant market position long after the formal monopoly ended. The profits from Telmex helped Carlos Slim, whose family owned 48 per cent of the capital and 71 per cent of the voting shares, to become the third-richest person in the world, with a fortune of $49 billion in 2006, behind only Bill Gates and Warren Buffet, according to *Forbes* magazine. Most of that fortune was the result of Slim's undoubted business acumen and skill at diversification. But Telmex's profits were partly the result of some of the world's highest telephone charges, as the OECD pointed out.[66] In Argentina, the phone company was split geographically into a duopoly, with one firm owned by Spain's Telefónica and the other by Telecom Italia. Menem's government made the mistake of setting many tariffs for privatised utilities in dollars. That meant they went up (or failed to fall) even when other prices and wages were falling during the final years of convertibility. (Kirchner's government went to the other extreme, freezing many tariffs.) In Peru, Telefónica was the dominant operator in fixed-line and mobile telephony, as well as cable television and internet connection. In Chile and Brazil, by contrast, great efforts were made to ensure competition among several telecoms providers and prices fell more sharply. In Brazil, mobile phone use grew massively. In the first two years after privatisation in May 1998, the total number of mobile lines increased from 4.5 million to 19 million, of which 3.4 million were owned by the poorest 45 per cent of the population (up from 270,000 in 1998).[67]

Across the region telecoms privatisation brought new investment, technological modernisation and huge increases in coverage. One study found that in countries which privatised, over the next three years the rate of growth of coverage (in relation to population) of land lines and mobile phones combined rose from 5 per cent a year to 14 per cent a year, the waiting list fell by half and the quality of service improved.[68] The cost of international calls tended to fall, while those of local calls rose, as cross-subsidies were removed. Mainly as a result of privatisation, Latin America had one-fifth as many lines as developed countries in 1999, compared with one-sixth in 1985. Both coverage and quality remained well below those in developed countries. But this was one area where the region was starting to close the gap.

Similarly, electricity privatisation led to lower prices in Argentina, Chile and Peru. In Brazil, it was plagued by problems stemming from the poor design of regulations. There was much trial and error when governments granted licences to private firms to build and operate infrastructure, such as motorways or power stations. One study of more than a thousand such concessions granted in Latin America during the 1990s found that in more than 60 per cent of cases their terms were substantially renegotiated within three years.[69] Chile finally got this right in the late 1990s, using private finance to build a modern motorway network.

In all, from 1990 to 2001, private investment in infrastructure in Latin America totalled a whopping $360 billion, $150 billion more than in East Asia.[70] But it came to be recognised that private investment would have to be supplemented by a revival of public investment, especially in areas such as water and transport. Nevertheless, on balance, privatisation of public services was clearly positive for Latin America. One recent detailed study concluded that infrastructure privatisations 'generally increased access to power, telephone services and water, particularly for the poor who, before privatisation, often had no services or paid higher prices for private services (particularly in the case of water). Although some privatised firms have raised prices, which has burdened lower-income households, the bottom line is still one of absolute gains in welfare for the poor.'[71] There were even signs that privatisation was becoming less unpopular. In the Latinobarómetro poll, respondents saying that privatisation had been 'somewhat' or 'very beneficial' fell from 46 per cent in 1998 to 21 per cent in 2003, before rising again to 32 per cent in 2005. The following year, 30 per cent of respondents pronounced themselves satisfied with privatised utilities, almost double the number of the 2004 survey.[72]

Privatisation was supposed to be only part of a broader attempt to sweep away the cobweb of regulations that had enmeshed private business under the old model. But little of this happened. There was little reform of labour markets, for example. In a few countries, steps were taken towards more flexibility by encouraging temporary jobs and by cutting the cost of layoffs. But in general unreformed labour laws meant that it was more difficult and expensive to hire and fire workers in Latin America than in developed countries.[73] The irony was that only a minority of the workforce enjoyed such protection. Around half of the labour force toiled in the informal sector, with almost no legal protection. Some deregulation happened in other areas. Salinas freed Mexico's ports, breaking the power of a trade union aristocracy which sub-contracted work to ill-paid casuals while pocketing large fees for doing nothing. In the first year of deregulation, the cost of services at Veracruz, the main port, fell by more than 30 per cent and the volume of containers handled rose by 47 per cent. After deregulation of Mexico's trucking industry, the number of licensed trucks rose by 62 per cent in two years, fees declined by up to 50 per cent and service quality improved.[74] Deregulation of transport was crucial to the export boom in Chile and Mexico. But these were exceptions. In general, business was hampered by a labyrinth of red tape. Latin America scored poorly in annual surveys of business conditions around the world by the International Finance Corporation, the World Bank's private-sector arm. These found that not only were labour laws in the region especially rigid, but legal requirements to start a business were often absurdly cumbersome and protection of property rights and creditors abysmal. To take a few examples, it took 152 days to start a business in Brazil, compared to just two days in Australia. In Bolivia, registering a business cost one-and-three-quarter times the average annual income, while in Denmark it is free. In Guatemala it took on average almost four years to enforce a contract in the courts, while in Tunisia it took less than a month.[75]

A balance sheet of the reforms

A quarter of a century after the debt crisis that give birth to the Washington Consensus, what is its record in Latin America? The first thing to say is that the initial fruits of economic reform were relatively disappointing. Take economic growth first: it did pick up in the 1990s. Stagnation followed from 1998 to 2002, but then strong recovery from 2004 onwards (*see* Chart 3). To what extent was this patchy record a direct result of the reforms? Measuring their impact on growth is not straightforward. For example, it is hard to disentangle the impact of reforms from that of the capital inflows they encouraged. According to José Antonio Ocampo of CEPAL, who offered a nuanced critique of the Washington Consensus from the left, since the 1970s the main determinant of economic growth was capital flows, not policies.[76] Yet almost as soon as the ink of that analysis was dry, this relationship seemed to break down. Since 2004 robust growth has coincided with only moderate net capital inflows, as governments took advantage of trade surpluses to reduce indebtedness. Much depends, too, on what period is used to assess the relationship between growth and the reforms. As Ocampo rightly points out, stabilisation often is (but should not be) confused with reform.[77] Stagnation and the rise in poverty in

Chart 3: Latin America, economic growth, 1980–2006
(GDP at constant prices, annual % change)

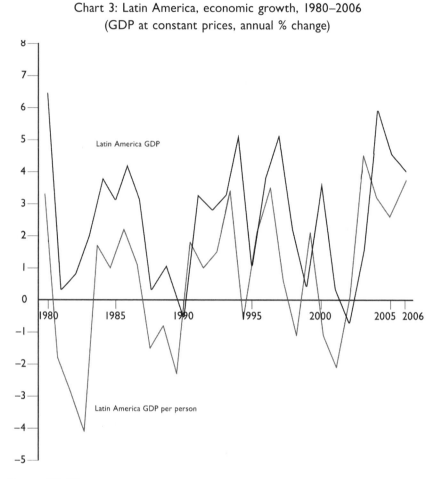

Source: ECLAC

the 1980s were the hangover from the debt-fuelled growth fiesta of the 1970s. Those who pin the blame for the 'lost decade' of the 1980s on stabilisation are merely stating a truism. The critics are unable to show that any alternative set of policies would have produced a better long-term outcome.

Some early studies suggested that the reforms added two percentage points to annual growth rates in the early 1990s. A later study, by researchers at the Inter-American Development Bank, found that the reforms had only a temporary effect in accelerating growth. Even so, they conclude that per capita income in Latin America in 2000 was 11 per cent higher than it would have been without the reforms. The main effect was to raise productivity in the region. In general, reforms delivered more growth in countries with better

Chart 4: GNI per person, Latin America and the world, Atlas method ($)

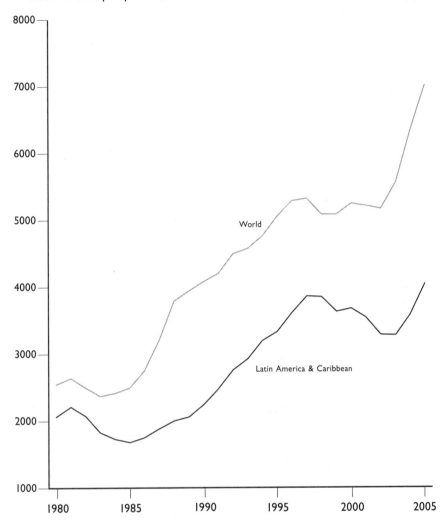

Source: World Bank
World Bank Atlas method: The World Bank's official estimates of the size of economies are based on Gross National Income converted to current US dollars using the Atlas method. GNI takes into account all production in the domestic economy (i.e. GDP) plus the net flows of factor income (such as rents, profits and labour income) from abroad. The Atlas method smoothes exchange-rate fluctuations by using a three-year moving average, price-adjusted conversion factor.

public institutions.[78] Take into account the slowdown from 1998 to 2003, and the record looks much less favourable. As recovery gained pace after 2003, another twist was added to the debate. On the one hand, just like the prior slowdown, recovery owed much to external conditions. As China industrialised, its demand for Latin American foodstuffs and minerals pushed their prices to record levels. Low world interest rates helped Latin America, too. On the other hand, after two decades of stabilisation and reform, many of the region's economies had emerged in much better shape to take advantage of such opportunities. In other words, there was a lag before the full effect of reform was felt, just as many believe that the steady growth in the British economy since 1993 owes much to the Thatcher reforms.

Given the ideal external conditions, growth in Latin America remained relatively disappointing – especially when measured against growth rates in China and India. That comparison was in part unfair: China is at a similar stage in its development to that of Brazil from the 1950s to the 1970s, of industrialisation based on drawing in the reserve army of rural labour and foreign capital. But it was true that, despite the revival of growth, too much remained unreformed in Latin America: the region is technologically and educationally backward, it still suffers from relatively low productivity, stifling business regulation, deficient transport facilities and weak public institutions. These factors appeared to limit sustainable growth in the region as a whole to around 4–5 per cent a year. But steady and stable growth at this pace would represent a great improvement on the past four decades or so.

Some critics, such as CEPAL, argued that the reforms themselves had weakened the region's productive capacity by accentuating 'dualism' in Latin America's economies. In other words, while a fairly small number of large companies (including subsidiaries of multinationals) became much more efficient, they had fewer links than in the past with the mass of small and medium businesses, many of which struggled.[79] Economic 'informality' and unemployment did increase as a result of stabilisation and reform. But unemployment fell steadily again after 2003. That is in line with trends elsewhere. In Spain, for example, which underwent reforms analogous to those in Latin America, unemployment rose above 20 per cent in the early 1990s; it was not until 2005 that it fell below 9 per cent, its level of 1980.[80] Ocampo argues that to raise growth and spread its benefits wider, government should adopt 'technology policies' and 'strategic visions' for different sectors, as well as helping small and medium firms.[81] To some that looked like old-fashioned industrial policy. But there was wide consensus that governments needed to get more involved in stimulating research and development, especially through collaboration between universities and the private sector – a national innovation strategy, as Williamson called it.[82]

The outstanding achievement of the reforms was the taming of inflation, and greater macroeconomic stability. It was not easy. Beating inflation was a long battle (*see* Chart 6). One way of interpreting the adjustment of 1998 to 2003 was that it was the price that was paid for having used overvalued currencies to bring inflation down. In 1999, as capital flowed out of the region, half a dozen countries abandoned pegged exchange rates in favour of floating ones. Instead of using the exchange rate to control inflation, they entrusted the task to Central Banks and monetary policy, adopting inflation targeting. In many countries, the new regime seemed to work well. The unweighted cross-country average inflation rate in the region fell from a peak of 1,206 per cent in 1989 to just 10 per cent by the end of the 1990s. By 2006, this average rate had fallen to 4.8 per cent, and for the first time since the 1930s no country suffered inflation of more than 20 per cent.[83] The average public-sector deficit in the region fell from 6.5 per cent of GDP during 1980 to 1990 to 1.3 per cent of GDP by 2005.[84] Excluding debt interest payments, the 2005 figure amounted to a surplus of 2.2 per cent of GDP.

Once low inflation was achieved, it opened up the possibility of bank credit and cheap mortgages for large numbers of Latin Americans who had been denied them for a generation – or had never had access to them. Strong growth in credit in Mexico and Brazil in the years after 2003 was a factor in faster economic expansion. Low inflation and reasonably disciplined fiscal policies served to boost the authority and credibility of economic policy-makers in many countries in the region. That was reflected in the risk premium on Latin American government bonds, which fell to around two percentage points above US Treasury Bonds in 2006 – its lowest-ever level. In addition, governments were able to break their dependence on foreign financing. By 2005, the governments of Mexico, Brazil and Colombia had switched more than half their debt to local currencies, as well as extending its term.[85] With surprising speed, they seemed to have overcome what Ricardo Hausmann, a Venezuelan economist, dubbed 'original sin' – emerging-market countries' traditional inability to borrow long-term in their own currency.[86] This owed much to the abundant liquidity in the world economy. Some argued that it also showed investors' disregard of risk. But the effect was that Latin America was insulating itself from any recurrence of the external 'shocks' it suffered in the 1980s and 1990s.

That new resilience stemmed in part from the second big achievement of the reforms: the growth in exports, after half a century in which their neglect had contributed much to the region's instability. Export growth in Mexico, Central America and the Caribbean had much to do with the establishment of assembly plants serving the United States' market. In South America, export growth depended more on natural resources. High commodity prices helped,

Chart 5: GNI per person, Latin America and the world, PPP exchange rates ($)

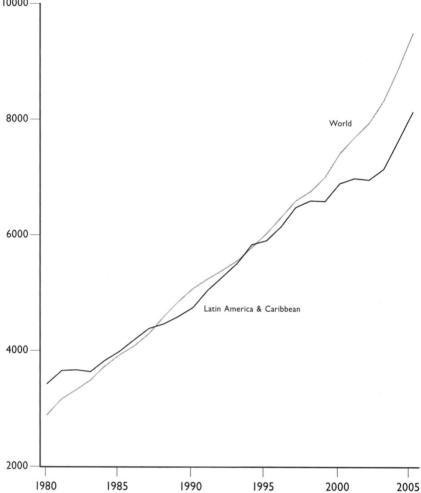

Source: World Bank

Purchasing power parity (PPP) conversion factors take into account differences in the relative prices of goods and services – particularly non-tradables – and therefore provide a better overall measure of the real value of output produced by an economy compared to other economies. PPP GNI is measured in current international dollars which, in principle, have the same purchasing power as a dollar spent on GNI in the US economy. Because PPPs provide a better measure of the standard of living of residents of an economy, they are the basis for the World Bank's calculations of poverty rates at $1 and $2 a day. The GNI of developing countries measured in PPP terms generally exceeds their GNI measured using the Atlas method or using market exchange rates.

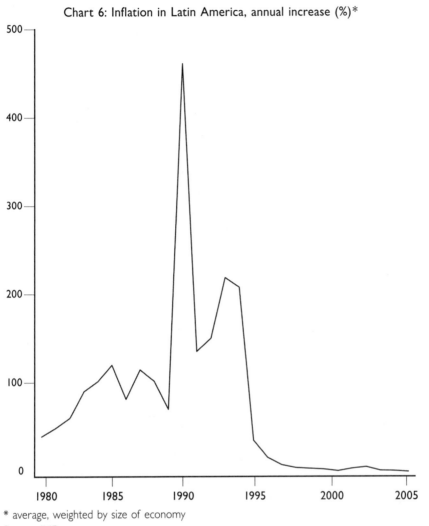

Chart 6: Inflation in Latin America, annual increase (%)*

* average, weighted by size of economy
Source: IMF

but were not the only explanation. Taken together, macroeconomic stability and better export performance held out hope that the next time the world economy is hit by financial instability, Latin America will not be the main protagonist.

The outlook in 2006 may have looked brighter than for a generation, but it had been a long and painful journey to recovery. The most powerful criticism of the reforms was that in the short term they had made Latin America more vulnerable to outside events. Some economists argued that the 'lost half-decade' was the result of what they called an 'external shock', and had nothing to do with the reforms themselves. But others were surely right when they pointed to the abrupt abolition of exchange and capital controls without prior reform of banking systems as a serious policy mistake. An early warning – which went unheeded – had been provided by banking collapses in Chile and Argentina in 1982–3, which followed the lifting of capital controls and freeing of interest rates by military regimes. An early remedy, which could have been more widely copied, was Chile's subsequent imposition of a tax on short-term capital inflows (which also helped to prevent its currency from becoming overvalued). Williamson himself later accepted that he should have included effective supervision of banks as an essential concomitant of financial liberalisation.[87] More broadly, critics such as Joseph Stiglitz argued that gradual, carefully sequenced reform would have avoided the social cost and policy mistakes of 'shock therapy'.[88] That is true – in a perfect world. The problem in the Latin America of the 1980s and 1990s was that governments faced economic emergencies. Naím, the Venezuelan trade minister, points out that reformers in his country did not adopt swift, drastic reforms because of a 'theoretical preference for traumatic shocks' but because of 'the practical impossibility of doing otherwise given the deterioration of the state apparatus'.[89] In addition, past experience showed that gradual reform tends to peter out in the face of pressure from powerful local interest groups who benefited from the subsidies and rents of the old model.

Another criticism is that the reforms were imposed in a uniform fashion, which took no account of national circumstances, and that they were rammed through undemocratically. A cursory examination shows that these criticisms do not hold up.[90] Some countries reformed drastically and quickly (Argentina, Bolivia and Peru), while others did relatively little (Ecuador and Venezuela). In Brazil and in Chile (after democracy was restored in 1990), reform was more gradual, and was preceded by the slow building of political consensus. Mexico signed NAFTA, but retained state monopolies in oil and electricity and the labour laws of the PRI. Even Chile kept its two largest companies – Codelco, the world's biggest copper producer, and Enap, an oil producer and distributor – in state hands. Brazil sold stakes in its oil company and invited private investment into electricity and oil exploration. But it retained three large state-owned banks, including a development bank which pursued industrial policies. The detailed formulae used to beat inflation varied. The politics of stabilisation and reform varied widely too. Certainly, in Mexico, Peru (under Alberto Fujimori) and, to a lesser extent, Argentina (under Menem), reforms were often decreed from on high, with little prior political debate. But both Fujimori and Menem were re-elected for second terms, as was Fernando Henrique Cardoso's reforming government in Brazil. Low inflation and rising social spending were democratic conquests, not dictatorial impositions.

Although he is often approvingly cited by left-wing opponents of reforms, Stiglitz himself concludes that 'the Washington Consensus policies were designed to respond to the very real problems in Latin America, and made considerable sense'.[91] In retrospect, the main problem with the Washington Consensus was not what was on Williamson's list, but what was not. Perhaps the most important missing commitment was to equity, to slashing poverty and inequality.[92] These concerns quickly moved to the centre of debate in Latin America. They were enshrined in the presidential declarations of the Summits of the Americas from 1994 onwards.[93] Whatever the rhetoric, the new consensus being implemented by many governments in Latin America maintains the tenets of the Washington Consensus and adds to it a greater emphasis on equity and on the role of the state in obtaining it.

Tackling poverty and inequality

In 1980, 40.5 per cent of Latin Americans lived below the national poverty line, and 18.6 per cent lived in 'extreme poverty', meaning that their income was not enough to allow them to nourish themselves adequately. Ten years later those figures had increased (see Chart 7). They fell between 1990 and 1997, rose slightly during the 'lost half-decade' and fell steadily thereafter.[94] Using the World Bank's international poverty line of $2 a day, around a fifth of Latin Americans were poor in 2004, down from a quarter in the early 1990s.[95] Only Chile managed a big and sustained fall in poverty, from a peak of 45 per cent in the mid-1980s to 13.7 per cent in 2006.

What explains this relatively disappointing performance? The first answer is that growth was not fast or sustained enough, at least until 2003. To have a rapid impact on poverty, annual growth needs to be around 6 per cent. That is because of Latin America's unequal income distribution. Contrary to widespread claims, there is little evidence that the reforms in themselves either increased poverty or widened income inequality significantly for the region as a whole. But neither, at first, did they reduce inequality. In the 1950s, income distribution in Latin America was already the most unequal in the world (see Table 4). Inequality widened again during the 1980s, mainly because of the rise in inflation and the lack of growth. The pattern in the 1990s was varied (see Table 5). Income inequality fell in Brazil and Mexico, but it rose in countries that had previously been more egalitarian, such as Argentina.[96] There is some evidence that the trade opening may have increased inequality slightly, but that is mainly because it stimulated technological modernisation. Technological change has widened the differential between skilled and unskilled wages in Latin America, as it has elsewhere. On the other hand, low inflation and cheaper imports have

Chart 7: Poverty in Latin America

Latin America, prevalence of poverty according to national household surveys in 19 countries: % of population (in brackets, % of population in extreme poverty)

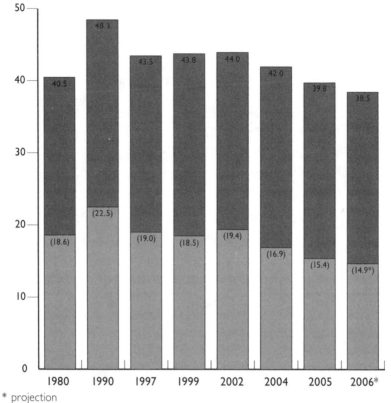

* projection

Source: UN Economic Commission for Latin America and the Caribbean (CEPAL)

Table 4: Income inequality by region, 1950–1992*

Gini coefficient

	1950	1960	1970	1980	1992
Africa	40.8	41.0	41.8	42.2	42.5
Asia	40.3	39.5	39.7	41.7	42.3
Latin America	52.4	52.8	54.2	54.7	54.8
Eastern Europe	35.8	36.1	36.3	36.5	36.9
Developed countries	39.8	39.8	38.9	38.6	39.2

* Distribution of household per capita income, weighted by population.

Source: World Bank (2004)

Table 5: Income inequality in Latin America, 1987–2005

Gini coefficient, selected countries

	1987	1989	1990	1992	1993	1997	2003	2004	2005
Argentina, main cities				0.450			0.528		
Bolivia, urban population					0.529		0.505	0.505	
Brazil			0.604					0.566	
Chile	0.561						0.546		
Colombia, urban population				0.500				0.553	
Mexico		0.527						0.499	
Peru					0.537	0.520			
Uruguay		0.424							0.450
Venezuela		0.425						0.454	

Source: World Bank; Michael Walton, Harvard University. Data derived from household surveys

tended to narrow income inequality. This improvement may not be fully recognised in the figures.[97]

Conservatives argued in the 1990s that growth alone would reduce poverty. But in the new consensus, there was a growing recognition that Latin America's widespread poverty and extreme inequalities might themselves be a drag on growth. Poor people, it was argued, were excluded from playing a full part in the economy because of their lack of education and lack of access to credit. Policies such as universal secondary schooling, wider access to higher education and greater public investment in infrastructure could both cut poverty and boost growth. Some added to that list land reform, if carried out in a peaceful and well-organised manner that did not threaten property rights.[98]

But only half the gap in inequality between Latin America and the rich countries is explained by the unequal distribution of education, capital, land and earned income. The other half is because the actions of the state reduce inequality in rich countries. The World Bank found that before taking into account tax and state transfers, incomes in the United Kingdom and Sweden were not much more unequal than those of Latin America.[99] In almost all Latin American countries, government spending on social programmes has increased substantially over the past 15 years. On average, social spending rose by 39 per cent between 1989–91 and 2002–3.[100] That was an achievement of democracy – but one made possible by the reforms, which freed resources previously squandered by state-owned companies. However, taxes in Latin America are not particularly progressive. And much social spending is regressive (i.e. it goes disproportionately to the better-off). That is especially true of pensions, public universities and energy subsidies. The net effect is that while state transfers reduce the Gini coefficient in the United Kingdom from 0.53 to 0.35, in Latin America they reduce it by only two percentage points.[101] Another reason for inequality is that the poor tend to suffer more in recessions, since they have no assets on which to fall back. To make matters worse, state spending in Latin America has tended to follow the economic cycle, rather than cushion it. Chile has adopted a counter-cyclical fiscal policy, under which the government saves during economic booms; as a result, it could increase spending when the economy slowed in 2000–2. And governments – in Chile, Mexico, Brazil and Colombia for example – have begun to implement targeted anti-poverty programmes. In 2006, some 50 million of the poorest Latin American families were enrolled in such programmes.[102]

For the poorer countries in the region, faster growth was more important than redistribution in cutting poverty and inequality. Elsewhere, the impact of low inflation, the achievement of universal primary education and better social policy started to make a difference. By one account, income distribution in Brazil in 2006 was less unequal than at any time since such data began to be collected in the 1960s.[103] Similarly, in Mexico income distribution was less unequal in 2004 than it had been in the late 1980s, and extreme poverty was falling fast.[104] What made these trends remarkable was that growth in both countries had lagged the regional average for most years since the late 1990s. Between them, economic reform and democracy were starting to lay the foundations for faster reductions in poverty and inequality. But not all governments in the region subscribed to the new consensus.

CHAPTER 7

THE POPULIST CHALLENGE

In 2001, on one of his many foreign trips, Hugo Chávez visited the editorial offices of *The Economist* in St James's Street in London. Over coffee and biscuits, he expounded on his globetrotting diplomacy aimed at sustaining the oil price, which had only recently climbed from the low levels of the late 1990s. Asked for his response to criticisms in Venezuela that he was concentrating all power in his own hands, he suddenly unleashed a lengthy diatribe, accusing his enemies of lying and his questioner of being an opposition propagandist. Already running late, he stopped on the way out to chat up the receptionists, two young black women, as if they were Venezuelan voters. Across the road, in Lancaster House, several hundred people were waiting for him to give a lecture. By the time Chávez arrived, more than half an hour late, the British foreign-office minister deputed to welcome him was already halfway through his speech.

Hugo Chávez is a man of many contradictions, and remains so after eight years in power. He is a compulsive communicator, a seducer of audiences in the manner of a televangelist, as Cristina Marcano and Alberto Barrera, two Venezuelan journalists, point out in a perceptive biography.[1] He has been compared to Zelig, the protagonist of a Woody Allen film who assumes the characteristics of whoever he is talking to.[2] Chávez can be cordial, warm and amusing. But he is also arrogant, prickly and paranoid – he was so even before a coup attempt against him in 2002. He believes in the accumulation of power through systematic confrontation. Even more than his bête noire, George Bush, Chávez takes the view that people are either with him or against him.[3] He is tactically reckless, but strategically calculating. His rhetoric is incendiary, but his actions are sometimes surprisingly timid. Some of these ambivalences were noted by Gabriel García Márquez, who interviewed Chávez shortly before he became president in 1998. He concluded that there were 'two Chávezes'. One was a potential saviour of his country. The other was 'just another despot'.[4] As Teodoro Petkoff, a newspaper editor and former planning minister, has noted, Chávez also enjoys that most precious of qualities for a politician – luck. This has notably included the upswing in the oil price since 1998. It has also been his good fortune to be consistently underestimated by his opponents.[5]

Chávez is the most controversial figure in contemporary Latin America. He claims that his 'Bolivarian Revolution' has replaced a corrupt representative democracy with a superior 'direct democracy', and is substituting 'twenty-first-century socialism' for 'savage capitalism'. His supporters argue that Chávez is not only successfully challenging globalisation and the hegemony of the United States but offering a better life to his country's poor. According to one foreign propagandist for his regime, 'a slow-burning revolution is now underway in Venezuela ... Latin America is witnessing the most extraordinary and unusual political process since the Cuban revolution nearly half a century ago.'[6] On the other hand, many of his opponents see Chávez as a dictator, albeit an elected one, and they have repeatedly tried to oust him. Some of them also draw the parallel with Cuba – though they are horrified rather than inspired by it. In Venezuela and in Latin America, Chávez's opponents are by no means confined to the right. Carlos Fuentes, the Mexican novelist and a persistent critic of George Bush, has said of Hugo Chávez that 'he passes himself off as a governing leader of the left when in truth he is a tropical Mussolini, disposing benevolently of oil wealth while sacrificing the sources of production and employment'.[7] One of Chávez's leading critics at home is Teodoro Petkoff, who was a guerrilla leader in the 1960s and went on to found a socialist party. Chávez, he says, 'represents a significant regression for democracy'. Outside Venezuela, his government 'is seen as a government of the left because it faces up to the gringos. But it has fascistic elements and practices, such as the use of selective violence and repression to corner the opposition in a ghetto.'[8]

Chávez himself claims that his 'Bolivarian revolution' is continental in scope. Certainly, he embodies the sharpest challenge to liberal democracy in Latin America. Whatever the defects of the prior regime in Venezuela – and they were many – Chávez's rule is less democratic, open and pluralist than that of his predecessors.[9] There are many reasons to believe that the effect of Chávez's policies, though masked by windfall oil revenues, will be to accelerate his country's long-term decline. Contrary to his claims, the 'Bolivarian revolution' does not form part of a seamless web of revolutionary nationalism enveloping Latin America. In countries such as Chile, Brazil and Mexico, governments are following other models, which combine elements of social democracy with market liberalism. Their policies look far more effective, progressive and sustainable than the Bolivarian revolution. But Chávez shouts louder than his neighbours, and his voice is heard abroad. So it is important to assess why he came to power in Venezuela, whether he really represents a fundamental rupture with his country's past, and whether his 'revolution' is likely to survive and be copied elsewhere in the region.

The blessing and curse of oil

Modern Venezuela is built on a lake of oil. Foreign oil companies began pumping the black stuff during the First World War. In December 1922, while drilling beneath the shallow waters of Lake Maracaibo, engineers working for Shell stumbled upon a fountain of oil gushing forth at the rate of 100,000 barrels per day.[10] For the next four decades, Venezuela was the world's biggest oil exporter (until it was overhauled by Saudi Arabia). Thanks to oil, between 1920 and 1980 its economy grew faster than any other in the world, at an annual average rate of 6 per cent.[11] Oil money transformed what had been a sleepy, rural country of coffee, cattle and cacao farms. Caracas became the most 'Americanised' capital in Latin America, studded with skyscrapers and criss-crossed by urban motorways crowded with big Chevrolets and Fords. Venezuelans glimpsed prosperity: in 1970, income per head was the highest in Latin America, outstripping that of Argentina.[12]

Venezuela was one of the five founding members of OPEC. But higher and more volatile oil prices from the 1970s onwards proved to be as much a curse as a blessing. Oil gave Venezuela a chronic case of what economists call 'Dutch disease':[13] an overvalued currency made it hard for the country's non-oil businesses to compete against imports or to export, and thus reinforced Venezuela's dependence on oil. Productivity languished and inefficiencies multiplied. Second, oil played havoc with fiscal discipline. Habituated to oil revenue, the government failed to collect taxes efficiently: by 1992, non-oil public revenue was just 5.6 per cent of GDP. When the oil price fell, governments turned to foreign loans and to debauching the currency so that oil dollars went further in bolivares.[14] As a result, after decades of price stability, Venezuela caught the Latin American inflationary disease.

The third curse inflicted by oil was political. Oil rendered public opinion hostile to even the mildest of austerity measures or economic reforms. Venezuelans were convinced that they lived in a rich country. If they were poor, they believed that this was because someone – corrupt politicians or foreign multinationals – must be stealing their wealth, rather than because of misguided policies or weak and ineffective institutions. This would make them uniquely susceptible to populist political messages – especially because after the mid-1970s they did get steadily poorer. The long boom came to a painful and symbolic end on 'Black Friday' in February 1983, when the bolívar was devalued. By 1985, income per head was 15 per cent lower than in 1973.

Under the presidency of Jaime Lusinchi (1983–89), Venezuela drifted deeper into an economic abyss, exacerbated when the oil price halved after 1985. The government struggled to carry on servicing its debt, which absorbed up to 70 per cent of export earnings. It imposed exchange controls under which importers of 'essential' goods were subsidised with cheap dollars. According to one estimate, over-invoicing or downright fraud under this scheme cost the state up to $11 billion – a figure that dwarfed subsequent corruption scandals.[15]

Economic decline exposed political weaknesses. A popular revolution in 1958 had ushered in a seemingly solid democracy in a country that had seen an almost uninterrrupted succession of dictators since Simón Bolívar. This democracy was moulded by a power-sharing agreement, called the Pact of Punto Fijo. It placed the two main political parties – the social democratic Acción Democratica (AD) and the Christian democratic COPEI – at the centre of political life.[16] It was designed to exclude the Communist Party, and to set limits to political competition. Its authors wanted to avoid the polarisation that marked a short-lived democratic interlude from 1945 to 1948, when an AD-dominated government had pushed through modernising reforms but its sectarianism had alienated business, the Church, the army and the other parties. Punto Fijo was similar to the National Front forged by Colombia's Liberal and Conservative parties in the same year.

For a quarter of a century, *puntofijismo* worked well. Both parties, and especially AD, were highly organised and disciplined. They controlled social organisations, such as trade unions and professional associations. Their leaders spun a vast web of patronage financed by oil revenue. The party in power would regularly consult the other, which functioned as a loyal opposition. Guerrilla movements were defeated and sections of the left brought into the system in a third party, the Movement to Socialism (MAS) founded by Petkoff. Both of the main parties backed the prevailing economic orthodoxy of state-led industrialisation. Business was fed cheap credit and tariff protection. Though generally speaking Venezuela aligned itself with the United States in the Cold War, its foreign policy displayed considerable autonomy. In his first term as president from 1973 to 1978, Carlos Andrés Pérez of AD began selling oil to Cuba, for example.

The system had several weaknesses which would eventually prove fatal. The armed forces were bought off with arms purchases, perks and a top-heavy command structure, and allowed to run their own affairs without civilian oversight. Political power was highly centralised: until 1989, state governors and mayors were appointed, not elected. Some social groups were not well represented by the two main parties. That was especially true of the urban poor. From the mid-1970s onwards Venezuela's economy failed to create anything like enough jobs to employ a rising population. The swelling urban informal sector was in practice excluded from a social protection system administered through trade unions. The civil service was underpaid, poorly trained, corrupt and politicised. As Moisés Naím, a minister in Pérez's second administration (1989–93), has pointed out, Venezuela's democracy spent far more than the Latin American average on social programmes. But in 1988 infant mortality was three times higher than in Chile, which spent only a third as much. Vaccination rates were half the regional average. Every few years, hospitals had to be re-equipped because of theft or neglect. Above all, the system depended for its smooth functioning on a rising level of oil revenue. But the ratio of government oil revenues to population fell from a peak of \$1,540 per person in 1974 to \$382 in 1992 (and \$315 by 1998).[17] By 1989, 53 per cent of Venezuelans lived in poverty, up from 32 per cent in 1982, and income per head had receded to its level of 1973.[18]

The rise of Hugo Chávez

Venezuelans quickly dubbed it 'the coronation'. For three days in February 1989, champagne flowed ceaselessly as waiters circulated with plates of lobster for hundreds of guests thronging the Teresa Carreño theatre, a brutalist concrete labyrinth next to the Hilton Hotel in the centre of Caracas. Middle-Eastern oil sheikhs rubbed shoulders with Fidel Castro, Spain's Felipe González and Dan Quayle, on his first foray abroad as vice-president of the United States. The motive was the inauguration of Carlos Andrés Pérez as president of Venezuela for the second time.[19] He had won AD's nomination against the wishes of the party hierarchy. Pérez was popular. Venezuelans remembered that in his first term (1974–79) he had nationalised the oil and iron-ore industries. He had poured oil profits into new state-owned heavy industries, including a Soviet-style complex comprising massive steel, aluminium and hydropower plants at Ciudad Guayana, deep in the interior. Those were the days when *Venezuela Saudita* ('Saudi Venezuela'), as it was dubbed, imported more Scotch whisky per head than any other country and Concorde connected Caracas to Paris. Pérez had only narrowly escaped corruption charges after his first term.[20] Many voters took the cynical view that having already enriched himself he would not need to steal. At a huge rally to close his campaign, he promised 'full employment' and insisted that 'we won't pay the debt at the cost of sacrificing welfare and development'.[21] He won 53 per cent of the vote.

Pérez inherited a bankrupt government and country. In 1988 the fiscal deficit was 9.4 per cent of GDP, the current-account deficit was the largest in Venezuela's history and the price of everything from bank loans to medicines and staple foods was artificially held down.[22] To take one example, petrol, at the equivalent of just 20 American cents a gallon, was cheaper than anywhere in the world except Kuwait. The difference with the average world price – and thus the implicit, indiscriminate, subsidy – was equal to 10 per cent of the national budget.[23] No matter that he had campaigned otherwise: Pérez realised that reform was unavoidable, as Fujimori in Peru and Menem in Argentina were to do shortly afterwards. He appointed a talented team of free-market technocrats who launched a radical programme intended to shift Venezuela from state-led import-substitution to export-led growth. But the president, a machine politician accustomed to 'administering abundance' as he had put it in the 1970s, proved a poor salesman for austerity and reform. And it soon became clear that the years of easy money had rotted the Venezuelan state to its foundations.

Within three weeks of the 'coronation', Venezuela was shaken by urban rioting on a scale hitherto seen in Latin America only in Bogotá in 1948 following the murder of Gaitán. The immediate trigger was a botched decision to double the petrol price. Not only did Pérez fail to explain the need for this, but officials also failed to enforce an agreement that bus operators would only raise fares by an initial 30 per cent.[24] On Monday 27 February – the end of the month when many people tended to be short of cash – commuters were faced with an abrupt doubling of fares. Small protests by radical students were joined by angry commuters. From the capital and its suburbs, the protests spread to a dozen other towns and cities, encouraged by live television coverage. By mid morning, the crowds began to loot shops. The Caracas police had only just ended their first-ever strike, and stood idly by as the slums were enveloped by chaotic and leaderless rage. The government seemed paralysed. After thirty hours of chaos, Pérez ordered the army to restore order. Over the three days of what became known as the *Caracazo* some 400 people were killed, according to a careful analysis by human-rights groups. Most were civilians shot by the security forces.[25] Some 3,000 shops, including 60 supermarkets, were destroyed in the Caracas area, most of them serving the *ranchos*, as the tightly packed slums that cling to the hillsides are called.

The *Caracazo* was a profound shock to a peaceful democracy. Pérez pressed on with the reforms, but he had been forced onto the defensive politically right from the outset. The reforms did produce growth. But they were incomplete: inflation remained stubbornly high, the fiscal situation remained fragile and labour laws unreformed. The government was slow to put in place an effective anti-poverty programme. A much-needed reform of bank supervision was held up by opposition in Congress, including from Pérez's own party. The riots had another unexpected consequence. Hugo Chávez, an army major, concluded that the conditions were ripe for his longstanding dream of overthrowing what he saw as a corrupt democracy. 'It was the moment we were waiting for to act,' he would say later.[26]

Chávez had long nurtured a sense of himself as a man of destiny. A typical Venezuelan *mestizo*, of mixed African, indigenous and European descent, he grew up in respectable poverty in Sabaneta, a small town in the depths of the Venezuelan *llanos* (plains) in Barinas state.[27] His father was a teacher, his mother a teaching assistant. Like so many other ambitious Latin Americans of modest provincial background, he joined the army as a way of getting ahead. Gradually, radical politics displaced baseball in his affections. But his initial inspirations were not Marx, nor even Fidel Castro. As a young cadet, he travelled to Peru for the 150th anniversary of the Battle of Ayacucho and was received by the president, General Juan Velasco Alvarado. Chávez was a fervent admirer of Velasco's military socialism, as he was of Omar Torrijos, the Panamanian strongman who negotiated a 1977 treaty wresting ownership of the Panama Canal from the United States. Through childhood friends and his elder brother, Adán, Chávez met leaders of small left-wing groups founded by survivors of Venezuela's guerrillas of the 1960s. From one of them, Douglas Bravo, Chávez adopted the image of a 'three-rooted tree' of radical nationalism drawn from Venezuelan history – an inspiration to which he constantly refers. The first root was Bolívar. What Chávez saw in the Liberator was not the conservative aristocrat who admired Britain and the United States. Rather, he imagined Bolívar as a radical anti-imperialist. The second root was Simón Rodríguez (who sometimes called himself Samuel Robinson), a tutor and friend of Bolívar and an eccentric educator, socialist and early champion of indigenous rights. The third was Ezequiel Zamora, a liberal general in Venezuela's endless 'federal wars' of the mid nineteenth century. One of Zamora's slogans was 'Lands and free men: horror to the oligarchy'. Chávez took him as a pioneer of agrarian reform, though he was a *hacendado*. Zamora died after being shot in the back by one of his own men – a fate which Chávez seems to fear. He is said to have confided to friends that he thinks himself to be the reincarnation of Zamora.[28] Chávez later added a fourth root to the tree: Pedro Pérez Delgado (whose nom de guerre was *Maisanta*), the son of a lieutenant of Zamora's and sometime social bandit whom Chávez claimed as his great-grandfather.

In 1983, the year of the 200th anniversary of Bolívar's birth, with three other young officers Chávez formed the Bolivarian Revolutionary Movement-200 (MBR-200). On the date itself, they gathered under a celebrated samán tree near Maracay where their hero had rested after a battle. There they repeated the oath of liberation that Bolívar is said to have sworn in the company of Simón Rodríguez after they had climbed Monte Sacro in Rome. Two years after the *Caracazo*, Chávez and his friends were promoted to the rank of lieutenant-colonel. That rank is popularly known in Latin American armies as *comandante*. And indeed, for the first time, they had command of troops – in Chávez's case a parachute battalion at Maracay, the army's main garrison just 70 miles (110 kilometres) south-west of Caracas. At last, they could put their conspiracy into effect. On the night of 3 February 1992, Chávez set off with 460 conscripts, telling them they were going on a training exercise. In fact, their destination was Caracas and the exercise was a military coup in which they were joined by four other lieutenant-colonels with some 1,900 further troops. The conspirators seized positions in the capital as well as in Maracaibo and Valencia, the country's second and third cities. But Pérez, their target, eluded them. The night before Pérez had returned from the World Economic Forum at Davos, where he had received the plaudits of international bankers and businessmen. He managed to broadcast a message denouncing the coup and rallying loyal troops. Ironically, given Castro's subsequent alliance with Chávez, one of the first messages from abroad supporting Pérez came from the Cuban leader.[29]

The coup failed. Chávez's bid to seize power from a democratically elected government had cost 20 dead (14 of them soldiers), and left several dozen wounded. But it turned into a political triumph. Pérez's defence minister allowed a defeated Chávez to broadcast, live, a brief call to his supporters to surrender. For the first time, Venezuelans glimpsed Chávez's innate skill as a communicator: 'Companions, unfortunately, *for now*, the objectives that we set ourselves in the capital were not achieved ... I assume responsibility for this Bolivarian military movement.'[30] This brief broadcast turned him into a hero to many citizens of an unhappy republic. The phrase 'for now', which he later said had been unconscious, seemed to signal a continuing movement. His ready acceptance of responsibility for his actions contrasted with the self-serving evasions of the politicians. He had crystallised popular disillusion with political leaders and corruption which, in hard times, had suddenly become unbearable to previously complaisant Venezuelans. He had managed to identify himself in the public mind with the sainted Bolívar, Venezuela's only unquestioned hero. He had exposed the weakness of the Punto Fijo state. The MBR-200 had been almost reckless in its preparations but had not been stopped – just as the interior ministry had failed to anticipate or respond to the *Caracazo*. The conspirators enjoyed much military sympathy. Officers' salaries had declined so that they could no longer afford cars or decent housing; a lieutenant was taking home the equivalent of $200 a month in 1991.[31] Months later, a group of senior officers staged a second, bloodier, rebellion. In several hours of fighting, in which Mirage fighter jets buzzed the capital, 142 civilians and 29 soldiers were killed. The rebels possessed a tape recorded by Chávez in prison, in which he called for the population to join the rising (though in the end this was not broadcast).[32] Repelled by the violence, they did not. But that did not save Pérez. His approval rating had dipped into single figures in opinion polls. In 1993, the hapless president was impeached. Ironically, given Chávez's subsequent massive off-budget financing and use of billions of dollars of public funds for foreign diplomacy, Pérez was sentenced to 28 months of house arrest for misappropriating a mere $17 million, which he said he had used in part to help Violeta Chamorro win the 1990 presidential election in Nicaragua.

Another irony surrounding the collapse of *puntofijismo* was that its final gravedigger was one of its original authors: Rafael Caldera, an elderly COPEI leader who had been Venezuela's president from 1969 to 1974. The Punto Fijo Pact had taken its name from that of Caldera's Caracas house, where it was signed in 1958. In February 1992, in a special session of Congress, he expressed sympathy for the aims of Chávez's coup attempt, though not the method. Breaking with COPEI, Caldera stood for the presidency in 1993 as an independent at the head of a coalition of 17 small parties, mainly of the left. He won, but with only 30.5 per cent of the vote. Caldera – who would be aged 83 by the time he left office in 1998 – tried vainly to turn the clock back. For the first two years of his government, he abandoned economic reform and reimposed controls. But within days of his taking office, the economy was dealt another heavy blow when Banco Latino, the country's second-largest bank, collapsed. That triggered a run on the financial system. Misguidedly, the Caldera government pumped liquidity into the stricken banks while leaving their owners in charge. In vain: much of the new money went swiftly abroad while 13 banks, accounting for 37 per cent of total deposits, duly went bust in 1994. The bailout cost the state the equivalent of 21 per cent of GDP.[33] The bank bust wiped out an important segment of Venezuelan business, while further undermining the credibility of democratic government.

Caldera eventually realised that he had little choice but to relaunch Pérez's reform programme. He renamed it Agenda Venezuela. It was implemented by Petkoff, whom Caldera had made planning minister. The government tried to raise oil output by offering risk contracts to foreign companies for the first time since nationalisation. Given more time, Agenda Venezuela might have restored faith in the system. But it was too late. Desperate for change, in the 1998 presidential election Venezuelans turned once again to the candidate who expressed the most radical rejection of the status quo, as Caldera and Pérez had seemed to in 1993 and in 1988 respectively. This time it was Hugo Chávez, whom Caldera had pardoned after he had served just two years in prison. The former coup leader had been persuaded, reluctantly, that elections were a more effective route to power than force. To that end, he formed the Movimiento V República (MVR, or Fifth Republic Movement), which brought together his military and civilian supporters. He was backed, too, by two smallish left-wing parties. He promised a Constituent Assembly, action against corruption, and wage increases. He won 56.2 per cent of the vote.

The battle for Venezuela

In proclaiming a 'Fifth Republic' in Venezuela, Chávez was not invoking General Charles de Gaulle.[34] Rather he was signalling his intention to dismantle the Punto Fijo system. His first act as president was to order a referendum on convoking a Constituent Assembly, in which his supporters won 66 per cent of the vote but 95 per cent of the seats. On paper, the new constitution the assembly wrote did not involve big changes. However, it did increase the powers of the president. It extended the presidential term from five to six years, and introduced the possibility of a second consecutive term. It scrapped some of the decentralising measures introduced after 1989. In economic policy, it was a bit more statist, reversing a partial privatisation of the pension system approved by the Caldera government. Above all, the assembly was a tool which enabled Chávez to take control of all the organs of state. The assembly proclaimed itself sovereign, replacing the Congress elected in 1998 and the supreme court. But in other ways, Chávez began cautiously, making few changes to economic policy. He even invited foreign bids to explore for natural gas, and completed the privatisation of telecommunications.

At first, Chávez enjoyed overwhelming popular support. In a fresh general election held under the new constitution in July 2000, he was re-elected with 59 per cent of the vote while his coalition won 99 of 165 seats in the new unicameral National Assembly. Yet in little more than a year thereafter he managed to arouse a mass opposition movement bent on his overthrow. Several things contributed to this. Perhaps because he was achieving little real change, Chávez picked a series of verbal quarrels with interest groups such as the media, the Catholic Church, the trade unions and private business. Despite his ample majority in the National Assembly, he sought and was granted extraordinary legislative powers. He issued a decree which suggested that he might subject private schools to politicised inspections. In December 2001, he used his legislative powers to issue, without prior consultation with those affected, 49 laws including measures on land use and oil contracts. In themselves, these laws were not especially radical, although the land law gave the government power to determine what crops should be grown. But they crystallised fears that Chávez was bent on becoming a dictator. In November 1999, at a meeting with students in Havana University during his first state visit to Cuba, he surprised Venezuelans by proclaiming that 'Venezuela is travelling towards the same sea as the Cuban people, a sea of happiness and of real social justice and peace.'[35] He publicly expressed sympathy for Colombia's Marxist guerrillas. In 2001, he launched the Bolivarian Circles, intended to be a grassroots organisation to defend his regime, paid for out of public funds. Though probably modelled on the 'Dignity Battalions' of Panama's General Manuel Noriega, opponents compared them to Cuba's Committees for the Defence of the Revolution. He had already put the army in charge of a new social programme, the Plan Bolívar 2000, which quickly became the target of corruption allegations. Finally, Chávez sacked the board of Petróleos de Venezuela (PdVSA), the state oil company, appointing a new one headed by a leftist academic and made up of low-ranking employees picked for their political loyalty.[36] Chávez accused PdVSA of having become a state within a state, acting in its own interests rather than those of Venezuelans. But his opponents saw the company as a rare example of meritocratic efficiency and feared its subjection to political control.

All this fuelled a massive opposition movement, centred on the middle class, which staged a series of strikes and massive street demonstrations. Some sectors of the opposition were undemocratic, some comprised the remnants of the old order resisting Chávez's determination to extinguish them, but the majority were convinced democrats battling against what they saw as imminent military or communist dictatorship. The government organised counter-demonstrations in support of the president. But Chávez's approval rating in opinion polls had sunk to around 30 per cent. He had lost the middle class and the political middle ground. Several of his closest allies turned against him, including two of his co-conspirators of 4 February and Luis Miquilena, an octogenarian former communist who had persuaded Chávez to contest the 1998 election and who had presided over the Constituent Assembly.

Events moved to a head in April 2002. The unions and Fedecámaras, an umbrella private-sector lobby, declared an indefinite general strike cum lock-out, seeking the restoration of the PdVSA board. Unrest in the armed forces was palpable.[37] There is much evidence that a conspiratorial movement within the armed forces had been planning a coup for months. On 11 April, hundreds of thousands of opposition supporters marched through the centre of Caracas towards the Miraflores Palace. Gunmen opened fire on the demonstration, killing several people. Many senior army officers refused to obey Chávez's order – reminiscent of that of Pérez during the *Caracazo* – to put troops on the streets to repress the crowds.[38] On the evening of 11 April, the army command asked Chávez to resign. There is controversy as to whether he in fact did so. By one account, negotiations over his resignation broke down. Certainly, he did not submit a written resignation. But Chávez did take Fidel Castro's advice, delivered in a telephone call that night, and opted to surrender rather than to resist or to die in his palace like Salvador Allende.[39] As he had done on 4 February, Chávez showed cold realism, choosing strategic withdrawal after losing a battle. Had the army turned power over to the National Assembly and agreed to let Chávez go to Cuba as he requested, he might still be there today. But there was a 'coup within the coup'. Pedro Carmona, the president of Fedecámaras, proclaimed himself president, named an ultra-conservative cabinet which excluded even his labour allies, decreed the immediate closure of the National Assembly and the supreme court, and the abolition of the new constitution which had been approved by a large majority in a referendum only 28 months previously. Carmona was backed by a coterie of senior generals and admirals. But they had no direct command of troops. The army command withdrew its support. As diehard *chavistas* from the Caracas slums rioted on the streets (something which the private television channels chose not to cover), General Raúl Baduel, the commander of the parachute brigade, sent three helicopters to collect Chávez from his confinement at a naval base on the Caribbean coast and return him to the Miraflores presidential palace once again.[40] In four days of chaos and confusion, some fifty people had died. In the end, it was the army that restored Chávez to power, just as it was the army that had eased him out days before.

The coup was swiftly condemned by other Latin American governments – but not by the United States. Under George Bush the United States had become increasingly supportive of the Venezuelan opposition, especially after January 2002 when Otto Reich was appointed to be the State Department's top diplomat for Latin America. Reich, who was born in Cuba, had worked in the Reagan administration in an office conducting propaganda on behalf of the Nicaraguan *contras*. Chávez had irritated the Bush administration not just with his anti-American rhetoric and his affection for Colombia's guerrillas, but also by visiting Saddam Hussein in Iraq in 2000, and Iran and Libya the following year. Chávez's government would later go to great lengths to assert that the coup had been dreamed up in Washington – perhaps to try to distinguish it from his own effort of a decade earlier. The 2002 coup was 'manufactured by the CIA', Chávez claimed.[41] There is no evidence of this. Rather, a State Department official said publicly in February 2002 that US diplomats had told dissident Venezuelan officers that they would oppose any coup.[42] However, this was obscured by the failure of Reich and the administration to condemn the coup when it happened – an extraordinarily short-sighted and selective failure to support democracy in Latin America which sent a dangerous message.

Chastened by the coup, Chávez temporarily backpedalled, restoring the old PdVSA board and making a half-hearted call for dialogue. But the coup weakened the opposition more than it did the government, undermining its international legitimacy. Chávez moved quickly to strengthen his control over the armed forces. Seven months later, the opposition's most uncompromising leaders once again marched into the president's trap. Many of the military officers who had backed the April coup began a public protest in a square in Altamirano, an upper-middle-class district of Caracas. At the same time, Fedecámaras and the trade unions began an indefinite general strike. They were soon joined by PdVSA workers. Oil output plunged. The dispute cost $50 million a day, and wreaked huge economic damage. But to the disappointment of the military rebels, the army sat on its hands. Chávez opted to sit out the strike whatever its costs. When it collapsed after two months, the president seized direct control of a shattered oil company, sacking 18,000 workers, including many experienced professionals. Some of those who replaced them were untrained loyalists.

In its quest to unseat Chávez, the opposition belatedly arrived where it should have begun. As the strike ended in February 2003, the opposition movement collected 3.2 million signatures for a referendum to recall the president – a device inserted into the constitution by Chávez. Had the referendum been held in mid-2003, by his own admission Chávez would almost certainly have lost.[43] The economy was reeling: mainly because of the strike, by December 2003 GDP had shrunk to less than 85 per cent of its level of two years previously. Despite the rise in the oil price, poverty had continued to rise under Chávez, peaking at 60 per cent in 2004.[44] Opinion polls showed support for the president at only 30 per cent.

An elected autocracy

Three things came to Chávez's rescue. The first was the spectacular rise in the oil price, to which his own actions had made a modest contribution but which was mainly attributable to war in Iraq and rising demand in China and India. By 2005, higher prices had quadrupled Venezuela's annual oil revenues compared with 1998.[45] Second, with Cuban advice Chávez finally came up with more effective social programmes. Third, Chávez used judicial manoeuvring and his control of the electoral authority to delay the recall referendum. The opposition was obliged to collect the signatures again in December 2003. That the referendum was finally held, in August 2004, owed much to pressure from the Organisation of American States (OAS) and other Latin American countries. By then the economy was recovering and the new social programmes, called 'missions', were up and running. Chávez survived the referendum, winning by 59 to 41 per cent in an election in which 70 per cent of registered voters turned out (compared with an average of 55 per cent in previous elections). Opposition claims of fraud were not endorsed by observers from the Carter Center and the OAS. But Chávez's vote was undoubtedly boosted by the government's drive to register 2 million new voters, many of them immigrants who had waited years for naturalisation.[46]

Buoyed by his referendum victory, Chávez moved quickly to consolidate an elected autocracy. He used his majority in the National Assembly to name 12 new judges to the supreme court and sack others seen as disloyal. Many opposition voters no longer trusted the electoral authority. That prompted many to stay away from a local election in which the *chavistas* won control of all but two state governorships. In an election for the National Assembly held in December 2005, most opposition parties decided on a last-minute boycott. As a result, the *chavistas* won all the seats in the assembly. But only 25 per cent of registered voters turned out. A year later, the shattered opposition managed to rebuild, uniting behind the presidential candidacy of Manuel Rosales, the social democrat governor of the western state of Zulia (whose capital is Maracaibo, the second city). A new electoral authority, while not independent, made efforts to deal with some of the opposition's complaints. Once again, Chávez won easily, with 63 per cent of the vote against 37 per cent for Rosales.

Beginning a new six-year term, the president announced an acceleration of his drive to achieve 'twenty-first-century socialism', and for the first time said publicly that he was a communist. He planned to change the 1999 constitution to curb the powers of state governors and of mayors, and to allow his own indefinite re-election (an echo of the 'president for life' of Bolívar's Bolivian Constitution of 1826). Chávez obtained from the National Assembly power to legislate by decree for 18 months. Venezuela still had some of the outward trappings of democracy. The government was not overtly repressive. But, little by little, freedoms were being chipped away. A new media law prompted some self-censorship at radio and television stations, according to Petkoff, who has spent the past few years editing an independent newspaper.[47] After the 2006 election, Chávez declared that the government would not renew the broadcasting licence of RCTV, the biggest opposition television station. The government conducted low-level harassment of opponents, bringing trumped-up charges against several of them. A proposed law would make it difficult for NGOs receiving foreign donations to continue to function. Those on the list of the 3.4 million people who signed the petition for the recall referendum found themselves liable to be sacked from government jobs and denied public services, from passports to loans and contracts. Opposition political activities faced intermittent and selective violence from *chavista* gangs drawn from the slums. Some businesses faced abrupt demands to produce property titles. By provoking the opposition and polarising the country, Chávez had gained near-absolute power, exercising personal control not just over the legislature and the judiciary, but over PdVSA and the armed forces.

'We're starting to build our own socialist model,' Chávez claimed in 2005. To get a glimpse of what this entailed, officials directed foreign visitors to Catia, a gritty district a few miles west of the Miraflores Palace. There, a defunct petrol-distribution depot had been turned into a 'nucleus of endogenous development'.[48] That meant a combination of workers' co-operatives and social service provision, all paid for by PdVSA. Three new buildings surrounded a central meeting area. One housed a well-equipped health clinic. In a second, the government installed scores of sewing machines for a co-operative of 180 women. Their first contract, in 2005, was to make red T-shirts and caps for Venezuela's diplomats to wear on a May Day march. The third building was a co-operative making shoes. The hillside above had been planted with maize by another co-op, this one of market gardeners. Some 1,200 people worked in the 'nucleus', which cost $6.6 million to build. Across the road there was a small but well-stocked new supermarket run by Mercal, a state company set up by Chávez to provide cheap food for the poor. Mercal operated on largely commercial lines, but some of its prices were subsidised, at a cost of $25 million a month to the government. Nearby was a centre for the education 'missions' set up by Chávez. One programme, officially completed, taught illiterate adults to read. Two others allowed people to finish their primary or secondary education; a fourth gave cramming courses – and the promise of a place in an expanded university system – to 286,000 teenagers who failed to complete secondary school. The first and perhaps most appreciated of the 'missions' was *Barrio Adentro*, under which 16,000 Cuban doctors and dentists, lent by Fidel Castro in return for cheap oil, worked as general practitioners in the *ranchos*, where medical services were all but non-existent. So the 'Bolivarian revolution' indeed provided the urban poor with services they previously lacked. But it did so in a clientelistic fashion, in return for political loyalty. The 'missions' represented a parallel state, accountable to nobody but Chávez. Their financing was opaque – and they were almost certainly unsustainable.

Even more than its predecessor, the Fifth Republic was dependent on oil revenue. Thanks to the steep rise in oil prices, the economy recovered rapidly after the strike: GDP grew at over 10 per cent a year in 2005 and 2006. The private sector made money again but was slow to invest, because of uncertainty about its future. It was hemmed in by a web of controls and intermittent threats to property rights. Price controls on staples led to shortages of some products in 2006, as they had in the late 1980s. Banks were required to earmark 29 per cent of their loans for farming and housing, at subsidised rates, and rates on other loans were capped (again just as they had been in the 1980s). In the countryside, the government launched a noisy war on the *latifundio*. By mid-2006, around a hundred private farms deemed 'unproductive' had been taken over by the government or by squatters.[49] They included parts of an estate owned by Britain's Vestey family. For all of Chávez's vociferous denunciation of an 'oligarchy' of *latifundistas*, the fact was that agrarian reform had already been carried out by Pérez in the 1970s. Venezuela is an overwhelmingly urban country, and the state itself owns more than enough idle rural land to settle the landless. At the start of his new term, in January 2007, Chávez nationalised the main telecoms company, CANTV, which had been privatised by Pérez and in which Verizon, an American firm, had a 28.5 per cent stake. He also said the energy industry would be nationalised. He had already obliged multinational oil companies to accept new contracts in which they became minority partners in joint ventures; the same was due to happen to their investments in gas and in refineries that upgrade the heavy oil of the Orinoco belt.

The main feature of 'twenty-first-century socialism' was a massive increase in public spending as a result of the huge rise in oil prices, as well as the bigger share of oil revenue the government took through taxes and royalties on its joint-venture partners. The central government's budget rose from 20 per cent of GDP in 1999 to 27 per cent of GDP by 2005.[50] But there was much off-budget spending too. Chávez obliged the Central Bank to turn over $6 billion of its foreign-exchange reserves to FONDEN, a slush fund under his control. In addition, PdVSA diverted several billion dollars from its investment budget to the same fund. In 2006 the government had an extra $21 billion at its disposal from these sources, according to one estimate.[51] Despite its huge oil windfall, until 2005 the government ran a fiscal deficit, and the public debt rose. Some of the money was lavished on new state companies, such as an airline; other planned state ventures included mining, iron and steel and cement firms, and tractor and computer factories.[52] Another chunk went on the government-funded co-operatives. In the first two years of this programme 6,814 'productive units' were created, and 264,720 participants given training, according to the government. In 2006 alone, officials planned to train another 700,000 people and create 28,000 new co-operatives or other community associations.[53] In this Chávez was copying Velasco's Peru which, in a similar top-down manner, sponsored hundreds of co-operatives. Only a handful survive today. So abundant did the oil money become that Chávez had plenty available to spend on promises of foreign aid designed to win allies and influence abroad. According to an estimate by an opposition newspaper, in the seven months to January 2006 alone Chávez made aid commitments totalling $25.9 billion.[54]

The reviving economy and the torrent of public spending finally began to cut poverty, from 49 per cent in 1999 to 37 per cent by 2005. Given the extraordinary increase in oil revenue, the record of the Chávez government in reducing poverty was not outstanding compared with that of several others in the region who lacked such wealth. The 'Bolivarian revolution' was enormously expensive, but all the evidence suggests that it was rather incompetent. Despite its cornucopia of resources, the Fifth Republic neglected Venezuela's basic infrastructure. This was dramatised in January 2006 when a viaduct carrying the motorway which links Caracas to the international airport and the port of La Guaira had to be closed because of subsidence (the viaduct collapsed weeks later). For several weeks, the half-hour journey from airport to city took five hours, until a temporary road cut that to three hours. Governments had known of the problem for two decades. Under Chávez, Venezuela has had six infrastructure ministers in seven years; the president normally shuffles more than half of his cabinet each year.[55] The social-welfare 'missions' were set up in parallel with a state health and education bureaucracy which remained unreformed. At 23 de Enero, a large public housing project dating from the 1950s and a stronghold of *chavismo*, the health clinic lacked X-ray plates and chemicals for pathology tests in January 2006. There were no medicines.[56] Violent crime increased steadily. The number of murders per year tripled between 1998 and 2005. Caracas became the most violent capital in South America. That was in large part because of the failure of the state to train its police forces adequately. The police themselves were responsible for many murders. In April 2006, the attorney general's office said that it was investigating 6,000 'extra-judicial executions'.[57] All the indications were that corruption was at least as prevalent, and probably much more so, than under previous governments. In a statement in 2005, Venezuela's Catholic bishops warned of 'wide and deep corruption in many areas'.[58] The difference with the past was that the auditor-general and attorney-general were no longer drawn from the opposition.

While opinion polls showed that many Venezuelans were dissatisfied with the government, Chávez himself remained popular, as the 2006 presidential election showed. His supporters tended to be poorer, darker-skinned Venezuelans. Many of them saw Chávez as one of themselves, and were linked to him by a quasi-religious bond. But many others merely valued the 'missions', the economic growth and the make-work programmes. Their loyalty was not unconditional. The big question for Chávez was what would happen if and when oil revenues fell substantially. By one estimate, the government would find it hard to sustain its levels of spending if benchmark prices fell much below $40 (others put that figure at $50).[59] Chávez has talked of expanding production, but there were doubts about Venezuela's capacity to do so. For the first time, institutional decay spread to PdVSA. After the 2002–3 strike, oil output fell. The company claimed that total national crude-oil production in 2005 was 3.3 million barrels per day (b/d), of which only 2.1 million came from fields operated by PdVSA and the rest from those managed by private companies. But according to the International Energy Agency, total output was only 2.7 million b/d. Chávez invited state oil companies to invest in Venezuela, including those from Iran and China. But it was not clear how much any outsiders would invest in Venezuela on the new contract terms.[60]

For all the defects of Chávez's regime, Venezuela in 2006 was not Cuba. Was it likely to become so? In 2004 Chávez had stated: 'We are not proposing to eliminate private property. Nobody knows what might happen in the future ... but at this moment it would be madness.'[61] The Fifth Republic adopted – and intensified – many of the economic policies that had brought down the Punto Fijo system when oil prices fell. The Venezuelan state continued to rely for political support on the distribution of oil revenue, it continued to neglect infrastructure and institutions, and it relied on a similar battery of economic controls. Just as its predecessor had provided social assistance to the organised working class, the Fifth Republic did so to the urban poor. But it could not give them sustainable jobs. Politically, Chávez had replaced the limited democracy of the Punto Fijo republic with a hybrid regime that, according to Petkoff, had 'one foot in democracy' and 'the other foot in authoritarianism and autocracy'.[62] Chávez reversed Punto Fijo's historic achievement of taking the armed forces out of politics. Instead of power being shared by two parties, it was concentrated in one man.

In the wake of the 2006 presidential election, Chávez announced plans to unify the MVR and the myriad *grupúsclos* that supported him into a single revolutionary party to be called the United Socialist Party of Venezuela. Hitherto, the absence of such a party had been a notable difference between Chávez's Venezuela and Castro's Cuba. The Bolivarian revolution rested on three pillars. One was the armed forces. In 2005, nine state governors were military officers, either retired or on active service; by one estimate, more than 500 senior government jobs were held by military men.[63] The second was Aló Presidente, his television chat show broadcast every Sunday. This usually lasted around five hours, but on occasion stretched to over seven hours. Chávez employs all his charm and *llanero* wit, telling jokes, interrogating officials, interviewing guests and generally getting his message across. The third pillar was Cuban political support. Cubans designed the 'missions', and provided specialist help in the form of doctors, sports trainers and literacy teachers. There were reports in 2006 that Cuba's intelligence service was assembling a national register of people and property. Some Cubans are reported to have been given Venezuelan nationality. A fourth potential pillar involved a planned new army reserve, supposed to be 1.5 million strong, and answerable directly to the president. This seemed to be a more ambitious – and armed

1 Simón Bolívar: the great Liberator left an ambiguous political legacy.

2 Francisco de Paula Santander, the forgotten liberal.

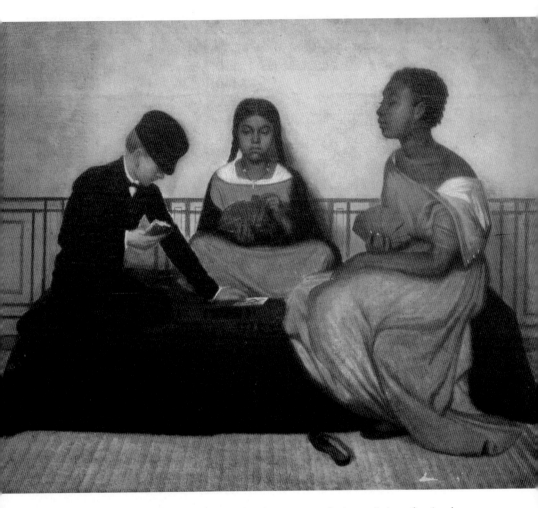

3 Francisco Laso's *Three Races or Equality before the Law*, an early denunciation of racism by a liberal Peruvian painter and writer.

4 Revolutionaries at Tampico – Mexico's revolution of 1910–17 created a corporate state.

5 Ernesto 'Che' Guevara (left) and Fidel Castro led a revolution in Cuba, but failed elsewhere.

6 In 1992 Hugo Chávez staged a failed coup against an elected government – something he would later suffer when in power.

7 Ricardo Lagos, a moderate socialist, in La Moneda.

8 & 9 Fernando Henrique Cardoso and Luiz Inácio Lula da Silva: contrasting reformers in Brazil.

10 Vicente Fox and Felipe Calderón: democracy finally arrived in Mexico in 2000.

11 A new, emerging middle class: proud first-time home-owners at a housing project in Mexico.

12 & 13 The changing face of Lima's shantytowns: Huáscar, San Juan de Lurigancho, 1985, and the Megaplaza shopping centre in the Cono Norte, 2004.

14 Bolivia's 'water wars': a protest in El Alto against water privatisation.

15 Child labour in the coca industry.

16 Álvaro Uribe, Colombia's man of destiny (watched by a portrait of Bolívar).

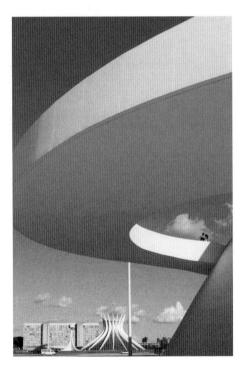

17 Oscar Niemeyer's buildings in Brasília: 'Le Corbusier took the right angle while I was concerned with curves'.

18 Evangelical protestantism – the new religion of Latin America's poor.

19 The Rio de Janeiro *favelas*: a failure of policing.

20 São Paulo: getting around by helicopter in Brazil's global city.

– version of the Bolivarian Circles. Its purpose was ostensibly to defend the 'revolution' against the United States, but it was probably intended as a means of intimidating the opposition.

For Venezuela, the big unanswered question was whether Chávez would ever allow himself to be freely voted out of office. Some of the regime's critics, such as Petkoff, trusted in the residual strength of Venezuela's democratic culture, and the influence of international opinion, as a restraint on the president. There was much polling evidence that a majority of Venezuelans valued democracy, and that they understood 'socialism' to mean social programmes, not Cuban-style communism. Strikingly, in the 2006 Latinobarómetro poll, 70 per cent of respondents in Venezuela agreed that democracy was the best system of government, down from 78 per cent in the 2005 poll but still a higher percentage than in all but four other countries in the region.[64] But according to another view, Chávez has 'virtually eliminated the contradiction between autocracy and political competitiveness' and 'has refashioned authoritarianism for a democratic age.'[65]

There was no longer a Soviet nuclear umbrella under which Chávez could shelter, as Fidel Castro did in 1962. For all his rhetorical attacks on the 'empire', the United States remained the main export market for Venezuela's oil. But in his search for allies abroad, Chávez did seem to be seeking to buttress himself against potential hostility in the Americas to any lifetime presidency. He offered oil to China, though transport costs and the need to adapt refineries to Venezuela's sulphurous crude meant that exports on any scale were probably several years away. He bought arms from Russia. And he made friends with Iran, defending its nuclear ambitions.

He increasingly seemed to see himself as Castro's successor. He conceived the Bolivarian revolution to be continental in scope, like its Cuban predecessor. Yet rather than a twenty-first-century socialist, Chávez most resembled some of the political figures from Latin America's past: the twentieth-century populists and the nineteenth-century military *caudillos*. Like Perón and the other populists, he has created a personalist regime, blurring the boundaries between leader, party, government and state. Like them, he used the mass-communications media effectively. Like them, he used elections as his route to power but ignored the checks and balances and pluralism inherent in democracy. Like them, he engaged in unsustainably expansionary economic policies. Like Rosas and the *caudillos* of the Argentine interior in the 1830s, he commanded a private army in the shape of the reserve. Like Rosas, as well as like Castro, he seemed to see himself as pretty much president for life. In a speech in 2005, he said that he did not intend to retire until 2030, the bi-centenary of Bolívar's death, by which time he will be 76. As long as the oil price remained high, the odds were that Chávez would cling to power for many more years. But given its inefficiencies, keeping the Bolivarian show on the road required ever more money. It is not hard to envision the regime imploding amid fights over corruption and cash. If the oil price were to fall sharply, Venezuela would face an appalling hangover. The Caldera government had belatedly established a fund to save windfall oil revenues, with the aim of cushioning the effect on the economy when the oil price falls. Chávez scrapped that arrangement, and spent like there was no tomorrow. The prospect facing Venezuela might not be that of turning into a second Cuba but a second Nigeria – a failed petro-state.[66]

Supporters of Chávez liked to claim that he was the leading figure in a uniform regional wave of anti-American leftism. Certainly, he was not alone in trying to extract more of the the rents from the oil industry. After a period in which low oil prices had given multinational oil companies much leverage in contract negotiations, they had to yield to 'resource nationalism' in many parts of the world. In Latin America, Evo Morales was Chávez's closest disciple. On Chávez's advice, he decreed the 'nationalisation' of Bolivia's oil and gas industry; he later signed new, tougher, contracts with the multinational companies involved in which they became sub-contractors of a revived state energy company. Like Chávez, Morales summoned a Constituent Assembly to rewrite the constitution, which offered the potential for him to put his supporters in charge of all the institutions of state. In Ecuador, Rafael Correa seemed set on following a similar course. What these countries had in common with Venezuela was the availability of revenues from oil or natural gas. So it was possible that their presidents might be able to imitate Chávez's strategy of appropriating those revenues and redistributing them to create a mass political clientele. But the scale of those revenues was far greater in Venezuela, and Bolivia and Ecuador were politically very fragmented. In Bolivia, Morales was backed by a genuine and variegated mass movement that was likely to be critical of any pretensions to one-man rule. Even if they wanted to imitate Chávez, it was not certain that either Morales or Correa could do so. Still less was this the case for Daniel Ortega in Nicaragua, with no oil or gas revenues. He seemed likely to try to maintain friendly relations with both Venezuela (to get its aid) and with the United States (for its Central American trade agreement). Elsewhere in the region there were several other policy models which combined social democracy and a market economy in differing, more progressive and more sustainable ways. By far the most successful was at the other end of South America from Venezuela, in Chile.

CHAPTER 8

THE REFORMIST RESPONSE

Twenty years ago, the Casablanca valley was a dusty place of sleepy farms through which traffic crawled on a narrow road linking Santiago, Chile's capital, with Valparaíso, its largest port. Today, the valley floor is carpeted with mile after mile of trim vineyards. They produce good quality white wine, in a country which until recently had been known in the world only for cheap but reliable *vino tinto*. A fast new toll motorway snakes through the valley and over the dun-coloured hills to the coast. It was built and maintained by private investment under a public–private partnership. Beside the motorway stands an unobtrusive white building that houses the laboratory of Vitro Centre Chile. Opened in 2004, the laboratory turns out partially fattened lily bulbs using up-to-date biotechnology. It is a joint venture among local private investors, a Dutch firm and Fundación Chile, a public–private technology agency. It began on a small scale, employing 43 people. But its founders hoped to be exporting lily bulbs to Holland within a few years, competing for a slice of a $750 million world market, and to have established a new high-tech flower-export business.[1] If they succeed, they will follow a long line of new export industries created in Chile in recent decades, such as fish-farming, wine, fruit and furniture. The country is making a successful living out of its natural resources, partly by adding value to them.

The Chilean model: reform deepened by democracy

Uniquely in Latin America, Chile has achieved sustained and rapid economic growth over the past two decades, and as a result has seen poverty fall sharply. Over that period (1987–2006) its economy grew at an annual average rate of 6 per cent. The equivalent figure for Latin America as a whole was just 2.8 per cent. Even in 1998 to 2003, when the rest of Latin America stalled, Chile still managed to grow at an annual average of 2.8 per cent – once again more than twice the regional rate. From 2004 onwards, growth has returned to an annual rate of around 4 to 5 per cent. Keep it up, and in another decade or so Chile will have achieved developed country status, with a similar income per head to Portugal, Greece or Spain today.[2] True, income distribution in Chile is much more unequal than in those countries. But poverty has fallen sharply, from a peak of 45 per cent of the population in the mid-1980s to 19 per cent by 2004 and 13.7 per cent by 2006.

It is an uncomfortable fact for democrats that the foundations of Chile's dynamic export-led growth were laid by General Pinochet – but only through a costly process of trial and error. Shortly after seizing power Pinochet entrusted the economy to the 'Chicago Boys', a group of neo-conservative economists trained at the University of Chicago. They implemented a drastic adjustment, which saw the fiscal deficit fall from 25 per cent of GDP in 1973 to 1 per cent in 1975, and a radical programme of structural reform. This included large-scale privatisation (though the copper and oil firms were kept in state hands), and the opening of a previously closed economy. Import tariffs were cut from an average of 110 per cent in 1973 to 14 per cent by 1979, and all restrictions on the financial system lifted. The Chicago Boys ignored the short-term social cost of their policies. They also made policy mistakes. In privatising, they paid no heed to competition or regulation. The result was that the economy came to be dominated by a clutch of highly indebted conglomerates centred on the privatised banks.[3] This mistake was compounded by a second one. Worried that inflation was slow to fall, in 1978 the government fixed the exchange rate. The peso quickly became overvalued, prompting an import boom and allowing the conglomerates to borrow dollars cheaply abroad. In 1982, Chile went bust, hit harder by the debt crisis than any other Latin American country. The economy shrank by 14 per cent. In 1983, real wages fell more than 10 per cent and unemployment climbed to 30 per cent (including people on a government make-work programme). The financial system collapsed, and was re-nationalised. The bank bailout would lumber the government with liabilities equivalent to 35 per cent of GDP.

In its aftermath, a new economic team implemented more pragmatic, gradualist policies. Tariffs were temporarily raised, some prices were indexed and inflation would not reach single figures until 1995. To prevent overvaluation of the exchange rate, which was pegged close to inflation, the government imposed a tax on short-term capital inflows. A second round of privatisation, which included the utilities and the pension system, was carried out with more attention to regulation. Growth resumed, and this time it was sustained. The reforms had worked – but they took much longer to do so than their authors had assumed. By the early 1990s, Chile could be hailed as a 'textbook example of an open economy'.[4]

The governments of the centre-left Concertación coalition that have ruled Chile since 1990 kept the broad thrust of the dictatorship's economic policies, deepened some of them and reformed others. That bestowed democratic legitimacy on the 'Chilean model'. Since 1990, income per head has more than doubled. Growth has remained high but has been less volatile than under the dictatorship. It has been driven by exports and by investment. In 1970, exports were equal to just 12 per cent of Chile's GDP; in 2005, that figure was 41 per cent. In the 15 years to 2003, exports almost quintupled, while the share accounted for by copper fell from 80 per cent in the 1960s to 40 to 50 per cent. Under Ricardo Lagos, a moderate socialist who was president from 2000 to 2006, Chile deepened its commitment to open trade, signing free-trade agreements with the United States, the European Union and South Korea. From the late 1980s onwards, the rate of investment climbed steadily to reach around 25 per cent of GDP, well above the regional average. Uniquely in the region, most of this investment has been financed by an increase in national savings, which rose from 8 per cent of GDP in 1985 to 27.1 per cent a decade later. Those savings came partly from a consistent budget surplus, partly from the privatisation of the pension system by the dictatorship, but mainly from high levels of savings and investment by business, encouraged by a 1984 reform which cut taxes on re-invested profits.[5] The Concertación governments placed greater emphasis on social policy, partly to repair the lack of social investment by the dictatorship and partly to try to reduce inequality. Their approach has been cautious. In 2004, public spending in Chile was only 22 per cent of GDP – the same share as in 1987, pointed out Nicolás Eyzaguirre, a Harvard-educated former IMF official who was Lagos's finance minister.[6] But rapid growth and a reduction in military spending meant, for example, that spending on education tripled in the decade after 1990. Under a government-backed housing programme, *campamentos* (shantytowns) were all but eliminated. Lagos set out to abolish extreme poverty in Chile, through a programme called *Chile Solidario*. His government also introduced unemployment insurance. The Concertación governments drew on private investment, operating under public contracts, to upgrade the country's infrastructure. More than 2,000 kilometres of motorways were built, and airport capacity tripled.[7]

What explains Chile's remarkable success? The first factor, without doubt, is effective economic policies. These assign clear roles to market and state. 'The market is essential for growth and democracy is essential for governance,' as Lagos has put it.[8] Under the Concertación, the state has concentrated on regulating markets, rather than intervening in them. Fiscal policy has long been prudent, and has become increasingly sophisticated. In contrast to Venezuela, Chile saves in a 'stabilisation fund' part of its windfall when copper revenues are high. As a result, alone in the region Chile was able to increase social spending during the recession (mild in its case) of 2000 to 2002, enabling it to break with its past cycles of boom and bust. Lagos codified this counter-cyclical fiscal policy in a rule. This requires the government to record a fiscal surplus of 1 per cent when the economy is growing at its potential (as defined by an independent panel of experts) and when the copper price is at its expected long-term average (as forecast by a second panel). If either figure is below par, the government can spend more. The surplus required under the rule is in part to defray the liabilities from the 1982 banking collapse.[9] This fiscal rigour means that public debt stood at just 12 per cent of GDP at the end of 2004, and has given Chile Latin America's best credit rating and some of its lowest interest rates. As the copper price went through the roof in 2005 and 2006, the government once again faced the challenge of trying to prevent the peso from appreciating too much. The response was characteristic. The administration of Michelle Bachelet, who succeeded Lagos as president in March 2006, announced that on top of the existing copper-stabilisation fund, it planned to set aside an amount equal to about 0.5 per cent of GDP per year in a pension-guarantee fund whose proceeds will be invested abroad.[10] But fiscal rigour and respect for markets has been combined with a dose of pragmatism – and even heterodoxy. The dictatorship did not privatise Codelco, the state-owned firm which is the world's largest copper producer, partly because some of its profits went to the armed forces for arms purchases. The Concertación governments have kept Codelco in state hands, but encouraged private (including foreign) investment in new mines and reduced the proportion of its profits spent on arms. Similarly, the controls on capital inflows were counter to IMF orthodoxy, but are now widely accepted to have helped Chile avoid financial instability (they were abolished when the Central Bank adopted a floating exchange rate in 1998).

As important as the policies themselves is the broad political consensus that sustains them. This was forged in negotiations over the transition to democracy after Pinochet lost a 1988 referendum on staying in power. From this consensus derives policy stability. In Chile, unlike in many other countries in the region, businesses can afford to make long-term investments, knowing that political surprises are highly unlikely. That applies equally to private investment in infrastructure, and explains why Chile has the most modern network of roads, ports and airports of anywhere in the region. This policy environment eventually spawned a dynamic business class in Chile, helped by deep capital markets. Though foreign investment is welcome, Chile is notable for a large number of home-grown companies, many of which have begun to invest in other Latin American countries.

A third factor is relatively solid institutions, such as the civil service and courts – a legacy of the country's long tradition of constitutionalism and the rule of law dating from Diego Portales. The core institutions of the Chilean state never became as subservient to political forces as in Peronist Argentina or in Venezuela.[11] When the reforms started, educational levels were reasonably high. And some of the groundwork for diversification had been laid. CORFO, a state development agency founded in 1939, and other state bodies such as the Institute for Fisheries Development (IFOP), helped to develop new industries such as fruit, forestry and fish-farming.[12] An important role, too, was played by Fundación Chile. This unique body was set up in 1976 as a joint venture between the government and ITT, an American conglomerate whose assets were expropriated by Allende. ITT's half of the Fundación's $50 million capital came from the compensation it was paid, and was an attempt to improve a corporate image damaged by allegations that it had conspired with the CIA against Allende. The Fundación helped develop the salmon and wine industries by bringing in foreign technology and consultants and setting up laboratories for quality control. Nowadays it concentrates on research and development and its application to business through start-ups in which it always seeks private partners and itself drops out once a business is viable. 'It's a new way of doing development policy, much more tied to markets and public–private partnerships,' according to Juan Pablo Arrellano, a former education minister who was the Fundación's director during the Lagos government.[13]

The conservative opposition claims that Chile's economy is losing some of its dynamism. In particular, it blames relatively high rates of youth unemployment on a labour law that increased collective-bargaining rights. But Chile still scores highly on the Index of Economic Freedom published each year by the Heritage Foundation, a conservative American think-tank. In 2006 it was ranked 15th, ahead of such European countries as Germany and Spain. Similarly, in its 2005 ranking of competitiveness, the World Economic Forum, a Swiss body, ranked Chile 23rd, well ahead of any other Latin American country. It commented that 'Chile continues to benefit from a combination of remarkably competent macroeconomic management and public institutions, which have achieved EU levels of transparency and efficiency: only 8 of the 25 EU members have stronger performances in the area of public institutions.'[14] The campaign for the presidential election of December 2005 revealed a widespread consensus in Chile that sustaining growth requires government action to improve the quality of education and to provide further stimulus for innovation and research and development. In 2004 the government pushed through a law setting up a national innovation fund to be paid for with a new royalty of up to 3 per cent on the profits of mining companies. Nowadays Chilean policy-makers like to compare their country with other small, open economies in the developed world, such as New Zealand, Ireland and Finland, rather than with its Latin American neighbours.

Chilean democracy has become increasingly self-confident. For much of the 1990s, the Concertación coalition had to govern in the shadow of Pinochet and his supporters, who exercised much influence over the army, business and the media. More than in most countries, the transition to democracy was a negotiation. Under this deal, Pinochet stayed on as army commander for seven years, the civilian government was saddled with a military-dominated national security council, and former military commanders were among nine appointed senators who gave the conservative opposition a veto over constitutional change. Pinochet's arrest in London in 1998, at the request of a Spanish court, proved to be a turning point. It emboldened Chile's judiciary to unpick parts of the amnesty that the dictatorship had granted itself for its abuses of human rights. By January 2005 some 300 retired officers, including 21 generals, were in jail or facing charges.[15] Lagos was both willing and able to adopt a more robust attitude than his two elected predecessors to making Chile 'a democracy above suspicion' as he put it. In 2005 the conservative opposition finally agreed to scrap the authoritarian clauses in the constitution. In other ways, too, Chile has become a palpably more relaxed place. The Lagos government pushed through laws abolishing the death penalty and film censorship, and legalising divorce (though abortion remains prohibited, even in cases where the mother has been raped or her life is endangered by the pregnancy). Talking in La Moneda, the palace where Allende had fallen, Lagos pointed to 'a wider cultural change in Chilean society' and 'a greater openness'.[16]

These changes were symbolised by the election of Michelle Bachelet as president in 2006. A paediatrician in her fifties, Bachelet came originally from the left wing of the Socialist Party and had spent part of her exile in East Germany. The main difference between her and Lagos was in her relative lack of political experience. As a candidate, she seemed hesitant on policy issues. But when asked about her life and how Chileans see her, she became animated, a note of passion entering her voice. Bachelet's father was an air force general who sympathised with Allende. He died of a heart attack while in prison after the coup; both she and her mother were briefly detained and ill-treated in Villa Grimaldi, the headquarters of the DINA, Pinochet's notorious intelligence agency, before going into exile in Australia and then East Germany. Rather than her socialist politics, what made her election remarkable in a country long held to be the most socially conservative in Latin America was that she is an agnostic and has three children by two different men, neither of whom she lives with. 'The polls show that more than half of Chileans think I'm the person who best represents Chile,' Bachelet said. 'I have a different sort of family, but one that is similar to a third of Chilean families.'[17] In her first year in office, Bachelet looked less than assured. She handed economic policy over to a competent American-educated team, but with only a couple of exceptions her first cabinet was as inexperienced as she was. She proclaimed her intention to promote a 'citizens' democracy,' with greater public participation in policy-making. But in May and June 2006, her government was shaken by protests by school students, backed by many parents and teachers, over the poor quality of education. It was the biggest display of discontent since the end of the dictatorship. With the state's coffers overflowing with record copper revenues, the protestors demanded that the government breach its fiscal rules and spend more on schools.[18] Yet the problem of education is as much one of management as of lack of money. The government stood firm, at some cost to its popularity.

Such disagreements are the lifeblood of a normal democracy – which is what Chile has at last become. Purists might argue that its transition to democracy will not be complete until there has been alternation of power. That is partly because some Chileans will remain unconvinced that the conservative opposition has itself embraced democracy, as Franco's supporters in Spain's Popular Party did. Yet one can hardly blame the government for not losing an election. Not only does Chile's democracy now look consolidated. Its combination of market and state, growth and social policies, stands as a more powerful and effective example to the region than Chávez's sound and fury. Lagos, in particular, repeatedly tried to distinguish Chile's path both from events elsewhere in the region and from the neo-conservative policies of his country's recent past. 'How much of what we are seeing in Latin America is related to the simplistic belief of a few people that distribution can only occur in the context of populism? In our experience this will end in failure in the long-run. And how many others think that growth is enough, and the rest will come naturally?'[19] Of course, some of the factors in Chile's success were not easily exportable. But other countries, such as Peru – another open economy based on mining and export agriculture – have adopted elements of them.

Brazil: reform through democracy

Mention Chile, a country of just 15 million people, in mighty Brazil, and you will be greeted with derision. Brazil has followed its own path towards development over the past dozen years but like that of Chile over the same period it has been marked by democratic pragmatism. After a decade of false starts, with the Real Plan of 1993–4 Brazil finally began to stabilise its economy and embarked on modernising reforms of the kind adopted earlier elsewhere in the region. Reform in Brazil has been slow and incremental, democratic and consensual. It has involved bottom-up institution-building rather than top-down dictation. By 2006 there were fears that the reformist momentum had been lost. But what has been achieved looks more solid than in some other countries.[20]

There were several reasons why reform came late to Brazil. Unlike, say, Argentina, Brazil enjoyed rapid and almost uninterrupted economic growth for three decades until 1980. And unlike Argentina, Brazil had found ways of living with inflation, chiefly by generalised indexation under which wages, prices, debt payments and so on were adjusted automatically for past price increases. It was an effective but insidious system which aggravated inequality. Inflation rose steadily, but the annual rate only broke into three figures in 1980 and into four figures in 1988. 'Inflation gave to many people (but not to the great mass of poor Brazilians) the illusion of abundance,' noted Fernando Henrique Cardoso, who would eventually end it.[21] Another delaying factor was that the 1982 debt crisis and the economy's subsequent stutters coincided with a protracted – and accident-prone – transition from dictatorship to democracy. The generals and their supporters allowed free elections for state governors in 1982, but then snubbed a popular campaign for a direct election for president three years later. That ensured that the first civilian federal government in two decades would be weak. Tragically, it was weakened further when Tancredo Neves, the leader of the opposition party of the Brazilian Democratic Movement (PMDB) and the man chosen as president by the Congress, died before he could take office. His vice-president, José Sarney, took over, but as a longstanding supporter of the military regime who had switched sides at the last moment, he lacked Neves's legitimacy. The election in 1989 of Fernando Collor de Melo, a young telegenic politician from the backward north-eastern state of Alagoas, proved to be another false start. His technically flawed stabilisation plan failed. His high-handed treatment of Congress backfired; he resigned to avoid impeachment for corruption. His only lasting achievements were to have slashed import tariffs and begun to privatise the state's vast holdings. He was replaced by his vice-president, Itamar Franco, an undistinguished PMDB politician from Minas Gerais.

A third problem was that reform in a federal democracy is inevitably slow and complex. Brazil is simply too large and diverse ever to be a 'delegative democracy' in which the president can decree far-reaching change from the top.[22] With the brief exception of Vargas's *Estado Novo*, Brazil has always resisted absolutism: it is not coincidental that its monarchy was a constitutional one, and that its dictatorship of 1964–85 chose to keep the Congress in being and limited its military presidents to fixed six-year terms. To make matters even more difficult for reformers, Brazil's fledgling democracy equipped itself with a new constitution in 1988 which was riddled with flaws. It entrenched the failing economic model of statist nationalism and corporatist privilege just when this was going out of fashion across the world. It even included a constitutional cap on interest rates, at 12 per cent – a provision inevitably honoured in the breach. It gave all those who had worked in the public sector for five years absolute job tenure and full pension rights even though they had not sat competitive exams. As politicians rushed to exercise their new scope for patronage, federal government spending on personnel increased from 2.5 per cent of GDP in 1986 to 4.5 per cent in 1989.[23]

The constitution was drawn up at a time when the federal executive was weak, both in relation to the Congress and to the directly elected state governors and mayors who secured an exaggerated devolution of power and money, free from corresponding responsibilities. Cardoso, a senator in the Constituent Congress, later said that this body 'reminded me a lot of my time [teaching at the University of Paris] in Nanterre in May 1968 when it was forbidden to forbid'.[24] In reaction to the dictatorship's shackles on political parties, the politicians in Brasília rejected any rules that might impose party discipline on legislators. But they kept the gross over-representation of poorer and more backward northern and north-eastern states introduced by the generals to diminish the weight of democratic and progressive opinion in São Paulo and the south. Unlike other federal states, such as the United States and Germany, Brazil allows less-populated remote areas to be over-represented not just in the Senate but in the lower house too (as does Argentina). According to population, São Paulo should have 110, rather than its current 70, seats in the Chamber of Deputies while Roraima, on the border with Venezuela, should have just one rather than its current eight. Over-representation of sparsely populated areas in the Senate is even greater in Brazil than in the United States: one vote for the senate in Roraima has equal weight to 144 votes in São Paulo.[25] The Congress was given the power to revise the constitution five years after it came into effect, by simple majority rather than the normal 60 per cent vote. But when it came, in 1993, that opportunity was not taken, because Congress was reeling from a scandal in which members of the budget committee were found to have taken bribes from construction companies. Of 30,000 proposed amendments, only five were adopted.[26] One of these further weakened the executive by cutting the president's term from five to four years.

For a dozen years after the debt crisis broke in 1982, no government managed to stabilise the economy for more than a few months and much of the public goodwill towards the new democracy was squandered. Yet just when Brazil appeared ungovernable in democracy, matters were in fact beginning to change.[27] In May 1993, Cardoso was Brazil's foreign minister. He was at a dinner party in New York when he received a phone call from Itamar Franco, the eccentric interim president, who said he was thinking of making him finance minister. The job was a poisoned chalice. Inflation would top 2,700 per cent that year. Franco had already got through three finance ministers in seven months. Cardoso later recalled that by the time he went to bed he thought he had persuaded the president to desist. Franco appointed him regardless.[28] It was that 'accident' that would lead to Cardoso, a brilliant and cosmopolitan sociology professor who lacked the common touch, being elected president of Brazil for two successive terms. As finance minister, Cardoso assumed the role of de facto prime minister. He assembled a team of talented liberal economists who came up with the Real Plan, a clever mix of budget cuts, a new currency and a mechanism to break price indexation and inflationary expectations. According to Cardoso, 'The root cause of inflation in Brazil was really very simple. The government spent more than it earned.'[29] The forecast federal deficit in 1994 was $20 billion of a total budget of $90 billion. Yet dealing with the problem was not simple at all. As Cardoso noted, 'The budget was a work of fiction. The accounts of the Central Bank and the Treasury were mixed together and nobody knew much about either of them.'[30] Apart from budget reform, the groundwork also included putting an end to federal 'loans' to state governments which were rarely repaid and renegotiating the foreign debt.

Cardoso's team correctly perceived that Brazilians were fed up with inflation and would support almost any measures to end it. They secured Congressional approval in 1993 for cuts in spending and in constitutionally mandated transfers to states and municipalities. But unlike previous failed stabilisation plans, the Real Plan did not involve either wage or price freezes. Its centrepiece was a 'virtual' currency, known as the Unit of Real Value, which operated alongside the devalued *cruzeiro* for several months. This allowed relative prices to adjust, and persuaded Brazilians that the new currency – the *real*, launched on 1 July 1994 – would preserve its value. It worked: annual inflation fell to two digits by 1995 and to under 2 per cent by 1998. Unlike many other countries in the region, Brazil vanquished inflation without a recession. The increase in the real value of wages sparked a consumption boom. Economic growth averaged 4 per cent a year from 1994 to 1997 despite interest rates remaining high.

Only weeks before the launch of the *real*, it had seemed inevitable that Luiz Inácio Lula da Silva of the left-wing Workers' Party (PT), narrowly defeated by Collor in 1989, would win the 1994 presidential election. The success of the Real Plan turned the race upside down. Cardoso realised that he would win the election during a campaign stop in Santa Maria da Vitória, a small town in the backlands of Bahia, in the impoverished north-east, on 11 July 1994. The townspeople in the square held up one-*real* notes and asked him to autograph them. 'The *real* rescued hope and trust, not just in the currency and economic stabilisation, but in the country', Cardoso wrote.[31] While Lula, because of his personal journey from poverty to leadership, was a symbol in himself, Cardoso was not, and needed the symbol of the *real* to win. Bringing inflation under control in itself caused a 20 per cent drop in poverty.[32] Lula, the PT and the rest of the left made the mistake of opposing the Real Plan. Its success meant that Cardoso won the election outright with 54 per cent of the vote. Yet achieving the new president's goals of consolidating economic stability, integrating Brazil's economy with the world, modernising the state and tackling Brazil's social problems would involve a lengthy – and in 2006 still unfinished – political battle.

Cardoso's battle to modernise Brazil

Cardoso was the leader of the Brazilian Social Democratic Party (PSDB), which in 1988 had broken away from the amorphous PMDB. The PSDB, with strong support in São Paulo, Minas Gerais and Ceará in particular, was a mainly middle-class party of professionals and technocrats. It had a clearer programme than the catch-all PMDB. Cardoso defined the PSDB as 'a centre-left coalition of committed democrats ... We advocated a blend of free-market reform and social responsibility' in the mould of Felipe González in Spain, Bill Clinton in the United States and Tony Blair in Britain.[33] To support Cardoso's candidacy, the PSDB had formed a coalition with the conservative Liberal Front Party, and with the smaller Brazilian Labour Party (PTB). In office, Cardoso invited the PMDB to join the government. In theory, Cardoso's government enjoyed the support of 70 per cent of the Congress, making constitutional reform easy. Yet, in practice, changing the constitution was a Herculean task. It involved rounding up the votes of 60 per cent of the total membership of each house of Congress. This majority had to be mobilised not just for formal votes on constitutional bills, in two consecutive sessions of Congress, but to defeat line-by-line amendments by opponents. Many nominal government supporters regularly voted against it when public spending or corporatist privileges were at stake. Ideally, the government should have moved swiftly to achieve lasting fiscal stability by reforming the structure and financing of government at all levels. But these tasks were complex and politically divisive.[34] Instead, Cardoso opted to give priority to more straightforward bills to roll back the state monopolies enshrined in the constitution. In 1995, Congress approved constitutional amendments ending the state monopolies of oil, gas distribution, telecoms and merchant shipping, and another one to guarantee the same treatment to foreign companies operating in Brazil as to local firms. In all, in eight years, Cardoso's two administrations secured the approval of thirty constitutional amendments, most aimed at creating a modern social democratic state and all tenaciously opposed by the PT and other, smaller, left-wing parties.[35]

Yet despite these successes, Cardoso's governments were dogged by the difficulty of mobilising political support for fiscal reform in the teeth of myriad special interests. After the initial squeeze at the start of the Real Plan, the budget deficit steadily rose again: the public-sector borrowing requirement reached 8 per cent of GDP in 1998. There were several reasons, but most came down to a characteristically Brazilian vice: for decades, the better-off had turned the state into a device for lining their own pockets while robbing the poor through inflation. Once inflation ended, the state could no longer evade the bill for its misplaced generosity. One egregious example was the pension system. This broke just about every rule known to actuaries.[36] There was no minimum retirement age. This mattered less when life expectancy was short. In the 1950s there were eight workers for each pensioner, but by the 1990s there were just over two. In the public sector, retirees could draw more than one pension and carry on working as well; the retirement pension was often higher than the final salary. By 1997 the total value of pensions paid to 2.9 million people in the public sector exceeded those paid to almost 17 million private-sector pensioners by the National Social Security Institute (INSS). The INSS itself went into deficit, partly because pensions went up every time the minimum wage increased. Total federal government spending on pensions increased from $5.5 billion in 1992 to $16 billion in 1996. The pension system was a prime example of the way in which public spending in Brazil was skewed towards the better-off: in 1999 the richest 20 per cent of Brazilians received 65 per cent of government spending on pensions, while the poorest fifth got just 2.4 per cent.[37] Yet a constitutional amendment that would have brought some rationality to the system languished in Congress for years. The end of inflation exposed a number of other 'fiscal skeletons' as they were called. The government absorbed some of the debts of the states in return for their commitments to cut payroll spending and avoid future indebtedness. It bailed out the state-owned Banco do Brasil, the country's largest bank, to the tune of $8 billion. At the same time – and contrary to the myth propagated by its critics on the left – the government expanded social spending, which amounted to 19.1 per cent of GDP by 2002, up from 17.6 per cent a decade earlier.[38]

Interviewed in his wood-panelled office in Brasília's Planalto Palace in March 1999, when his government was reeling from a forced devaluation, Cardoso admitted ruefully that if he had had his first term again 'I would be much more severe in controlling federal spending and in encouraging state governors to do the same.'[39] The price of loose fiscal policy was that the economic team headed by Pedro Malan, the shy, pipe-smoking finance minister from 1995 to 2001, came to rely on an overvalued currency and high interest rates to consolidate its victory over inflation. To make matters worse, throughout Cardoso's two terms, Brazil was hit by periodic bouts of financial instability, in which the price of shares and bonds would plunge, and vast sums of money would leave the country. The origins of these episodes was usually external: Mexico's devaluation of 1994–5, the instability of several East Asian countries in 1997–8, Russia's default of 1998 and Argentina's collapse of 2001–2. But they affected Brazil badly because of its fiscal vulnerability (which they aggravated) and because of its pegged exchange rate. Under the system adopted in 1995, the *real* depreciated by some 6 per cent a year against the dollar; by 1997, many economists reckoned it was overvalued by about 20 per cent, and Brazil's current-account deficit had climbed to 4.2 per cent of GDP. When the Asian crisis hit and nervous investors began to yank their capital out of Brazil, the Central Bank doubled its benchmark interest rate (to a stratospheric 44 per cent) to defend the exchange rate. But this jacked up the cost of rolling over the ever-growing public debt, which leapt from a comfortable 28 per cent of GDP in 1995 to 44 per cent in 1998. In January 1999, days after Cardoso had begun his second term, his government was finally forced to float the *real*. After a few anxious weeks, financial order was restored, with the help of a loan from the IMF and a skilful new Central Bank president, Arminio Fraga, who had previously worked on Wall Street for an investment fund operated by George Soros. To restore confidence in the currency, the Central Bank temporarily increased interest rates again, while the government launched a raft of fiscal measures. This worked: inflation was contained and the economy grew in 1999, albeit by only 1 per cent. But high interest rates and the devaluation itself pushed the public debt (much of which was in dollars) to over 50 per cent of GDP, while interest payments on the debt peaked at a massive 6 per cent of GDP.[40]

Given its cost, the delay in devaluing the *real* was a matter of fierce debate in Brazil. The most common criticism is that Cardoso gave priority to winning a second term, for which he first had to secure Congressional support in 1997 for a constitutional amendment to allow re-election. In his memoirs, the president himself says that he was aware as early as 1995 of the need to loosen the exchange-rate peg. In retrospect, he says, he should have done so in early 1998. He gives three reasons for the failure to do so then, or at any other point in his first term. He wanted to wait for a moment when international financial markets were calm. His economic team was badly divided over the issue. Lastly, he argues, 'In an economy that was still partly indexed and with the vivid memory of decades of inflation, the fear of a relapse into the inferno of hyperinflation tormented us. We remained victorious and immobile.'[41] These arguments are plausible. Eliana Cardoso (no relation of the president), who left the economic team because of her disagreement with the exchange-rate policy, concurred that 'a graceful exit strategy was simply not available ... As long as reserves and capital flows are available, the temptation to continue to use the exchange rate to keep inflation under control seems irresistable.'[42]

In the wake of the devaluation, the government put in place a new set of macroeconomic policies. As well as the floating exchange rate, these included targets for inflation and for the primary fiscal surplus (i.e. before debt payments). These were underpinned by the approval in 1999 of a Fiscal Responsibility Law, which had the status of a constitutional measure, and which codified all the public-finance reforms of the Cardoso era, placing strict limits on the indebtedness of all levels of government. Months earlier, stung into action by the devaluation, Congress at last approved two long-awaited constitutional reforms. One was a watered-down pension reform. The other was a reform of the public administration, which required governments at all levels to reduce their payroll spending to 60 per cent of their revenues within two years, and allowed them to sack workers to do so. But the devaluation had a high political cost. Cardoso lost much of his previous popularity and his government lost the initiative in Congress amid infighting among some of his key supporters. A promising economic recovery was derailed in 2001, partly by a drought-induced energy shortage and partly by the knock-on effect of Argentina's troubles. One final episode of financial instability lay ahead in 2002, when investors began to worry about Lula winning the election. Their fears turned out to be misplaced – Lula opted to maintain Cardoso's economic policy framework. But they were understandable given the last-minute nature of Lula's conversion to macroeconomic prudence.

In headline terms, the Cardoso government's economic record was disappointing: the economy grew at an annual average rate of just 2.3 per cent between 1995 and 2002, while unemployment rose from 4.4 per cent to 7.5 per cent over the same period (or to 11.2 per cent using the new, more realistic methodology adopted in 2001). Yet conquering inflation was a historic achievement, and dealing with its aftermath was a long and messy job. Unlike in many other Latin American countries, devaluation was not followed by a banking crisis. That was in large part thanks to a well-executed programme, known as PROER, which cleaned up the banking system without bailing out miscreant or irresponsible bank shareholders, at a net cost of just 3 per cent of GDP.[43] Officials argued plausibly that behind the disappointing growth figures lay a process of structural change in the economy which would bear fruit in the medium term. Having abandoned its past introversion, Brazil was becoming much more integrated with the world. More than $170 billion in foreign direct investment poured in, much of it attracted by a large-scale privatisation programme. The reduction in trade protectionism forced Brazilian firms to become more efficient. Productivity, which declined in the 1980s, rose at an annual average rate of 1.1 per cent in the decade after 1994.[44]

The devaluation triggered an export boom: Brazil's exports rocketed from $51 billion in 1998 to $137 billion in 2006, as industries as diverse as cars and agriculture modernised.

Much to his annoyance, Cardoso's opponents in the PT sneeringly dubbed him a 'neoliberal'. In his memoirs, he goes to great lengths to rebut this, insisting that, 'If we did anything in the ten years that I was minister or president, it was to rebuild the administrative machine, give greater consistency to public policies, in summary to remake the state.'[45] What characterised the Cardoso government's reforms was pragmatism, in which the freeing of markets was combined with measures aimed at creating a modernised, regulatory state. That spirit was epitomised in the privatisation of Telebras. Whereas Mexico and Argentina had turned state telecoms monopolies into private ones, Brazilian officials introduced competition from the outset. Similarly, the government kept Petrobras, the oil company, in state ownership but subjected it to market discipline by floating 40 per cent of its shares. The state retained around a third of the banking system. The government used BNDES, the state development bank, to pursue an industrial policy (though some would argue that instead of subsidising capital it should have spent more on education). Cardoso also put much stress on reforming social policies. He won approval for a constitutional amendment which obliged state and municipal governments to boost teachers' salaries and classroom equipment in the poorest areas. Primary-school enrolment increased to 97 per cent of the relevant age group, while secondary enrolment increased by 70 per cent. The government also initiated targeted anti-poverty programmes, and a large-scale agrarian reform that saw 80,000 families a year receive land. Yet the economic disappointments and intermittent financial turmoil of the second term meant that Cardoso was unable to see his chosen successor, José Serra, his health minister, elected. In October 2002, at the fourth attempt, Luiz Inácio Lula da Silva won the presidency with 53 million votes to Serra's 33 million in a run-off ballot.

Lula: continuity, change and corruption

For Brazilian democracy, Lula's was a historic victory. In the country of social injustice, his life story was a saga of triumph over adversity worthy of a *telenovela*. He was the seventh child of a dirt-poor family from the north-east. Aged seven, he made the boneshaking journey in a *pau de arara* (an open-bed truck known as a 'parrot's perch' because passengers must cling to an overhead rail) to join his father who had migrated to São Paulo. He was the first in his family to complete primary school, but his formal education went no further. After a series of odd jobs, he entered a government training scheme, becoming a lathe operator at a metalbashing firm. He first came to public notice as the leader of the metalworkers' strikes during the later years of the military dictatorship. Out of those strikes would eventually come the Partido dos Trabalhadores (Workers' Party), in which trade unionists were joined by community activists nurtured by Catholic liberation theology and by leftist academics. Though never formally a Marxist party, for two decades or more after its foundation in 1979 the PT espoused far-left policies, such as debt default, nationalisation of the banks and wholesale redistribution of wealth. But successive electoral defeats persuaded Lula and his key ally in the party, José Dirceu, the PT's president, to move to the centre and seek alliances. That process suddenly gathered pace during the 2002 campaign. Weeks before the vote, Lula met Cardoso and signalled his assent to an IMF loan which committed the next government to stick to responsible fiscal and monetary policies.[46] 'I changed. Brazil changed,' Lula repeated during the campaign. His television commercials, made by a professional marketing man, projected the soft-focus message of 'Lula, peace and love'. It was a return to the pragmatism of his days as a trade union leader – except that the candidate had donned Armani suits. That union background marked Lula out from Latin America's many more utopian leftists. José Sarney, the conservative former president who would become his ally, was reported to have said of Lula that he was 'a man who knows the value of 3 per cent.'[47] Lula is affable, speaks to ordinary Brazilians in homespun metaphors, and is by nature a negotiator rather than an ideologue, a reformist not a revolutionary. 'Each day, even if we advance a centimetre, we are going forward – without any miracles, without breaking away from our international commitments, simply doing what needs to be done,' he said in 2004.[48] But Lula's own personal history allowed him to stake a claim to be much more than just an ordinary politician. He was one of the few leaders who could speak both to the world's plutocrats at the World Economic Forum in Davos and to discontented anti-globalisers at the World Social Forum, which originated in his own party's stronghold of Porto Alegre.[49]

On the night of his electoral victory, Lula claimed before ecstatic supporters thronging São Paulo's Avenida Paulista that Brazil had rejected 'the current economic model, based on dependence, in favour of a new model of development'. But in practice Lula continued the main thrust of Cardoso's economic policies. In the weeks preceding his victory, Brazil's financial markets had yet again suffered an attack of nerves: the *real* lost around 40 per cent of its value in the six months before the election, falling to 3.8 to the US dollar.[50] That in turn caused prices to rise and sent the public debt, much of which was denominated in dollars, spiralling to a peak of 66 per cent of GDP. Lula moved quickly to calm the markets' nerves. Antonio Palocci, the new finance minister, was a former Trotskyist turned pragmatist who as mayor of Ribeirão Preto, a city in São Paulo state, had privatised some municipal services. He immediately announced a tightening of fiscal policy. To head the Central Bank, Lula named Henrique Meirelles, a former chief executive of BankBoston who was a member of the PSDB. The Bank nipped inflation in the bud by yanking up interest rates yet again. The government moved quickly to push a second pension reform through Congress. Lula's calculation was plain: a year of pain followed by three years of gain. He also knew that debt default would be disastrous for Brazil: most of the public debt was held by Brazilian banks and pension funds, not foreign investors.

'It is infantile to blame the IMF for these measures. We are taking them because they are in Brazil's interest,' Palocci told a packed meeting of financiers at the Bank of England.[51] The government's economic orthodoxy brought anguished disillusion to the PT's left: half a dozen of its legislators, led by Heloísa Helena, were expelled and set up a far-left splinter party. But it paid off: the economy grew by 5 per cent in 2004. Although it slowed again the following year, as the Central Bank kept monetary policy tight to meet its inflation target, growth picked up again in 2006. The government was helped by favourable conditions in the outside world. High world prices for commodities helped Brazil's exports, while cheap money in rich countries encouraged investors to seek out the higher returns offered by emerging markets. By the end of 2006, Brazil's finances were in far more robust shape than four years previously. The *real* had strengthened to around 2.15 to the dollar (by May 2007 it had reached 1.95). The risk premium – the spread over the interest rate on American Treasury bonds – demanded by investors for holding Brazilian bonds fell from some 25 percentage points to just two. The public debt (net of government assets) fell to 49 per cent of GDP. The government retired most of the dollar debt, and replaced it with paper in *reais*. In November 2005 it paid off its debt to the IMF early. Despite the strength of the currency, the export boom meant that Brazil's current account moved into surplus in 2003 and stayed there. In late 2005 the Central Bank began cutting interest rates steadily.

In the 2002 election campaign, Lula had pledged himself to eliminating hunger. The PT had long criticised Brazil's social policies as inadequate. Yet once in government it got off to an oddly unconvincing start. Lula had promised a scheme called *Fome Zero* ('zero hunger'), an old-fashioned and inefficient plan for food stamps. After a year in which they achieved little beyond setting up a plethora of overlapping social ministries, Lula's officials came to recognised the value of a clutch of targeted cash-transfer schemes for poor families established during the Cardoso government. They consolidated five of these into *Bolsa Família* ('Family Fund'), which they swiftly expanded. By late 2006, this reached 11 million families, or one in four. It paid them

95 *reais* (US$44) a month.[52] *Bolsa Família* was 'the most important income-transfer programme in the world', according to Lula.[53] His government also increased the real value of the minimum wage by 25 per cent. 'How many countries have achieved what we have: fiscal responsibility and a strong social policy at the same time? Never in the economic history of Brazil have we had the solid fundamentals we have now', he claimed, arguing that the country was now ready for 'a leap in quality'.[54]

In other ways, Lula's government was hugely disappointing. That was especially so in its management of the government bureaucracy (where it placed thousands of party militants in jobs regardless of qualification), and above all of Congress. The PT had done less well than Lula in the 2002 election, winning only 91 of the 513 seats in the lower house of Congress. Lula was less skilful than Cardoso in building a solid governing coalition. He kept nearly all the important ministries in the hands of the PT. He could count on the support of a handful of small left-wing parties. He, or rather José Dirceu, his chief of staff, also struck deals with several rent-a-parties. But in 2005 the government was rocked by revelations about those deals. After the head of one of these parties was implicated in a bribery scam at the federal postal service, he retaliated with claims that the PT was paying a monthly stipend, dubbed the *mensalão*, to dozens of members of Congress from allied parties in return for their votes. Much of the money was channelled through an advertising man who received many government contracts, and who was then found to have repaid part of a bank loan taken out by the PT. The scandal forced the resignations of Dirceu, a dozen other senior officials and the entire top leadership of the ruling party. What made it all the more reprehensible was that the PT had long presented itself, sanctimoniously, as holding a monopoly on political ethics in Brazil. To make matters worse, Palocci was forced to resign as finance minister in 2006 over corruption claims stemming from his period as mayor of Ribeirão Preto.[55]

Lula insisted that he knew nothing of the *mensalão*. Many Brazilians, especially poorer ones, appeared either to give him the benefit of the doubt, or to conclude that his party was no more corrupt than any of the others. Much of Brazil's press took a different view, and became implacably hostile to Lula. The scandal damaged the PT's standing among the middle class. But economic stability and *Bolsa Família*, together with the affection that many poorer Brazilians felt for their president, won Lula a second term at an election in October 2006, in which he secured 61 per cent of the vote in a run-off ballot. Whereas in 2002, Lula had polled heavily in Brazil's more developed south and south-east, this time he owed victory to the votes of the poorer, more backward north and north-east. Normally governing parties do well in Brazilian elections, but the scandals cost the PT seats. It only partially replicated Lula's gains among the poor in the north-east.[56] At the outset of his second term, Lula formalised an alliance with the centrist, catch-all PMDB, still one of the largest parties in Brazil but one with a voracious appetite for patronage and pork.

Overall, progress outweighed disappointment in Brazil. Much had been achieved over the previous dozen years. The proportion of the population living in poverty had fallen from 43 per cent in 1993 to 30.7 per cent in 2005. Income distribution was less unequal than at any time in the previous three decades.[57] These achievements were the result of price stability and democratic social policy, notably universal primary education and anti-poverty measures. The incomes of the poor rose steadily, and they bought more: prices of food and medicines fell in 2004 and 2005. That was all the more remarkable since rapid economic growth still proved elusive. In Lula's first term, growth averaged just 3.3 per cent a year while the world economy grew at 4.8 per cent.[58] This was partly because of the continued reliance on high interest rates for price stability, and to compensate for relatively lax fiscal policy. The government piled up primary fiscal surpluses, but once debt payments were taken into account, the public finances were still in overall deficit. The debt burden was gradually falling, but it remained heavy: interest payments continued to cost the government up to 5 per cent of GDP.

Critics argued that the Lula government should have made a far more aggressive effort to reduce the debt while conditions in the financial markets were benign. Even after the reforms, the annual deficit in the public-sector pension system still cost taxpayers the equivalent of 4.5 per cent of GDP. Too much public spending was still constitutionally mandated, giving the government little room to re-jig it to favour the less well-off. Instead of fixing this and cutting wasteful spending, of which there was much, the government relied on higher tax revenues to achieve its primary surpluses. The result was that the tax burden, all told, amounted to 35 per cent of GDP in 2006 – a higher figure than in the United States. Since the 1988 constitution, governments issued an average of 37 different tax rules per day, according to the Brazilian Institute of Tax Planning.[59] Around 40 per cent of employment was still in the informal economy. So the tax burden on legal businesses was stifling. It was one reason why investment was still relatively low, at around 16.3 per cent of GDP in 2005. Another reason was that public investment remained derisory. The Cardoso administration set up arms-length regulatory agencies to attract private investment to telecoms, roads and electricity. The Lula government mistrusted these, changed the rules and failed to attract significant investment. The result was potholed roads, clogged ports and a big deficit in drinking water and sewerage. These problems were aggravated by institutional failures and political corruption. After four years in Brazil as the World Bank's representative, Vinod Thomas mused: 'People wonder why, after so many years of so much investment in roads with external financing, the country is not yet able to maintain these assets, even though there are large taxes on gasoline to finance investment.'[60] Logistics costs in Brazil are twice as high as in developed countries, he noted.

Much else remained partly or wholly unreformed. The burden of regulation was as stifling as that of taxation. Rigid labour laws deter companies from hiring more workers. The agency charged with policing monopolies and promoting competition was slow and insufficiently independent. Despite the trade opening of the 1990s, Brazil remained relatively protectionist. Imports faced an average tariff of 13 per cent and bureaucratic obstacles. The *mensalão* scandal, and the difficulties of constructing legislative majorities, pointed to the need for political reforms. In the 2006 election, no fewer than 21 parties won seats in the lower house of Congress, a record. The mounting threats to the security of citizens from organised crime and everyday violence pointed to the need for reforms of police, prisons and judiciary.

In his memoirs, Cardoso writes with feeling that: 'The struggle to bring greater rationality to the public finances and to contain inflation is like the myth of Sisyphus: no sooner has it ended than it starts again.'[61] Brazil's economic drama over the past decade can be summed up simply: the cost of sustained political resistance to fiscal discipline was punishingly high interest rates that sacrificed economic growth and private consumption to the fiscal privileges of relatively better-off groups. Nevertheless, with stability achieved, economic growth was gradually edging up and Brazil was becoming a less unequal country. Its combination of stability, relative economic openness and democratic social reform lacked the dynamism of Chile, but its progress in reducing poverty and inequality looked far more sustainable than Venezuelan populism. What made Brazil's progress all the more remarkable was that it was the fruit of the patient construction of democratic consensuses.

Mexico: reform stalled by democracy

A couple of kilometres to the north of the Zócalo in Mexico City lie the ruins of Tlatelolco, Tenochtitlán's twin city in Aztec times. Tlatelolco was the site of what was at the time the largest market anywhere in the Americas. It was also the scene of the final act in the Spanish conquest of the capital.[62] All that is left are the depleted bases of a dozen or more temple platforms set in a sunken garden. The site is overlooked by the monastery church of Santiago Tlatelolco, its austere baroque bulk fashioned by the Spaniards from the reddish black volcanic stone of the ruined temples. Beyond the church rises the ugly early 1960s concrete tower that housed the Mexican foreign ministry until 2006, when it moved to a taller building of glass and steel in the city centre. On the other three sides stand the apartment blocks of a government housing project from the same era. The raised open space of concrete flagstones between the buildings is called the Plaza de las Tres Culturas or the Square of the Three Cultures – indigenous, Spanish colonial and republican *mestizo*. In the ideology of the Institutional Revolutionary Party (PRI) these fused more harmoniously than in the architectural clashes of the square. At least so claims the stone plaque overlooking the garden: 'On August 13th 1521 heroically defended by Cuauhtémoc Tlatelolco fell into the power of Hernán Cortés. It was neither a triumph nor a defeat. It was the painful birth of the *mestizo* people that is Mexico today.'

More recently the square was the site of another act of bloodshed, one that in retrospect would also come to be seen as marking another painful birth – that of Mexican democracy. In 1968 the student protests that began in Paris and swept campuses across the world from Berkeley to Berlin found an echo in Mexico. Students and their professors took over the National University and the Polytechnic in Mexico City. Many of the leaders admired Che Guevara, but above all the movement stood for freedom of political expression.[63] The president at the time, Gustavo Díaz Ordaz, was a narrow-minded authoritarian. Even as the student movement was fizzling out, he saw in it a threat to Mexico's image in the world: the Olympic Games were due to open in Mexico City in mid-October. On the evening of 2 October, a march by a few thousand students was due to end with a rally in the square at Tlatelolco. As the marchers prepared to listen to speeches, watched by the army, members of a government-organised plain-clothes paramilitary squad, acting as agents provocateurs, fired on the crowd from a balcony in one of the apartment blocks, wounding the army general in charge. That prompted the army to rake the square with fire from armoured cars, bazookas and machine guns as well as small arms. The exact death toll is still not known. Contemporary newspaper accounts talked of up to 28 dead and 80 wounded. The student movement itself put the figure at 150 civilians and 40 members of the security forces killed. The *Guardian*, a British newspaper, claimed that 325 people were killed.[64] After the massacre, the regime's characteristic response was denial, captured by Rosario Castellanos, a poet, in lines carved into a second stone monument in the square, this one unveiled on a rainy evening in October 1993 on the 25th anniversary of the massacre:

> ¿Quién? ¿Quiénes? Nadie. Al día siguiente, nadie.
> La plaza amaneció barrida; los periódicos
> dieron como noticia principal
> el estado del tiempo.

Y en la televisión, en el radio, en el cine
no hubo ningún cambio de programa,
ningún anuncio intercalado ni un
minuto de silencio en el banquete
(Pues prosiguió el banquete.)

Who? Whom? Nobody. The next day, nobody.
The square awoke swept clean; the newspapers
gave as the main news the state of the weather.
And on the television, on the radio, in the cinema
there was no change in the programme,
no special announcement, nor a
minute of silence at the banquet
(For the banquet indeed continued).[65]

Nevertheless, the massacre of Tlatelolco would prove to be a profound shock to the PRI system. It punctured the official myth of consensual political order. It alienated the middle class who had been the system's greatest beneficiaries – Octavio Paz, the poet, was the first to respond, resigning as Mexico's ambassador to India. It would cause future governments to react in ways that eventually would further destabilise the system. As Enrique Krauze, a historian, puts it: 'There had been a profound loss of legitimacy on that dark night of Tlatelolco ... Though the deep-seated cult of authoritarian government in Mexico would not recognise the fact, 1968 was both its highest point of authoritarian power and the real beginning of its collapse.'[66]

In the decades after the Second World War, Mexico had enjoyed rapid economic growth. This reached its apogee under the long stewardship of Antonio Ortiz Mena as finance minister from 1958 to 1970. During that period, private investment was favoured, real wages rose at an annual average rate of 6.4 per cent, the exchange rate was fixed at 12.5 pesos to the dollar, the public debt was low and the budget in balance. Ortiz Mena called it 'stabilising development'.[67] It was jettisoned by Luis Echeverría, who succeeded Díaz Ordaz as president in 1970. As interior minister in 1968, Echeverría was complicit in the massacre of Tlatelolco and the repression of the student movement. As president, he proclaimed a 'democratic opening' but only within narrow limits: there was a second student massacre in 1971, and the government launched a secretive 'dirty war' against peasant guerrillas in the Sierra Madre del Sur. At the same time, he appeared to embrace many of the ideas of the student leaders. He posed as a champion of the third world, and launched rhetorical attacks on businessmen (whose investment slowed as a result). He redoubled efforts to co-opt the universities and the middle class by throwing public money at them. The total number of public-sector jobs expanded by a staggering amount, from 600,000 in 1970 to 2.2 million in 1976.[68] He paid for the breakneck expansion of the state by printing and borrowing money. Over his term, foreign debt increased sixfold while the real value of wages halved as inflation took off. José López Portillo, Echeverría's successor, initially seemed to promise more moderate government. But the discovery of a huge oilfield offshore in the Gulf of Campeche allowed López Portillo to resume the policies of Echeverría, until falling oil prices and rising interest rates caused the public finances to collapse like a house of cards.

If Tlatelolco had damaged the PRI's political legitimacy, the devaluation, debt default and bank nationalisation of 1982 undermined its claim to economic competence. Yet the PRI's retreat from power and the transition to democracy in Mexico would be extremely gradual and occupy almost two more decades. It had formally begun with a political reform in 1978, which legalised the Communist Party and other left-wing groups. The opposition was allowed to win a quarter of the seats in the Chamber of Deputies the following year. However, the established order did not lightly surrender power to a divided but increasingly determined opposition to its right and left. Miguel de la Madrid, who as president from 1982 to 1988 had to cope with the wreckage left by López Portillo, was an economic liberal. He began to return the economy to the policies of Ortiz Mena and 'stabilising development'. But he did little to reform politics. The government's response to a devastating earthquake in the centre of Mexico City in 1985 showed a characteristic mixture of denial and incompetence. Among some 370 buildings that collapsed was one of the blocks of flats at Tlatelolco, killing 700 people. In all, 20,000 people were killed and another 180,000 were left homeless. In many cases it was left to unofficial volunteers to rescue survivors from the rubble and care for the homeless. Out of this tragedy came a powerful grassroots movement for urban renewal, a novelty in a country where the state left little room for independent civic organisations.[69]

De la Madrid eschewed an opportunity to move towards democracy and fair voting when he failed to intervene after the National Action Party (PAN), the conservative opposition, was fraudulently denied an overwhelming victory in an election for governor of the northern state of Chihuahua in 1986. He also exercised the traditional presidential prerogative of choosing his successor, Carlos Salinas. That prompted the most serious split in the PRI for almost half a century. Cuauhtémoc Cárdenas, a former governor of Michoacán and the son of Mexico's most revered president, had rallied much of the PRI's left wing against de la Madrid's liberal economic policies. When Salinas was revealed as the PRI's presidential candidate in 1988, Cárdenas opted to run against him for a clutch of small left-wing parties. The election marked another milestone in the PRI's steady loss of credibility. Salinas was declared the winner with 50.4 per cent to 31 per cent for Cárdenas, but only after the interior ministry's computers tallying the count shut down for several hours. Before the plug was pulled on the computer system, Cárdenas had been ahead.[70] Massive demonstrations against electoral fraud took place across the country. Cárdenas probably spared Mexico a bloodbath when he urged his supporters to channel their anger into forming a new Party of the Democratic Revolution (PRD).

Salinas: *perestroika* without *glasnost*

Salinas made a determined attempt to rebuild the PRI system by restoring its lost reputation for economic competence while updating its mechanisms of political control. Though his father had been industry minister in the 1960s, Salinas seemed to be a new kind of PRI politician. He had a doctorate in political economy from Harvard. Although prematurely bald, he was aged just forty when he became president. He spoke softly, but with a hint of steel. He liked to describe himself as a consensus-builder and negotiator.[71] But he was ruthless and hyperactive. He surrounded himself with a clutch of liberal economists with doctorates from American universities. They were charged with modernising Mexico. The finance minister, Pedro Aspe, brought inflation down and renegotiated the foreign debt, restoring stability and a modicum of economic growth after years of debt-induced stagnation. Salinas boldly challenged several political taboos: he put aside the PRI's history of anti-clericalism by restoring relations with the Vatican, and ordered an end to six decades of land reform, instead granting members of *ejidos* (communal farms) the right to obtain individual title to their plots. For these reforms, he secured the support of the PAN. In the most iconoclastic move of all, he challenged the deep-rooted anti-Americanism of Mexico's political leadership by opening negotiations for a free-trade agreement with the United States and Canada.

This whirlwind of economic modernisation attracted much praise abroad. But some of the reforms were less liberal (let alone 'neoliberal') than they seemed. Salinas left intact the state monopolies of oil and electricity, excluding energy as well as many services from NAFTA. Telmex, the telecoms company, was transformed from a public monopoly into a private one. Foreign banks were barred from the bank privatisation. The president relied on many of the institutions, levers of power and clientelistic networks of Mexico's corporate state. Private business was especially loyal. At a dinner in 1993 that would become infamous, Salinas sat down with two dozen of Mexico's richest businessmen, most of them beneficiaries of privatisations or other favours. He asked for $500 million for the PRI to fight the 1994 election. Most were happy to stump up their alloted $25 million.[72] Inflation was reduced partly through the *pacto*, an incomes policy negotiated with business and with Fidel Velázquez, the general secretary of the Confederation of Mexican Workers (CTM), the main trade union. Under this arrangement, real wages halved in the decade to 1992. In that year, the CTM held its Congress in Mexico City's sports arena. It was an event worthy of the Kremlin's gerontocratic heyday. In front of a giant portrait of Salinas, scores of elderly union leaders sat in tiers on a podium, their heads protruding like coconuts in a shy. To well-orchestrated cheers, Velázquez was re-elected for an eighth consecutive six-year term at the age of 91. No vote was deemed necessary.[73] In deference to Don Fidel, Salinas did not touch the restrictive labour laws.

Salinas did make a few gestures towards political modernisation. He set up a National Human Rights Commission. For the first time, the PRI surrendered its monopoly of state governorships, PAN victories being accepted in Baja California and Chihuahua. But in many other cases, Salinas would wait to see the strength of opposition protests. He sometimes intervened not to recognise an opposition victory but to force the 'winning' PRI candidate to resign, to be replaced by a presidential appointee. In all, he removed 17 governors in 14 of Mexico's 31 states.[74] Salinas felt obliged to enact an electoral reform. This created a Federal Electoral Institute (IFE). Although nominally independent, it was still controlled by the interior minister, who chaired its general council.[75] The president could count on a pliant media, dependent on government money. Those he could not co-opt, Salinas coerced. Early on, he imprisoned the powerful leader of the oil-workers' union, ostensibly for corruption but in reality for having favoured Cárdenas. The PRD complained that 250 of its activists were killed during Salinas's term. Officials continued to reject criticisms of the lack of political reform. 'There isn't a unique model for democracy,' Salinas insisted in an interview at Los Pinos, the modernist presidential complex in Chapultepec Park. 'What there is, is the requirement to respect freedoms and to allow equality of competition – that's what we're working on and that's what we're committed to.'[76] A senior aide was more candid. Referring to the parallel between the government's economic reforms and the contemporaneous dismantling of communism in the Soviet Union, he said bluntly: 'The Soviet Union shows that it is not easy to do *perestroika* and *glasnost* at the same time. The worst of all worlds would be to be left with neither, and without a government or society that functions.'[77]

Salinas also tried to rebuild the PRI's support among the poor. Migration to the cities and the growth of the informal economy meant that millions of Mexicans had slipped through the ruling party's corporatist net of peasant, trade union and professional organisations. To reach them, Salinas created the National Solidarity Programme (Pronasol). Over his six-year term, this swallowed $18 billion, or around 40 per cent of total public investment. It handed out money for building health clinics, school classrooms, rural roads and community development projects. In an attempt to bypass what officials saw as a sclerotic bureaucracy and cut corruption, the money went mainly to mayors, backed by newly created Solidarity committees. The programme was closely identified with Salinas himself. Under its auspices, almost every week he would leave Los Pinos and criss-cross the country. In elaborately choreographed trips by plane, helicopters and convoys of 4x4s, he would whisk to half a dozen events in a day, opening drinking-water schemes or health clinics in dusty villages and handing out property titles in urban shantytowns. Poverty experts criticised the programme for not reaching the poorest and for its lack of co-ordination – the new clinics might lack doctors for example. But above all it was designed to be politically effective. It made Salinas popular and helped the PRI to win comfortably a mid-term election in 1991.[78]

In the end Salinas over-reached himself. Even before the end of his term, his attempt to rebuild the PRI and its regime began to unravel. Some of his advisers talked of turning the PRI into the Solidarity Party. Together with his choice of Luis Donaldo Colosio, a gentle and loyal associate, as the presidential candidate for 1994, this stirred fears that Salinas would seek to remain in charge, breaking an unwritten rule of the system. Undercurrents of corruption eddied around the presidential family. All this exploded into the open with three (still-unresolved) murders. The elderly cardinal-archbishop of Guadalajara was killed by drug traffickers as he arrived at the city's airport. Then Colosio himself was shot dead by a lone gunman at a campaign rally in Tijuana – a political assassination of a gravity unmatched in Mexico since the murder of Álvaro Obregón by a Catholic fanatic in 1928. Months later, Francisco Ruiz Massieu, the PRI's general secretary and former husband of Salinas's sister, was the victim of a contract killing in the centre of Mexico City.

These murders were not the only violent challenge to political order. On 1 January 1994, the date that NAFTA came into effect, several hundred Indian guerrillas seized the colonial town of San Cristóbal de las Casas in the southern state of Chiapas in the name of the previously unknown Zapatista Army of National Liberation (EZLN). As Carlos Fuentes, the novelist, put it, just when Mexico was moving closer to North America its rulers were forcibly reminded that parts of their country still belonged to Central America. Chiapas had never known democracy – the PRI regularly won elections there with more than 90 per cent of the vote. Unlike in the rest of Mexico, the state's ranchers and coffee *hacendados* had successfully resisted land reform, and now Salinas had ended any chance of it. Militarily, the Zapatista uprising would be brief. After more than a hundred people were killed as the army drove the rebels out of San Cristóbal and other towns, Salinas quickly declared a unilateral ceasefire. Far from shoring up authoritarianism as some of its critics feared, NAFTA constrained the regime's ability to unleash repression because it focussed the outside world's attention on Mexico. Initially, at least, the Zapatistas attracted widespread sympathy, thanks in part to the semiotic skills of their leader, a ski-masked former university teacher of Marxist philosophy who styled himself Sub-Comandante Marcos.[79] They would gradually be rendered irrelevant, in large part because of Marcos's inability to adapt to the arrival of democracy.

Days after Ernesto Zedillo took over as president on 1 December 1994, the cracked edifice of *salinismo* came tumbling down. The political turmoil of an electoral year had caused Salinas and Aspe to abandon their previous macro-economic prudence. Monetary policy was loosened and the government began to finance itself with *tesobonos* (short-term dollar debt). The political violence gave investors the jitters: money was flying out of the country. When Zedillo took office on 1 December, outstanding *tesobonos* were equal to twice the value of the Central Bank's reserves.[80] Once again, as it had at the end of each presidential term since 1976, political handover coincided with economic turmoil, pointing to the regime's post-Tlatelolco instability. Three weeks later, after a botched attempt to widen the exchange-rate band under which the peso had gradually devalued against the US dollar, Zedillo's government let the currency float. After weeks of drift, with the help of loans from the United States Treasury and the IMF, the government managed to stabilise the economy and recovery quickly followed. But the cost had been heavy. The exchange rate was stabilised by means of high interest rates, wage controls, and increases in VAT and in government-controlled prices. The economy slumped: GDP contracted by 6 per cent in 1995, but domestic demand fell by 14 per cent and would not recover its level of 1994 for three years. To make matters worse, many of the newly privatised banks faced collapse. Many of their new owners were inexperienced; in one or two cases they were corrupt. They lent recklessly, in some cases to insiders and/or in dollars. Having benefited from lax regulation under Salinas, they received generous treatment from Zedillo when they got into difficulties. In essence, they were allowed to pass to the government their non-performing loans, some of which were to their own directors. And the government offered unlimited deposit insurance. The Zedillo administration did belatedly tighten supervision and accounting standards, and lifted the ban on foreign commercial banks. By 2006 foreign banks accounted for more than four-fifths of the system. In all, the bank bailout cost the taxpayer around 20 per cent of GDP.[81]

The bailout reflected the government's weakness. It was 'the best deal we could get. We spent years battling to make the economic numbers add up and to restore confidence', according to Liébano Sáenz, Zedillo's chief of staff.[82]

The new president was an unexciting technocrat, lacking Salinas's political skills. But he had some important qualities: he was honest and decent, he believed in economic reform and he was a democrat. 'The time has come for democracy to extend to all areas of life in our society,' he said in his inaugural address to Congress.[83] Right from the outset, he said that he preferred the rule of law to the unwritten rules of presidential supremacy, that he would maintain a 'healthy distance' from the PRI and that he would not choose his successor.[84] This amounted to a voluntary abdication of authoritarianism. He would later partially retreat from this, but it was far too late for any significant restoration of presidential power. Zedillo took two other crucial steps towards democracy. Within days of his taking office, Congress approved a judicial reform that created an independent and powerful Supreme Court. In 1996, after painstaking negotiation achieved consensus on the main points among the three main parties, the Federal Electoral Institute was reformed to become wholly independent of government, along with its sister organisation, the electoral tribunal. The government also pushed through a reform granting independence to the Central Bank. It took timid steps to loosen the state monopoly over energy, but beyond a few private companies building power stations these didn't amount to much in practice.

In February 1995, in the depths of economic turmoil, Zedillo broke another of the unwritten rules of the system: he ordered the arrrest of Raúl Salinas, Carlos's elder brother, for the murder of his former brother-in-law, Ruiz Massieu. The murder investigation degenerated into a gothic farce. But, months later, the Swiss authorities froze about $130 million they found in secret bank accounts belonging to Raúl, some opened with a false passport. Swiss officials claimed that some of this money came from the drug trade. There had been whispers for years that Raúl had been enriching himself through embezzlement and influence-peddling. A federal investigation found that some of the money in the accounts had been transferred by Carlos Salinas while president.[85] In 2005, Raúl Salinas was released from prison on bail after an appeal court quashed his conviction for murder, but he remained under investigation in Mexico and France for illicit enrichment.[86]

Zedillo could restore Mexico's fortunes but not those of the PRI. If the 1982 debt crisis damaged its reputation for economic competence, this was destroyed by the 1994–5 debacle. As most Mexicans saw their living standards plummet, they were angered by the bailout of the billionaire bankers and by the revelations of corruption at the top. The PRI itself turned against the economic reforms, which had radically reduced the scope for political patronage. At a party convention in 1996 to shouts of 'down with neoliberalism' new rules were approved which required the party's presidential candidate to have held elected office – a changed aimed at disqualifying the reforming technocrats. In the mid-term election of 1997, for the first time the PRI lost its majority in the lower-house of Congress. Cuauhtémoc Cárdenas gained partial retribution for 1988 when he was elected as the first-ever governor of the Federal District (the inner core of Mexico City), a post that had hitherto been filled by presidential appointment. In 2000, after 72 years in power, the PRI would finally lose the presidency.

Fox: gridlocked democracy

Vicente Fox was ideally equipped to end the rule of the PRI. A farmer who had been the manager of Coca-Cola's Mexican operations, Fox came late to politics. In 1991 he was denied victory in an election for governor of the central state of Guanajuato by fraud; he won four years later and almost immediately launched a presidential campaign. His popularity obliged the PAN, a party of conservative lawyers, to choose this rough-edged businessman as its candidate. He was thick-skinned, determined and a natural media performer. His campaign was simple but devastatingly effective: he promised *el cambio* ('the change'), but not adventurism. He appealed to democrats across the political spectrum.

On the face of things Fox's victory seemed to set the seal on Mexico's transition from authoritarian politics and an inward-looking state-dominated economy to an outward-looking, globalised liberal democracy. But in many ways he turned out to be a disappointing president, partly because that transition was both more complicated and less complete than it appeared.[87] Fox stoked expectations, promising more economic reforms and growth of 7 per cent a year, but was unable to deliver much of either. Just as he moved into Los Pinos, Mexico's economy was hit by two blows from outside. In the United States the dotcom bubble burst, slowing industrial production on both sides of the border. NAFTA had helped Mexico recover swiftly after 1995, but it had tied the country's fortunes ever more closely to those of the United States' economy. At the same time, China joined the World Trade Organisation, marking the arrival of a powerful competitor to Mexico for footloose manufacturing plants. These twin blows caused three years of economic stagnation and the loss of some 700,000 jobs, most of them in the *maquiladora* (assembly) plants producing goods for export. The private sector responded, cutting costs. Although some *maquiladoras*, especially in low-value businesses such as textiles and toys, moved to China, Mexico continued to attract investment in higher-value goods, such as cars and electronics. Growth picked up in the second half of Fox's term. But the economy continued to be held back by many vestiges of the corporate state. Labour productivity remained low, at only about a third of that in the United States. Despite NAFTA, much of the domestic economy was dominated by monopolies or oligopolies. Some were state-owned, such as Pemex, the grossly overmanned and inefficient oil firm. Others were privately owned, such as Telmex, the dominant telecoms firm. The cost of restricted competition was tangible: on average, telecoms costs were higher than in China or Brazil as well as in the United States; in 2006 Mexico had fewer telephones per head than Brazil although it privatised eight years earlier. Electricity costs are disproportionately high too, despite big subsidies to the state-owned power companies.

NAFTA has tended to accentuate the gap between the prospering north of the country and the backward, poorer and more indigenous south. Public policies failed to bridge the gap. Although Fox promised an ambitious programme of infrastructure development (mainly roads and electricity) for the south, called Plan Puebla-Panama, not much happened. The government did nothing to encourage alternatives to subsistence farming nor to reform education so that it offered equality of opportunity. In some cases, this was not for want of trying. Fox sent reforms of energy, taxes and labour laws to Congress. But the PAN lacked a legislative majority, and the president lacked the political skills to fashion consensus. There was an underlying political problem. Unlike in Spain or even in Chile, the end of authoritarian rule was not accompanied by a concerted effort to fashion new democratic political institutions. Power has rapidly seeped away from the presidency – to state governors and mayors, to an independent media and above all to Congress and the party leaders. In principle, that is both democratic and positive. The problem is that there are no rules to encourage co-operation among these different actors.

Yet as he left power in 2006, Fox could point to some solid achievements. During his presidency Mexico enjoyed greater political freedom than perhaps at any other time in its history. He maintained economic stability: inflation dropped to just 3.7 per cent in 2006; in the second half of his six-year term, growth picked up, averaging almost 4 per cent a year. A few years of single-digit inflation transformed the financial markets with surprising speed, as Guillermo Ortiz, the Central Bank's governor noted. In 2000, the credit-rating agencies began to award investment-grade status to Mexican government debt. In 1999, the maximum term of government bonds was one year, and most were either denominated in US dollars or linked to inflation. In October 2006, the government was able to issue a thirty-year peso bond whose yield was not linked to inflation. A conservative fiscal policy meant that in 2006, the government only absorbed 16 per cent of national savings, down from 80 per cent in 2000. That has helped everyone else borrow more cheaply. Bigger Mexican companies can now raise money cheaply with peso bonds of their own. The banks finally started lending again as interest rates came tumbling down. A re-organised government housing fund, together with bank mortgages, triggered a house-building boom. Across Mexico, new housing estates sprouted. A quietly expanding middle class saw tangible benefits from stability. At the same time, innovative social policy helped to tackle extreme poverty. The Zedillo government replaced Salinas's Solidarity programme with a less politicised and more effective targeted anti-poverty scheme called *Progresa*. This gave a small monthly stipend to mothers provided they kept their children in school and took them for regular health checks. Normally each Latin American president feels the need to re-invent the wheel. But Fox kept *Progresa*, changing its name to *Oportunidades*, and expanded it so that by 2006 it was reaching 5 million families, or around a quarter of the total population.

Calderón by a whisker

The presidential election of 2006 reflected the fine balance in Mexico between progress and frustration. The campaign was dominated by Andrés Manuel López Obrador, the candidate of the centre-left PRD. As governor of the Federal District, he kept himself constantly in the public eye, with new roads, non-contributory pensions for the elderly and a daily early-morning press conference at which he set the political agenda. He combined this practical action with lacerating criticism of Fox and of the rich and powerful in Mexico. He promised to govern for the poor, and railed against the bankers and businessmen who he said had benefited from crony capitalism. He slammed the economic policy of the past two decades as 'a failure' that delivered 'zero per capita growth' (in fact, per capita income did grow between 1983 and 2005 but at the unimpressive rate of around 0.5 per cent a year). He said he would maintain fiscal balance ('you can't have deficits') but implausibly said he would finance a big increase in public investment merely by cutting bureaucratic waste.[88]

For many months, as López Obrador led the opinion polls, the only question in Mexican political circles was whether he would be a second Hugo Chávez or a second Lula. In reality, the answer was neither. He resembled Argentina's Néstor Kirchner in his profound lack of interest in the world beyond his own country; he took pride in not having a passport. His political mentor was Echeverría. López Obrador had spent his formative political years in the PRI, leaving to join Cárdenas in 1988. His detractors saw in López Obrador a throwback to the PRI's authoritarian populism of the 1970s. In a country where politics was long dominated by backroom deals, López Obrador was a politician of the public plaza in the tradition of South America rather than Mexico. He sometimes showed scant regard for the law, and two of his senior aides were implicated in corruption. However, when Fox's government tried to remove him from the presidential race by bringing criminal charges against him in 2005 for a minor violation of planning law by the city government, the effort rebounded. It was widely seen as disproportionate, politicised justice and merely boosted his popularity. But López Obrador made mistakes of his own, such as insulting Fox and staying away from a first campaign debate. For all his political skills, he was a polarising figure who scared middle-of-the-road democrats. Many of them switched their support to Felipe Calderón, who had beaten Fox's own nominee to be the candidate of the PAN. Though lacking in oratorial charisma, Calderón was a solid and well-prepared politician. Fairly or not, he portrayed López Obrador as a 'danger to Mexico', a second Chávez; Fox and the country's top businessmen weighed in on his behalf.

When Mexico voted on 2 July, Calderón (PAN) won with 35.9 per cent of the vote against 35.3 per cent for López Obrador (PRD), a margin of just 233,831 votes out of 42 million. The PRI's Robert Madrazo, an old-style political boss but an economic pragmatist, polled a meagre 22.2 per cent. So confident of victory had López Obrador's campaign been that Manuel Camacho, one of his closest aides, wrote in an article published the day after the election that the voting had taken place 'in exemplary fashion' and that 'democracy is going to win'.[89] Nevertheless, when the result was adverse, López Obrador immediately cried fraud, though he never produced any plausible evidence. He demanded a vote-by-vote recount, even though two counts of the votes had produced a similar result. To get his way, he launched a campaign of 'civil resistance'. For seven weeks, his followers camped out in the Zócalo and along Reforma, Mexico City's grandest avenue. The electoral tribunal ordered a recount of 9 per cent of the ballot boxes – those in which López Obrador's campaign claimed that most irregularities had occurred. But this only shaved 10,000 votes from Calderón's margin of victory.[90] Even so, López Obrador refused to concede defeat. 'To hell with your institutions,' he cried, calling Fox 'a traitor to democracy' and Calderón a usurper. He proclaimed himself Mexico's legitimate president.

But by then, most Mexicans had stopped listening to him. His actions in defeat seemed to prove right the fears of his detractors. His attempt to emulate Bolivia's Evo Morales and use street protests to topple an elected president failed. His followers did not make up the mass social movement he claimed. Talking to those camped out in Reforma, it was clear that many of them were clients of the political machine he had built while governor of the Federal District. There was much irony and little truth in his claim that the 2006 election was a repeat of 1988. The truth was that Mexico's independent electoral authorities passed a severe test in 2006, with only a few glitches. The irony was that many of López Obrador's closest aides were, like him, former

PRI officials who had been complicit in the fraudulent campaigns of the past. In the view of Héctor Aguilar Camín, a historian, the protests of 2006 were those that the PRI didn't stage when it lost power in 2000. 'Alternation in power had happened very cheaply for us. It's the first protest against this young democracy, done by the ex-priistas of the PRD.'[91] It passed almost unremarked by López Obrador that the PRD had secured its best-ever result in Mexico's Congress in the 2006 election. The party's six state governors, and many of its legislators, began quietly to work through the institutions he disdained, negotiating legislation with the new government.

The narrowness and disputed nature of his mandate meant that Calderón faced a difficult task in governing Mexico, let alone pushing through pending reforms. But he had certain advantages. Unlike Fox, Calderón was a party man through and through. Aged only 44 in 2006, he had much political experience, having headed the PAN's congressional caucus. A lawyer, he also had technocratic credentials, having studied economics and, at Harvard, public administration. He faced a more favourable economic situation than Fox had inherited (although once again a new government in Mexico took office with the US economy decelerating). Such was Mexico's financial strength that the peso and stockmarket sailed through the election and its aftermath without blinking. Even without further reform, Mexico's economy could grow at a steady 4 per cent or so over the next few years, according to Francisco Gil, Fox's finance minister.[92] He drew a parallel with Spain, which like Mexico opened up its economy and cast off authoritarian rule. Like Mexico, Spain suffers from weak productivity but has achieved sustained economic growth by combining manufacturing exports to a large and rich neighbour (the European Union, in its case) with dynamic construction and tourism industries and a strong banking system. Spain, however, had stronger institutions and a more educated population than Mexico when it embarked on democracy. And Mexico needs to grow faster than Spain if it is to achieve a rapid reduction in poverty. Such is the lack of opportunity that each year during Fox's government some 500,000 Mexicans risked the increasingly hazardous border crossing to migrate to the United States. The task facing Calderón was to create a more dynamic economy by demolishing the remaining vestiges of the corporate state and to help to fashion more effective democratic institutions.

In the quarter of a century since the 1982 debt crisis, and especially in the past dozen years, Mexico has changed radically. It is a much more democratic, pluralist and open society than it was under Salinas, let alone under López Portillo. Yet the economic reforms remained partial, and their success was only partial too.

CHAPTER 9

CHANGING SOCIETIES

Walk down the side of the presidential palace in Lima, cross the River Rímac on a stone bridge built in 1610, turn right past the colonial-era bullring at Acho and you are transported from the remnants of viceregal splendour into the grubby, dynamic chaos of twenty-first-century urban Latin America. Hundreds of brightly painted minibuses and battered Volkswagen Beetles operating as self-appointed taxis vie to take you to San Juan de Lurigancho, a broad desert valley surrounded by grey Andean foothills that stretches north-eastwards for miles. Settlement only began there in the 1960s; by 1980 the district had a population of 260,000.[1] Today, the municipal district of San Juan de Lurigancho is home to more than 830,000 people, or more than a tenth of metropolitan Lima. It is only the largest of a score of 'shantytown' districts grouped in three *conos* ('cones') that project into the desert to the north, east and south of Lima.

The foundation of these squatter settlements was graphically described by Norman Lewis, a British travel writer, who visited Peru in 1972:

The new arrivals, urban slum-dwellers who could no longer afford to pay their rent, or Indians to whom conditions in places like these were sybaritic compared to the destitution of the Altiplano, simply marked out their claims, knocked four stakes into the ground and nailed straw-matting to them to make an enclosure ... Dust covered everything, including the repellent strips of *charqui* (dried meat) and the blackened slices of cow's heart on the food stalls. Everything was squalid and makeshift. There was filth and foraging pigs in the streets, water stored in oil drums and bought at racketeering prices, and all the sicknesses one would expect to find in such a place. And yet hope was not absent. The government had given these people nothing whatever, but they had come together and turned themselves into a smoothly working community.[2]

In the 1980s, wave after wave of families fleeing the 'dirty war' between *Sendero Luminoso* and the army erected their *esteras* (huts of straw-matting), moving further up the valley and the hillsides. A study of Huáscar, a neighbourhood of San Juan de Lurigancho, by Emma Raffo, a Peruvian anthropologist, recorded that in 1984, eight years after its foundation, most houses were barely half-built and the streets were unpaved. There was electricity, whose installation was paid for in part by the inhabitants themselves, but no drinking water or sewerage. Nobody had property titles.[3]

These were difficult years in Lima. The terrorist war of *Sendero Luminoso* coincided with, and aggravated, an economic maelstrom of depression and hyperinflation. In 1992, per capita income in Peru had fallen to 70 per cent of its level of 1981, and two-thirds of Peruvians lived in poverty.[4] Government services broke down. *Sendero Luminoso*'s attacks against the power grid meant that for several years Limeños only received electricity one day in two if they were lucky. Rubbish accumulated by the roadside, the few parks in the city were reduced to dusty wastegrounds and public health deteriorated. This collapse of basic state services was dramatised in 1991 when Peru suffered an outbreak of cholera, a disease that had been eradicated from the Americas in the 1920s and whose causes are poverty and poor sanitation. Between 1991 and 2000, 5,040 people died of cholera in Peru (more than 80 per cent of them in the first three years of the outbreak); 7,716 died elsewhere in Latin America (and one in the United States) as the disease spread as far afield as Mexico and Argentina before gradually being controlled.[5]

Today, the *conos* of Lima show many outward signs of progress.[6] The Northern Cone, the oldest-established with a population of 2.3 million, is home to some 20 per cent of Lima's middle class, according to one estimate.[7] Megaplaza, a modern shopping mall, opened there in 2002, after an investment of $50 million. Its 45,000 square metres of retail space include two department stores, a multiplex cinema and restaurants. Its promoters plan a similar mall in the eastern suburbs.[8] In San Juan de Lurigancho the main avenues are asphalted right to the end of the valley, with trim grass in the central reservations. There is a hypermarket on the main avenue, while other streets are lined with *cebicherias* and *chifas* (seafood and Chinese restaurants, respectively), small general stores, car-repair workshops, gyms and private schools advertising English lessons. There is a profusion of evangelical Protestant churches and two Mormon temples. Most houses have electricity, water and sewerage; the smell of excrement no longer pervades the district. On the distant hillsides, there are still *esteras* and huts of wood or brick belonging to the poorest or the most recently arrived. But in Huáscar, all the streets are paved and the neighbourhood is dotted with small parks. Most of the houses are of brick and concrete and comprise two or three storeys; some are finished and faced with whitewashed cement.

This progress has been achieved through a mixture of collective action and individual initiative. Obtaining public services involved a long fight by neighbourhood associations. The women in Huáscar organised *comedores populares* (community kitchens), receiving support from NGOs, the Church and eventually the government. San Juan de Lurigancho is home to hundreds of textile, furniture and footwear businesses, many of which are informal but some of which are successful exporters. Some entrepreneurs in Huáscar have prospered. Noemí Medina arrived there in 1982 from northern Peru 'when this was an *estera*' she says, gesturing to her comfortable three-storey house.[9] She was a community leader, a co-ordinator of the *vaso de leche* ('glass of milk') programme, a scheme introduced by a left-wing mayor of Lima in the 1980s under which poorer children were given free breakfasts. In 1986 she bought a sewing machine with a small loan from an NGO and began making bras. Today, she has eight sewing machines in a workshop on the flat roof of her comfortably furnished three-story house. She employs eight workers, who make more than 1,000 items of baby-clothes a week which she sells under her own brand name. Her younger son helps her with sales and marketing; he has a law degree from the Catholic University, one of Lima's most prestigious and expensive universities. Her story is one of hard work mixed with occasional strokes of good fortune. As a teenager she studied dressmaking and later attended a secretarial course and another in design. She has had several low-cost loans from micro-credit institutions and one from a commercial bank. When Mario Vargas Llosa unsuccessfully ran for election as Peru's president in 1990, his Libertad party sent a business-school professor to teach management classes in Huáscar. 'I went to all the classes and learned a lot,' says Ms Medina. 'How to administer the workshop, the stockroom, the value of each thing, how to separate the accounts of the business from those of the home.' An evangelical Protestant who belongs to Catedral de la Fé, a church founded in Argentina in 1984, she says that 'God has always helped me in everything and I always pay my tithe', donating clothes to those poorer than herself.

Most people in Huáscar have not been as successful as Ms Medina. In follow-up fieldwork in 2006, Emma Raffo found that many of those she had interviewed in the 1980s remained poor, dependent on casual or informal work, the men as building workers or in the textile workshops, the women in domestic service or as seamstresses. More positively, nearly all have finished building their houses. They have piped water and sewerage as well as electricity. Nearly all of them have refrigerators and telephones as well as the ubiquitous colour television; a few have computers. For all of them, their house is their most important asset. Though they have property titles, none would contemplate offering the houses as a guarantee for a loan. In some cases rooms are rented out or used for small businesses. In others, married children have set up home on the second or third floor. Unlike their parents, they will not have to start from scratch, invading land and living for years without basic services. In most cases the children have received more education than their parents. Some of the children, usually the youngest in the family, have completed university degrees (often with financial help from elder working siblings). Some families manage to save a little, money that is used when someone suffers illness or requires an operation. There is much expectation that the younger generation will be better-off than their parents. Some youngsters have migrated to Europe or the United States – a source of sorrow but also of pride. The younger generation is less deferential than their parents, and has high expectations.[10] One poll found that 75 per cent of respondents aged 15 to 29 wanted to leave, with the United States, Chile and Spain as the most favoured destinations.[11] The family remains a vital network for pooling resources. But it is not immune to the strains and frustrations of poverty. Across Latin America, a quarter of all families are headed by women.[12] Men often come and go. Machismo has not noticeably been weakened by modernity. Domestic violence is a widespread, and often unrecognised, problem. In San Juan de Lurigancho, a group of NGOs has set up a refuge for battered women, but such facilities are rare.

Peru regressed further than almost anywhere else in the region in the 1980s. Its economy has been growing again since 1992, and rapidly (an annual average of over 5 per cent) since 2002. But only in 2006 did it start to generate many new jobs. Despite the growth, poverty has fallen only modestly, from 54 per cent in 2001 to 51.6 per cent in 2004; extreme poverty fell faster, from 24.1 to 19.2 per cent.[13] Much of the growth comes from high prices for mineral exports and a boom in the capital-intensive mining industry. But some of it stems from the rise of labour-intensive agriculture on the Pacific Coast. The top-down co-operatives imposed by Velasco's agrarian reform were split up into family-owned plots by spontaneous decision of the co-op members in the 1980s. A new breed of commercial farmers with small and medium-sized holdings has come into being. They produce for export asparagus, artichokes, mangoes and a host of other crops, just like their counterparts in Chile.

For the first time in a generation, Peru has a good chance of sustained economic growth and rapid falls in poverty. But there is a missing element. The country's core public services – health, education, transport and the police – are of poor quality, and an anti-poverty programme was only just getting off the ground. Too many people lack the skills and capacities needed to get a decent job, even if one were available. In Huáscar, for example, the health centre from the 1980s has been turned into a small hospital, with 36 beds for obstetrics and gynaecology, 40 beds for emergencies, basic medicine and surgery. It has one ambulance. But it is the only hospital in the whole of San Juan de Lurigancho. According to Dr Mario Ruiz, the hospital's director, the district has the highest rate of tuberculosis in Peru.[14] The Fujimori government allocated half the money needed to build a TB ward, but then the senior officials at the health ministry changed. The ward has been abandoned, unfinished. The government of Alejandro Toledo (2001–6) set up a system under which the government pays the cost of tests, X-rays and medicines for poorer patients, but Dr Ruiz said the money frequently arrives in arrears. Patients said that they have to pay the petrol for the ambulance, and for most medicines. The hospital has 54 doctors, but they only work in the mornings; in the afternoons they cross the road and practise privately in modest consulting rooms. Education in San Juan de Lurigancho is little better than healthcare. A shortage of school buildings and of money means that state schools operate a two-shift system, accommodating primary classes from eight a.m. to one p.m. and then secondary school from one p.m. to six p.m. Teachers lack facilities and time to prepare classes. Primary classes have up to forty pupils. Teachers say that only a minority of children come from two-parent families.[15]

In the 1980s, a youthful Alan García of the moderately populist APRA party wrecked Peru's economy with his reckless dash for growth. In 2006, García was elected again. He was older and seemed wiser, and ran on a platform of moderate change. That Peruvians preferred him to Ollanta Humala, a radical populist army officer in the mould of Hugo Chávez, was a sign that many believed that things were moving in the right direction and that they had something to lose. But the southern Andes, the poorest area of the country, voted overwhelmingly for Humala. The task facing García was to sustain and increase economic growth while improving public policies to ensure that its benefits reached places like San Juan de Lurigancho and the southern Andes. That meant reforming education, healthcare, social policies and other functions of the state. This challenge was particularly acute in Peru, but it applied almost everywhere else in the region.

Urban, mobile and expectant

Public policy may be falling short in San Juan de Lurigancho, but such places embody the gigantic process of social change that has transformed Peru and many other countries in the region over the past two generations. The migrants who streamed to Lima and other coastal cities were leaving behind conditions of servitude, misery and isolation in the Andes. The city has not offered jobs to all of their children, and the services they receive may be deficient, but most are far better-off than they would be in rural areas. The presence of the migrants and their descendants has democratised the country from the bottom up. Peru still bears the traces of a caste society with a racist white elite. But the march of *mestizaje* is unstoppable, the elite is less white and less homogenous than it was in the 1970s and there is more social mobility. The *conos* of Lima have become 'melting pots that fuse the distinct regional traditions' and 'the powerful centre of a new *mestizaje* of predominantly Andean colour, generating cultural styles, economic options, organisational systems and creating the bases of a new institutionality', argued José Matos Mar, an anthropologist of Andean Indian descent in an influential book originally published in Peru in 1984.[16] Matos Mar is a man of the left, but his view of the informal economy as an emerging and alternative legal order was similar to that which Hernando de Soto would express in 'The Other Path' two years later.[17] This *mestizaje* has its counterpart in politics. Disdaining the political establishment, the *conos* voted for outsiders, such as Alberto Fujimori and Alejandro Toledo, though they shunned Ollanta Humala in 2006. At a local level, too, they have made their voice heard. In San Juan de Lurigancho, four of the nine mayors since local elections were restored in 1981 have been imprisoned for corruption or theft. But recent mayors have been more effective. The district council and the mayor meet regularly with a consultative group of community leaders and NGOs to discuss policy on health, education, women, children, the environment and public security. 'There has been some progress,' said Ketty Pelaez, a community leader. 'People have understood that there's a system, though whether they participate is another matter.'[18]

In the past half-century or so, Latin American societies have become overwhelmingly urban. In 1940, more than 60 per cent of the population lived in the countryside. Today, according to the United Nations, 76 per cent live in cities, making Latin America among the world's most urbanised regions. Migration is a search for opportunity, an expression of choice. Urban life offers many more possibilities of receiving modern services than the peasant farming that many migrants (or their parents) left behind. Latin America's swelling megacities are theatres of social inequality but also of social progress.

When Margaret Thatcher flew over São Paulo in 1992 on a trip to Brazil after she had left office as Britain's prime minister, she exclaimed in awed surprise at its serried ranks of skyscrapers stretching to the horizon: 'Why didn't anybody tell me about this?'[19] The largest city in the southern hemisphere, São Paulo's population grew at a dizzying 5 per cent a year during Brazil's economic 'miracle' of the 1960s and 1970s. North-easterners such as the young Lula da Silva joined a new wave of foreign migrants, as Lebanese and Koreans followed the Germans, Italians and Japanese who arrived in the late nineteenth century. São Paulo became the largest industrial centre in the southern hemisphere. Car factories like Volkswagen's Anchieta plant, a vast industrial cathedral, were built in its suburbs. It was said that São Paulo was home to more German industrial firms than any other city in the world. Some of the migrants were unable to get industrial jobs and ended up in miserable *favelas* on the outskirts. But the city also spawned a large middle class. São Paulo's headlong growth was in part the hypertrophic consequence of inward-looking economic policies. Brazil's economic opening of the 1990s was painful for greater São Paulo, which in 2006 had a population of 18 million. Some traditional industrial firms could not compete; new industries emerged elsewhere, often in mid-sized towns; much of the car industry moved to new factories in neighbouring states. São Paulo has re-invented itself as a financial and service centre, the only truly global city in Latin America. The world's third-largest civilian helicopter fleet ferries businessmen to and from gleaming skyscrapers above the congested streets. The city and its satellite towns are studded with shopping malls and hypermarkets.

Unemployment in greater São Paulo peaked at 21 per cent in 2004, but had fallen to 14 per cent by late 2006.[20] There are continuing enclaves of misery and crime. But, as in Lima, there has been progress despite slow economic growth. A study in 2005 of low-income families in four districts on the periphery of Greater São Paulo carried out by the Fernand Braudel Institute found that 96 per cent of them lived in houses of cement-covered bricks, rather than the wooden shacks of the 1970s.[21] São Paulo has avoided the depths of the chronic drug-related violence of Rio de Janeiro, a city which has yet to recover from losing its status as Brazil's capital in 1960 and where the *favelas* climbing over the hills above the opulent beachfronts of Copacabana, Ipanema and Leblon symbolise a society that was too long complacent about social inequalities. Nevertheless, a study of residents in three Rio *favelas* in 2001 found that 96 per cent had piped water and electricity (compared with figures of 33 per cent for water and 48 per cent for electricity in 1969); that 73 per cent of the children were more educated than their parents; and that 74 per cent of the children earned more than the minimum wage, compared with 45 per cent of their parents. But fear of crime, the police and drug traffickers had increased.[22]

Across Latin America, in 2002 nine out of ten households had access to potable water (up from 83 per cent in 1990) and electricity, while three-quarters had access to improved sanitation (up from 69 per cent in 1990).[23] Access to basic public services has transformed the lives of many Latin American families over the past few decades, though this is not properly counted in the statistics on poverty and inequality. Urbanisation has gone hand in hand with more access to education; a more mobile and demanding society has gone hand in hand with democracy. Today's urban Latin Americans have much higher expectations than their rural forebears. They demand more of governments. They are organised in different ways than in the past. In most countries, trade unions are much weaker than they were in the 1970s. But thousands of social movements, community groups and NGOs have arisen to press for better housing or services, for land reform, human rights and women's rights, or for environmental protection. 'Civil society', to use the fashionable term for the tapestry of social movements, voluntary associations and pressure groups, is vocal, robust and lively in many countries. That, too, is relatively new: had Alexis de Tocqueville strayed south during his celebrated investigation of 'Democracy in America', he would have found few of the voluntary organisations that so impressed him in the early United States.

Class divisions have become much less rigid. A study in 1996 by Nelson do Valle e Silva, a sociologist at a Rio de Janeiro university, found that fully half of Brazilians had moved to a higher socio-economic category than that of their parents (though 11 per cent had slid to a lower one). Even Brazil's elite is not a closed group: it doubles in size each generation and about one in five of its members are the children of rural labourers.[24] At the bottom, a greatly expanded urban working class is no longer predominantly made up of unionised factory workers: in most Latin American countries the informal sector of small unregistered businesses makes up 40 to 50 per cent of the workforce. There are frequent laments that the middle class is shrinking and being squeezed. That reflects the decline in jobs in the public sector in the 1980s and 1990s and of the perks and privileges that often went with them. But more broadly, the middle class is both expanding and changing in character. Fernando Henrique Cardoso, a sociologist as well as politician, has noted that middle-class groups 'linked to the market and not to the state are more numerous and have more modern aspirations and demands'. They include managers and owners of small businesses, and many professionals in the media, entertainment, leisure and financial industries; many have risen from families of lower status.[25] This new middle class is starting to blur the traditional divide between a small rich elite, which nowadays is less homogenous than myth would have it, and the poor masses. Economists at the World Bank and Argentina's University of La Plata have made a rare attempt to measure the size of the middle class, which they define as people with an income of four to eight times the international poverty line of $2 per day (adjusted for local purchasing power). They conclude that in the 2003–5 period around 17 per cent of Latin Americans qualified, up from 15 per cent in 1992–5 (the year of measurement varied across countries). The increase was doubtless blunted by the 'lost half-decade' of economic stagnation of 1998–2002. But the trends were clear: while the middle class shrank in Argentina and Venezuela it increased in Mexico and by more than the average in Brazil and Chile.[26] According to another estimate, the number of Mexican families with incomes of between US$600 and US$1,500 per month rose from just over 5 million in 1992 to more than 9 million in 2004.[27]

Perhaps the most characteristic change in Latin America's social structure compared with a generation ago in qualitative terms is the emergence of an expanding and socially ambitious lower middle class. Its members have much more access to consumer goods than their parents. In the Braudel Institute study all the households surveyed had refrigerators and colour televisions (often more than one). Nearly half had mobile phones, and 29 per cent owned a car. Some 30 per cent of respondents owned DVD players, and another 22 per cent planned to buy one soon. Much of this was financed by high-cost consumer loans – a potential problem.[28] The ubiquity of refrigerators and other consumer goods contrasts with Eduardo Galeano's assertion in *Open Veins of Latin America*, that still-influential anti-capitalist tract, that 'the consumers to whom big auto and refrigerator plants direct their products are only 5% of the Latin American population. Hardly one in four Brazilians can really be considered a consumer.'[29]

Even in Bolivia, the move from countryside to city has provided opportunities. Take the case of Felipe Copaja, the man of Aymara descent who owns a small workshop in a side-street in El Alto.[30] He was born in an Indian village on the Altiplano. His parents were peasant farmers. 'Because of poverty, they came to work in El Alto,' he said. 'But they continued to go back and forth. They sold weavings and handcrafts.'[31] When he was ten, Felipe came to El Alto, where he completed secondary school, trained as a mechanic and set up his own business. Though dissatisfied with corruption and what he called impunity (i.e. the lack of the rule of law), he said that racial discrimination is less pervasive than it was. 'I've done quite well,' he declared. His daughter was due to start studying medicine at La Paz's San Andrés University, the city's oldest seat of higher education. His son hoped to follow her to university.

The search for opportunity

That quiet journey of social mobility is repeated across the region, even if not everyone makes it. Finding jobs for these proud new university graduates is one of the many challenges facing the region's democracies. It is made particularly acute by demographic change. The region's population grew explosively for several decades until the 1960s, as improvements in public health meant that life expectancy increased and infant mortality declined. The birth rate then began to fall, amongst other things because of improvements in education, especially of girls, and the spread of contraception. But there are lags involved in what economists call the 'demographic transition' from a growing population to a stable one (there are also big variations from country to country). Until about 1995 the absolute number of children in Latin America continued to grow – requiring big investments in extra school places. There is currently a 'bulge' of young adults seeking employment. This may be one reason for high levels of crime in recent decades. The advantage is that the 'dependency ratio' – the number of those too young and too old to work compared to the labour force – is low at the moment, and will be for another two decades or so. That means that social spending will be relatively low and pension obligations ought to be manageable during this period. Thereafter Latin America will quickly run into the problems of an ageing population that are common in the rich world.[32]

One response to the lack of opportunities at home has been emigration. Countries that imported people have begun to export them. Migration robs Latin America of some of its brightest, but brings remittances and new ideas. According to estimates by the Inter-American Development Bank (IDB), in 2005 some 22 million Latin Americans worked in the developed world while another 3 million to 5 million were in neighbouring countries within the region (for example, there were many Bolivians in Argentina, Nicaraguans in Costa Rica, Guatemalans in Mexico, Haitians in the Dominican Republic, Colombians in Venezuela and Peruvians in Chile.) The IDB reckoned that these workers sent to family members back home remittances totalling almost $54 billion in 2005 – or more than the combined total of foreign direct investment and foreign aid for the whole region. These funds are an important source of support for millions of poorer families.[33] The World Bank put the total figure for remittances to Latin America and the Caribbean at $48.3 billion in 2005 – a tenfold increase in real terms since 1990. Some $21.8 billion went to Mexico, but remittances were even more important to the smaller economies of Central American and Caribbean countries, accounting for more than 50 per cent of Haiti's GDP and above 10 per cent in Honduras, El Salvador, the Dominican Republic, Nicaragua and Guatemala. But the bank cautions that the net effect of remittances on economic development is relatively small. It estimates that for each percentage-point increase in the share of remittances in GDP, the proportion of the population living in poverty falls by 0.4 per cent.[34] And migration has human and economic costs, often depriving children of one or both parents and the labour force of some of its more enterprising members. In addition, there are the rising dangers of the journey itself: 472 people died trying to cross Mexico's northern border in 2005, up from 254 in 1998, according to the United States Government Accountability Office.[35]

A more traditional response to lack of opportunity has been the informal sector. Visit almost any city in Latin America and the central districts will be clogged with street vendors, peddling anything from clothes to pirate DVDs to health remedies or construction materials. They are just the most visible segment of a massive informal economy of unregistered businesses. According to estimates by the International Labour Organisation, the informal sector accounted for 48.5 per cent of total urban employment in Latin America in 2005.[36] That figure was slightly down on 1995 (50 per cent). But it was higher than in 1990 (43.6 per cent), though some of that increase may be down to the fact that a higher proportion of adults (especially women) now take part in the labour market.

Why is the informal sector so big? That is a matter of much debate. One school of thought blames over-rigid labour laws that make it expensive to hire and fire workers. Another highlights the failings of the legal system and the labyrinthine complexities of registering a business. But perhaps the most important factor is that, for the unskilled, the formal sector offers little chance of a decent career. There is much research that shows that many workers choose to work for themselves. They pursue the dream of running their own business, often after spending a few years picking up the rudiments of it by working in a formal job.[37] The informal sector is a result both of low productivity and lack of job-creation in the formal sector, but also of the profusion of unskilled workers. That is a legacy of the past neglect of education in the region: in 2000, for example, only 20 per cent of adult Latin Americans had any secondary schooling at all.[38] In turn, the scale of the informal sector acts as a drag on total productivity in the economy and denies the state potential tax revenues. There are several reasons to believe that in the medium term the informal sector should shrink. Research shows that many of the new jobs created since the opening up of Latin American economies to international trade go to more skilled and educated workers. International experience, such as that of Spain, shows that employment grows gradually but steadily after the kind of structural adjustment that Latin America has undergone. But governments can speed the process, both by making it easier to legalise businesses and above all by improving the education and training of the workforce.

A rebellion against poverty and discrimination

Cotacachi is a small, pleasant town in a verdant valley between two towering volcanoes, a couple of hours' drive north of Ecuador's capital, Quito. Since 1996, its mayor has been Auki Tituaña, an economist who wears the traditional pigtail, white felt hat and poncho of the Quichua-speaking Indians of the Ecuadorean Andes. Aged 39 when interviewed in 2004, he recalled that as a child his mother would drag him into the road to let a *mestizo* pass on the pavement. When Indians came down from their plots in the hills to the market, town officials would confiscate their ponchos and hats as a means of press-ganging them to sweep the streets without pay. Such discrimination has been challenged by new organisations of Latin Americans of indigenous and African descent. There is less racism than there was, but those who suffer it are more conscious and less tolerant of it. 'The *mestizo* has begun to look on us with greater respect, but they still don't see us as equal partners,' Mr Tituaña said.[39]

From the Mexican revolution onwards, governments in several countries recognised the cultural legacy of indigenous people and made paternalistic efforts to improve their lot. The aim was assimilation. Indian peoples, it was tacitly thought, would disappear under the twin processes of *mestizaje* and urbanisation. They did not. There are generally estimated to be around 40 million Latin Americans who define themselves as indigenous people. Some 90 per cent of them are in just five countries: Mexico, Guatemala, Ecuador, Peru and Bolivia. Mexico has the largest number (some 14 million) but they make up the largest proportion of the total population in Bolivia and Guatemala (perhaps a majority in each country). Many live in extreme poverty; they are amongst the most disadvantaged people in the region, with less education, poorer health and worse living conditions than those who are not indigenous.[40] In both Guatemala and Peru, indigenous people made up the bulk of victims of 'dirty wars' involving left-wing guerrillas and the security forces. Yet they retain a powerful cultural identity. Until recently, indigenous people rarely organised politically along ethnic lines; if they did at all, it was as *campesinos* ('country people', i.e. peasant farmers). The first sign of that changing came in Ecuador in 1990, when a newly formed confederation grouping Indian peoples from the Amazon and the Andes staged a national 'uprising', blocking roads and obliging the government to negotiate. The Zapatista rising, though led by a white former university professor, drew worldwide attention to the grievances of Mayan Indians.

What is behind this rise in ethnic militancy, and what does it portend for Latin American democracy? Poverty and discrimination are not new for indigenous peoples. What has changed is the political environment. In the 1970s Catholic bishops and priests played an important role in training indigenous leaders in several countries. The return or achievement of democracy gave indigenous people political rights, often for the first time. Then globalisation kicked in. The quin-centenary of Columbus's 'discovery' of the Americas focussed attention on the continent's original inhabitants. An international network of activists and NGOs provided financial and other support to indigenous organisations, their leaders and their protests. The Indian cause was given legal force by Convention 169 of the International Labour Organisation (ILO). Most Latin American governments signed it, committing themselves to guarantee indigenous people equal rights as well as to respect their lands and traditions.[41] Some scholars argue that 'neoliberalism' was another factor in the rise of ethnic militancy, both because of the dismantling of the corporate state and its replacement by a liberal philosophy of individual rights, and the opening to investment in mining and oil by multinationals, which often took place on indigenous lands.[42] But the corporate state had rarely done much for indigenous people, and state-owned mining and oil companies had rarely been sensitive to their land claims in the past. Rather, liberal democracy has offered Indian groups the chance to participate in politics more effectively. They have formed political parties in Bolivia and Ecuador. Their advent is part of a broader eclipse of class politics by those of identity.

In a round of constitution writing in the 1990s, the ILO's provisions were incorporated in ten countries, including Bolivia, Ecuador and Peru. Governments, long committed to the aim of racial integration, came to recognise that they rule multicultural societies. The basic, and justified, demand of many of these movements was for equal treatment. Calls for local autonomy and collective rights were potentially more complicated. Some of these demands were met by democratic local government, as in Cotacachi. The appeal to collective rights was in part a defence mechanism, and the expression of a desire to maintain a traditional way of life and all its rich cultural legacy. It also harked back to the *República de Indios*, the caste society of the colonial period. The risk was that it would become a way to entrench modern-day *caciques* and *curacas* and become a cover for the suppression of individual rights, such as in forced marriages. Some indigenous groups carry the stamp of the far left, and their attitude to democracy was ambivalent. In both Ecuador and Bolivia, protests in which indigenous organisations played a prominent part have twice toppled elected presidents. But the recourse to such agitation also showed that in many countries indigenous people were still struggling to be treated as full and equal citizens. The indigenous movements might succeed in negotiating better terms of entry to a globalised world. Or they might lead to the undemocratic trampling of individual liberties within the Andean *ayllu* or Mexican *ejido*, and they might nudge the wider society away from liberal democracy and economic openness.

The term 'Indian' is of course a colonial imposition, and derives from a geographical misunderstanding to boot. But its embrace by some of the indigenous activists was a way of generalising their condition beyond that of each linguistic sub-group. It is also a shifting, socially defined category. Two decades ago, Evo Morales would have described himself as a *mestizo*, and in many ways he is one. But the new politics of ethnic identity signalled that for the first time in centuries, race and racial discrimination had become an explicit and urgent issue to be tackled by the new democracies.

That applied also to the descendants of African slaves, who by one count make up some 30 per cent of Latin Americans.[43] Like indigenous peoples, blacks were more likely to be poor. In Brazil, for example, blacks earned 30 per cent less than whites with the same level of education. Yet until recently it was widely believed in Brazil that blacks were poorer because of their class, not their race: *o dinheiro branqueja* ('money whitens'), the Brazilian saying went. Centuries of miscegenation – and the absence of any official colour bar – means Brazilians are a multi-hued rainbow nation. Traditionally, Brazilians' self-image is that they are whiter than others might see them. In the 2000 census, 54 per cent described themselves as white, 38.4 per cent as *pardos* or *mulatos* (i.e. mixed) and only 6 per cent as *negros* (blacks). That self-image was paralleled in the notion of 'racial democracy', officially adopted by republican governments. Getúlio Vargas encouraged expressions of African culture, both in music (*samba*) and religion (*candomblé* and *umbanda*), and these became an integral part of Brazilian national culture.[44] *Feijoada*, a stew of beans and cheap cuts of pork that is Brazil's national dish, has its origins in the slave quarters.

Discrimination might not have been officially encouraged but it existed, expressed in job advertisements that required 'good appearance' or in the ubiquitous second, service lift in middle-class apartment blocks to which servants were relegated. A study in São Paulo in 1995 found that blacks were twice as likely to die violent deaths as whites, and that 42 per cent of black men who died were aged 20 to 49.[45] Around the same time, the city's justice secretary, who was black, complained that he had been stopped four times in a year by police who suspected him of having stolen his official car.[46] In the restored democracy of the past two decades, race has finally made it onto the political agenda in Brazil, pushed there by small, mainly middle-class groups of black activists.[47] Some Brazilians began to describe themselves as blacker than others might see them. The Cardoso government conducted a survey on race in 1999 and found that blacks and browns, though 45 per cent of the total population, made up 64 per cent of the people below the poverty line. A 25-year-old white Brazilian had on average 8.1 years of schooling while a black Brazilian of the same age had just 6.1 years. The government began to implement what Cardoso called 'an eclectic mix of affirmative action policies'.[48] Government ministries began to introduce racial quotas for jobs. Affirmative action gathered momentum under Lula. For the first time, a black judge was appointed to the Supreme Court (though it transpired that in the early twentieth century the court had two *mulato* judges, both of whom had been seen as white).[49] Various city governments introduced racial quotas and so did some public universities. That was controversial.

Some Brazilians worried not just that affirmative action would introduce political clientelism into meritocratic institutions, but that race would become a divisive problem in a way that it had not been before in republican Brazil. But the new political consensus seemed to be that racial discrimination was one of the roots of Brazilian inequality and injustice. Elsewhere in the region, this debate was less advanced. But other countries, such as Colombia and Peru, moved to make racial discrimination illegal. They sometimes even tried to enforce it – an upmarket discotheque in Lima was fined after it refused entry to a dark-skinned Peruvian.

The neglect of the countryside

Visit the highlands of southern Mexico, Guatemala or the Andes and the picture becomes depressingly familiar. Especially away from the coasts, rural areas in Latin America tend to be poor and lack good roads, schools and healthcare. Governments have long tended to neglect the countryside, either because they lacked the means to do otherwise, because they were pursuing industrialisation or, nowadays, because the voters are mainly in the cities. Yet this may be a mistake. Latin America is less urban than the official statistics suggest. These treat villages of 2,000 people in remote areas as 'urban'. The OECD applies a more realistic definition of 'rural': all places that have fewer than 150 inhabitants per square kilometre (0.4 square miles) and are more than an hour's travel from the nearest city of more than 100,000 people. By that definition, some 42 per cent of Latin Americans live in the countryside according to the World Bank.[50] It argues that public spending has been too biased towards urban areas and to subsidies to richer farmers. It wants governments to spend more on rural education and roads and on farm-related research and development. Where they have done so in the past the results were positive. Take Colombia's coffee belt. Its capital, Manizales, is a clean modern city of 380,000 people, 2,250 metres up in the central cordillera of the Andes. The surrounding hillsides are full of neat, brightly painted farmhouses linked by asphalted roads, home to a rural middle class.[51]

Some would argue that governments also ought to be carrying out land reform. Landholding remains very unequal in many countries – in Brazil 1 per cent of rural landowners possess half of farmland (though that includes large tracts of Amazonia that are unsuitable for agriculture). In countries such as Brazil, Bolivia and Paraguay, democracy has seen the emergence of powerful movements of landless would-be farmers. Brazil's Movimento Sem Terra (MST) has gained many admirers abroad. (Noam Chomsky, an American leftist, has called it 'the most important and exciting popular movement in the world'.)[52] In the mid-1990s the MST attracted the sympathy of many urban

Brazilians who saw it as a symbol of their country's social injustice. It was even favourably portrayed in a Globo television soap opera. This sympathy peaked after police in the northern state of Pará massacred 19 MST members. (In all more than a thousand rural activists have been killed in Brazil in the past two decades.) That prompted the Cardoso government to launch a huge land reform programme. According to government figures, between 1995 and 2002 some 20 million hectares – a territory the size of the Benelux countries – were distributed to 635,000 families; this was five times more than had received land in the previous twelve years. The government created a land registry, introduced a tax on idle land and approved a summary procedure for its expropriation.[53] The Lula government continued the programme along similar lines.

The MST complained that the pace of land distribution was nowhere near fast enough. Others worried that it might be too fast. The beneficiaries face all the problems of small-scale family farming. For example, at Pirituba, an MST settlement in upstate São Paulo, some farmers were making only around US$150 per month a dozen years after moving onto the land (though they also grew much of their food). To provide jobs and to stop their children leaving the land, they wanted government support to develop agro-industrial projects, such as fish- and fruit-farming, according to Ilda de Souza, the leader of a co-operative there.[54] Some of the MST members were recruited from the ranks of the urban unemployed and had no background or experience in farming. The risk is that land reform becomes a disguised welfare programme – and a more expensive one than *Bolsa Família*, the government's main targeted anti-poverty programme. Land reform is costly: Cardoso spent $7 billion on it in his first term alone. In theory, after a few years its beneficiaries are supposed to become 'emancipated', with their own land titles, like other farmers. But in practice, very few settlements have made that step, which the MST resists. It was also hostile to a pilot programme under which cheap loans were given to would-be farmers to buy land. Although the MST likes to paint the picture of a countryside in the grip of retrograde *latifundia*, in fact much Brazilian agribusiness is modern and efficient. That did not stop MST activists from invading productive holdings; it broke into a forestry plantation operated by Votorantim, a Brazilian conglomerate, three times in 2005, destroying a tree nursery. To many Brazilians, it became increasingly unclear whether the movement's aim was land reform or social revolution.

Land reform was repaying 'a debt from the past' as Cardoso put it. The tragedy was that it didn't happen earlier, when ownership of land was a more important factor in Latin America's political and social inequalities. In some other countries, such as Mexico, Venezuela, Bolivia and Peru, comprehensive land reforms were carried out in the middle decades of the twentieth century. In Brazil that did not happen – until a restored and far more inclusive democracy decided that it was a political imperative.

A revolution in prayer

Social change has even affected that most traditional of Latin American institutions, the Roman Catholic Church. In the 1960s, liberation theology shook the Church out of its lethargy. It became more or less official doctrine when a conference of Latin American Bishops held in Medellín in 1968 declared that the region was in a state of 'structural sin' and 'institutionalised violence' and that the task of the Church was to pursue an 'option for the poor'. Liberation theology was heavily influenced by dependency theory; it would have its most visible political impact in Central America among Nicaragua's Sandinistas and El Salvador's FMLN, and in forming many outsiders' views of Latin America and its problems.[55] Across the region, the liberation theologians worked through Christian base groups and trained a generation of community leaders, most of whom are now in late middle age. They were influential in the founding of the MST and of many other social movements. Revolutionary priests can still be found in Latin America. But liberation theology failed in its effort to create a mass 'popular' church that would pursue socialism, as its promoters wanted. That was partly because Pope John Paul II and the Vatican hierarchy successfully isolated the liberation theologians through the preferment of conservatives (some of them ultra-reactionaries) as bishops. But it was mainly because ordinary Latin Americans were resistant to the 'popular' church.[56]

In the *favelas* and shantytowns from São Paulo to Lima and in the highland villages of Mexico and Guatemala, it is evangelical Protestantism, not 'popular' Catholicism, that is winning converts and changing social attitudes among the region's poor. The evangelicals were at first denounced by the left as agents of authoritarian reaction and of *Yanqui* imperialism. That image was given some credence by the crew-cut Mormons pounding the Latin American streets, the presence of American televangelists such as Jimmy Swaggart on the region's television channels and the prominence of such 'born-again' Christians as Efraín Ríos Montt, Guatemala's bloody military dictator of 1982 to 1983. Some scholars, such as David Lehmann, a Cambridge social scientist, do see the evangelicals as 'an enterprise of cultural conquest'. But Lehmann argues that the evangelicals embrace the United States 'not so much [as] a political or geographical unit, but rather [as] a land of wealth and Protestantism, "land" here being used, as in "land of milk and honey", in a slightly fabulous way.'[57]

Today there are thousands of different evangelical churches and sects. Many are of home-grown Latin American inspiration; even those that are not have acquired a local character. Their politics are varied but are nearly always directed rather narrowly at promoting the interests of their own churches. What they have in common is a stress on teetotalism, hard work and progress through individual effort without neglecting charity for the less fortunate. Whereas the liberation theologians and their base communities focussed on trying to change society, the evangelical Protestants offer individuals counselling and succour with the concrete problems of their everyday lives. They well express the driving ambition of the lower middle class. They have acquired a mass audience among the poor, among black Brazilians and indigenous Guatemalans, and also among women. They preach the importance of the family as a stable unit in which men should assume their responsibilities; they are less tolerant than Catholics of male infidelity. The response of the Catholic Church has been the charismatic revival movement, founded in the United States in the 1960s. Like many of the evangelical churches, it is a Pentecostal movement that emphasises the spontaneous experience of the Holy Spirit and the opportunity for individuals to change their lives. Denounced as middle class by its detractors among the liberation theologians, like evangelical Protestants the charismatics offer support to the upwardly mobile. In places like São Paulo they draw hundreds of thousands to open-air masses.

In Guatemala, some 30 per cent of the population is now Protestant; six out of ten of the remaining Catholics are charismatics. Fraternidad Cristiana, a homegrown Protestant church, planned to open in 2007 a temple that was said to be the largest building in Central America, complete with a 'Burger King drive', seating for over 12,000 and parking for more than 3,500 cars, all at a cost of $20 million.[58] At least 15 per cent of Brazilians are now Protestants. In some ways, the Pentecostals are agents of modernisation in Latin America, preaching individual initiative, hard work and entrepreneurialism. At the same time, they have obvious flaws: they have their share of fraudsters, and many of their religious practices – speaking in tongues, miracles and the like – seem mediaeval. But in ways that are often overlooked, they are changing Latin America, and especially some of its poorer places. So much for the contention that the Counter-Reformation still dominates the lives of the Spanish-speaking peoples, as Claudio Véliz could argue as recently as 1994.[59]

The media finds a new message

Latin America's mass media, too, have changed much over the past quarter-century. In the early 1990s, as Carlos Salinas was propelling his country into the North American Free Trade Agreement, finding out what was happening in Mexico was about as easy as it was in the Soviet Union. Televisa, a private company, had acquired a near-monopoly on television, with four national channels, in return for its loyalty to the regime. Its evening news programme was the mouthpiece of Los Pinos, the presidential office. It offered upbeat daily reports of the president's doings. The opposition, especially its leader, Cuauhtémoc Cárdenas, was simply ignored, except for occasional smear reports alleging that he was linked to violence. Salinas later privatised the state channel, Televisa's only competitor: it was bought by Ricardo Salinas Pliego (no relation, but a friend) who ran a chain of white-goods shops. (Salinas Pliego was investigated for corporate malfeasance by the US Securities and Exchange Commission in 2005.) In those days, Mexico City had a dozen daily newspapers. All had small circulations, and all were kept alive by government payments. *Proceso*, a newsweekly, was more independent, but survived by being impenetrably dull. There were only three other independent news media in the whole of the country, all in far-flung cities: *El Norte* in Monterrey, *El Diario de Yucatán* in Mérida, and *Zeta* in Tijuana.

In Brazil, things were not all that much better. The Globo TV network owed its expansion to its relationship with the dictatorship. Globo notoriously failed to cover massive street demonstrations calling for a direct presidential election in 1985 (rather than the dictatorship's preferred option of an election in Congress). In 1990, it did all it could to stop Lula winning the presidency and get Fernando Collor, the telegenic but hitherto little-known governor of the small state of Alagoas, elected instead. Only a few years earlier, in Brazil and many other countries dictatorships imposed censorship; defiant independent journalists faced exile, imprisonment or worse.

Such treatment continues only in Cuba, where 29 independent journalists were arrested in 2003 and given prison terms averaging 27 years after summary trials; in 2006, 24 were still in jail. Elsewhere the media landscape looks very different. In Mexico, television remains a duopoly, but news is less propagandistic in tone. The press is free and independent. Though there is much sensationalism and poor journalism, there are two or three serious newspapers, providing a range of comment and analysis. In Brazil, Globo has matured into a much more democratic outlet; much of its output is of good quality. The Brazilian press has carried out ceaseless investigations into corruption in all branches of government. In Peru, each Sunday evening viewers can choose from three or four lengthy current affairs programmes, offering investigative reports, interviews and analysis. Several of Peru's print media are fiercely independent. Across the region, thousands of radio stations provide the main source of information for many Latin Americans. Although only 16 per cent of Latin Americans had internet access in 2006, this figure was growing fast, and with it a host of local news websites and blogs.[60] Internet cafes are ubiquitous, from shantytowns to Andean villages.

There were still some concerns. In parts of Latin America, journalism is a dangerous trade. According to the Committee to Protect Journalists, a New York-based body, 39 journalists were killed in Colombia between 1992 and 2006 because of their work – more than anywhere else over that period except Iraq, Algeria and Russia. Many of the Colombian victims fell in a brave battle against drug traffickers and their allies in paramilitary groups. El Espectador, one of the two main Bogotá daily newspapers, closed in 2004. It had never really recovered from reprisals against it by Pablo Escobar, after the paper had revealed his role in the drug trade. In 1986 its editor, Guillermo Cano, was murdered by a gunman acting on the orders of Escobar. Four years later, the paper's offices and print works were damaged by a massive bomb. The paper's circulation in Medellín, Colombia's second city, was restricted by intimidation against distributors. As the centre of power of the drug trade shifted to Mexico in the early years of this century, the media there started to face similar threats, with 13 journalists killed between 1992 and 2006. Journalists in remote areas of Brazil and Peru were also vulnerable. Normally it was journalists in provincial towns reporting on local corruption or abuse who were most at risk. Their killers were rarely brought to justice. A second, related problem was self-censorship as a means of survival, a growing practice in Colombia.

In some countries, media freedom faced threats from government. That was especially so in the case of Venezuela.[61] Defamation laws were a concern in several countries. In Argentina, many media companies depended unhealthily on government. They piled up dollar debts during the 1990s. When the peso was devalued in 2002, they secured a law from the government that declared that the media were part of Argentina's cultural patrimony and thus could not be taken over by foreign creditors. Government publicity made up an important source of revenue for several Argentine newspapers and journalistic programmes on television. In Latin America, as in many other parts of the democratic world, media companies were often linked to large conglomerates with other business interests. That gave rise to potential conflicts of interest. In Colombia, television news programmes used to be assigned to the two main parties. Now they are in the hands of such conglomerates.

At the same time, modern media groups emerged in several countries. They took a professional approach to news; some of them pursued investigative journalism. Investigations by La Nación of Costa Rica turned up evidence that three of the country's former presidents had received bribes. One of the former presidents, Miguel Angel Rodríguez, was forced to resign from the post of secretary-general of the Organisation of American States; he faced criminal charges in Costa Rica. In some countries, however, readers and viewers had a hard time distinguishing muckraking from calumny, and claims of grand larceny against the public purse from petty theft. The risk was that they would conclude that politicians were irredeemably corrupt as a species – a stance that is false and that undermines democracy. Overall the media remained one of the more widely trusted institutions of Latin American democracy.[62] It played an important role as a watchdog, and in reflecting the debates about economic and social policy in the region. It was also an important ingredient in the emergence of 'open societies' in Latin America. These societies placed new demands on the region's states, demands which they often struggled to meet.

CHAPTER 10

EVOLVING STATES

The state of Oaxaca in southern Mexico is a corrugated land of forested mountains scored by brown, serpentine rivers. Such are its geographical contortions and ethnic diversity that its 3.4 million people are divided into 570 separate municipalities, more than twice as many as in any other Mexican state. One of them is Santiago Tlazoyaltepec, reached by a drive of a little less than two hours from the state capital up a precipitous dirt road flanked by cool forests of pine and evergreen oak. Like many of the settlements established by the Mixtec people (whose name means 'people of the clouds' in their own language), Tlazoyaltepec straggles along the tops of sinuous mountain ridges. Rather than a town, it is a clutch of separate ribbon villages with a total population of some 10,000 people. The world owes the domestication of the turkey to the Mixtecs. But today, they scratch a living from small *milpas* (maize fields). Ask how things are going, and the answer is a repetitive lament: *no hay trabajo* ('there's no work').

Even so, people are living a little better nowadays, concedes Panfilo Santiago, the municipal councillor in charge of education, a short, thick-set man whose Spanish is delivered in a strong Mixtec accent. One reason is that many of the younger people have gone north, to the United States or to the tomato fields of Baja California. They either return richer, or send money back home. The relative prosperity of families where someone has gone to *el norte* ('the north') is displayed in the status symbols of the Mixtec highlands: a big Ford or Chevrolet pick-up parked outside the door and, increasingly, a two-storey concrete house in place of a wooden hovel. The second reason is that some 70 per cent of people in Tlazoyaltepec are enrolled in an anti-poverty programme begun under the name of *Progresa* by the government of Ernesto Zedillo, and expanded and renamed *Oportunidades* by his successor, Vicente Fox. The scheme pays mothers a modest monthly allowance provided they keep their children at school and take them for regular health check-ups. The payments are small, but rise with the age of the children. By 2006 about 5 million families in Mexico, or one in four, received support from *Oportunidades*. One of them is the Velasco family in Tlazoyaltepec. María Elena Velasco, aged 32, has two young children that she is bringing up on her own because her husband is working in Baja California. She receives 360 pesos (about US$35) every two months from *Oportunidades*. 'It helps a bit,' she says. 'We'd like it to be more, but it helps.'

Progresa was designed by Santiago Levy, an outstanding Mexican technocrat. He says that while he was teaching at Boston University he looked at two different strands of the academic literature on poverty, one concerning nutrition and human capital and the other on income distribution.[1] He put them together in *Progresa*. Though similar schemes were pioneered by some local governments in Brazil in the 1990s, *Progresa* was the first large-scale example of what have come to be known in the jargon of development as 'conditional cash-transfer' programmes or CCTs. It replaced a hotch-potch of other subsidies and transfers. While alleviating poverty in this generation, its main aim is to prevent it in the next generation. The idea is to ensure that in 15 to 20 years' time all young Mexicans complete secondary school (in 2002 only around 40 per cent of the relevant age group did), so that they can get better jobs. The programme is starting to achieve these aims. Poverty is falling: according to government yardsticks, the proportion of Mexicans whose income was insufficient for them to feed themselves adequately more than halved (to 18.2 per cent of the population) between 1996 and 2005.[2] What made this more remarkable was that economic growth was slow between 2000 and 2005. Independent evaluations have found that as *Progresa/ Oportunidades* was rolled out across Mexico, drop-out rates in secondary schools fell significantly. It also had an impact in reducing child labour and improving child health.[3]

In Brazil, the Lula government's conversion to the idea of a CCT scheme was reinforced when James Wolfensohn, the president of the World Bank, arranged for Santiago Levy to go to Brasília and talk to Lula about *Progresa/ Oportunidades*.[4] By late 2006, Brazil's *Bolsa Família* reached one family in four – a similar percentage to *Oportunidades* in Mexico.[5] Similar schemes were set up in half a dozen other countries, including Colombia. The details varied. Argentina's programme, known as *Jefes y Jefas de Família* and expanded in 2002 to cope with mass unemployment, had fewer conditions and higher benefits. The decision as to who received it was in large part sub-contracted to political leaders, who used the scheme to assure themselves a loyal following.[6]

By contrast, across the Andes *Chile Solidario* focussed specifically on the very poorest who usually slipped through social safety-nets. According to Yasna Provoste, a Christian Democrat of Andean Indian descent who was the minister responsible for the programme from 2004 to 2006, 'our mission is to incorporate families who are most excluded from the institutions. Those in extreme poverty didn't know about social networks, rights or benefits. Their poverty was reproduced generationally.'[7] *Chile Solidario* covered some 290,000 families in 2006. It involved much input from a network of more than 2,500 social workers. They made frequent visits to the beneficiaries to ensure that they knew about and made use of a wide range of social programmes covering housing, education and income. One beneficiary of the programme was Olga Durán, a 35-year-old single mother in Peñalolen, a suburb on Santiago's eastern fringe. Sprawling up the slopes towards the snowcapped Andean cordillera which, when pollution allows, can be glimpsed from Chile's capital, Peñalolen is a mix of lower-middle-class respectability and enclaves of poverty, with new housing estates adjoining older, single-storey dwellings. Ms Durán lives in a two-room wooden hut behind one of those single-storey houses, which is occupied by her mother. She moved there after being stabbed by her husband, from whom she is now separated. Through *Chile Solidario* she studied baking and won a grant to set up a small food stall. Her eldest son was able to stay at school, where he did well, winning a scholarship to study electronics. 'Little by little I'm moving forward,' says Ms Durán.[8]

These conditional cash-transfer schemes formed a central part of an evolving, though still incomplete, Latin American welfare state. The region's nation-builders, from the PRI to Perón and Vargas, bequeathed expensive European-style social-security entitlements – but not the means to pay for them. These entitlements covered the middle class and the organised working class, but excluded the masses of the urban and rural poor. In Latin America as a whole, at the peak in 1980 social-security programmes covered only 61 per cent of the population.[9] The new social assistance programmes, such as *Oportunidades*, were more closely targeted at the poor. They were also more democratic than the populist programmes of Perón or Chávez: they were based on the notion that every citizen as an *individual*, rather than as a member of a political client group, had a right to education, health and a minimum social safety-net, irrespective of their political loyalties. They often involved collaboration between national and local government. *Chile Solidario*, for example, relied on household data which municipalities were legally required to draw up. In many cases, the programmes were subject to careful audit and evaluation.

The CCTs were not a panacea. Some analysts worried that they might create a culture of welfare dependency. But the payments are small. A bigger worry, expressed by Levy, is that as free health insurance, pensions and other benefits began to be attached to *Oportunidades*, this might remove any incentive to join the formal economy.[10] The answer was gradually to merge non-contributory social assistance schemes with a reformed social-security system. But reforming social security required a dedicated political effort to tackle vested interests. In Mexico, for example, the social-security institute (known as IMSS) is in some ways organised for the convenience of the powerful trade union of its own workers. Of each peso contributed by workers or the government to the institute, 17 centavos went to pay the pensions of the institute's own staff in 2006. According to Levy, who tried and failed to reform the IMSS during Fox's government, that figure would rise to 30 centavos over the following decade.[11] Others feared that clientelism would inevitably creep into the operation of the CCTs. Such worries aside, the CCTs looked more sustainable than Chávez's oil-financed, top-down 'missions'. The CCTs were a Latin American invention and were eagerly copied in Africa and Asia. But they were not enough on their own. They could help poorer parents to keep their children healthy and at school. They could not guarantee good schools and hospitals, or the other basic services of the modern state.

The limping leviathan

Prior to the liberal reforms of the past quarter-century, the Latin American state seemed almost omnipotent, both economically and politically. Yet this leviathan had rotting entrails and feet of clay. 'The state is useless,' was the withering verdict of Fernando de la Rúa, Argentina's president from 1999 to 2001, after he took office.[12] Rather than an ideological statement this was a factual description. In the period from the mid-nineteenth century to the 1930s, most Latin American countries achieved a stable administration that exercised the basic function of the state, of control over the national territory. That process was uneven: states were relatively sophisticated in the southern Cone but weaker than average in Central America and some of the Andean countries. These fledgling states normally had to overcome local or regional rebellions. Geography was always a challenge to state-building until the advent of air travel. Laurence Whitehead cites an 'extreme' but illustrative case in the 1920s, of a Bolivian official appointed to administer his country's rubber-producing provinces in the Amazon lowlands. This official would leave La Paz for the Chilean coast, take a ship through the Panama Canal to England and then a return boat to Manaus, and proceed upriver to his post where he would find that the local currency was sterling rather than the Bolivian peso.[13]

From the Second World War onwards, the nation-builders and the populists greatly expanded the state apparatus. Governments assumed responsibility for education, health and social security for the first time. The state grappled with the national-security demands of the Cold War and the developmentalist project of controlling the national economy. Public employment grew. But for all its vaunting ambition, the Latin American corporate state suffered from two basic weaknesses. The first was that a professional, technical approach to public administration often lost out to 'patrimonialism' (the capture of public institutions by private interests) and/or clientelism (the use of public resources, or award of public employment, to sustain a political following).[14] The result was inefficiency and corruption.[15] Social-security systems, in particular, were often grossly over-staffed and inefficient, and were sometimes treated as cash cows by governments. Public employment was often used as a tool of political patronage. Nowhere was this more true than in Argentina. In his second government (1952–55), Perón required senior civil servants to become members of his ruling party.[16] Perón assembled an unstable coalition of corporatist trade unions and conservative provincial *caudillos*. Its price was much feather-bedding. Provincial and municipal governments increased their share of total employment in Argentina to 8.7 per cent by 1985.[17]

The second, related weakness was the inability of these states to command sufficient tax-raising capability. Direct taxes on income and property were often resisted, or evaded, by the wealthy. Instead, states came to rely on inflationary financing and debt. More and more tasks were placed upon the state, but without the resources required to carry them out. By 1980 Latin America suffered 'over-extended, inflexible, unresponsive, voracious and over-political bureaucracies', as Whitehead put it.[18] A surfeit of public employment went hand in hand with a growing deficit in the provision of public services and deterioration in their quality.

Democracy and economic reform required a different kind of state, one that was less ambitious but more service-oriented, efficient and inclusive. Instead of occupying the commanding heights of the economy and exercising political control through corporatism, what was needed was a state which concentrated on providing public goods – education, healthcare, public security, equality of opportunity – and on regulating markets, privatised services and the environment. Over the past quarter of a century, considerable progress has been made in this direction. The shortcomings of Latin American states remain notorious. But reform has been sufficiently wide-ranging as to merit the description of a 'silent revolution' according to an account prepared by researchers at the Inter-American Development Bank.[19]

Democratisation prompted the reform of electoral authorities and efforts to reform judiciaries.[20] It also brought decentralisation and more social spending. In 2004 local and regional governments carried out 19.3 per cent of public spending, up from 13.1 per cent in 1985. Stabilisation stimulated the reform of economic policy-making bodies, the area where most progress was made. Many countries reformed their budgetary institutions, and a dozen imposed legal restrictions on the fiscal deficit. Several countries set up counter-cyclical stabilisation funds in which to save part of any windfall from commodity prices. A dozen countries gave greater legal or operational independence to their central banks in the conduct of monetary policy.

Tax systems were reformed with the aim of simplifying them and reducing evasion. On average, the rate of corporate tax fell from 42 per cent in 1986 to 30 per cent by the late 1990s. The top rates for personal income tax fell too, while average VAT rates rose from 10 per cent in the early 1990s to around 15 per cent. These changes made tax systems less of a drag on economic efficiency. But by relying on indirect taxes, they did nothing to make tax systems more progressive (i.e. to use taxes as a means to make the distribution of income more equal). Overall, most tax systems in the region had little direct impact on income distribution.[21] The bigger problem was that many countries still did not gather enough taxes to finance a modern state able to provide basic services and opportunity for all. According to one study, total taxation as a share of GDP in Latin America rose from an average of 14.2 per cent in the early 1990s to 16.1 per cent by the end of the decade (these figures exclude social-security contributions and local-government taxes). That figure remained well below the developed-country average of 29 per cent.[22] As always, the average concealed huge variation. Brazil and Uruguay collected more taxes than the average for countries of their income level. In Brazil, in particular, the tax burden rose steadily over the two decades after 1985, to become an oppressive burden on business. Including social security, government of all levels was collecting 35 per cent of GDP in 2006. But tax revenue was extraordinarily low in countries such as Mexico, Colombia, Guatemala and Peru. In Mexico, governments long relied on (volatile) oil revenue to make up the shortfall: in 2006, tax revenues were only around 15 per cent of GDP, though total government revenues were 23 per cent.[23] In Colombia in the early 2000s the central government's tax take (excluding social-security contributions) was just 13 per cent of GDP, in Guatemala 10 per cent and in Peru 12.4 per cent, though in all three cases the figure was higher than in the late 1980s.[24] The share of the economy accounted for by government tends to rise with income and economic development. Even so, where the tax take is less than a fifth of GDP it is hard for the state to command sufficient resources to provide basic public goods, or for it to redress the extreme inequality of income and opportunity that is characteristic of Latin America. For example, in some countries a needed rise in social spending came at the expense of public investment in infrastructure, such as roads, ports and safe water. There was scope to increase local property taxes in many countries, and to reduce evasion of income taxes and of VAT. But if some governments had to tax and spend more, most also had to spend better, from the standpoint both of efficiency and of equity.

All too often, the basic administrative functions of the state, from registering businesses to implementing government policy, are inefficiently carried out.

Governments often found it easier to create new agencies than reform existing ones. In Peru, Fujimori created effective new tax and competition authorities but left unreformed the education, health and interior ministries. In Mexico, Zedillo's government set up an elite Federal Investigation Agency (known as AFI and modelled on the FBI) but left untouched a battery of corrupt and incompetent federal, state and municipal police forces. In many countries there were islands of excellence in the public administration. In Brazil, for example, the foreign ministry acted as a bureaucratic elite – diplomats would be seconded to run other ministries or executive agencies. But these agencies often operated in a sea of mediocrity. In a pioneering effort to evaluate administrative efficiency, the Inter-American Development Bank found that Brazil, Chile and Costa Rica (in that order) had the most effective state bureaucracies, coming closest to the ideal of a professional civil service whose decisions were impersonal and where hiring, promotion, dismissal and salaries were based on merit rather than patronage.[25] The rest of Central America and Peru were the most distant from this ideal.

Pockmarked by corruption, inefficiency and a lack of professionalism, the average Latin American state was a far cry from that of Singapore or South Korea. It was ill-equipped to carry out the industrial and other development policies which critics of the Washington Consensus wished to entrust to it. There were some efforts to reform the core public administration. Both Mexico and Chile approved laws to make the civil service more professional. In Brazil the proportion of civil servants with university degrees rose from 39 per cent in 1995 to 63 per cent in 2001.[26] However, this meritocratic approach was partially reversed by the Lula government, which placed many Workers' Party members in public jobs. According to some senior diplomats it even compromised the professionalism of Itamaraty, the foreign ministry. In an unusually vehement public criticism, Roberto Abdenur, who retired as Brazil's ambassador to Washington in 2006, told *Veja*, the country's leading newsweekly: 'There is a generalised sentiment that diplomats today are promoted in accordance with their political and ideological affinity, and not their competence ... Itamaraty needs to recover its professionalism, safe from ideological stances, intolerant attitudes and party-political identification with the dominant political force of the moment.'[27]

Similarly, decentralisation led to examples of excellence – and counter-examples of misgovernment. One of the best-known of the former was the Brazilian state of Ceará. When Tasso Jereissati, a young reformist from the PSDB, was elected governor in 1987 he broke with the corrupt, clientelistic pattern of government in Brazil's poor north-east. He began by cleaning up the state's finances.[28] He eliminated 40,000 jobs (out of a total payroll of 146,000) which were held by non-existent 'ghost' workers.[29] At the same time, the state government launched a far-reaching community-health programme. It hired 8,400 women as community-health promoters, and trained and supervised them. Each of them visited around a hundred families a month, offering help and advice with oral rehydration therapy, vaccination, pre-natal care, breastfeeding and monitoring the growth of babies. Before 1987, only 30 per cent of Ceará's 178 municipalities had a nurse, let alone a doctor or health clinic. As a result of this programme, vaccination coverage for measles and polio rose from 25 to 90 per cent of the child population by 1992. Infant mortality fell from 102 per thousand live births in 1987 (double the Brazilian average at the time) to fewer than 30 per thousand in the early 2000s. According to one of the reformers who worked with Jereissati, 'What's different from other states has been the way of approaching the management of the public sector, with criteria of efficiency, rationality in the investment of resources, planning on technical grounds instead of cronyism and the sharing out of jobs among political friends.'[30] The PSDB and its allies continued to run the state for the next 20 years. They improved education and attracted private investment in new industries, such as shoe-manufacturing and fruit-farming. By 1999, 95 per cent of children under 14 were attending school and so were four out of five 17-year olds. Poverty remained high, though it fell from more than 70 per cent in 1987 to below 50 per cent. But the state was laying the long-term basis to escape from poverty through better health and education.[31]

At municipal level, Bogotá was a similar example of good practice. In the 1980s, Colombia's capital was chaotic, congested and violent, with poor public services. A series of reforming mayors, including Liberals Jaime Castro and Enrique Peñalosa, Antanas Mockus, an independent, and Lucho Garzón, a moderate socialist, transformed it into one of the best-governed cities in Latin America. Castro sorted out the city's finances. Peñalosa began a modern mass-transport system in a city of almost 7 million people that had previously lacked one. The Transmilenio, as it was called, was copied from Curitiba in Brazil, another innovative and well-governed city. It involved articulated buses running along dedicated carriageways with fixed stops resembling railway stations. It cost about $10 million per kilometre to build – much cheaper than a metro. It cut travelling times, congestion and pollution significantly. The city government also created new parks and libraries. It built new secondary schools in poorer districts, and got private schools to manage them under a scheme similar to charter schools in the United States. It also took steps to improve teacher training. Bogotá's murder rate fell sharply, partly as a result of national trends, but helped, too, by citizen education campaigns pioneered by Mockus, which included stronger regulation of alcohol and guns.

Decentralisation was not problem-free. In Colombia and elsewhere it brought some fiscal difficulties. In some cases, money was devolved without corresponding responsibilities; in other cases, the reverse occurred. In Peru, many mayors spent their new funds on bullrings or other ostentatious public works, while education and health, which in contrast to Colombia were still in central-government hands, languished. In Brazil, the multiplication of municipalities was a voracious claim on the public finances. Since the 1988 constitution, more than a thousand new municipalities were created as local government became a growth industry. But the region also has many success stories in local government, of urban regeneration and development and innovative transport schemes. At local level, as at national level, good government could make a difference. In Ecuador, whose national governments were generally unimpressive, there were effective mayors of both left (Auki Tituaña in Cotacachi, for example) and right (Jaime Nebot in Guayaquil).

The actions of government did serve to reduce inequality in Latin America, though not by as much as they do in the developed world. In the 1990s, contrary to the myth propagated by some critics of the reforms, social spending increased substantially in the region. CEPAL found that social spending per head increased on average by 50 per cent in real terms between 1990–1 and 1998–9, and then continued to increase slightly despite the economic slowdown of 1998–2003. The increase was general, but it was highest in those countries with the lowest spending at the start of the decade (including Colombia, the Dominican Republic, Guatemala, Paraguay and Peru). In 2002–3, on average social spending was equal to 15.1 per cent of GDP, up from 12.8 per cent in 1990–1. But the average concealed a range from 19 to 21 per cent of GDP in Uruguay, Argentina and Brazil to 5 to 7 per cent in Ecuador, El Salvador and Guatemala.[32] Much of the increase in spending went on pensions, but some of it went on education and health as well as the targeted anti-poverty programmes. Much spending on pensions and on traditional social-security systems goes predominantly to the better-off. So does public spending on universities, which traditionally get a disproportionate share of the education budget. In Brazil, for example, the poorest 20 per cent of the population received only 3 per cent of social spending on unemployment insurance and 2.4 per cent of spending on pensions.[33] On the other hand, the conditional cash-transfer schemes and the expansion of coverage in schooling and in basic healthcare went disproportionately to the poor.

A start has been made in fashioning more effective and inclusive democratic states in Latin America. But much remains to be done. That is particularly true in two areas that are worth considering in detail: education on the one hand, and public security and the establishment of the rule of law on the other.

The classroom gaps

The school at Tunibamba Llacta, a hamlet near Cotachachi in the Ecuadorean Andes, consists of two huts next to a football pitch carved out of a mountainside and scuffed bare of grass.[34] It is surrounded by maize fields and small, red-tiled farmhouses. There are just two teachers for 75 pupils. One of them is José Menacho, a young Andean Indian who wears his long black hair pulled back from his handsome copper-coloured face into a pigtail. On the board, he draws a dog. *Allku*, he repeats to his class of five- to eight-year olds, some of whom are paying attention. He then draws a sun (*inti*, he writes) and a hot pepper (*uchu*). He is teaching reading and writing in Quichua, his pupils' first language. Bilingual teaching in primary schools began in Ecuador in 1988. Educationalists thought it would improve the performance of children of indigenous descent. Activists hoped that it would preserve the language. But the scheme suffers from a lack of qualified teachers and educational materials. In Ecuador, indigenous 10-year-old children score 20 per cent below their peers in language and maths.[35] In Mexico, 1.2 million primary pupils receive bilingual education in 54 different tongues. But there is a similar lack of competent teachers. As in Tunibamba Llacta or in rural Peru and Bolivia, in the Mixtec highlands primary-school classes take in children of widely differing ages.

The first big problem with Latin America's education systems is that they are failing to provide equality of opportunity. There is little sign of a gender gap, with girls and boys scoring more or less equally on years of schooling and test scores (except in Guatemala where fewer girls than boys are at school).[36] But there are big differences in educational attainments between rich and poor, rural and urban children and by race. In the mid-1990s, the richest 10 per cent of Latin American adults had about 11 years of education on average, while the poorest 30 per cent only had six years. In Mexico, only 1 per cent of all those in higher education are from the poorest 20 per cent of the population, according to John Scott of CIDE, a Mexico City university.[37] Indigenous and black Latin Americans are much less likely than their peers to complete primary school. In rural areas in countries such as Peru and Bolivia, teacher absenteeism is common. Children often only attend school for around a hundred days a year and for less than two hours a day.[38] But lack of equity is not the only problem.

When it comes to the educational level of its workforce, Latin America lags not just the rich world but East Asian countries and other countries of similar incomes. At the start of the twenty-first century, the average Latin American adult had just 5.8 years of schooling – compared with 10.5 years for South Koreans and 7.9 years for Malaysians.[39] That is a crucial competitive disadvantage in a world where knowledge has become increasingly important to economic growth. This educational gap also contributes to income inequality: the differential between skilled and unskilled wages has widened in Latin America, as it has elsewhere, because of technological change.

Fortunately, there are many signs of change. Democratic governments in many countries have made huge efforts over the past 15 years to increase school enrolment. In the decade from 1995, the percentage of children entering and completing primary and secondary education has risen faster than in any other part of the developing world. But there is still more to be done in expanding coverage. On average, 95 per cent of children in the relevant age group were enrolled in primary school by 2003, up from 90 per cent in 1995. The big change was in secondary-school enrolment, which rose from 33 per cent of the relevant age group to 64 per cent over the same period.[40] An outstanding example was Brazil, which went from being a regional laggard to above average. By 2005, almost all young Chileans completed secondary school, up from 50 per cent in 1990. But regionwide, enrolment in secondary schooling and in pre-schooling (60 per cent in 2003) is lower than it should be given the income levels of Latin American countries. At successive Summits of the Americas, governments committed themselves to achieving universal primary education by 2010, and to have 75 per cent of youngsters completing secondary school by then. Most are on course to achieve that. But the goal should be to ensure that all Latin Americans complete 12 years of schooling – the minimum needed to get a decent job in globalised economies.

As coverage increased, more attention began to be focussed on the abysmal quality of schooling in the region.[41] In 1995 Colombia and Mexico took part in an international study of maths and science education carried out by the International Association for the Evaluation of Educational Achievement (IEA), a body based in Belgium. Colombia was placed 41st out of 42 countries, ahead only of South Africa; at the last minute, Zedillo's government blocked publication of Mexico's results, which were later revealed to have been worse than Colombia's. In the next set of IEA tests in 1999, Chile took part. Though regarded as a regional leader in education, its results were no better than Colombia's; out of 38 countries, Chile scored ahead only of the Philippines, Morocco and South Africa. That performance was below the level that might have been expected given Chile's income per head. In another standardised international test, that of the OECD's Programme for International Student Assessment (PISA) held in 2003, the three Latin American participants (Brazil, Mexico and Uruguay) fared little better. They all scored near the bottom in reading, maths and science in the tests, which involved 15-year olds in 41 countries. Around half of the Latin American students had serious difficulties in using reading to extend their knowledge and skills. Three-quarters of the

Brazilian pupils, two-thirds of the Mexicans and nearly half the Uruguayans could not apply basic mathematical skills to explore and understand an everyday situation. By contrast, only around a fifth of students in OECD countries had similar difficulties. In a regional test of primary school pupils in 11 Latin American countries carried out by UNESCO in 1997, Cubans performed significantly better than pupils elsewhere in the region.

What is going wrong? Peru's educational performance highlights the problems. Enrolment in Peru is amongst the highest in Latin America, a creditable achievement for one of the region's poorer countries. But Peru came at the bottom of the class in the PISA tests in 2000, well below even the other Latin American participants. Conditions in San Juan de Lurigancho point to one of the difficulties: class sizes of 35–40, and schools used for primary classes in the morning and secondary classes in the afternoon. 'We need fewer children in the classroom and more hours of teaching,' says Sonia Chuquimango, who teaches at the Miguel Grau primary school.[42] The teachers complain, with reason, that they are poorly paid. Ms Chuquimango's salary is 1,100 soles per month (around $330) in 2006. Some teachers work two shifts a day; many have another job outside teaching on which they are equally reliant. That is a consequence of the fiscal impoverishment of the state in Peru inflicted by the grandiose developmentalism of the Velasco military government of 1968–75, and Alan García's reckless dash for growth in the 1980s. Successive governments carried on building schools. Fujimori, in particular, built many in small towns and villages in the Andes. But the state lacked sufficient tax revenue to pay the teachers properly. Until the 1990s, governments relied on inflation to square the circle. In the early 2000s, teachers' salaries were worth only a third of what they had been three decades earlier, according to Richard Webb, a former governor of Peru's Central Bank and a development consultant. That has had a disastrous effect on teacher motivation. 'The government pretends to pay us and we pretend to teach,' was how one teacher expressed it in fieldwork carried out by Webb.[43] The response of these professional workers to the erosion of their salaries has been a militant trade unionism. The union has resisted outside evaluation of teachers and schools. The Toledo government raised teachers' salaries but failed to insist on a quid pro quo of reform.

Many of these factors are present elsewhere in the region. Countries such as Brazil and Mexico spend a similar amount on their education system per pupil as Poland or Hungary but get much poorer results. The biggest problem is the way that education is organised. East Asian countries, such as South Korea, that have achieved a spectacular expansion of educational coverage and high test scores take a centralised approach to schooling. But that approach has failed in Latin America. The education ministries are normally the largest employer – Peru has 300,000 teachers for example, and Mexico 1.4 million. Hiring of teachers and educational bureaucrats is often based on political connections rather than merit. Giant bureaucracies breed giant trade unions. Mexico's Educational Workers Union is the largest trade union in Latin America. In practice it is often the union, not head teachers, parents or local authorities, that decides on the hiring and (very rarely) firing or redeployment of teachers. In many countries, teachers are not properly trained, but the unions have resisted evaluations of their professional capacities. 'Control of bad teachers is very limited,' admits Enrique Rueda, the leader of the Oaxaca branch of the union.[44] Long strikes are common – the Oaxaca teachers have struck almost every year, and did so for six months in 2006. But governments normally continue to pay salaries during strikes. In Mexico head teachers and school inspectors belong to, and are appointed by, the union.

In many of the election campaigns of 2005–6, education was one of the main issues of public debate. The consensus among educationalists is that Latin America needs better-quality teachers, a longer school day, rigorous teacher evaluation, strong community involvement in schools, universal pre-schooling and good quality textbooks.[45] These are the things that Cuba got right in its education system. But traditionally, Latin American education has been over-centralised and under-regulated. Many of the necessary reforms would give schools more local autonomy but would subject them to greater accountability, by setting and enforcing national standards. Change is under way. By 2001, 17 countries in the region had introduced national tests to evaluate student learning, up from four in 1990. Several countries, including Brazil and Mexico, also set up evaluation agencies. Some are also experimenting with greater school autonomy. In the 1990s the state of Minas Gerais in Brazil set up local school boards in which parents were involved, and gave them responsibility for part of the school budget and the power to appoint the head teacher. In subsequent national tests, Minas Gerais got some of the best results in the country. The education ministry is no longer seen as a political booby prize, with ministers changing every few months. Paulo Renato Souza, who oversaw the spectacular improvement in Brazil's education coverage, was education minister for all eight years of Cardoso's two terms.

There have also been experiments with private-sector involvement in schooling. These include Bogotá's charter schools. In several countries, Fe y Alegría, a Jesuit-founded educational movement, runs state schools, with good results. In Chile, the Pinochet dictatorship introduced a quasi–voucher scheme, under which private bodies receive public money to run public schools. Some 40 per cent of pupils now go to these schools, which do not charge fees but are allowed to charge for extras. Research is not conclusive as to whether this system has made schools more effective or not. But there is some evidence that it has increased social stratification, with middle-class pupils gravitating to the privately run schools.[46]

The private sector provides around two-thirds of university places in the region. Only around a fifth of Latin Americans receive any higher education. Yet until the 1990s, governments tended to spend disproportionately on public universities. They were seen as an important political constituency. Some, such as the University of São Paulo or the University of Chile, or some faculties of the University of Buenos Aires or the National Autonomous University of Mexico, are centres of excellence. They charge no fees. Entrance is by competitive examination. Their students tend to be drawn from the richer sections of the population, as are those of the top private universities. Students from poorer families tend to go to private universities of poorer quality, which have mushroomed in the past two decades. In the past 15 years, much of the increase in the education budget has gone to schools. But Mexico still lavishes five times more money on each student in public universities than on each pupil in primary schools (compared with twice as much in the other OECD countries). Brazil spends around a quarter of its education budget on the public universities. That is inequitable. There is a strong case for charging fees to richer students, and for a subsidised student loan scheme to attract poorer students.

Unlike some macroeconomic reforms, remedying Latin America's educational deficits cannot be achieved overnight. It is a long-term endeavour. Seen in that light, by the mid-2000s there was evidence of progress as well as of its lack. In Santiago Tlazoyaltepec, María Elena Velasco's father, who lives in a wooden shack and has a small *milpa* and a few sheep, only went to school for two years. Her mother, who speaks little Spanish, had no schooling at all. María Elena and her brother completed the six years of primary school but only managed a year of lower-secondary schooling before dropping out. She is determined her children should do better. There is no high school in Tlazoyaltepec, so that means taking them 'to the valley', to the city of Oaxaca, she says. 'Who knows how I'll do it but I'll have to. If I work as a cleaner I'll earn 50 pesos a day.'[47]

Legalism and lawlessness

Attached to the Texan city of El Paso but a long way from anywhere else, Ciudad Juárez has attracted hundreds of thousands of Mexicans to its export assembly plants where they make everything from car parts to television remote-controls for export to the United States. Here the Rio Grande, which divides the two cities, is for much of the year a shallow stream, its broad bed encased in concrete levees. On its north bank rises the tall metal fence, backed every few hundred metres by a green Border Patrol 4x4, that has interrupted the free flow of people northwards but not that of goods, including illegal drugs. Cross the bi-national bridge to the east of the city centre and not much visibly changes as you head south into the industrial parks and shopping malls of Juárez. But follow the fleets of white-painted works buses that leave the *maquiladora* plants as the shift changes in the late afternoon to deliver the workers to their homes in the poor, western *colonias* that sprawl over the hills and gulches of the Chihuahua desert, and the contrast is sharper. A winding two-lane road, only recently asphalted, hugs the south bank of the Rio Grande, past small concrete huts of one or two rooms built on foundations of old tyres. Across the river, the rush-hour traffic roars along Interstate 10. But the biggest difference between the two sides of the river is less immediately tangible than the gap in public infrastructure or in living standards: it is in the degree to which the rule of law is applied.

In recent years, Juárez has become notorious for the murders of women. Some 450 women and girls were killed between 1993 and 2006.[48] Their beaten or mutilated bodies were often found dumped on waste ground. Some of the deaths were the result of domestic violence or of robberies. But at least 90 of the killings seemed to have a sexual motive. They gave rise to lurid hypotheses of serial killers, 'snuff' movies and/or macabre initiation rites practised by organised rings linking local drug traffickers, police and politicians. Human-rights groups talked of the killings as 'feminicide' or hate crimes. 'They kill them because they are women and because they are poor,' says Esther Chávez, a feminist accountant who set up Casa Amiga, a counselling centre and women's refuge in the city.[49]

But they also killed them because they thought they could get away with it. Several men were arrested and imprisoned for the sexual crimes, but human-rights groups insisted that they were innocent, and had been tortured into confessing. Campaigning by activists on both sides of the border finally forced the federal government to intervene. The federal attorney-general's office reviewed the cases. It found that 177 local officials involved in investigating the murders had been negligent, though it also said that many of the cases had been solved. President Fox sent 1,200 federal police to the city to re-train the local force. A special commissioner was appointed to co-ordinate local, state and national authorities and to mobilise funds to address the city's social problems. New parks were created, and roads paved in the shantytowns. The killings in Juárez were unusually grisly, and because they attracted publicity, the government reacted. But the problems of criminal impunity and police corruption that Ms Chávez and others complain of were by no means confined to Juárez.

Latin American societies have long suffered a paradox. From Iberian colonialism, they inherited a formalistic legalism. Yet this coexisted with widespread lawlessness. One manifestation of this paradox was the size of the informal economy. Another was that across the region, crime – and especially violent crime – rose steadily in the 1980s and 1990s. In 1990, Latin America and the Caribbean had a homicide rate of 22.9 per 100,000 people; by the early 2000s, the figure had risen to 25.1.[50] In both cases, it was higher than in any other region except Africa. In Chile, Peru and Uruguay the murder rate was lower than in the United States. But some Latin American societies are among the most violent in the world. In the early 2000s, Colombia, El Salvador, Venezuela and Brazil all had murder rates that were much higher than the regional average. In some years in certain cities – Medellín and Cali in Colombia, Guatemala City, and parts of Rio de Janeiro and São Paulo – the figure was over 100 homicides per 100,000 people.[51] Echoing Ciudad Juárez, 524 women were murdered in Guatemala in 2004 according to the national police.[52] Kidnapping was also disproportionately common in Latin America, especially in Colombia, Mexico, Brazil and Venezuela. Fear of violent crime was even more pervasive than its reality. Year after year, the Latinobarómetro polls showed that crime, violence and personal insecurity were the second most important public concern in the region, after poverty and unemployment. In the 2006 survey, they were seen as the biggest problem, ahead even of economic issues, by respondents in Colombia, Venezuela and much of Central America. They were, too, in Argentina, still a relatively safe country – a backhanded compliment to the vigour of the country's recovery from economic collapse.[53] Massive public demonstrations against crime brought hundreds of thousands of people on to the streets of Mexico City and Buenos Aires in 2004. Many of them were middle class, alarmed by the spread of kidnapping and hold-ups at traffic lights. But many were less well-off: most crime in Latin America, as elsewhere, involves the poor robbing and/or killing the poor. Several conservative politicians were elected president mainly or partly because they promised to get tough on crime and violence. They included Álvaro Uribe in Colombia, Tony Saca in El Salvador in 2004, and Felipe Calderón in Mexico. As well as the human suffering involved, violence carried an economic cost, and was an impediment to development. According to one estimate, Latin America's income might be 25 per cent higher if the level of violence were similar to that in the rest of the world.[54] Another calculation suggested that in the 1990s violence cost Colombia two percentage points of economic growth each year, scaring off investors and tourists.[55]

There were several common factors behind the prevalence of violent crime. They included the pace of urbanisation and the economic dislocations of the 1980s and 1990s. But there were two more specific parts of the explanation. The first was the relative weakness and/or inefficiencies of the police, the courts and the prisons. But perhaps the most important factor in the increase in crime was externally generated: the demand for illegal drugs, and especially cocaine, in the United States and later in Europe and elsewhere brought into being vast and powerful organised crime networks. Over time, drugs began to be sold and consumed within Latin America as well. These two factors fed off each other. The drug trade – as well as corruption, crime and the informal economy – flourished precisely because of the weakness of the state and the rule of law in the region, to which it in turn made such an important contribution. It formed a massive millstone around the neck of Latin American democracy.

These factors meshed with local ones. In Central America, for example, in the aftermath of civil war both guns and unemployed young males were plentiful. In addition, youth gangs (known as *maras*) emerged in the 1980s among the children of Central Americans who had migrated to Los Angeles to escape war and poverty at home.[56] In the 1990s, some of these youths began to return to Central America, either because of the arrival of peace or because they were deported after committing crimes. They took the gangs with them – to El Salvador, Guatemala and Honduras in particular. Estimates of total gang membership in Central America ranged from 70,000 to 300,000 in 2006. Though most were small, neighbourhood outfits, some turned to serious crime, including extortion and drug dealing and trafficking. Starting in 2003, governments in these three countries responded with *mano duro* (literally 'harsh hand') policies, which included making it an offence merely to belong to a gang and incarcerating thousands of youths in overcrowded and out-of-control prisons. That tended to make the problem worse, driving the gangs to become more organised and violent. Murder rates in the three countries, which had begun to fall in the late 1990s, rose again. They included some cases of the murder of suspected gang members by police taking the law into their own hands.

In the *favelas* of São Paulo and Rio de Janeiro, the arrival of crack cocaine in the 1990s aggravated pre-existing lawlessness derived from chaotic urbanisation. A study of Diadema, a poor municipality on the southern outskirts of São Paulo whose population grew at an average rate of 16 per cent *a year* between 1950 and 1980, compared conditions there to those of the 'Wild West' in the United States. Lack of secure land tenure, the absence of effective government and weak local organisation all bred violence. As settlements were legalised and local government became more effective, violence began to fall in the early 1990s. Then it rose again sharply, reaching a terrifying peak of 141 murders per 100,000 people in 1991. The explanation was that drug dealers had moved in.[57] The problem was even worse in Rio de Janeiro, where most of the 700 *favelas* came under the control of the drug mobs.

In Colombia and, to a lesser extent, Peru, the drug trade provided finance for armed groups that challenged democratic rule. Before turning in more detail to the Colombian case, it is worth signalling two regional trends in the response to crime. The first is a tendency towards the privatisation of policing and justice. The second is a more helpful counter-trend of police and justice reform. Both stem from the flaws of the police and justice systems. Historically, the police in Latin America have tended to be a subordinate branch of the armed forces.[58] In many cases, they still are. In Brazil, for example, the main police force is known as the *polícia militar* ('military police'); though administered by the state governments, it is an auxiliary branch of the army, regulated by the defence ministry. This military connection has meant that the police have tended to use (sometimes lethal) force all too readily, and has made its reform more difficult.[59] Their main job has been the preservation of political control and public order, rather than the prevention and detection of crime. They serve government rather than the public. Their professional status and salaries are low, training is inadequate and corruption is common. Though each force tends to be over-centralised in its command structure, there is often duplication among rival forces. Overall numbers are often inadequate. Mexico, for example, had some 400,000 police in hundreds of different forces in 2006. On average, policemen had just six years of education, received only two weeks of training and were paid just $370 a month; some 35 per cent of them were officially thought to use drugs, and two-fifths left the force each year.[60] In many countries, the police were feared and mistrusted by the public: in the 2006 Latinobarómetro polls, fewer than four in ten respondents expressed any confidence in them.[61]

As a result, in many countries crimes are often neither reported nor properly investigated. According to research by CIDAC, a think-tank in Mexico, 96 per cent of crimes went unpunished between 1996 and 2003 – an extreme case, perhaps, but not unrepresentative.[62] Only around 8 per cent of some 50,000 murders committed each year in Brazil are successfully prosecuted. In Colombia in the 1990s, only around 40 per cent of murders were investigated, and only one murder in ten resulted in an arrest.[63]

Worse, the police themselves are sometimes responsible for violent crime. Reports by groups such as Human Rights Watch and Amnesty International, as well as their local counterparts, have regularly charted the use of deadly violence by police against civilians. In a notorious case in 1997 in the São Paulo suburb of Diadema, for example, a dozen police were videotaped by local residents as for three nights running they set up a roadblock to beat and extort money from passing motorists, shooting one dead.[64] In Argentina, the Buenos Aires provincial force has a particularly bad reputation. Several of its officers were found to have taken part in the bombing of a Jewish welfare centre in Buenos Aires in 1994 in which 86 people were killed, as well as in the unrelated murder of a press photographer.[65] Many of its commanders took bribes – often shared with local political leaders – in return for turning a blind eye to drug trafficking and other criminal activity. In Mexico it is widely assumed that many municipal and state police forces are working for the drug gangs rather than against them.

Given the shortcomings of the police, citizens have sometimes sought private solutions to violent crime. In several countries the rich have retreated to gated communities. Private security guards often rival the police in numbers. In Brazil, a proposal to ban the sale of guns and ammunition was defeated in a referendum in 2005. According to one estimate, there are perhaps 17 million guns in Brazil, around half of them unregistered.[66] The poor sometimes take justice into their own hands: lynchings are not uncommon in Guatemala, and rural Peru and Bolivia, and occasionally take place in the Lima shantytowns. Residents in some poor districts of Lima erected their own gates across their streets. Vigilantism has a long history in the region. For example, in Diadema, in the 1970s and 1980s vigilantes known as *justiceiros* killed supposed wrongdoers. They were tolerated by residents, who saw them as the only means of controlling crime. Police, on or off duty, sometimes doubled as vigilantes. In Rio de Janeiro, where on many counts there has been less progress than in São Paulo, in about 90 of the 700 or so *favelas*, armed militias, made up mainly of former and off-duty police, had expelled the drug traffickers by early 2007, often in violent battles.[67]

In Peru, peasant farmers formed vigilante patrols known as *rondas campesinas*. These were originally a defence against rustlers. During the guerrilla campaign by *Sendero Luminoso* in the 1980s and 1990s these *rondas* were promoted and supported by the armed forces as part of a successful counter-insurgency strategy. The largest and most notorious example of vigilantism was the paramilitary armies in Colombia. Some of these groups were formed by landowners in response to murders and extortion by left-wing guerrillas. Others evolved from the groups of gunmen hired by drug gangs. They defended landowners and rural towns from guerrillas, but by imposing their own reign of terror.

On the other hand, almost every country in the region saw attempts to reform the police and the courts. In Central America, these included the creation of new civilian police forces in El Salvador and Guatemala as part of peace agreements that ended civil wars. In South America, reforms were generally aimed at turning the police into a professional force with specialist skills, through changes in recruitment, training and management. Reformers also tried to strengthen oversight and monitoring of police violence, and to generate greater community involvement in policing and security. At the same time, some local governments began to treat violence as a public-health problem. This approach was pioneered in Cali, Colombia's third city with some 2 million people. Murder rates in the city had climbed from 23 per 100,000 in 1983 to 85 by 1991 and to a peak of 124 by 1994. That was partly the doing of the Cali 'cartel' of drug traffickers and their war with their rivals in Medellín. In 1992 the city's then mayor, Rodrigo Guerrero, a public-health specialist, ordered an epidemiological study of violence to establish how, where and when people were being killed. This was followed up with an education campaign, earlier closing times for bars and a ban on the carrying of handguns at weekends.[68] These measures managed to reverse the increase in violence, though only to around the 1991 level. This approach was expanded by Antanas Mockus, Bogotá's mayor, with greater success. The combination of such measures, President Álvaro Uribe's security build-up and a peace agreement with the paramilitaries produced a dramatic fall in the murder rate.

In Brazil, several states experimented with community policing. The most developed of these experiments was in the state of São Paulo.[69] The new plan involved more patrolling in selected areas, the establishment of permanent 24-hour police posts, extra training and counselling for police involved in violent incidents. The state government also seized more unregistered guns and cut the number of gun licences it issued from 70,000 a year to 2,000. Murders in the state fell sharply, from a peak of almost 13,000 in 1999 to 9,000 in 2004. In Diadema, the new approach was complemented by the city government, which set up its own municipal police force and, as in Colombia, restricted alcohol sales. By 2003 the murder rate in Diadema had fallen to half its 1999 peak.

In Peru, a group of civilian officials made a bold attempt to reform the police during the presidency of Alejandro Toledo.[70] The police in Peru were in some ways effective: through dogged intelligence work they had managed to capture Abimael Guzmán, the leader of *Sendero Luminoso*, and to dismantle several kidnapping gangs. But they were widely seen as corrupt, regularly demanding bribes from citizens, and they were failing to deal with day-to-day crime. When the reformers arrived in office, the security forces were discredited by the corruption and abuses of Alberto Fujimori and his sinister intelligence chief, Vladimiro Montesinos. The new team purged some 1,300 officers and cut almost by half the numbers of generals and colonels in an absurdly top-heavy force. They eliminated much graft, set up a special anti-corruption office, reformed training procedures and introduced promotion by merit rather than years of service. One of their first measures was to set up a police ombudsman to deal with the grievances of the lower ranks, a measure aimed at improving morale. They also transferred around a thousand officers from administrative and other duties to police stations in Lima. Under a new law, they set up citizen-security committees, involving the police, local governments and community organisations. Polls showed that the police began to rise in public esteem. But the reforms faced fierce resistance, both from police commanders and from members of Toledo's party who wanted to place supporters in jobs in the interior ministry. Toledo eventually discarded the reformers, and many of the changes were reversed. The reforms had been conceived as a package. 'You can only do community policing if the population sees decisive leadership in cleaning up the police,' according to Gino Costa, the interior minister in 2002–3 and one of the leading reformers. 'The great lesson is that you need political will and continuity.'[71]

Like education, police reform was a long-term project. But there were enough successful experiments to indicate that it could be done. It was more difficult to shake up judiciaries, which were often autonomous and had a strong corporate ethos aimed at preserving their privileges rather than providing a better public service. Nevertheless, since the 1980s nearly every country in the region has attempted judicial reforms. The aims have included increasing the political independence of the judiciary, making it more efficient, modernising the legal system, widening access to the law and improving respect for human rights. Yet these aims sometimes involve trade-offs: a more independent judiciary may be less efficient, and wider access may increase the backlog of cases, for example. Reform has been most effective at the top: supreme courts in countries such as Argentina, Brazil and Mexico have become more independent and more professional, dealing with fewer, more important cases than in the past. In Colombia, a constitutional court created under a new constitution in 1991 has developed sweeping powers of judicial review. Access to justice has been broadened by mechanisms such as *defensorías del pueblo* (ombudsman's offices) which have been set up in 15 countries. One review of judicial reform in the region notes than even its critics agree that on average judiciaries are more independent, case-management is more efficient, judicial resources have increased and human rights are more protected.[72] That judgement, of course, does not mean that there are not many problems. Justice is too often slow, venal, arbitrary or simply non-existent. One of the most glaring shortcomings is that in several countries a majority of the inmates in unreformed, overcrowded and violent prisons are held on remand without having faced trial. The unexpected flip side of São Paulo's relative success in tackling drug gangs was the emergence of a powerful criminal syndicate inside the state's prisons. In May 2006 the *Primeiro Comando da Capital* ('First Command of the Capital') was responsible for five days of mayhem followed by retribution, in which some 150 people, a quarter of them police, were killed, 82 buses torched and 17 bank branches attacked. This trial of strength between the mob and the state was apparently provoked by the transfer of several hundred of the *Comando*'s adherents to a more remote jail.[73] Another big problem is that in a handful of countries armed groups pose a violent challenge to the rule of law. That was especially so in Colombia.

'Lead or silver'

Enrique Low Murtra wanted nothing more than to leave his job as Colombia's justice minister to open a law office and return to his previous career as a university teacher. 'I would like to imagine that vengeance is not eternal. To be exiled, like Scipio, from one's own country seems to me to be an injustice,' he said.[74] A gentle, avuncular man who had once been a supreme-court judge, he was still only 49. He spoke softly as the rain pattered down outside his office in a colonial mansion in Bogotá in March 1988. But he would indeed suffer exile – and worse. Two months earlier, on the instruction of Colombia's president, Virgilio Barco, Low Murtra had signed warrants for the arrest and extradition to the United States on drugs charges of the five leading members of the 'Medellín cartel'.[75] They included Pablo Escobar, perhaps the world's most ruthless and notorious drug baron. Faced with constant death threats, the minister sent his daughter out of the country. 'Even going for a haircut has become a problem,' he said. So intense did the threats become that, in July 1988, Barco sent him to Switzerland as ambassador. That did not save him. In 1991, he was back in Colombia, working as he had hoped as a law professor at the University of La Salle. No longer in government service, he had no bodyguards. He was gunned down at the entrance to the university.[76]

Low Murtra's assassination was just one of thousands of murders inflicted on Colombia by the drug trade. It had begun quietly in the 1970s with marijuana and then cocaine. Few people in Colombia bothered much until the traffickers began to use their cocaine wealth to go into politics. Pablo Escobar, who had begun life as a car thief and small-time hoodlum, became the alternate to a Liberal congressman. A reformist faction of the Liberal Party, led by Luis Carlos Galán, denounced the infiltration of 'hot money' into politics. When Rodrigo Lara Bonilla, a member of Galán's group, was appointed justice minister in 1983, he started cracking down on the drug trade, with enthusiastic support from the US Embassy. After the traffickers attempted to smear Lara Bonilla, he denounced Escobar by name in a session of Congress. Weeks later he was shot dead by a hired assassin on a motorbike as he was being driven in his ministerial car in Bogotá.[77] It was the start of ten years of warfare of terrifying intensity by the Medellín drug mob against the Colombian state and others they saw as a threat to their business. The victims included judges, politicians and journalists, as well as hundreds of policemen and ordinary Colombians. The carnage reached a crescendo in 1989, when three presidential candidates (including Galán, the likely winner) were murdered and an Avianca jet with more than one hundred passengers on board was blown up in mid-flight between Bogotá and Cali. The country's politicians had had enough: a constituent assembly, called into being to reform Colombia's constitution, voted to ban extradition – the fate most feared by the traffickers. The new government of César Gaviria negotiated the surrender of Escobar and his henchmen. But after 13 months in comfortable confinement near Medellín, Escobar escaped hours before he was to be moved to a maximum-security jail. After a desperate manhunt lasting 16 months that involved half a dozen different US government agencies, Escobar was finally cornered and killed in Medellín in December 1993.

Escobar famously offered those who stood in his way the choice of *plomo o plata* ('lead or silver'), a bullet or a bribe. Either way, the rule of law was the loser. The drug trade enveloped Colombian democracy in violence and corruption. To defeat Escobar, the Colombian state recruited some dubious allies. These included not just his foes in the Cali drug mob, who were less flamboyant and more businesslike than their counterparts in Medellín; they also encompassed a criminal gang called *Los Pepes* (short for 'people persecuted by Pablo Escobar'), whose leaders included the brothers Fidel and Carlos Castaño, who would become leaders of the United Self-Defence Forces of Colombia (AUC), as the umbrella group of the right-wing paramilitaries was known.[78] The Cali drug barons gave money to the 1994 election campaign of Ernesto Samper, whose presidency was dogged by his battle to clear his name in the face of American hostility. And the dismantling of the 'Medellín cartel' had no effect on the flow of cocaine to the United States and Europe.

Richard Nixon was the first American president to declare a 'war on drugs'. But this only got serious under George H W Bush, after an explosive increase in the use of crack cocaine in the United States.[79] In 1989, in a televised speech to the nation, he singled out cocaine as 'our most serious problem'. He committed the US armed forces, whose commanders were seeking a new role after the end of the Cold War, to this new battle. He offered unprecedented amounts of aid to the Andean countries. He urged upon them a three-pronged strategy for the eradication of coca, the hardy shrub from whose leaves cocaine is extracted; the use of the security forces to interdict processing facilities and trafficking routes; and 'alternative development' of legal crops in or near drug-producing areas. Almost two decades and several billions of dollars later, the drug warriors could point to a series of tactical victories, in particular places at particular times. The total amount of land under coca, as surveyed by the CIA and by the UN, reached a peak in 2001 of around 200,000 hectares and then fell somewhat. But the flow of cocaine was never seriously interrupted, and its street price in the United States, having fallen in the 1980s and early 1990s, remained more or less constant thereafter.[80]

There were three reasons for that. The first was what came to be called the 'balloon effect' – squeeze the drug trade in one place and it will expand elsewhere. That applies to transport routes as well as coca production. Both the trade and drug consumption have spread far and wide. Latin American countries are now cocaine consumers, while drug gangs control many of the slums from Tijuana to Rio de Janeiro. As power in the drug business, like in many other industries, moved closer to the consumer, Mexico's drug gangs began to mimic the wealth, firepower and turf wars previously confined to their Colombian counterparts. Drug-related murders soared in Mexico (to 2,100 in 2006). Felipe Calderón's first initiative as president was to send thousands of army troops to the most affected areas and to expand the federal police. However, it was not clear whether the government would carry out the radical purge and reform of the police that Mexico needed.

The second reason was the modernisation and professionalisation of the drug industry: for example, the bulk of coca cultivation shifted from Peru to Colombia in the early 1990s, and the original drug 'cartels' were replaced by a host of small, flexible networks, some of them run by accountants, lawyers or other professionals. There was also evidence that coca growers had raised their productivity. But the third and most important explanation was the peculiar economics of an illegal trade for a good that continued to be much in demand in the United States and Europe despite its prohibition. As Peter Reuter, an economist at the University of Maryland, has pointed out, prices at each stage in the long chain that turns a coca leaf on an Andean hillside into a gram of cocaine on the streets of the Bronx or the City of London are determined mainly by the need to reward risk-taking, rather than by the cost of production. That is why the price of a kilo of pure cocaine (measured in relation to its equivalent in coca leaf) rises by a factor of roughly 200 times between the coca farm and the street.[81] Most of the increase occurs once cocaine has entered the United States or Europe – because law enforcement is tighter and risk is thus higher. So even if repression in the producer countries succeeds in increasing leaf prices, this has little effect on cocaine prices.

Both the drug trade and the American-sponsored 'war' against it have been very costly for the Andean countries. American aid has been feeble in relation to the scale of the problem. Involving the armed forces and the police in fighting the drug trade has sometimes corrupted them. It has also drawn resources away from other priorities, such as citizen security. It has required democratic governments to use heavy-handed repression of peasants who are trying to earn a better living by growing coca. Such repression has sometimes produced a nationalist reaction. The rise of Evo Morales to Bolivia's presidency owed much to the American insistence on eradicating coca. Some Mexicans were irritated when the Americans pressed Vicente Fox into vetoing a law legalising the consumption of small quantities of drugs. Large-scale aerial spraying of coca crops with weedkiller by Uribe's government in Colombia has brought claims that legal crops have been affected, too, and of environmental damage (though producing cocaine itself involves the large-scale use of more toxic chemicals).

But as long as cocaine remains illegal, officials argued, the costs for the Andean countries of ignoring it were higher than those of fighting it. Visit any drug town in the tropical lowlands of Peru or Colombia, and it is clear that cocaine brings squalor, violence and insecurity as well as easy money. Even if only a fraction of the profits from the trade return to the producer countries, that is still big money – perhaps $2 billion to $5 billion a year in Colombia in the 1990s. The Latin American organised-crime syndicates generated by the illegality of the drug trade have global reach. They are immensely powerful, wealthy and well-armed. By their nature, they pose a huge danger to the rule of law and the democratic state in their home countries. And the profits to be had from cocaine have provided a ready source of cash for illegal armed groups.

Democratic security in Colombia

At first glance, San Vicente del Caguán looked like any other small cattle town on the fringes of the Amazon basin. On its stiflingly hot, bustling streets, lined with half-finished houses of concrete and brick, Japanese pick-ups and motorbikes jostled with horse-drawn carts. From early afternoon, Mexican *rancheras* blared out from the loudspeakers of the numerous brothels. What made San Vicente unusual in 2001 was the presence in the main square of a small office of the FARC – the Revolutionary Armed Forces of Colombia, the largest and longest-lasting leftist guerrilla army in Latin America.[82] For three years, the government of Andrés Pastrana allowed the FARC to control a Switzerland-sized swathe of mountains, jungle and grassland around San Vicente. The FARC had demanded this 'demilitarised zone' as a condition for getting peace talks going. But the talks made little progress. The FARC used them for propaganda purposes. They held public hearings on how to reduce unemployment, while carrying on their war with increasing savagery.

That war began in the 1960s, but has undergone several changes in character. The FARC's origins lie in peasant self-defence groups organised by the pro-Moscow Communist Party during the conflict between Liberal and Conservative supporters known as *la violencia*. They were driven to what became the 'demilitarised zone' by the army. Even today, most of the FARC's guerrillas are of peasant origin, according to Alfonso Cano, who himself is not but who is in charge of political affairs in its ruling secretariat.[83] Sociologically, the FARC can be seen as representing the interests of two particular groups of Colombian peasants: some among the small-scale farmers who colonised 'internal frontiers' and whose farms were threatened by cattle barons; and farmers and day-labourers in the coca industry. The FARC combines peasant stubbornness with narrow dogmatism. Its lifelong leader, Manuel Marulanda (known as *Tirofijo* or 'Sureshot') is in his 70s; he is not known to have visited a city larger than Neiva (population: 250,000) in southern Colombia. Though the FARC was nominally the military wing of the Colombian Communist Party it quickly came to dominate the party: it imposed its doctrines of 'prolonged popular war' (learned from the Vietnamese) and the 'combination of all forms of struggle' (i.e. military action plus legal politics) on the party, which has shrivelled into insignificance. It also began to espouse 'Bolivarianism', a gaseous populist nationalism.

The FARC's original justifications for its armed struggle were land and opposition to the power-sharing pact between Liberals and Conservatives known as the National Front, which ended *la violencia*. Yet Colombia has long since become mainly urban, the power-sharing pact ended formally in 1974 (and in practice in 1986) and the country's democracy has been the subject of almost continuous political reform. Peace agreements saw three small guerrilla groups lay down their arms in 1990 to 1991 – but not the FARC or the ELN, its smaller rival of originally guevarist inspiration. A new constitution followed in 1991, designed to open up politics to new parties and to decentralise power. The FARC had taken part in peace talks launched by President Belisario Betancur (1982–6) and set up a political party called the Unión Patriótica. This won 4.5 per cent of the vote in the 1986 presidential election. But over the next five years more than a thousand of its members were murdered, including two of its presidential candidates. Most were killed by the right-wing paramilitaries, who at the time had close links with some army commanders. The FARC cited this as proof that it was excluded from democracy. But its opponents noted that while appearing to accept democracy, it had carried on building up its army during the truce under Betancur with the aim of seizing power militarily.[84] For that reason some army commanders opposed Betancur's orders for a ceasefire and the release of guerrilla prisoners and began to work with the paramilitaries. The FARC had also got into the drug business in a big way, as well as extortion and kidnapping. By 2001, the best estimates were that it was making $250 million to $300 million a year from drugs (while its paramilitary foes were making perhaps $200 million).[85] In a lengthy interview, Cano admitted that the FARC received money from *retenciones* (i.e. kidnaps). When asked about drug income he said this was 'everywhere in the world economy'.[86]

By the 1990s, the FARC's actions had much more to do with plunder and a self-sustaining militarism than with any residual social grievances. Drug money helped the FARC to expand greatly, from perhaps 5,000 fighters in the early 1980s to a peak of around 20,000 in 2002. (The ELN, which engaged in kidnapping and later drugs, had around 5,000 fighters at its peak.) In the mid 1990s the FARC began to operate in larger units. It inflicted several humiliating defeats on the armed forces, in which small detachments were overrun by forces of several hundred guerrillas and some 500 police and troops were taken prisoner. The guerrillas also launched devastatingly inaccurate and bloody home-made mortar attacks on police posts in small towns, as well as frequent sabotage attacks against infrastructure. They would erect roadblocks on main highways, abducting motorists for ransom. The armed forces were far too small and too immobile to respond effectively: commanders noted that the security forces would have to expand some thirtyfold to achieve the same ratio of troops to territory that El Salvador's army enjoyed during that small country's civil war of the 1980s.

The drug-fuelled growth of the FARC exposed the weakness of the security forces and of the state – the flip side of Colombia's aversion to militarism and its tradition of civilian government. The relative impotence of the army prompted an expansion in the guerrillas' polar opposite, the AUC paramilitaries. 'The AUC exists because [the] armed forces have not done their institutional duty of guaranteeing lives, property and honour,' Carlos Castaño, one of its leaders, told the *Washington Post*.[87] The paramilitaries counted on the complicity of some politicians and army officers. They proceeded to act with even greater savagery than the FARC. They used terror to control territory, massacring groups of villagers whom they held to be collaborating with the guerrillas. Trade union leaders were targeted, partly because of the past enthusiasm of some of them for armed struggle.[88] So were human-rights workers. Journalists and social scientists were the targets of both the AUC and the FARC. By the late 1990s, the government's writ ran over only about half of a vast country, although that half included the cities where most Colombians lived. Indeed, hundreds of thousands of Colombians fled to the cities to escape a conflict that had become a self-sustaining war for territory to plunder. Insecurity began to affect the hitherto vigorous economy: combined with the new constitution's fiscal liberality, that triggered a sharp recession in 1999 and unemployment climbed to 20 per cent. A million or so Colombians moved abroad in the late 1990s. There were widespread fears that Colombia was on the way to becoming a failed state.

When Andrés Pastrana, a personable former television news anchor from a prominent Conservative family, succeeded Samper in 1998 he took two important decisions. One was to open peace talks with the FARC. And the other was to seek a strategic alliance with the United States. He was more successful in the second of these. Under Plan Colombia, drawn up jointly by

Colombian and American officials, the United States granted Colombia some $500 million to $700 million a year in mainly military aid between 1999 and 2006. Most of this went on some seventy helicopters and the training and equipping of new army battalions. The aim was to fight the guerrillas (and the paramilitaries) by fighting drugs, and so squeeze their finances. Pastrana also began the task of expanding the armed forces, and of turning a conscript force into a professional army.

While the state was strengthening its defences, so was the FARC. Its politics were remarkably intransigent. Not for it the compromises with democracy made by the Central American guerrillas of the 1970s and 1980s. 'Our struggle is to do away with the state as now it exists in Colombia, preferably by political means, but if they don't let us then we have to carry on shooting,' said Cano. The FARC would not demobilise in return for 'houses, cars and scholarships' or a few seats in Congress. 'This country will be saved when we have the chance to run the state.'[89] To that end, even as it supposedly talked peace, the FARC carried on its war. According to the armed forces commander, General Fernando Tapias, it used the 'demilitarised zone' as a logistical base: 'They are supplying, equipping and training with no action by the state to hinder them.'[90] With the talks going nowhere and the FARC continuing to stage brazen kidnappings of politicians and others, Colombians became disillusioned with a 'peace process' that wasn't. In 2002, with an election looming, Pastrana called off the talks and sent the army back to San Vicente and its environs. The 'demilitarised zone' did serve one purpose. 'It has allowed the country and the world to see the government's willingness to seek a negotiated settlement, and the opposition to democracy of the insurgents,' as General Tapias put it.

The presidential election saw a crushing victory for Álvaro Uribe Vélez. A lawyer and Liberal former governor of Antioquia, the economically important area around Medellín, Uribe was an austere, intense figure. His father, a cattle farmer, had been kidnapped and murdered by the FARC. He campaigned on the slogan of *mano firme, corazón grande* ('firm hand, big heart'). He seemed to believe that he was a man of destiny: he promised that he would be 'the first soldier of Colombia' and would double the size of the security forces. In normal times, this uncompromising message would have been electorally unattractive in Colombia, a country whose mainstream politics were moderate, consensual and mistrustful of a powerful state. But these were not normal times. Uribe, running as an independent against his own party's official candidates but with the support of the Conservatives, captured the national mood.

Uribe's 'democratic security' policy involved a big military build-up. In his first four years he expanded the security forces by a third, adding more than 60,000 troops and 30,000 extra police. He continued Pastrana's work of turning the army into a salaried, professional force. He extended the state's control over more of Colombia's vast territory, placing permanent police detachments in 150 municipalities (of a total of 1,100) which had lacked them. He created a force of some 20,000 part-time 'peasant soldiers' (later renamed 'popular soldiers') for local guard duties. Six new mountain battalions of the army occupied the high Andean massifs which had served as transit corridors and strategic refuges for the FARC. He also turned the army into an offensive force, creating nine new mobile brigades. All this was micro-managed by the president himself. He recounted with glee to visitors that his Friday-night relaxation was to stay at his desk until two a.m., ringing police and army commanders across the country to quiz them about security in their areas.[91] Each weekend he would set off to remote towns or villages and hold public meetings to discuss local problems. All this changed the strategic balance in the war. The FARC were driven from much of central Colombia, forced back to remote jungles and to operating in smaller groups. Several thousand guerrillas deserted, individually or in small groups. Officials reckoned that the FARC's fighting strength had been cut to around 12,000 by the end of 2006.[92]

The weakening of the FARC enabled Uribe's government to persuade the paramilitaries to demobilise. The terms on which they did so were controversial. Under the Justice and Peace Law approved in 2005, those of their leaders who were accused of crimes against humanity were required to give a voluntary account of their actions and, if convicted in the courts, would face a reduced sentence of no more than eight years' confinement in a special facility (perhaps a prison farm). The government also had a powerful lever over those of the AUC leaders who were wanted on drugs charges in the United States: it would suspend extradition only while they co-operated. Officials argued that the law was a reasonable compromise between peace and justice, given that the paramilitaries had not been militarily defeated. Uribe insisted that the AUC chiefs would not be able to get away with intentional omissions in their statements because the government 'has made visible those involved in atrocities'.[93] But human-rights groups complained that the law was too lenient in not requiring a binding confession and in not ensuring that the paramilitaries dismantled their criminal networks. Colombia's Constitutional Court agreed: it put more teeth into the law, requiring full confessions on pain of forfeiting reduced sentences. Whatever its imperfections, the process quickly appeared to acquire momentum. In late 2006, 57 paramilitary leaders were jailed pending court hearings. No fewer than 25,000 people registered as victims of the paramilitaries. Mario Iguarán, the attorney-general, said that charges might eventually be brought against 300–400 paramilitary leaders.[94] The government's intention was to apply the same terms to the guerrillas – something that the FARC might well find hard to swallow.

Uribe took the same tough approach to the drug issue as he did to security. With American support, he unleashed a massive programme of aerial spraying of coca fields. According to measurements by the United Nations Office on Drugs and Crime, by 2004, the area under coca had fallen to half its 1999 peak before drifting up again thereafter. But there was no discernible effect on the supply price of cocaine in world markets. The spraying was controversial; in 2006 the government switched tactics and put more emphasis on manual eradication and on the development of alternative economic activities. Predictably, Plan Colombia had proved to be far more effective as a counter-insurgency plan than as an anti-drug plan, though it been sold to the American public as the latter.

Uribe's democratic security policy certainly made Colombia a safer place. According to official figures, the murder rate fell steadily: whereas 28,837 people were killed in 2002, the figure for 2006 was 17,277 (or 41 per 100,000).[95] The number of kidnappings fell over the same period from 2,883 to 687. Critics disputed the figures, but there was little doubting the overall trend. The main roads became safe to travel again. Greater security brought a boom in investment. Economic growth reached 6 per cent in 2006. Uribe's supporters saw him as the saviour of his country. Most Colombians tended to that view. In opinion polls, respondents regularly gave the president an approval rating of 60–75 per cent. His popularity and political success allowed him to persuade Congress to change the constitution to allow him to stand for a second consecutive term. In a country that historically had been deeply suspicious of an over-mighty executive, this was perhaps his most surprising achievement. In 2006, he was duly elected by a landslide for a second term: he won a thumping 62 per cent of the vote. That was almost three times as much as his nearest challenger, Carlos Gaviria, who represented a coalition of the peaceful, democratic left – a novelty for Colombia. But it was soon clear that Uribe's second term was going to be far more difficult than the first.

Some high-ranking army officers had long been guilty of collusion with – or at least turning a blind eye to – the paramilitaries. Several of the most important paramilitary leaders were former army officers. These links undermined the legitimacy of the state. Support for the paramilitaries was not the policy of the armed forces as an institution, nor of the government, and such cases became increasingly rare. But thanks to investigations by journalists and prosecutors the penetration of politics and of state institutions by the paramilitaries began to be laid bare, becoming a political scandal (dubbed *parapolítica* or 'parapolitics' by Colombians). The former head of the civilian intelligence agency from 2002 to 2005 was accused of collaborating with the AUC. The Supreme Court ordered the arrest of a dozen legislators for the same reason; nearly all were supporters of the president. The investigations revealed that in some areas of the Caribbean coast in particular, the paramilitaries had seized control of local politics, murdering, intimidating or bribing those who stood in their way. They used that control to extort commissions from public contracts. They also controlled much of the drug trade in the area. These developments seemed to echo the claim made by some of Uribe's critics on the left that the president was himself in league with the paramilitaries. There was no evidence of any personal link. However, he was sometimes guilty of poor judgement in his choice of friends and collaborators. Uribe insisted that the scandals were only coming out because of the climate of greater security and because of the demobilisation of the paramilitaries and the investigations under the Justice and Peace Law. There was some truth in that. *Parapolítica* had little effect on Uribe's popularity at home. But it did severe damage to his standing abroad, especially in the United States. The Democrats, who had won control of the US Congress, had become increasingly hostile to Plan Colombia. They made it clear that they would not quickly ratify a free-trade agreement with Colombia. That was potentially a big setback for Uribe and for his country.

Colombia's transformation was remarkable but remained fragile. The FARC was not defeated. Some Colombian officials claimed that its leaders were receiving succour in Chávez's Venezuela and in Ecuador. After Rafael Correa's victory in Ecuador they felt surrounded by hostile governments. The security forces needed further strengthening if new criminal groups were not to spring up where paramilitary demobilisation had left a vacuum of territorial control. Between 1.5 million and 2.5 million Colombians had been uprooted by conflict, and many of them were surviving in poverty in the cities. There was a strong case for a land reform which would have settled some of the displaced people on land bought or grabbed by drug traffickers and paramilitaries. But Uribe showed little interest in this. Partly because of the strength of its democratic institutions, such as the courts and the independent attorney-general, Colombia had stumbled into an effort to bring war criminals to justice on a massive scale and with almost no outside support. The man of destiny had strengthened the authority of the democratic state. But by seeking a second term he had vested that authority in himself. He had not groomed a political heir, nor institutionalised many of the changes he had wrought. Much hung on who came after him. But the main barrier between Colombia and normality was the continuing failure of cocaine prohibition in consuming countries around the world. Politicians in the United States and Europe cavilled at granting aid to Colombia's embattled democracy, or at helping its legal economy to expand through trade. Meanwhile, their countries' cocaine consumers continued to pump money into Colombia's illegal armies.

CHAPTER 11

THE STUBBORN RESILIENCE OF FLAWED DEMOCRACIES

Like many Latin American airports, that of El Alto – which serves Bolivia's capital, La Paz – has in the decades since its construction been enveloped by urban sprawl. It is now surrounded by dusty streets lined with houses of concrete and brick in varying stages of completion. The airport shares its name with a satellite city which in 1980 had less than half its current population of 700,000. In those days, the airport bordered pasture dotted with small adobe farmhouses. The passenger stepped out, breathless, on to the tarmac of what, at 4,000 metres above sea level, is the world's highest commercial airport, to be greeted by an uninterrupted view of the Cordillera Real, a line of majestic snowy peaks that march away north-westwards towards Lake Titicaca. To the south stretched the infinite bleakness of the Altiplano, the high-altitude plain that covers much of western Bolivia. La Paz, sprawling over the flanks of a vast volcanic crater that plunges down from El Alto, is the world's largest Andean Indian city. Many of its streets were – and still are – used as markets. The vendors were nearly all Indian women. They were dressed in bowler hats and knee-length flounced skirts known as *polleras* – the costume of seventeenth-century Spanish peasants imposed upon them by the viceroys and long since adopted as a symbol of cultural identity. Some sat cross-legged in the street in the fierce midday sun, minding a sheet of blue polythene on which were laid out only a few neat mounds of mandarins – half a dozen for a few pesos. At the other extreme of al fresco retailing, on the lower reaches of Avenida Buenos Aires, tightly packed stalls groaned under the weight of cassette players and televisions, smuggled in defiance of import restrictions.

In March 1980, La Paz was tense.[1] After 15 years of military rule, the armed forces had turned over power to a rickety, interim civilian government. The city was abuzz with rumour. The previous November a coup attempt had failed, but only after 200 people were killed and 125 more 'disappeared'.

Another coup was in the air: a prominent local journalist who denounced this had just been murdered. In July 1980 the coup duly came, just weeks after a centre-left coalition had won a clear mandate in an election. It soon became evident that the new regime was led by army officers with close links to the drug trade. Once again, a window of opportunity for democracy seemed to have slammed shut. But it was to be the last successful military coup against a civilian government in Latin America – or at least the last one that installed a military dictatorship. Though brutal and corrupt, the *junta* proved short-lived, partly because its links to the cocaine trade aroused the hostility of the United States. In 1982 it collapsed, allowing the elected centre-left government to take office. The new president, Hernán Siles Suazo, was a leader of the 1952 revolution and had held office in the 1950s. This time he presided over chaos. Like the rest of the region, Bolivia was bankrupt. The government resorted to printing money on a massive scale. In 1985 inflation peaked at a rate equivalent to 25,000 per cent a year. In return for a five-dollar bill, the visitor would receive long, tightly packed bundles of greasy and tattered banknotes, tied together with string or rubber bands. As well as moneychangers, the streets were thronged with almost daily demonstrations by miners and other workers demanding wage increases to compensate for inflation. In an obscure office in the Central Bank, a concrete and glass skyscraper that soared incongruously over the low, whitewashed buildings of the city centre, sat a representative of the International Monetary Fund, an urbane German. He was happy to pass the time of day with a visiting freelance journalist, doubtless because nobody else would listen to him.

Against this unpromising background, an unlikely experiment began. An early election in 1985 brought to power for the third time Victor Paz Estenssoro, the leader of the 1952 revolution, who was by then aged 78. Advised by a young American economist called Jeffrey Sachs, his government swiftly ended hyperinflation by raising petrol prices and closing the fiscal deficit.[2] Paz Estenssoro went on to dismantle many of the economic institutions he had erected a generation earlier. He liquidated chronically loss-making state-owned industries and, after the world tin market collapsed, Comibol, the state mining firm, laying off thousands of workers. Subsidies, import controls and protective tariffs were all slashed or abolished. Government authority was restored: when the militant miners marched on La Paz, they were stopped halfway and without bloodshed by a state of emergency and army tanks. Bolivia thus followed Chile in using free-market reforms to conquer hyperinflation, but it was the first country in the region to do so as a democracy. In all this, Paz Estenssoro's lieutenant was the planning minister, Gonzalo ('Goni') Sánchez de Lozada, a wisecracking, cigar-smoking mining magnate. Goni had been brought up in the United States and spoke Spanish with a curious mixture of soft Andean throatiness and an American drawl. In 1993 he was elected president. To attract foreign investment, he devised a variant of privatisation which he called 'capitalisation'. Under this scheme, through a bidding process private companies injected capital investment into state-owned firms in return for a 50 per cent shareholding and management control. Foreigners took over not just the telecoms company, the railways, the national airline and electricity companies but also the oil and gas industry, a nationalist totem. Over-riding sixty years of mercantilist xenophobia, he signed an agreement with Brazil to build a pipeline to export Bolivian gas to São Paulo. As he prepared to leave office in 1997, Goni was ebullient. Having created a new natural-gas industry, he forecast that Bolivia would soon enjoy 'Asian rates' of economic growth.[3] He spoke proudly of his social reforms, too. The state's shares in 'capitalised' companies were used to endow a new private pension system and to make an annual payment (of $248 in 1997) to all Bolivians aged over 65. He decentralised power and money to local government. His vice-president, an Amerindian intellectual, promoted bilingual education, so that Indian children would receive some of their initial schooling in their first language.

Not only had Bolivia become an unexpected advertisement for the Washington Consensus; as power alternated after each election between coalitions of centre left and centre right, democracy seemed to take root. A country that had so long been the continent's unstable, suffering heart seemed to have become a success story. Yet that appearance proved deceptive. In the 1990s, the economy grew at only half the 8 per cent a year Goni had promised. That was not enough: the population was expanding at 2 per cent a year, and income distribution was very unequal. In 2001 annual income per head was under $950, and 63 per cent of Bolivians were poor, according to the World Bank. Then growth petered out, as the economy was hit by Argentina's collapse, a regionwide recession, and by a big US-backed campaign to eradicate all illegal coca. Coca had long been grown in the Yungas, close to La Paz, for such traditional uses as chewing (the mild narcotic effect is a welcome antidote to the cold) and coca tea (which helps tourists adapt to high altitude). In the late 1970s coca spread to the Chapare region near Cochabamba, where it was sold for the drug trade. The American eradication campaign was supplemented by modest aid to develop alternative crops in the Chapare, such as bananas, palm hearts and pepper. But these only paid a third as much as coca, and employed fewer people.[4]

In 2002, Goni was again elected president. But this time he had a narrow mandate, and the country was in a surly mood. The best hope of kickstarting faster economic growth lay in vast deposits of natural gas – the largest in Latin America outside Venezuela. These had been discovered since privatisation, just as Goni had forecast. He pressed ahead with a project, promoted by a consortium of foreign companies, to export the gas via a Chilean port to Mexico and the United States. This made economic sense, but it touched both the electrodes of Bolivian nationalism: hostility to Chile (dating from the War of the Pacific) and resentment at the exploitation of the country's natural resources by foreigners (dating from the colonial silver mine at Potosí). The result would be an explosive political short-circuit. To make matters worse, the government had to try to reduce a large budget deficit. According to Goni, the drug 'war' cost Bolivia 5 per cent of GDP; the transitional cost of the pension reform to the government amounted to another 5 per cent. The president went to Washington for help. 'I said to Bush that I needed $150 million otherwise I was going to be seeking political asylum in the coming year. They gave $10 million,' he recalled later.[5] Goni suffered a first shock in February 2003, when protests against tax rises were backed by a police strike. In the resulting disorders 27 people were killed, several public buildings were torched and foreign businesses looted. Eight months later, rock-throwing crowds of demonstrators, organised by far-left groups opposed to the gas export plan, blockaded the roads through El Alto for a fortnight, cutting La Paz off from the airport and the rest of the country. When the government ordered the army to open the roads, 59 people were killed in the resulting clashes. Abandoned by Congress, Goni was forced to step down. He was taken by helicopter to the airport, and to a life of exile in the suburbs of Washington DC – just as he had warned Bush might happen. Constitutional forms were preserved: power passed to the vice-president, Carlos Mesa, an articulate historian who had previously hosted a popular television programme. But in June 2005 he suffered the same fate as Goni. After three weeks of roadblocks in El Alto and elsewhere, organised by the same leftist groups who now wanted full and immediate nationalisation of the gas industry, Mesa resigned. The president of the Supreme Court took over as Bolivia's third president in as many years, and called an early election for December 2005.

The election was won emphatically by Evo Morales, the most widely supported of the protestors' leaders. Of Aymaran Indian descent, he led both the cocaworkers' unions in the Chapare and a left-wing party called the Movement to Socialism (MAS). Morales secured 54 per cent of the vote in an election in which 80 per cent of those registered turned out – by far the largest mandate since democracy was restored in 1983. He ran on a platform of nationalisation of oil and gas, a constituent assembly to entrench indigenous rights and an end to coca eradication. He was, he repeatedly said, the United States' 'worst nightmare'. Ironically, Morales was very much a creation of the United States and its 'war on drugs'. When he launched his first presidential campaign, in 2002, he was a relatively minor figure. But he received an unexpected boost when Manuel Rocha, the American ambassador, said that if Morales won the United States would cancel all aid to Bolivia (which averaged $100 million a year). Bolivians saw this as a crude intervention in their democracy and gave Morales 22 per cent of the vote. Morales is often referred to by outsiders as Bolivia's first indigenous president. Yet he left his Andean village as a young man and headed for the coca fields of the Chapare. In the 1980s the Chapare was booming, pulling in Bolivians from all over the country, and was a melting pot of *mestizaje* comparable to Potosí in the early seventeenth century.[6]

Morales is culturally a *mestizo*, and his politics are derived from Bolivia's tradition of radical syndicalism, though he was less lettered than the miners' leaders of the past, many of whom had read Marx and Trotsky. His political home is the headquarters in Cochabamba of the Federación del Trópico, as the cocaworkers' union calls itself. This occupies part of an unfinished six-storey office block of raw concrete opposite a scruffy park near the centre of the city. Shortly after eight a.m. on a weekday morning in January 2004, supplicants began arriving at the office. By the time Morales turned up two hours later, a couple of dozen were lined up waiting for a word with the leader. Several women sought scholarships for their sons; a group of teachers came to discuss a strike; a lawyer warned Morales about a bill in Congress to allow double nationality, which he claimed was a device to increase American influence in the country. Like most urbanised men of Andean Indian descent, Morales wore ordinary western clothes. He cut an unsmiling but not unattractive figure, with a boyish shock of black hair. From his original syndicalism, Morales's political ideas have evolved into a vague blend of dependency theory, utopian socialism, anti-globalisation rhetoric, indigenous rights and the pragmatism of a trade union leader. What he was seeking, he said, was 'a refoundation' of Bolivia through a Constituent Assembly, to create 'a new country, without discrimination or exploitation, where indigenous, *mestizos* and *blancoides* ["whitish people"] live together'.[7] Bolivia was rich but it was impoverished because its wealth is in the hands of multinational corporations, he claimed. He said he wanted 'a mixed economy'. Foreign companies would no longer hold oil and gas deposits in concession. These would pass to Yacimientos Petrolíferos Fiscales Bolivianos (YPFB), the state hydrocarbons company. But multinationals would be encouraged to sign service contracts with YPFB to operate the fields. Morales insisted he was a democrat, though one who favoured 'participatory democracy'. He said he admired Fidel Castro and Hugo Chávez – he was a frequent visitor to Caracas – but also Lula ('how he combines the mixed economy is very intelligent'). Morales himself gave an impression of being relatively pragmatic. But he also had a record of shifting further left under pressure from the streets.

In office he was true to those words – with all their contradictions. He appointed to his cabinet activists from social movements with little experience of governing. In his inaugural speech he hailed Che Guevara and Fidel Castro, but also gave signs that he wanted an accommodation with the United States. After a relatively moderate start, at the end of April he travelled to Havana, where he formalised an alliance with Chávez and Castro. On his return home, he led army troops into a gasfield operated by Brazil's Petrobrás and declared the nationalisation of the oil and gas industry – provoking a furious reaction in Brazil. Six months later Morales beat a partial retreat, signing new contracts with Petrobrás and other companies. These gave YPFB formal control over the gas and its marketing, and increased royalties on the multinationals beyond the 50 per cent imposed by Mesa. At the same time, he signed an export agreement with Argentina that potentially offered the companies the incentive to increase gas output. The new taxes increased government revenues by around 7 per cent of GDP in 2006, but much of the money went to regional governments under the current constitution. It was not clear by the end of 2006 what the future held for private investment in gas in Bolivia. Meanwhile, Morales set up a Constituent Assembly to rewrite the constitution. This made slow progress, as did his plans for land reform. He faced a powerful opposition movement, based in Santa Cruz and other eastern areas, which demanded regional autonomy. Morales gave every impression that he would like to imitate the elected autocracy and 'twenty-first-century socialism' of Hugo Chávez. But it was far from clear whether Bolivians would allow him to do so.

Evo Morales represents one face of Latin American democracy today. It is an ambivalent face. On the one hand, the movement of which he is a leader bundled two presidents from office without regard for the constitution or democratic political procedures. It saw the streets, not the Congress, as the venue where political conflicts should be resolved. It was wedded to economic policies – nationalisation and greater state control over the economy – which have failed not just around the world but in Bolivia itself. In all of these ways, it was retrograde. On the other hand, the election of Morales underlined that democracy in Bolivia, and in Latin America, no longer excludes those who claim to stand for radical change and to represent the poor majority and indigenous people. Like many Bolivians, Morales saw his country's democracy as having been hijacked by corrupt and self-serving traditional parties. Like the populist leaders of the past, he has pursued a road which combines electoral politics with popular mobilisation. Like them, he has pursued 'resource nationalism'.

Elsewhere in Latin America, democracy is far more robust and has plenty of less ambivalent leaders. Bolivia is an extreme case, not the mean. But many other countries share to some degree at least some of Bolivia's weaknesses: political fragmentation, the weakness of political parties, a populist challenge to liberal democracy, the difficulties that reformers face when they must rely on traditional political bosses, and a relatively disappointing economic performance. As in Bolivia, if often not to the same extent, democracy must battle against widespread poverty, inequality, ethnic differences and racism, as well as the drug trade and pressure from the United States to eliminate it. And as in Bolivia, there is ambivalence or hostility towards privatisation and foreign investment, especially in natural resources.

The long and winding road to democratic consolidation

There are many definitions of democracy. At its simplest, in Joseph Schumpeter's phrase, it is 'that institutional arrangement for arriving at political decisions in which individuals acquire the power to decide through a competitive struggle for the people's vote'.[8] Others have identified three main elements in this arrangement: regular, free and competitive elections; the existence and enforcement of constitutional rules to ensure civil and political rights; and mechanisms to ensure that nobody is unreasonably excluded from exercising those rights and from participating in elections.[9] Yet democracy also involves considerations about how government is exercised, not just how it is chosen. Many writers have stressed the importance of restraints on the state and on the executive power, in order to hold them accountable to citizens and to guard against despotism. Elections can be decreed, but the everyday practice of democracy involves the gradual accretion of rules, habits and institutions. Robert Dahl, a noted democratic theorist, lists six political institutions required by modern democracies: elected officials; free, fair and frequent elections; freedom of expression; alternative sources of information; 'associational autonomy'; and 'inclusive citizenship'.[10] Getting from the mere replacement of dictatorship with an elected government to this full institutional panoply has often been envisaged as a transition, a journey whose destination some political scientists have called 'consolidated democracy'. Arrival means not just that democracy should be stable but also that it should ensure that its citizens should enjoy the rule of law, backed by an effective state capable of regulating the market and providing public goods (e.g. security and clean air).[11]

The quality of democracy is not just a matter to excite academics. Consolidated democracies tend to be better than dictatorships not just at protecting human rights but also at generating wealth and opportunity for their citizens. In the short term, the relationship between democracy and development may not be clear-cut. Dictatorships can sometimes push through economic reforms more swiftly than democracies. Yet in the long-run, democracy and successful market economies are mutually reinforcing.[12] That is not least because only democracies have the legitimacy to offer a long-term guarantee of property rights. They tend to be better at enforcing the rule of law and at fostering education, both of which are needed for sustained economic growth. Market capitalism tends to produce a large middle class of property owners who have an interest in education, freedom, participation and the rule of law. Conversely, it is no coincidence that stable democracies all have market economies, since a command economy is inimical to political pluralism and competition. But, as Dahl has pointed out, the close association between democracy and market capitalism conceals a paradox, in that market economies generate inequalities in 'political resources' (i.e. influence and access).[13] The undue influence of the rich and powerful poses a special challenge to democracy in egregiously unequal societies such as those of Latin America. Indeed, on the more exacting definitions of democratic 'consolidation' much of Latin America has fared less well than the southern and eastern European states with which it formed part of what Samuel Huntington called the 'third wave' of democratisation, beginning in the 1970s.[14] Nevertheless, in most Latin American countries democracy has shown considerable resilience.

The region's democracies were subjected to a severe stress test during the 'lost half-decade' of 1998–2002, which saw unemployment rise, real incomes fall and progress in reducing poverty halted. Democracy held up – but not unscarred. There was some increase in instability, with eight elected presidents being ousted before the end of their term since 1998. But half that number came from just two countries (Bolivia and Ecuador), and two more were of doubtful legitimacy, having won rigged elections (Fujimori in Peru in 2000 and Jean-Bertrand Aristide in Haiti). Public support for democracy suffered. The Latinobarómetro poll found in 2004 that some 55 per cent of respondents 'would not mind a non-democratic government if it could solve economic problems'.[15] In the same poll, 71 per cent of respondents thought that 'the country is governed for the benefit of a few powerful interests'. Economic recovery and the electoral marathon of 2006 brought a recovery in support for democracy. But many democratic institutions were still held in relatively low esteem. In the 2006 poll, only 36 per cent expressed any confidence in the judiciary (up from 20 per cent in 2003) and 27 per cent in the legislature (up from 17 per cent in 2003). The figure for political parties was just 22 per cent (though that was double the 2003 number).[16] These polls suggest that many Latin Americans remained potential fodder for populist *caudillos* promising magical solutions to economic problems. In Peru, Ecuador and Bolivia, a large minority did not separate their disapproval of the government from their attitude to the democratic system. Rather than trusting in the political system, some social groups – including Mexican farmers opposed to a new airport on their land, Brazil's landless movement, Bolivia's social movements and Peruvian groups opposed to mining – have seen mobilisation and sometimes-violent protests as the means by which to achieve their demands. Yet in 2006, Latinobarómetro found that 57 per cent of respondents thought that voting was the best way to change things against 14 per cent who favoured participating in protest groups. These opinion surveys pointed to the underlying resilience of democracy: they suggested that roughly half of Latin Americans have remained convinced democrats through the ups and downs of the economic cycle, with only around 15 per cent preferring authoritarian government. Around a third of respondents are indifferent or did not respond. Only in Paraguay have more respondents favoured authoritarianism than democracy – and even that changed in 2006. Across the region, some 70 per cent of respondents in 2005 agreed with the statement that 'democracy may have problems, but it is the best system of government' and that only with a democratic system can their country develop.[17]

Across the region there are striking variations in the solidity of democracies. Three groups are discernible: countries with consolidated democracies, those where democracy is consolidating, and those where it is unstable or under threat. Many political scientists suggest that only two nations in Latin America have consolidated democracies, and both are small: Uruguay and Costa Rica. Chile now has a strong claim to join them: in the past few years its civilian governments have finally shaken off the shackles placed on them during the transition from the dictatorship of General Augusto Pinochet. In many respects – save two important ones – Colombia might claim a place on this list. The problem is that its guerrillas do not accept democracy as the 'only game in town'[18] and the democratic state still struggles to impose the rule of law across the whole of the national territory. These four countries have two characteristics in common. With the partial exception of Colombia, their population is ethnically more or less homogenous – they lack the racial divide of Brazil or Peru. Another is that they had gone furthest towards establishing democracy a century ago. They had long experience of 'oligarchical democracy', to employ that helpful oxymoron.[19] In other words, these countries succeeded in institutionalising rules for political competition early on, although important social groups, especially the rural poor, were excluded. Only when these rules were established, and when economies were developing, was the whole population brought into the system. Uruguay was a pioneer in establishing universal suffrage and a welfare state. These were achieved in Costa Rica through a revolution in 1948. To preserve the tradition of peaceful political competition which they believed had been threatened, the victors of the revolution, José Figueras and his social-democratic National Liberation Party, abolished the country's small army. That helped to ensure that in Costa Rica, unlike Uruguay and Chile, democracy was not overthrown in the 1970s. Alone in Latin America, Costa Rica makes it to Dahl's list of the world's 22 'older democracies'.[20]

The puzzling absentee from the list of consolidated democracies is Argentina: in the 1920s its democracy was at least as advanced as any of the others, but it then suffered many reverses. The preservation of constitutional rule during the economic collapse of 2001–2 was a hopeful sign. But the country suffered from a lack of strong opposition parties and Peronism's continuing tendency to politicise the judiciary and the public administration. Argentina bucks the comforting notion that the practice of democracy over time will lead to its consolidation. But on the whole, this notion seems plausible. When assessing the prospects for democratic consolidation, the initial conditions do matter – as they do for liberal economic reforms.

Colombia and Argentina belong in a second group of countries, in which one might also include Brazil, Mexico, the Dominican Republic, and perhaps Peru. They all appeared to be moving towards the consolidation of democracy. That they are not there yet was in most cases because of the patchy application of the rule of law and the state's weaknesses in providing public goods and effective regulation of markets. Paraguay and El Salvador are still in the early stages of democratic transition, in which power has remained in the hands of parties which dominated, in one guise or another, under authoritarian rule. Honduras and Nicaragua have seen the alternation of power but are hampered by widespread poverty.

The third group, of unstable or threatened democracies, includes Venezuela. There a seemingly solid representative democracy has 'unravelled', to borrow from the title of a recent book on the country.[21] Depending on what the Morales government does, the same might happen in Bolivia. Ecuador is chronically unstable, with no fewer than seven presidents between 1996 and 2007. In Guatemala, democratic governments were struggling to establish the rule of law and had failed to raise enough taxes to pay for an effective state. Haiti is a failed state under the care of the United Nations. The election of René Préval as president in 2006 offered some hope of a fresh start.

So democratic consolidation has proved harder and slower than many hoped. In most countries the issue is not so much democracy's survival as its quality. Political scientists have come to recognise that countries can embark on a transition to democracy without ever arriving at the journey's end of consolidation. They have come up with a plethora of adjectival prefixes to describe this condition, such as 'pseudo', 'low-intensity', 'incomplete' or 'shallow' democracies.[22] Laurence Whitehead, another theorist of Latin

America's democratic transition, has suggested an alternative yardstick, that of 'viability'. He argues that 'like a plant in inhospitable soil, a democratic regime may be able to adapt and survive, but only by accommodating to local realities'.[23] Some of these realities may be undemocratic, leading to a regime that is formally democratic but rests on hybrid foundations. Whereas 'consolidation' is seen as a linear journey, Whitehead views 'viability' as cyclical and therefore reversible. As long ago as 1994, O'Donnell, the Argentine political scientist, warned of 'delegative' democracies in which 'whoever wins the presidential election is authorised to govern as they see fit, restricted only by the crude reality of existing power relations and by the constitutional term-limit on their mandate'.[24] Yet the opposite fear is increasingly raised: that weak presidents are placing 'governability'[25] in jeopardy.

The pendulum stops

Difficult though it is to achieve consolidation, the current democratic wave in Latin America is qualitatively different from those that went before, in at least four ways: the pendulum between dictatorship and democracy has stopped; universal, effective suffrage has at last been achieved; and decentralisation has deepened democracy. These three factors have combined to give citizens a more tangible stake in democracy than in the past. Last but not least, Latin American societies, and not just political systems, are becoming more democratic. Democracy has 'put down roots', as Fernando Henrique Cardoso, Brazil's former president, puts it.[26]

That said, the region's still-flawed and sometimes feeble democracies face some formidable obstacles. They must struggle against poverty, inequality and an external threat to the rule of law in the form of the drug trade. They face high expectations from their electorates. And their inheritance includes undemocratic political habits and practices. Whitehead is surely right that at least in some countries democracy may become denatured by adapting to a hostile environment. But in most countries, and especially the larger ones, there is a reasonable prospect of relatively rapid democratic consolidation over the next decade or two – provided that electorates resist the populist temptation.

The fact that democracy has survived nearly everywhere is often taken for granted. It should not be. The story of Latin American democracy over the past quarter-century or so is as much about what didn't happen as what did. Given the region's history, the almost complete absence of military coups is striking. In only three cases have presidents been ousted by military interventions. Two involved Jean-Bertrand Aristide in Haiti, overthrown in 1991 and again in 2004, when the United States and France arranged for him to be flown out as a rebel band advanced on Port-au-Prince – a move he later denounced as a coup. The third was in Ecuador in January 2000, when the army high command ordered Jamil Mahuad to resign, installing his vice-president in his place, after several junior officers had joined an uprising by indigenous Ecuadoreans who occupied the Congress building. There were a few other military interventions in politics. In 1992, Alberto Fujimori, Peru's elected president, used army tanks to shut down the country's Congress and its courts in an *autogolpe* ('self-coup').[27] There were several attempts at a coup in Paraguay in the 1990s, all of which failed. In Venezuela, Hugo Chávez and his supporters staged two coups against the elected government of Carlos Andrés Pérez, in 1992 and 1993. They helped to create a climate in which Pérez was impeached for corruption a year before the end of his term.[28] Chávez himself was briefly toppled by a coup in April 2002, before being restored to power by loyal troops.[29]

These were the exceptions. In most countries, coups have not been attempted, even in circumstances of social breakdown that would certainly have prompted military intervention in the past. That goes for Argentina during its economic collapse of 2001–2, when middle-class savers and unemployed workers temporarily joined in protests whose slogan was *que se vayan todos* – 'kick all the politicians out'. That message might once have been taken as a green light by ambitious generals. Bolivia is a similarly striking case. In May 2005 when thousands of protestors blockaded roads across the country, forcing Carlos Mesa to resign, the country's politicians were divided as to who should replace him. In the past, that kind of chaotic power vacuum would inevitably have triggered a military coup. On this occasion, however, the armed forces quietly but firmly threw their weight behind the selection by Congress of the head of the Supreme Court as interim president with a mandate to call an early election.

This absence of open challenge to democracy was partly because the external climate had changed. Ever since Ronald Reagan, in his second term, decided that democratisation was the best policy for managing the conflicts of the final years of the Cold War in Latin America, the United States has opposed military coups against elected governments. The egregious exception to this record was the short-lived coup against Chávez in Venezuela, which the United States failed to denounce and appeared to support (though this was vehemently denied).[30] Aristide's overthrow in Haiti seemed to be another exception. Regional forces have played a role, too. Brazil and Argentina, for example, acted in concert with the United States to prevent a coup in Paraguay in 1996. In the aftermath, the Mercosur trade group, of which Paraguay was a member along with Brazil, Argentina and Uruguay, adopted a 'democracy clause' which called for the suspension of a member country in the event of any interruption of constitutional rule.

Yet the main reasons for the relative security of democracy were internal. In most countries, memories of the economic failure and repressive rule of most of the military governments of the 1970s appeared to have inoculated the body politic against any early repetition. That was particularly true in Argentina, where more than anywhere else the armed forces were discredited by their record when in power. The absence of coups was also a sign that democratic governments had weakened the power of the armed forces, though this was a gradual, uneven and contested process. Argentina apart, the transition to democracy was negotiated between moderate civilian politicians and the generals, rather than being imposed by military defeat or revolution. The armed forces tried to retain fat budgets, pet projects, and 'reserve powers' over the political process.[31] In many countries, those pretensions have been foiled, as civilians have asserted control over the military. The issue of holding the soldiers to account for the crimes of the dictatorships has been particularly difficult, but progress has been made in many countries. Across the region, unified defence ministries replaced separate self-governing ministries for each service. Most defence ministers nowadays are civilians (in Colombia, Chile, Argentina and Ecuador, recent ministers have included women). Progress has been made, too, in settling border disputes, often in spite of reservations from the military. Democratic governments in Brazil and Argentina scrapped incipient nuclear weapons programmes and agreed to joint inspection of nuclear facilities. After democracy returned to Chile, its government negotiated with Argentina a settlement of two dozen boundary disputes – an issue which had brought the two countries' dictatorships close to war in 1978. Peru's Fujimori was a questionable democrat, but he did settle his country's border dispute with Ecuador, which had thrice been a motive for skirmishes of varying severity. In relation to the size of their economies, Latin American countries spend less on defence than those in any other region in the world. In 2004 defence spending accounted for just 1.3 per cent of GDP, down from 1.8 per cent in 1995.[32]

Even so, the army retained an unhealthy degree of power in several countries, such as Peru, Ecuador, Guatemala and Venezuela. The United States sometimes pushed armies to play a prominent role in the 'war' on drugs (and more recently some Latin American governments have done so of their own volition). In Brazil, the main police force – the *policia militar* or gendarmerie – of each state was placed under the control of the armed forces during the military regime, a disposition confirmed by the 1988 constitution. In Chile, a country whose leaders feel surrounded by instability, military spending is higher than the regional average. General Pinochet sold arms to Ecuador during its war with Peru behind the Chilean government's back – something for which Chile apologised in 2005. (Argentina, too, sold weapons to Ecuador, a transaction in which the desire for kickbacks apparently outweighed strategic motives). Colombia's armed forces have been strengthened by American military aid and by a big military build-up. They remain under civilian control. The generals tenaciously resist submitting their officers accused of human-rights abuses to civilian courts. They argue, plausibly enough, that they are fighting an internal war – one on a scale that none of the dictatorships faced. But holding the army to stricter account would strengthen Colombia's case for outside military aid. The odd man out in the region is Hugo Chávez's Venezuela, whose government, although elected, is in many ways a military regime, and where the defence budget is rising steeply.

Votes for everyone, at last

Latin America has had a liberal constitutional tradition for almost two centuries as we have seen, even if this was often honoured in the breach. But in the nineteenth century, voting was typically limited by property and other qualifications to 5 to 10 per cent of the population. Now, for the first time, elections involving universal suffrage have become routine. In 1912 Argentina became the first country to introduce universal male suffrage (though it excluded immigrants). Voting rights were rapidly extended across the region from the 1930s onwards.[33] Women gained the vote between 1932 (Uruguay) and 1967 (Ecuador). But property and literacy requirements were retained in several countries, in effect denying the vote to many of the poor.[34] In Peru, illiterates (who included many Andean Indians) did not gain the vote until 1979. In Brazil they were not enfranchised until 1985 (three years later the voting age was lowered to 16 in Brazil).

Most Latin Americans have taken advantage of the right to vote. In the 11 presidential elections held between November 2005 and December 2006, on average 72.1 per cent of those eligible cast votes – a slight increase on the average turnout of 69.9 per cent for elections held between 1978 and 2004.[35] True, voting is compulsory everywhere except Colombia and Nicaragua, but only in four countries are sanctions applied to those who don't vote. The average turn-out for 1978 to 2006 conceals wide variations, from 90.7 per cent of those registered in Chile to 44.5 per cent in Colombia.

Suffrage is not only universal, it is also more effective than in the past. Electoral fraud has now become the exception rather than the norm. Nowhere illustrates this more clearly than Mexico. Carlos Salinas's election in 1988 was merely the most dramatic example of the way in which voting under the PRI system was neither free nor fair.[36] Apart from irregularities in the count, the vote was hardly secret. Polling booths consisted of flimsy stands, often set up in the street. The PRI's fraudulent methods inspired a whole lexicon: its techniques included stuffing ballot boxes with bundles of votes (known as *tacos*), moving voting places at the last minute (called *el raton loco* or mad mouse), supplying its supporters with credentials to vote at more than one polling station (*el carrusel*), manipulating voter-registration lists, and doctoring the count. Mexico's electoral reform of 1996, which created an independent electoral authority, was the crucial final step in achieving the alternation of power in the country. Although the authority's credibility was damaged among some Mexicans by the narrowness of the 2006 election result, it is likely to recover. The main worry in Mexico is that in some states the local electoral authority remains under one-party control.

Mexico apart, there have been only isolated cases of electoral fraud in Latin America over the past two decades. These include the Dominican Republic under Joaquín Balaguer, a civilian aide to Trujillo, who dominated political life from the 1960s into the 1990s. Investigations in Colombia showed that in some parts of the Caribbean coast right-wing paramilitaries carried out electoral fraud in congressional elections in 2002 and 2006. Perhaps the most blatant case was in Peru in 2000, when Alberto Fujimori sought an unconstitutional third consecutive term. To secure it, he manoeuvred to sack three dissenting judges from the Constitutional Tribunal, bribed television stations to refuse paid advertising from his opponents and to slant their coverage, and slandered his rivals in government-sponsored tabloid newspapers. This effort was masterminded by Vladimiro Montesinos, Fujimori's closest aide, who used the National Intelligence Service to spin a vast web of bribery and extortion. The regime did its best to manipulate the vote count.[37] The opposition candidate, Alejandro Toledo, pulled out of a run-off ballot, saying that the election was not free and fair, a judgement backed by international observers. Within months, Fujimori's regime collapsed, the president seeking refuge in Japan as video evidence of Montesinos's racketeering emerged. Toledo won a fresh election the following year. The fraud had failed.

In Venezuela, the opposition claimed that Hugo Chávez's victory in a 2004 recall referendum was fraudulent. These claims were never proven. Jennifer McCoy, who led the Carter Centre's efforts in Venezuela, declared the vote 'secret and free'. But she added that the electoral council's 'lack of openness, last-minute changes and internal divisions harmed public confidence in that vital institution both before and after the vote'.[38] In December 2005 the main opposition parties expressed their lack of confidence in the electoral authority by pulling out of an election for Venezuela's parliament, the national assembly, in which only 25 per cent at most of the electorate turned out to vote. A new electoral authority, though still containing a majority of government supporters, made some efforts to address the opposition's concerns. Manuel Rosales, the opposition candidate, accepted defeat in the 2006 presidential election.

Plural politics, deeper democracies

What gives the current period of democratic government its unique character is the combination of universal suffrage with the removal of the military veto over politics – and thus the end of the pendulum swings between dictatorship and democracy. The most obvious consequence has been that the left has been able to take and hold power through the ballot box – which in turn has encouraged many on the left to embrace democracy and to adopt more responsible policies.

In the early phase of the democratic wave, in the 1980s, centre-right governments were elected in many countries (Hernán Siles in Bolivia and Alan García in Peru were exceptions). Politicians of the centre-right were the main beneficiaries of the failure of state-led development, revealed by the 1982 debt crisis. The electoral success of the centre-right was important in cementing the commitment of business groups to democracy. Since the economic slowdown of 1998–2002, the region has seen a moderate shift to the left, though not everywhere. This began with the election of Chávez in Venezuela in 1998 and of Lula in Brazil and Lucio Gutiérrez in Ecuador in 2002, and continued with the victories of Kirchner in Argentina in 2003, and of Tabaré Vázquez in Uruguay and Martín Torrijos in Panama in 2004. The presidential elections of 2005–6 confirmed the ascendancy of the moderate left, whose candidates won in five countries: Honduras, Chile, Costa Rica, Peru and Brazil. There were four victories for the radical or populist left, in Bolivia, Nicaragua, Ecuador and Venezuela. And in two countries, Colombia and Mexico, the centre-right triumphed.

Where it happened, this leftward shift was in part a natural response to hard times and an expression of frustration at the disappointing fruits of the reforms of the Washington Consensus. But it had at least as much to do with the alternation in office that is a healthy sign of normality in a democracy – and is wholly new for Latin America. The Latinobarómetro poll suggests that the region's underlying political stance has shifted only slightly to the left.

Two sharply different 'lefts' have emerged in Latin America in recent years.[39] One is social-democratic and pragmatic. It accepts capitalism and the importance of macroeconomic stability, but wants to complement these with social policies, more public investment and a few nods towards industrial policy. This left was exemplified by Lula's government in Brazil, by Ricardo Lagos in Chile and in Uruguay by Tabaré Vázquez and the Frento Amplio ('Broad Front') coalition. The other left is one of radical populists and socialists: it is nationalist, anti-American and anti-capitalist. It was epitomised by Chávez, but its other adherents included Nicaragua's Daniel Ortega, the Sandinista leader, parts of the FMLN in El Salvador, some of the indigenous leaders in Ecuador, and radical social movements such as Brazil's Movimento Sem Terra (landless movement). The left wing of Brazil's Workers' Party, strengthened (but within a weakened party) by the party-financing scandal that enveloped the Lula government in 2005, also falls into this camp. Néstor Kirchner, Argentina's president, in true Peronist fashion straddles both groupings. Morales in Bolivia hails from the second camp, but gave mixed signals during his early months in office.

The removal of the veto against the left is not the only way in which Latin American democracy has become more representative. For the first time, everyone can vote and anyone can be elected to office, not just the traditional political elite. The region's Congresses are slowly becoming more diverse places. Across Latin America, the percentage of congressional seats held by women increased from 8 per cent in the late 1980s to 15.5 per cent by 2003, before dropping slightly to 14 per cent in 2007.[40] More Latin Americans of Indian descent have been elected to Congress, or as mayors, than ever before in Bolivia, Ecuador and Guatemala. The trend may be positive but, like women, indigenous and black Latin Americans are still under-represented, and in some cases grossly so. Racial definitions have an element of subjectivity. But by one count only 15 out of 513 members of Brazil's lower-house of Congress in 2004 were black, though black and *pardo* (brown) Brazilians account for 44 per cent of the population.[41] In Guatemala, Mayan Indians made up 66 per cent of the population but only 14 of the 113 members of Congress in 2002.

On occasions in the past, presidents came from outside the 'white' upper-middle class. But diversity in the social background of political leaders is now becoming the norm. Lula was an obvious example. Alejandro Toledo, Peru's president from 2001 to 2006 was born in an Andean Indian village and grew up as one of 16 children speaking Quechua, before winning a scholarship that would eventually take him to Stanford University and a teaching job at a Lima business school. Like Lula, Toledo had once worked as a shoeshine boy. Evo Morales herded his family's llamas, before moving from the Altiplano to the lowland Chapare region to grow coca. Lucio Gutiérrez, a former army colonel elected as Ecuador's president in 2002, is of modest provincial lower middle-class background, like Venezuela's Hugo Chávez, but the army has long been a means of social mobility in the Andean countries. In 2006, Michelle Bachelet in Chile became only the third woman to be elected president in Latin America – and the first who was not the widow of a prominent public figure.

As well as becoming more diverse, democracy is becoming deeper through decentralisation. The Spanish and Portuguese monarchies imposed a centralised system of government. In the Spanish colonies there were municipalities, and their *cabildos* (councils) were often elected among the local whites. But at least until the Bourbon reforms they had little power or money. Despite the rhetoric of nineteenth-century Liberals, power remained fairly centralised in the republican era. Only Brazil and Argentina were genuinely federal republics. Under the PRI, Mexican federalism was an elaborate fiction. That is now starting to change: state governors have formed a lobby group and are pushing for a greater share of national revenues. Across the region the biggest change has been at municipal level. In 1980 only three countries in the region chose their mayors by direct election. In 2005, 17 did while in six others they were chosen from among directly elected local councillors.[42] Local governments in many countries now have substantial powers and resources. In Colombia, for example, they account for a fifth of government spending. This process has not been free of problems. It has contributed to political fragmentation, and has not been exempt from fiscal irresponsibility. But there are many positive sides to it. Across the region once-decaying cities are undergoing regeneration in the hands of effective mayors.

In some countries there are still barriers to equitable political representation. Perhaps the most glaring is the over-representation of remote and backward states or provinces in Brazil and Argentina. Another problem is that some countries have erected stiff barriers to entry into politics. In Peru, under an absurd and undemocratic law enacted by Fujimori, to appear on the ballot parties must obtain legal registration, and for that they must gather 100,000 signatures. Journalistic investigations found that the parties of both Fujimori and Toledo had forged many thousands of signatures prior to the 2000 election. That was hardly surprising. The real scandal was that during Toledo's government the Congress showed no desire to repeal the law, since the parties represented there benefited from the reduction of political competition. In Nicaragua, the Sandinista opposition forged an unholy alliance with Arnoldo Alemán, a former president convicted of corruption who controlled the ruling Liberal Party, to pass a measure that makes it hard for presidential candidates from new parties to get on the ballot. In Mexico, Jorge Castañeda, a political scientist turned politician, made determined, but unsuccessful, efforts to overturn a provision which requires presidential candidates to represent a legally registered party, barring independents. In all of these cases the ostensible purpose was to prevent political fragmentation. That aim would be better served by setting a German-style threshold, under which parties must gain a certain minimum share of the vote to obtain legislative seats. In 2004, Colombia approved a political reform which did this, as has Peru.

As well as becoming more representative, Latin American democracy is also becoming more participatory. It is dangerously mendacious to see these as competing alternatives, with 'participatory democracy' as being superior to the representative kind. Pure participatory democracy is impossible at anything beyond the most local level, as John Stuart Mill noted in 1861: 'Since all cannot, in a community exceeding a single small town, participate personally in any but some very minor portions of the public business, it follows that the ideal type of a perfect government must be representative.'[43] Those who claim otherwise, such as Hugo Chávez does rhetorically at least, are in fact arguing for a plebiscitarian rule in which 'the people' are called upon to bless periodically the exercise of authoritarian power – a larger-scale version of the tyranny of the manipulated mass-meeting. Yet participatory devices can complement and deepen representative democracy. Many of the new constitutions that almost all Latin American countries drew up in their transition to democracy partook of that spirit. Referendums – on anything from gun control, as in Brazil, to oil and gas policy, as in Bolivia – have become a regular feature of political life in many countries in the region. In Mexico, Chile and elsewhere, parties have taken to choosing their presidential candidate in open primaries, in which any citizen can vote. At local level, the 'participatory budgeting' espoused by the Workers' Party (PT) mayors of Porto Alegre in Brazil has been widely imitated across the region. It calls for spending priorities to be drawn up at a series of neighbourhood meetings. This can lead to spending being more equitable and effective. In 2004 the PT lost control of Porto Alegre, but José Fogaça, the new mayor, retained the system.

Castrated presidents, fragmented parties

Cardoso is right when he says that Latin American democracy is putting down roots, but they are in soil that is not uniformly fertile, with many boulders. Apart from poverty and inequality, some of the obstacles to democracy are found in the region's political systems themselves. Democratic institutions are often poorly designed, political parties are relatively weak, and pre- or anti-democratic forms of political behaviour survive. These weaknesses affect not just the quality of democracy but the effectiveness of government.

Latin America has a long tradition of presidential rule. But many countries lack the stable two-party system that in the United States has allowed presidentialism to function fairly smoothly. That two-party system is the result of a British-style, first-past-the-post electoral system. Uniquely, Latin America combines presidentialism with legislatures elected by proportional representation (PR). In continental Europe, where PR is common, it is associated with parliamentary regimes in which multi-party coalition governments are the norm. Latin America's awkward mix of presidentialism and PR has contributed to a pattern in which presidents lack legislative majorities, stimulating conflict between executive and legislature.

Some political scientists have argued that this pattern was a factor behind the democratic breakdowns of the 1960s and 1970s, and have called for Latin America to adopt parliamentarism. This has prompted a lively academic debate – one with a few faint practical echoes.[44] The problem is that presidentialism fits naturally with Latin America's cultural tradition of personal leadership, from Aztec *tlatoani* to Spanish viceroy to republican *caudillo*. Significantly, the debate has been liveliest in Brazil, which had parliamentary government under its constitutional monarchy in the nineteenth century, and briefly from 1961 to 1963. Brazil's Constituent Congress of 1987–8 discussed adopting a parliamentary regime. The matter was put to a referendum in 1993 in which another option was to return to constitutional monarchy. But presidentialism won easily (with 55 per cent of the vote against 25 per cent for parliamentarism).[45] Peru's constitution of 1979 incorporated a prime minister, but one who lacked the power to dissolve Congress and call a fresh election – the sanction that encourages compromise in multi-party parliamentary systems. Bolivia makes a nod to parliamentarism. Under its constitution, if no presidential candidate wins 50 per cent of the popular vote, the Congress must choose between the top two contenders. Until 2002, this helped presidents to assemble a viable governing coalition. The problem – until Morales's victory – was that it robbed the president of a strong popular mandate. In Mexico, where no party has had a majority in Congress since 1997, some politicians talked of the virtues of France's semi-parliamentary government.[46] The result of Latin America's awkward hybrid – of presidentialism plus proportional representation and multi-party systems – has been the dispersal of power. Rather than healthy checks and balances, this has often resulted in mere gridlock.

One response to that has been a crude assertion of presidential power, riding roughshod over the legislature and judiciary – a tradition begun by Bolívar. This is what O'Donnell meant by 'delegative democracy'. There have been some recent examples. Fujimori in Peru used army tanks to shut down the country's Congress in 1992, to local acclaim and international condemnation. He claimed that the politicians were blocking anti-terrorist legislation and his economic programme. He also declared the judiciary in permanent 're-organisation', filling it with stooges. Fujimori faced exceptional circumstances. These included the hyperinflationary economic chaos bequeathed by Alan García's presidency, and the vicious insurgency by *Sendero Luminoso* (Shining Path), a fundamentalist Maoist group, which brought the loss of some 70,000 lives in a 'dirty war' with the security forces from 1980 to 1993. Fujimori's heavy-handed methods worked – but only for a while and at a long-term cost to Peru's democracy. He crushed the Shining Path, stabilised the economy, and built many schools and health clinics in Andean villages. He legitimised his *autogolpe* ('self-coup') with a new constitution approved by referendum, which concentrated powers in the presidency and, unprecedentedly, allowed him to stand for (and easily win) a second term. But he was ever the elected autocrat. In an interview in 1995, when he was about to start his second term, he was pressed as to whether the way to make permanent the transformation in Peru's circumstances he had wrought was to devolve power to new democratic institutions. Three times he dodged the question.[47] He claimed that he governed according to 'technical' rather than 'political' criteria – an answer reminiscent of Porfirio Díaz's motto of 'little politics, much administration'.

If Fujimori's regime was the archetype of 'delegative democracy', the term also fits that of Hugo Chávez. To a lesser extent, it applied to Carlos Menem's government in Argentina (1989–99). Menem packed the Supreme Court with cronies (as every previous Argentine president since Perón had done, with the notable exception of Raúl Alfonsín.) He made frequent use of decree powers. So too has Kirchner; he also removed political opponents from the Supreme Court, but has adopted a more open process for the appointment of its justices. Another high-handed president was Fernando Collor, who froze Brazilians' savings by decree. But the legislature had its revenge when Collor was impeached for corruption. Some analysts saw the abandonment in several countries – Argentina, Brazil, Peru, Venezuela and Colombia – of constitutional bars on a sitting president seeking a second consecutive term as another sign of an over-mighty executive. Against that it could be argued that when voters were lucky enough to find a president they liked, they should have the chance to keep him or her in power. In Brazil, Colombia and, perhaps, Argentina, there were sufficient institutional restraints on the presidency to make the potential benefits of re-election outweigh the costs. That was not the case in Peru or Venezuela. In practice, second terms often proved a disappointment, as they were in the case of Menem, Fujimori and, to a lesser extent, Cardoso and Uribe.

'Delegative democracy' was the exception, not the rule. Whatever his or her constitutional strength, the reality is more often that of a Latin American president castrated by political fragmentation. As noted, this phenomenon is not new: a review of 71 South American presidents elected in relatively fair contests from 1930 to 1990 found that in an 'overwhelming majority' of cases their parties lacked a legislative majority.[48] A study in 2005 of the previous two elections in 18 countries found that on average the president's party had a majority in the lower-house of Congress in only three cases (Chile, Honduras and Nicaragua). In a further six, the president's party had 40 per cent or more of the seats (Argentina, Costa Rica, the Dominican Republic, Guatemala, Peru and Uruguay).[49] Mexico after Vicente Fox displaced the PRI in 2000 was an extreme case of gridlock. Although the president's conservative National Action Party had 37 per cent of the seats in the lower-house, Fox proved unable to build sufficient political support from other parties to push through his ambitious programme of economic and political reform.

Elsewhere, presidents were sometimes skilful in building coalitions, as Cardoso did in Brazil between 1994 and 2002. Others battled to try to secure ad hoc majorities for specific measures. Often this involved offering pork and patronage: legislators would extract public works for their home patch or government jobs for followers. Sometimes presidents could not even count on much loyalty from their own parties: in Nicaragua, Enrique Bolaños, an honest businessman elected in 2001, was estranged from his party which resented his decision to prosecute his predecessor, Arnoldo Alemán, for corruption. In some countries, however, legislatures played a fairly effective role both in scrutinising governments and in crafting legislation. That was true of Brazil, Chile, Colombia and Uruguay in particular, according to a study by the Inter-American Development Bank.[50] But often legislatures were weakened by high turnover among their members. In the United States around 90 per cent of members of Congress win re-election. In Latin America, only in Chile and Uruguay did at least half of congressional deputies win immediate re-election (but the figure in both cases was fewer than 60 per cent); in Argentina and Peru, fewer than 20 per cent did. In Mexico and Costa Rica, immediate re-election of members of Congress is constitutionally banned.[51]

These difficulties in assembling effective governing coalitions and experienced legislatures have thrown the spotlight on the shortcomings of political parties in Latin America. Political scientists have long seen political parties as the bedrock of democracy, both expressing and channelling interests.[52] In Latin America they are flourishing in quantity but not necessarily in quality. The standard academic study of party systems in the region, edited by Scott Mainwaring and Timothy Scully and published in 1995, found striking differences in the degree to which these were institutionalised. By 'institutionalisation', the authors meant four things: that patterns of party competition show some regularity, that parties have stable roots in society, that parties and elections are widely seen as legitimate, and that parties have an independent organisation and are not merely personal vehicles for political leaders.[53] On these criteria, Costa Rica, Chile, Uruguay, Venezuela and Colombia all had institutionalised party systems, while Peru, Brazil, Ecuador and Bolivia did not. Yet this finding is in some ways misleading. Just a decade later the party system in Venezuela and, to a lesser extent, Colombia, looked much less institutionalised and Brazil's rather more so. The underlying point is that party systems in Latin America are evolving rapidly: in some cases that is happening in ways that would seem to weaken the prospects for effective democratic government but in others it reflects adaptation to changed socio-economic and political realities.

Only a handful of countries preserved in the twentieth century the two-party systems (usually of Liberals and Conservatives, albeit sometimes under different names) that were characteristic of the nineteenth-century republics. They included some of the more solid democracies: Uruguay, Costa Rica and Colombia. In Colombia and Uruguay party allegiance ran deep, being passed from generation to generation within families as a badge of identity, as if it were support for a football team. Yet in the twenty-first century, two-party hegemony has collapsed or is under strain in all of those countries. In Uruguay, the Frente Amplio coalition won the presidency in 2004, breaking a duopoly of the Colorado ('Red' or Liberal) and Blanco ('White' or Conservative) parties dating back more than a century. In Costa Rica, corruption scandals that implicated three former presidents shook public trust in the two main parties. That was especially so for the Social Christian Party, which governed for eight years until 2006. In the 2006 election its presidential candidate won just 3.5 per cent of the vote. In Colombia, the Conservative Party withered to a disparate series of regional groups. The Liberals were stronger, but deeply faction-ridden. In 2002, Uribe, a lifelong Liberal, ran successfully for the presidency as an independent. He governed with the support of an informal coalition including many Conservatives and some Liberals. In Venezuela, a dramatic case, the two parties which dominated political life from 1958 to 1998, the social democratic Acción Democratica and the Christian democratic COPEI, were reduced to small, squabbling rumps by *chavismo*.

Only in Honduras has a two-party system survived. In Chile, something close to it has evolved since the end of the Pinochet dictatorship in 1989. Chile was unique in developing a European-style multi-party system by the mid-twentieth century, with strong Socialist, Communist and Christian Democrat parties. The electoral system bequeathed by the dictatorship, which discriminated against third parties, and the memory of tragic consequences of political division in 1973, encouraged the Socialists and the Christian Democrats to join with others to form a single centre-left coalition called the Concertación. In practice this has operated almost as if it was a single party. The same was true of the two-party conservative opposition alliance – at least until each party ran its own presidential candidate in 2005. In Argentina, by contrast, the Peronists (technically, the Justicialist Party) are hegemonic, but factionalised, with pronounced rightist and leftist tendencies. The Peronists apart, the party system is composed of myriad small provincial parties – the successors to the federalist *caudillos* of the early nineteenth century. Argentina thus lacks a coherent opposition. Mexico has a relatively stable three-party system, but as noted this has yet to show that it can generate effective government. It was a sign of the vigour of Fox's conservative National Action Party that Felipe Calderón won its primary nomination in 2005 against the opposition of the president.

In other countries, political loyalties have been far more volatile. Peru is in appearance an extreme case of party volatility. Four parties dominated politics in the 1980s: APRA; Acción Popular, a reformist party led by Fernando Belaunde, the president from 1963 to 1968 and 1980 to 1985; the conservative Popular Christian Party (PPC), and the United Left. Between them, they obtained 94 per cent of the vote in 1985. Ten years later, with Fujimori at the height of his power, they won just 7 per cent. And yet those who pronounced these parties dead exaggerated: in 2006, APRA returned to power with Alan García, while two of his three main opponents were Lourdes Flores, whose Unión Nacional Party was a direct descendant of and barely distinguishable from the PPC, and Acción Popular's Valentín Paniagua (standing for a coalition).

Similarly, to outward appearances, Brazil is an 'exceptional case of party weakness', as Mainwaring has put it.[54] In the 2002 election, no fewer than 19 parties won seats in the Chamber of Deputies; the most successful, the Partido dos Trabalhadores (Workers' Party or PT) of Lula da Silva, won just 18 per cent of the seats. In 2006, 21 parties won seats; the largest, the centrist PMDB, won 17 per cent of the seats. Many, though not all, of the other parties are 'catch-all' outfits, lacking ideology. That is why around a fifth of the 513 deputies in the lower-house normally switch parties after they are elected, some more than once. Legislators' strongest loyalties are often reserved for two non-party attachments. One is to their state, where most politicians build their political careers. They see their main task as funnelling pork from Brasília to their home patch. The other is to powerful cross-party sectoral lobbies. The largest of these, the *ruralistas* or farmers' lobby, had around 130 supporters in the 1994–8 Congress – more than the biggest party.[55] Others include *municipalistas* (ex-mayors or town councillors); the football lobby, financed by the Brazilian Football Confederation; and evangelical protestants. Many hoped that the rise of the PT, which claimed a monopoly on party discipline and ethical politics, would change all that. It did not, as the *mensalão* scandal showed.[56] The PT also encouraged more than 100 deputies to leave opposition parties and join small pro-government ones.[57]

Yet parties do matter in Brazil, and not just the PT. Cardoso's Party of Brazilian Social Democracy has become a fairly cohesive centrist party of technocrats. The conservative Liberal Front Party also functioned as an effective national party. Even during the most confusing period of Brazil's restored democracy, from 1988 to 1994, party discipline prevailed in 88 per cent of votes in the legislature.[58] From 1994 onwards, first under Cardoso and then from 2002 under Lula, Brazilian governments notched up a creditable record of legislation – although the process was neither easy nor swift.

A new politics

So parties are less weak than sometimes meets the eye. Even so, more-institutionalised party systems would be desirable. What lies behind their relative lack of institutionalisation in much of Latin America? One answer is the electoral system, especially in Brazil. Its version of proportional representation uses 'open' party lists, in which voters choose an individual candidate rather than a party. Each state is a single, often vast, constituency. Paradoxically, that means that candidates tend to rely on getting large numbers of votes from a small area, reinforcing their tendency to focus on local matters once in Brasília. A second factor in Brazil is that in the past parties tended to be top-down appendages of the state. That has meant they have found it difficult to survive regime change. The parties of the monarchy died with it, the Republican parties which dominated politics in the states between 1889 and 1930 did not survive Getúlio Vargas; and those of the 1945 to 1964 democracy perished when the military regime decreed a party re-organisation in 1965, creating a two-party system.

There are broader forces at work. One is that in the new democratic era, voters have been merciless in punishing parties that are held to have failed in their management of the economy. The Radical Party, part of Argentine political history since the 1890s, was for most practical purposes killed off by the 2001 to 2002 economic collapse. That was ironic since the policies that brought Argentina to disaster were those of the Peronist administration of Carlos Menem. In Mexico, the debt crisis of 1982 and the bungled devaluation of the peso of 1994 were central to the decline and fall from power of the PRI. Peru's ruling Acción Popular won just 6 per cent of the vote in the 1985 election. Bolivian voters in 2005 punished the MNR for what they saw as the failure of Goni's 'neoliberalism'. The same applied to Acción Democratica in Venezuela in 1993. In 2002 Colombia's Conservative Party paid the price for presiding over the country's first recession in half a century, even if much of the blame lay with the preceding Samper administration. Voters were more lenient with presidents who, having campaigned against applying 'shock therapy' to inflation, proceeded to implement drastic economic stabilisation plans – provided these worked. Thus Menem in Argentina and Fujimori in Peru were re-elected.

Several other factors have affected parties. The decline in ideological commitments after the Cold War made it harder to motivate party militants and made voters more fickle. The ubiquity of television means that party organisation is less important for winning elections than it used to be. To these universal factors must be added others specific to Latin America, where the fragmentation of politics mirrors that of society. Modernisation and industrialisation have rarely penetrated all corners of society: the old is never wholly eliminated by the new, but coexists uneasily with it. Take Ecuador: nineteenth-century Conservative and Liberal parties compete with various versions of mid-twentieth-century populism, a social democratic party, two parties of Christian democratic inspiration, various Marxist outfits and a twenty-first-century indigenous party. All retained a segment of the electorate. Meanwhile, the rise of the informal economy in Latin America has weakened parties that based their appeal on organised labour or business groups. Venezuela is perhaps the clearest case of this: much of Chávez's hardcore support comes from the swelling informal sector, whose members missed out on the social benefits channelled through trade unions or professional associations under AD and COPEI. Politics is not always national: decentralisation has sometimes given new force to regional political leaders or movements and undermined national party discipline.[59] Another factor is that to the extent that the populist parties so prevalent in the region rely on charismatic leadership, they run the risk of fading away with their founders. The region's political leaders have a habit of dying with their boots on: in 2006 Raúl Alfonsín clung to leadership of Argentina's moribund Radicals at the age of 79; Leonel Brizola, a political disciple of Getúlio Vargas was planning yet another failed presidential campaign when he died in 2005, aged 82; Daniel Ortega saw off all attempts at the political renewal of Nicaragua's Sandinistas, allowing him to return to power in 2007, almost 17 years after losing it. Some are inspired by the example of Salvador Allende, who won the presidency at the third attempt, or Lula, who won after three successive defeats.

One result of these changes has been the rise of a characteristic new Latin American political figure: the outsider, with no links to traditional parties. This phenomenon has been especially prevalent in the Andean countries, but not confined to them. Alberto Fujimori was the archetype. A university rector with no previous political experience, he formed an ad hoc party and rose from nowhere in the opinion polls just a month before the election of 1990. He capitalised on popular disillusion with a political establishment which had failed to defeat either inflation or terrorism. The year before, Ricardo Belmont, the owner and host of a television station, was elected as mayor of Lima as an independent. Similarly, Alejandro Toledo managed to become the vehicle of opposition to Fujimori while lacking a serious party. There was an echo of the outsider in Álvaro Uribe's crusade for the presidency against his party's official candidate. But Uribe was an experienced professional politician. That was not true of Venezuela's Hugo Chávez nor Lucio Gutiérrez, an army colonel involved in the 2000 coup against Mahuad and elected as Ecuador's president in 2002. Ollanta Humala, a nationalist former lieutenant-colonel, ran a similar campaign in Peru in 2006. Ecuador's 2006 presidential election featured contrasting outsiders: Rafael Correa, a left-wing academic whose only political experience was a brief stint as finance minister, defeated Álvaro Noboa, a banana magnate who was Ecuador's wealthiest man. In Argentina, Néstor Kirchner owed his election in 2003 to a combination of the inside backing of Eduardo Duhalde, his predecessor and Peronism's then-political boss, and the perception that as governor of Santa Cruz, a remote Patagonian province, he was untainted by the failures of the country's political establishment. In turn, the main claim to fame of Mauricio Macri, who emerged as Kirchner's strongest opponent in a Congressional election in 2005, was that he was president of Boca Juniors, Argentina's most popular football club.

A particularly troubling kind of personalistic political leadership was that of rich men putting their money to work for political advantage. Álvaro Noboa came close to winning his country's presidency in 2002 and again in 2006. Similarly, Sebastián Piñera, one of Chile's wealthiest businessmen – he was one of the owners of LAN, the national airline – was only narrowly defeated by Michelle Bachelet in a presidential election in 2006. Unlike Noboa, at least Piñera eventually recognised the conflicts of interest he would face should he have won, offering to sell his assets. These two men put up most of the money for their own campaigns. Less fortunate candidates relied on other people's money, either from the public purse or from private sources. As they became the recognised route to power, Latin American elections became increasingly expensive. Nowhere more so than in Brazil: though research on the subject is sketchy, according to one estimate the 1994 campaign is estimated to have cost $3.5 billion to $4.5 billion, compared with $3 billion for the 1996 election in the United States (though the strength of the *real* at the time inflates the Brazilian figure).[60] That is despite free television time for candidates. The expense is partly a function of party weakness: much of the money goes on making individual candidates known through marketing, ranging from T-shirts to rock concerts. Unlike in the United States, much of the money comes from relatively few large corporate donors. And much of it is not declared. As a result, campaign-finance scandals have become a regular part of Brazilian political life. New rules restricted campaign spending in 2006, though it was not clear how effective they would be. Public financing of election campaigns is often touted as a safer alternative. Yet in Mexico and Argentina this system has served to breed small, parasitic parties which feed off the taxpayer.

It would be wrong to suggest that organised parties are giving way to purely personalistic political leadership. As some older parties born in the era of state-led development withered away, new forces were born which reflected twenty-first-century political realities in Latin America. In Colombia, a new moderate left party, the Polo Democrático Alternativo, which rejected guerrilla violence, emerged, winning the mayoralty of Bogotá in 2004. Brazil's PSDB and some elements of Chile's Concertación emerged as a possible model for a new type of party, one based on a combination of professional politicians and technocrats (qualities often united in the same person). Torcuato di Tella, an Argentine sociologist, has argued that there is a long-term tendency towards the formation of bi-polar political systems, with the formation of two dominant parties or alliances, one of the left and the other of the right, in place of the preponderance of populist or centrist parties.[61]

Another new phenomenon was the partial replacement of class-based alignments with a new politics of ethnic identity. In Bolivia, 50 out of 130 deputies elected to Congress in 2002 were said to be 'indigenous' (of which 30 were elected for Morales's MAS). Previously, Congress contained only a dozen or so 'indigenous' deputies. For the first time, interpreters were hired to provide translation into Spanish from Aymara, Quechua and Guaraní, since several legislators chose to give their maiden speech in an indigenous language.[62] In Bolivia, the extent to which the Indian majority has in fact been excluded since the 1952 revolution is arguable. From the 1950s onwards, many Indians took an active part in politics, but defined themselves as *campesinos* (peasant farmers), miners or trade unionists. In Ecuador, indigenous groups set up a national organisation (the Confederation of Indigenous Nationalities of Ecuador or CONAIE) in the 1980s. This at first agitated for land; then it decided to launch a political party, called Pachakutik ('reawakening' in Quechua but also the name of the greatest of the Incas). In 2004, Pachakutik held 19 out of 215 municipalities, five provincial governorships (out of 22) and ten of the 100 seats in Congress. It backed Lucio Gutiérrez, the winner of the 2002 presidential election, and took two cabinet jobs. It later fell out with Gutiérrez, a former army colonel who had been involved in the coup of 2000 and was himself overthrown in 2005.

The rise of indigenous movements was just one way in which Latin American societies, in addition to political systems, had become much more democratic by the twenty-first century compared with thirty years before. The caricature of a small white elite governing over brown or black masses was largely that – even in countries like Peru or Brazil which had not experienced a national revolution. Voters are more educated, more urbanised and better informed than in the past. The Latinobarómetro poll shows that support for democracy tends to rise with the level of education. These trends have tended to weaken, though not eliminate, clientelistic politics. So too has the reduction in the size of the state as a result of liberal economic reform: that means that parties have fewer government jobs or subsidies to offer to supporters. Clientelistic practices – of swapping votes for favours – have a long history in Latin America, and have taken many forms. At their crudest, they involve paying for votes in cash or kind. At a campaign rally for César Gaviria, the Liberal candidate in Colombia in 1990, an onlooker noted that the party's political bosses 'can fill any vacuum in support from the poor as they always do, with what they're doing now – rum, fiestas and money'.[63] In a more sophisticated way, organised clientelism was at the root of the appeal of populist parties. Now, in countries such as Brazil, voters have developed a habit of using the ballot box to punish mayors or governors who devoted a disproportionate share of their revenues to public employment rather than services or investment. In 1998, of the 15 state governors who were re-elected for a second term, 13 had managed to limit their state's wage bill to 60 per cent or less of total revenues; of those who stood again and were not re-elected, none had managed to restrict their payroll to that extent.[64] Clientelism, like populism, is far from dead. Politics everywhere involves trading favours. Until the quality and quantity of education in Latin America improves, and until poverty and inequality diminish, some voters will continue to be tempted both by the clientelistic promise of votes for favours and the miracle preachings of populists. The difference is that they no longer hold anything like a monopoly in Latin America's democratic politics.

CHAPTER 12

THE LONELINESS
OF LATIN AMERICA

The small state of Tlaxcala, in the highlands east of Mexico City, was home to the people who would become Hernán Cortés's most important allies in his assault on the Aztec capital of Tenochtitlán. More recently, Tlaxcalans have had to respond to a different sort of invasion, one of cheap Asian textiles. That this involved painful change was clear from a visit to the state in 1992, five years after Mexico's government had begun to open the economy to international trade and just when it was negotiating the North American Free Trade Agreement (NAFTA) with the United States and Canada:

> Only birdsong disturbs the silence inside the La Josefina textile factory ... Yards of cotton cloth still hang from its lines of looms, stopped in mid-weave when the factory shut a year ago and its 100 workers were laid off. The nameplates on the machines explain what happened. They are from a bygone Lancashire: the cast iron looms were made more than a century ago by John M. Summer of Manchester, J. Dugdale & Sons of Blackburn and G. Keighly of Burnley. The spinning machines came from Dobson & Barlow Ltd, Bolton, in 1912, and the carding equipment from Platt Bros of Oldham in 1920. Since 1881, La Josefina had made yarn and cotton cloth for the Mexican market. It closed because its machines, though still in perfect working order, could not compete with modern, electronically controlled rivals ... 'Yarn came in from India, Korea and Taiwan at half the price we sold at,' Valentín Rangel, La Josefina's administrator, says. 'We were caught out, technologically backward and without the capital to renew our machinery.'[1]

A dozen years later, Tlaxcala was no longer just an industrial museum. The state's main roads were studded with new factories. Some supplied the expanding Volkswagen plant nearby at Puebla, the German car giant's main production site for North America. Turn off into the hills, and there is much evidence that life is improving in what was long a poor area, dependent on peasant farming and textiles. In rural villages, two- and three-storey houses of brick and concrete are replacing the small huts of a decade ago (though, as elsewhere in rural Mexico, the *Oportunidades* programme and remittances from migrants both play their part). According to Humberto Alva, the state government's secretary for economic development, income per head in Tlaxcala doubled in the ten years to 2005, reaching US$6,000 a year.[2] Even so, in the presidential election of 2006 Andrés Manuel López Obrador, and not Felipe Calderón, was the most voted candidate in Tlaxcala, as in every other state in Mexico's centre and south. López Obrador did not call openly for a return to the statist protectionism of the past. But he did call for a renegotiation of NAFTA to suspend the requirement on Mexico to lift the remaining tariff on the import of maize and beans by January 2008. Had López Obrador become president it is likely that he would have encouraged Mexico to look inward again: he showed little interest in, or knowledge of, the world beyond his own country.

Many Latin Americans, just like people elsewhere, are ambivalent towards globalisation. For some of them, the past quarter of a century has brought more pain than gain. Hundreds of thousands of workers lost their jobs in factories like La Josefina. Baroque labour laws offered no protection against economic realities but nor did they provide unemployment insurance to ease economic adjustment. Many new jobs have been created, but they have often gone to younger and better-qualified workers. This applies even in Mexico which, thanks to NAFTA, is one of the most globalised countries in Latin America. Mexicans were encouraged to believe that NAFTA would deliver instant prosperity (just as voters in the United States were told that it would end Mexican migration). Its achievements have inevitably been more modest, but it has done all that could reasonably be asked of it. A study by the World Bank found that NAFTA had a larger-than-expected impact on Mexico's trade, the inflow of foreign investment and the productivity of its economy. Without NAFTA, the study found, Mexico's total exports would have been about 50 per cent lower and foreign direct investment about 40 per cent less. The 'main conclusion ... is that the treaty helped Mexico to get closer to the levels of development of its NAFTA partners.'[3] Mexico's non-oil exports tripled in the first six years after the agreement came into effect, and continued to rise steadily thereafter. Thanks to NAFTA, and in sharp contrast to Venezuela, Mexico has managed to diversify its economy. Oil accounted for just 13 per cent of its total exports in 2005, down from 62 per cent in 1980. Rather than the oil price, Mexico's economy began to move to the rhythm of industrial production in the United States.

In northern Mexico in particular many places bear NAFTA's visible imprint. Take Ciudad Juárez. It may have become notorious for drug trafficking and violence, but it has also become one of the biggest industrial cities in North America. Industrial parks, shopping malls and brand-new housing estates in faux-colonial style stretch out endlessly into the Chihuahua desert, taking up roughly twice as much space as a dozen years ago. Monterrey, the industrial hub of north-east Mexico, has become a handsome city of swirling freeways, glass office blocks, innovative universities and frequent international conferences. Detroit's troubled carmakers, as well as their Japanese rivals and Volkswagen, are quietly expanding in Mexico. Mexico trains more engineers each year than the United States, China or India, according to Rafael Rangel, the rector of Monterrey's Instituto Tecnológico.[4] A non-profit university, the Tec, as Mexicans call it, had thirty campuses across the country in 2006, many of them linked to small-business incubators. With government partners, it was building a technology park on a patch of shrubland next to Monterrey airport. Rangel sees great potential for Mexico in industries such as aerospace, white goods, food, biotechnology and pharmaceuticals.

The World Bank study of NAFTA also found a positive, but smaller-than-expected, impact on Mexican wages and income per head. But in the popular mind, the impact of the trade agreement has been hard to separate from that of the peso collapse and recession of 1994–5 that so closely followed its implementation (but which were not directly related to NAFTA). The problem was not the trade agreement but the lack of public policies to ensure that all Mexicans could take advantage of it. The north of the country has long been more prosperous than the south, which is more rural and has more people of indigenous descent. But over the past decade the gap is widened. That is partly because the north is more entrepreneurial. It is also because it has better schools, roads and other transport links. The absence of motorways and railways along Mexico's coasts means that goods from the south bound for the United States must pass through the bottleneck of Mexico City, climbing to 2,500 metres above sea level. Get round that bottleneck, and transport costs for the south could fall by up 25 per cent. The south, where rainfall and labour are abundant, could be the market-garden of North America, producing fruit and vegetables for export rather than relying on subsistence farming of maize and beans. But export farming has been concentrated in the north, helped by cheap electricity for irrigation – a government subsidy which cost around $450 million in 2005, or more than the budget of Mexico's main rural-development programme.[5]

Some Mexican politicians contrast their own country's slow convergence towards the living standards of its North American partners with the rapid progress of Spain and other relatively new entrants to the European Union.

They conclude that Mexico would be much better off if NAFTA included EU-style structural and regional development funds. But there is no political will in Washington for that kind of aid (the fact that Mexico collects so little tax revenue from its citizens would make it hard to justify anyway). NAFTA represented the furthest that either Mexico or the United States was prepared to go to integrate with each other. In a more or less explicit quid pro quo, Mexico excluded the energy industry, and thus its state-owned energy monopolies, from the agreement while the United States barred EU-style freedom of movement of labour. Under Vicente Fox, Mexico spent six years fruitlessly trying to reach a bilateral agreement on migration. Despite the vocal anti-immigration lobby in the Republican Party in the United States, it is not impossible to imagine a future grand bargain in which chapters on energy and migration were added to NAFTA.

Torments in the name of freedom

The broader point is that the United States has been unwilling to provide the kind of external sponsorship of Latin American development that the EU has offered to Europe's southern and eastern periphery. The Bush administration insouciantly called on the European Union to admit Turkey as a full member while failing to offer Mexico anything like the same deal. That was unfortunate: even Eurosceptics would have to admit that the one unalloyed achievement of the EU has been its successful enlargement. The EU offers prospective members not just a market and aid but an incentive to import the rule of law and other institutions. In other words, the EU has underpinned democracy as well as development in the European periphery. That was especially so for Spain, as Latin Americans noted. José Ortega y Gasset, a Spanish philosopher, had argued as long ago as 1910 that 'Spain is the problem, Europe the solution'. That was tantamount to saying that 'there is not a Spanish road to modernity, that Europe should come and cure us of our demons because we don't know how to do so', as Emilio Lama de Espinosa, an international relations specialist, has put it.[6]

In the Americas, for better or for worse, the motivation for that kind of integration between the developed north and the developing centre and south is absent. Some of the reasons for that absence derive from history and geography. Fortunately, the New World lacks the long history of inter-state wars that convinced Europe's leaders that integration was the route to peace as well as prosperity. And the distances in the Americas are so much greater: most of the European landmass would fit inside Brazil alone, for example; Bolivia, one of the smaller South American countries, is twice the size of France. Even if the United States were willing to play the role of external sponsor of development it is far from clear that Latin American countries would in practice welcome it. As one of its senior diplomats put it, the EU is 'a highly developed system for mutual interference into each others' affairs'.[7] Yet Latin American countries have proved deeply reluctant to share sovereignty – even with each other, let alone with the Colossus of the North.

What the United States has offered to the rest of Latin America, fitfully, has been NAFTA-style trade agreements. Had matters gone according to the plan approved at the Miami summit in 1994, an agreement of this nature would by now have encompassed the whole region in the form of the Free Trade Area of the Americas (FTAA). Several things doomed that vision. The most important was the stalling of the Doha Round of world-trade talks that were supposed to free trade in agriculture – a vital cause for Brazil, Argentina and other South American countries. The United States insisted that it could only eliminate subsidies to its farmers in the context of a global, not regional, deal on agriculture. A less ambitious FTAA might still have been possible but neither Brazil nor the United States was prepared to push hard for it. As the FTAA talks became moribund, each of them sought to build its own trading web in the region. A free-trade agreement between Chile and the United States came into effect in 2004. Another with Central America, to which the Dominican Republic signed up, was due to come into force as DR-CAFTA in 2007. Peru, Colombia and Panama negotiated similar accords. But the Democrats, who gained control of the US Congress in the mid-term elections of 2006, were lukewarm, at best, about further trade deals, and it was not clear that these would be approved.

They are called 'free-trade agreements' (FTAs) but these are in reality preferential deals and for the Latin American signatories they are a third-best option. They were far less beneficial than a global trade deal; a united Latin America would have had more bargaining power in the FTAA negotiations than individual countries could exercise in bilateral deals. Of all the executive agencies in Washington, the Office of the United States Trade Representative is perhaps the most beholden to special interests in the US Congress. For example, Florida farmers excluded free trade in sugar from DR-CAFTA; for no good reason the United States insisted that the trade agreements should bar the imposition of selective controls on capital inflows of the kind Chile successfully used to stabilise its economy. Yet even with these limitations, many Latin American governments concluded that a third-best deal with the US was better than none at all. The main motivation for Peru and Colombia was to render permanent preferences granted to non-commodity exports from four Andean countries by a 1991 law which was due to expire in January 2007 (it was temporarily renewed to allow time for the FTAs to be approved). They looked at the foreign investment NAFTA had attracted to Mexico and hoped to be able to replicate it. And while FTAs with the United States do not involve the wholesale import of democratic institutions they do have the effect of 'locking in' some of the free-market reforms – which is why they are so bitterly opposed by the far left – and the commitment to economic stability.

Bolívar presciently observed in a letter to the British representative in Bogotá that the United States seemed 'destined by Providence to plague America with torments in the name of freedom'.[8] His comment nicely summed up his own mixed feelings of admiration for and distrust of the United States, and that country's combination of idealism and heavy-handedness in its dealings with its southern neighbours. The latter-day Boliviarians have a cruder view. They peddle the grossly exaggerated notion that Latin America as a whole has been forever under the thumb of the United States. In fact, the US has never paid much attention to South America. The larger countries of Latin America show almost as much diplomatic independence towards the United States as do those of Europe. That is not to ignore that US intervention has had a significant – and often negative – impact in the countries of the Caribbean rim, with Cuba and Guatemala being the clearest examples. The asymmetries of power between the two Americas have generated a certain arrogance in US behaviour and corresponding resentment in Latin America. Behind such attitudes lies a mutual lack of knowledge and comprehension. Latin American attitudes towards the United States are inevitably complex. On the one hand, ordinary Latin Americans admire the prosperity and freedoms of their northern neighbour – and yearn to migrate there. On the other, some members of Latin America's elites, justifiably or not, often see the US as a threat; they fear cultural invasion, political interference and economic domination.[9] But in practice, for most Latin American governments the United States is a fact of life to be managed and an opportunity to be made the best of. For many, it is their main export market (especially for higher value-added manufactures) and source of aid.

While in the past they had condemned *Yanqui* interventionism, many Latin American politicians came to lament what they saw as a lack of US engagement with the region. As a presidential candidate in 2000, George W Bush had gone to Miami to deliver a campaign speech in which he promised to take Latin America seriously. As an adopted Texan with a Mexican sister-in-law and a smattering of bad Spanish, Bush seemed to have a genuine personal interest in the region. In September 2001 he invited Vicente Fox to the White House and amidst the pomp and junketing of a state visit said that the United States had 'no more important relationship' than that with its southern neighbour. Days later the terrorist attacks against the United States changed Bush's priorities. Latin Americans, having suffered 'pre-emptive unilateralism' from the United States in the past were unsympathetic to the war in Iraq. The Bush administration, in turn, felt betrayed by Chile and (especially) Mexico who, as temporary members of the UN Security Council, hewed to an anti-war line.

Plan Colombia, and the democratic imperatives behind it, was ill understood in the rest of Latin America. More visible was the constant low-level bullying of the 'war on drugs'. Of course cocaine consumption was not confined to the United States. But the US continued to account for more than 40 per cent of estimated cocaine users, with 25 per cent in Western Europe and 15 per cent in Latin America itself.[10] Prohibition had demonstrably failed to eliminate demand. But around the world, few politicians had the courage to admit that. Instead, they talked of reducing the harm associated with cocaine consumption. That was of no help to producer or transit countries. As long as cocaine was demanded and remained prohibited, it would continue to be supplied by the trafficking gangs. They in turn provided the back-up which made it more profitable for farmers to grow coca than cocoa, coffee or other alternative crops. In Colombia and Peru, in particular, aid for alternative development remained tiny in relation to the scale of the problem. Instead, US policies obliged Latin American governments to declare 'war' on a segment of their farmers. Europe, for the most part, sat comfortably on its hands, smugly criticising US policies, while its own cocaine consumers continued to finance the likes of Colombia's FARC and its paramilitaries. The drug trade exploited the weakness of the rule of law in Latin America, but it added to it significantly. The best hope for Latin Americans was to focus their efforts on targeting trafficking gangs on the one hand and promoting rural development on the other. But that required more aid, and more policy flexibility. And all it might achieve was a gradual reduction in drug-related violence, lawlessness and corruption.

As well as the 'war' on drugs, Latin Americans had other gripes. Rightly or wrongly, the Bush administration was accused of being unhelpful when Argentina's economy collapsed in 2001 (though it came smartly to the rescue when Uruguay and Brazil wobbled the following year). Frustration was fuelled by the perception during Bush's first administration that nobody very senior in Washington was in charge of policy towards the region – a perception heightened by the apparent US endorsement of the failed coup against Hugo Chávez in Venezuela in 2002, and the failure to come to the aid of Goni in Bolivia the following year. To make matters worse, on the two issues that mattered most to many Latin American governments – trade and migration – policy was largely determined on Capitol Hill by the US Congress rather than by the White House.

Despite all this, relations between the United States and most of Latin America were not as bad as was sometimes claimed or as they often had been in the past. In Bush's second term, policy towards the region became more pragmatic. The administration sought to reduce Chávez's influence in the region through quiet diplomacy rather than the rhetorical aggression that had marked much of Bush's first term. In a five-country week-long tour of the region early in 2007, Bush talked of poverty and social injustice and invoked the memory of Kennedy's Alliance for Progress. He established a good personal relationship with Brazil's Lula. Thomas Shannon, a career diplomat who became the State Department's top official for the region in 2005, insisted that the United States would try to work with left-wing leaders who were democratically elected, such as Ortega in Nicaragua and Morales in Bolivia.[11] Missing was a clearer commitment that those countries that stuck to the path of democratic reform would reap the benefits of a close alliance, especially in the form of more-equitable trade deals and, for the poorer ones, greater development aid.

Global dreams and dilemmas

It has long been true that the further south you go in the Americas, the less powerful is US influence. For Brazil and Argentina, the European Union is a more important trade partner and source of investment than the United States. Many Latin Americans still yearn for Europe to act more generally as a counterweight to the United States in the region. A generation of politicians and writers who sojourned in Paris's *Quartier Latin* during the 1960s and 1970s argued that Latin America has more in common with the social democratic values of Europe than with hard-driving Anglo-Saxon individualism. That is debatable. But it was true that on many issues, ranging from policies towards Cuba and drugs to support for the UN and multilateralism, many Latin American governments tended to be closer to European positions than those of the United States. There was much bonhomie expressed at quadrennial EU–Latin American summits, which began at Rio de Janeiro in 1999 with the oxymoronic declaration of '55 priorities' for this transcontinental partnership. In practice, relations were low-key. Europe was too distracted by problems closer to home to show much interest. Spain was the big exception. Through the annual Iberoamerican summits begun in Guadalajara, Mexico, in 1993, it tried with some success to position itself as the main point of contact of Latin America with Europe. Its banks and utility companies began to invest heavily in the region in the late 1990s. They often seemed to overpay for local rivals; several lost heavily in the Argentine collapse and the regional slowdown. But they went on to reap handsome profits as Latin America recovered after 2003.

More recently, some Latin Americans have seen salvation in the rise of Asia, and of China in particular. China fever reached a peak in the region in

November 2004 when the country's president, Hu Jintao visited Argentina, Brazil and Chile, promising to lay out billions of dollars in investment in infrastructure to facilitate the import of the commodities that his country craves. Shortly afterwards, Hugo Chávez visited Beijing, where he stated improbably that Bolívar would have felt great affinity for Mao Zedong and added that China would invest heavily in Venezuela's oil industry. Partnership with China, the assumption seemed to be, was a liberating alternative to depending on the United States. That was particularly odd since China's imports from Latin America, far more than those of the US, are disproportionately concentrated in raw materials (traditionally disdained by the left). Much of China's investment and aid was tied to contracts for its own construction firms.

Nevertheless, the rise of China and India transformed the economic outlook for Latin America in the 2000s. Its main impact was to raise prices for the region's commodity exports, in many cases substantially, benefiting South America in particular; China alone has accounted for more than 50 per cent of the increase in global demand for many commodities since 2002. Second, trade with China became increasingly important. Though China accounted for just 6 per cent of Latin America's total exports in 2005, that was up from less than 2 per cent in 1999. China was especially important as an export market for Chile and Peru: it took more than 10 per cent of those countries' total exports in 2005; for Argentina the figure was 8 per cent.[12] Chinese direct investment involved a similar story of rapid growth from a low base: it totalled some $4 billion in 2004.[13] Chinese companies bought stakes in oilfields in Ecuador and Venezuela and mines in Peru. In 2007, an Indian firm, Jindal Steel and Power, agreed to invest $2.1 billion to develop a large iron-ore deposit in Bolivia.

But as well as hopes, the rise of China and India raised fears, especially in Mexico and Central America, whose textile and electronic assembly plants faced low-wage competition. More broadly, it gave greater urgency to the question of how Latin America can prosper in a globalised world. In many ways, Latin America is no longer the most advanced region of the developing world; nor is it the only one that attracts foreign investment as it was in the 1960s. Its wage levels are too high to compete with China in basic manufacturing: the average monthly manufacturing salary in the early 2000s was $120 to $150 per month in China and India compared with $1,112 in Argentina, $882 in Chile, $860 in Brazil, $670 in Mexico and $262 in Bolivia.[14] Yet Latin America's educational levels are no better than those of China and are much worse than South Korea's, and the region lacks India's large numbers of English-speaking graduates.

Latin America's main advantage in low-value-added manufacturing is proximity to the United States' market. But that applies mainly to Mexico,

Central America and the Caribbean basin. Between 1989 and 2002 textile and clothing exports from Latin America to the United States increased by a factor of 6.6, raising the region's share of total US imports for the sector to 27 per cent. But that growth was partly because of trade preferences. The Latin American share of the market declined after most of the barriers to the export of Chinese textiles were removed in 2005. Latin American clothing manufacturers will only survive if they can make the most of their ability to get goods on shelves more quickly than their Chinese counterparts. That depends on improving transport links and expanding the scale of manufacturing to lower unit transport costs.[15] Between 2000 and 2004, one in four *maquila* assembly plants left Mexico; most of them were textile and other low-value labour-intensive businesses which re-located to China, according to AT Kearney, a consultancy. But growth has since resumed for the *maquiladora* industry, and the firms that stayed made big efforts to cut costs and become more efficient.[16]

Despite the pessimistic message that is often heard from the region, most of the larger Latin American countries have quietly adapted to the opportunities of globalisation, even if they have yet to make the most of them. The private sector has led the way. It is not just in Mexico that manufacturing industry has modernised. In Brazil, too, that is true of many companies. A handful of homegrown multinationals have emerged in each country: Brazil's CVRD became the world's second-largest mining company when it bought Canada's Inco for $13.4 billion in 2006; weeks later, CSN, a steel firm, narrowly lost a bidding war with India's Tata Steel for Corus, an Anglo-Dutch steelmaker; while Gerdau, another steelmaker, and Embraer, a maker of regional jets, both have factories abroad. Mexico's Cemex is the world's third-biggest cement company, with factories in fifty countries; Mexican beer has become a big export industry (Corona and Sol are two of Latin America's few international brands); Grupo Mexico, a mining company, bought Asarco, a big American competitor. Grupo Maseca is making tortillas in China; and América Movil, the mobile arm of Carlos Slim's telecoms empire, has become the largest cellphone operator in Latin America. Tenaris, an industrial group of Italo-Argentine origin now based in Luxembourg, is the world's largest manufacturer of seamless steel tubes for the oil industry. In addition to these companies with global reach, there are a number of *multilatinas* operating in several countries in the region. Many Latin American manufacturers that survived the changes of the past two decades are 'leaner and meaner' and have become suppliers to rich-world multinationals, as one recent study argued.[17] In Colombia, for example, manufacturing industry increased its productivity by 46 per cent between 1992 and 2000, and increased the share of its output that it exported from 7 to 20 per cent over the same period.[18] In many other countries, there are viable manufacturing niches.

But for much of Latin America the path to prosperity inevitably involves making the most of a rich natural-resource endowment. The rise of India and China has had the effect of increasing the share of commodities in Latin America's exports. Yet that is not necessarily a bad thing. The World Bank noted in a report published in 2002 that countries such as Australia, Canada, Finland and Sweden all based their development on natural resources and are still net exporters of resource-based products. This historical record and recent Latin American experience shows that 'what is important is not *what* countries produce but *how*'. Farming, mining and forestry all have high-tech elements that can generate spillover effects elsewhere in the economy. 'Such industries can become knowledge industries,' the Bank argued.[19] That requires public policies that stimulate education and research and development as well as transport infrastructure. It also means remaining open to foreign investment to take advantage of global technological progress, as well as an effective system of property rights.

Mining and oil can easily become a curse rather than a blessing. There is a case for nationalising these resources: their production involves rents (monopoly profits) which state-ownership in theory can capture for the public good. This 'resource nationalism' was first ignited by Lázaro Cárdenas in Mexico, and is echoed by Hugo Chávez in Venezuela, by Evo Morales in Bolivia and by Rafael Correa in Ecuador. Yet in Latin America the potential benefits from resource nationalism have often been hijacked by particular interest groups, by trade unions (such as the oil-workers union in Mexico), bureaucrats and politicians. A wealthy state does not automatically create a wealthy country. Oil has often created dependence rather than an opportunity for diversification. And when prices are low, state natural-resource companies have often been a drain on the public purse; they have rarely been technological innovators. Whether or not they are in state ownership, mining and oil should be important sources of the tax revenues required to pay for the education and infrastructure needed for economic diversification. It is easy enough to increase taxes on natural resources when prices are high. The trick is to do so in such a way that takes account of the economic cycle and that does not send the message that private investors of all kinds risk finding that the terms on which they operate may change at a moment's notice.

If China was becoming the world's workshop and India its back office, Brazil is its farm – and potentially its centre of environmental services. Associated in the outside world with deforestation, much Brazilian agribusiness is high-tech and highly efficient. The vast majority of Brazilian soya is grown not on deforested land but on the limitless savannahs of the centre-west. Brazil is the world's largest exporter of beef, coffee, orange juice and sugar and on present trends soon will be of soya, poultry and pork. The country has no shortage of suitable farmland. Agriculture occupies 60 million hectares; it could cover another 90 million hectares without touching rainforest, according to Embrapa, the main government agricultural research institute.[20] What stops it from doing so is in part rich-country agricultural protectionism. Even so, Brazil's farm exports grew at over 6 per cent a year between 1990 and 2003, twice the rate of those of the EU and the United States. The secret is not just abundant land and permanent sunshine, allowing two or three harvests a year: it is also several decades of research and development by Embrapa, universities and private bodies. Brazil invested in agronomists, sending them abroad to study; back home again, they created plant varieties and animal strains that would thrive in the tropics. A similar research effort (in part by foreign carmakers) has made Brazil the world leader in plant-based fuels. In 2005, nearly two-thirds of the cars sold there had flex-fuel engines, allowing them to burn any combination of petrol and ethanol. Brazil's ethanol from sugar generates eight times as much energy per hectare than corn ethanol in the United States.[21] Other countries – notably Argentina, Chile and Peru – were making a similar success of farming for export.

Further development of agriculture means grappling with environmental concerns. Alongside old-fashioned farm protectionism, concern over climate change is adding a new version: opposition to 'food miles'. Yet growing food efficiently is good for the environment; the idea that food should not be traded internationally is no more logical than opposition to 'manufacturing miles'. For Brazil, the task is to make the most of its environmental assets. Since the Amazon rainforest benefits the world as a whole and not just South America there is growing discussion of how the world might pay for its conservation. Preserving the environment is economically beneficial for tourism, another industry where Latin America has a big advantage compared with parts of Asia. This lies not just in beaches: Latin America and the Caribbean have 116 UNESCO world heritage sites compared with 33 in China and 26 in India, for example.[22]

The main lesson is that while the world is an unfair place and agricultural protectionism is a particular burden for Latin America, countries' destinies are largely in their own hands, as Cardoso argued in the 1960s. Chile is the best example of a country that is successfully adding value to its natural resources. It has also placed more emphasis on becoming a global trader than on regional integration. Not surprisingly, many Chileans look to countries like Finland, Ireland or New Zealand as a role model, rather than to Argentina or Venezuela. But if regional integration can help Latin America to engage with the world, so much the better.

Ploughing the sea

In much high-flown rhetoric, the left in Latin America asserts that it is the champion of regional integration. In this, it lays claim to the mantle of Bolívar, an aristocratic conservative but a man who believed that the newly independent republics – or those of the northern Andes at least – had to stick together as a matter of survival. Bolívar's desire for strong government led him to reject federalism. He would find that confederalism was even less suited to South America. The short-lived union of Gran Colombia expressed his integrationist dream. In 1830, as the Liberator, stricken with tuberculosis and with disillusion, made his last journey to a proposed exile pre-empted by his death at Santa Marta beside the Caribbean, he received the news that Ecuador had followed Venezuela out of Gran Colombia. It came hard on the heels of the murder of Sucre, his most loyal general. In a letter to Ecuador's first president he penned his own famously bitter epitaph:

> You know that I have ruled for twenty years, and I have derived from these only a few sure conclusions: (1) America is ungovernable, for us; (2) Those who serve revolution plough the sea; (3) The only thing one can do is to emigrate; (4) This country will fall inevitably into the hands of the unrestrained multitudes and then into the hands of tyrants so insignificant they will be almost imperceptible, of all colours and races; (5) Once we've been eaten alive by every crime and extinguished by ferocity, the Europeans won't even bother to conquer us; (6) If it were possible for any part of the world to revert to primitive chaos, it would be America in her last hour.[23]

Bolívar's contemporary acolytes usually stop at point 2 or 3, omitting their hero's warning against democracy, populism and petty *caudillismo*. They construe the text as a denunciation of a narrow-minded oligarchy uncaring of the need for Latin American unity against the United States.

It would be more useful to ask why integration has proved so difficult in practice – and what its purpose should be. After all, the region has been relatively free of the inter-state conflicts that have dogged so many other parts of the world. That is one reason why for much of Latin America's history, regional integration was not a priority. Nor was it a realistic possibility: many countries spent the nineteenth century and much of the twentieth occupied in the most basic task of nation-state building, of controlling vast territories of broken geography (something which Colombia has not yet fully achieved even today). For example, it was only with the march of coast-hugging Brazilians to Amazonia and the centre-west, beginning in the 1970s, that Brazil has felt any great need to engage with its Spanish-speaking neighbours.[24] Until 1985, apart from a couple of border encounters, only three Brazilian presidents had ever visited Argentina (and only two Argentine rulers had made the trip the other way). In the 1960s, schemes such as the Latin American Free-Trade Association increased trade, especially in manufactures, through selective preferences. But their intention was only to widen protected markets, in a doomed effort to make import-substitution work better. The Central American Common Market made fitful progress in linking five small economies, while the five-nation Andean Pact (later renamed Andean Community) could rarely agree to a set of policies and stick to them.

Mercosur, formed in 1991 by Argentina, Brazil, Paraguay and Uruguay, promised to be different. It involved two of Latin America's three largest economies. It was formed by democratic governments who were committed to trade liberalisation and sound macroeconomic policies. Its philosophy was 'open regionalism', not the building of a protectionist fortress. It set out to create not just a free-trade area but an EU-style customs union, with a common external tariff and a common foreign trade policy, under a strict timetable and a clear set of rules. The idea was that companies could set up anywhere in the four countries and gain seamless access to a market of $1 trillion, achieving the economies of scale that are so often elusive in Latin America. At first all went well. Trade among the four countries grew swiftly, to $20.3 billion in 1998 when it amounted to a quarter of their total exports; local companies and multinationals re-organised their activities on a regional basis. Outsiders began to take note of what touted itself as the world's fourth-largest integrated market, after NAFTA, the EU and Japan.[25] Chile and Bolivia joined the free-trade area as associate members of Mercosur. When Paraguay's government was threatened by an upstart general, the group agreed that democracy should be a requirement for membership. Mercosur began talks with the EU on a free-trade agreement to parallel the FTAA.

Then things began to go wrong, as first Brazil devalued and later Argentina's economy collapsed. By 2002 trade among Mercosur's four full members had fallen to half its 1998 level; it would not surpass that level until 2005, but by then intra-Mercosur exports represented only around one-eighth of the four's total exports.[26] Far from pressing ahead with implementing the agreed rules, more and more ad hoc exceptions were punched in both the free-trade area and the putative customs union. These were blessed by presidential diplomacy, which papered over rising disenchantment. A dispute-settlement tribunal was eventually set up, along with a small permanent secretariat in Montevideo. But there were several underlying tensions. Paraguay and Uruguay felt permanently snubbed as Brazil and Argentina tended to do bilateral deals. But Brazil's disproportionate size meant that this arrangement was not as effective as the

'Franco-German axis' of co-equal giants that long drove the EU. For Brazil, Mercosur was more a geopolitical project of Itamaraty, the powerful foreign ministry, than a priority for the private sector of São Paulo, let alone that of the north-east. Itamaraty gave priority to widening Mercosur, whereas the other three founding members had more to gain from its deepening. In practice, all of them were reluctant to make the sacrifices of sovereignty required to make a common market work – even on such relatively minor matters as establishing a common customs code and sharing customs revenue.

Under Lula and Argentina's Néstor Kirchner, presumed political affinity seemed to replace 'open regionalism' as the guiding philosophy of Mercosur. Several experienced diplomats in both Brazil and Argentina lamented the naivety of this approach.[27] But it was shared by Hugo Chávez. He pulled Venezuela out of the Andean Community in protest at the negotiation by Peru and Colombia of FTAs with the United States. Although Colombia, not Brazil, was the most important market for Venezuelan industry, Chávez rushed to join Mercosur. With unwise alacrity, Venezuela was accepted as a full member, although Chávez was hardly a man known for his commitment to sharing sovereignty and accepting rules. Mercosur's disarray had already been dramatised when Kirchner gave his support to protestors who repeatedly blocked the main bridge between his country and Uruguay during the southern-hemisphere summer of 2006. The protests were over the building of two large paper plants on Uruguay's bank of the eponymous river that marks their boundary. Argentina's government claimed that these would pollute the river and that it had not been properly consulted. However, the blockades were a violation not only of the spirit of Mercosur but of Article 1 of the Treaty of Asunción (which requires the free circulation of goods between the four member states). They came just when Argentina tourists normally flock to beaches in Uruguay. Officials in Uruguay said the protests cost the country $400 million in the first year.

The issue of energy integration summed up how far Mercosur had moved from economic rationality. In the 1990s the Mercosur countries and their associates spent years and much money joining up their energy grids. But Kirchner's refusal to raise energy tariffs meant that Argentina, an important natural-gas producer, faced shortages. In 2004 he unilaterally and without notice began to cut exports of gas to Chile and halted exports of electricity to Uruguay.[28] Meanwhile, Petrobras invested heavily in developing Bolivia's natural gasfields and building a pipeline to São Paulo. After the national-isation, Petrobras switched the bulk of its investment budget elsewhere. Following their new political criteria, the Mercosur presidents entertained an absurd scheme promoted by Chávez to build an 8,000-kilometre (5,000-mile) pipeline to take natural gas from Venezuela to Buenos Aires, at a probable cost of $20 billion. Not only would it be far cheaper to ship liquid natural gas over such a distance, but the pipeline would also slice straight through the Amazon rainforest. In addition, while Venezuela claimed to have vast reserves of natural gas, these were largely undeveloped and PdVSA, the state energy firm, lacked experience with gas. In 2006 Venezuela began to build a far shorter pipeline to *import* natural gas from Colombia.[29]

The divided states of Latin America

Bolívar's name means little outside the northern Andes, let alone in Brazil or Mexico.[30] Yet Hugo Chávez conceived of the Bolivarian revolution as a Latin American, not just Venezuelan project. In an effort to win allies and neutralise diplomatic pressure against it from the United States, Chávez used part of his oil windfall to buy influence abroad. This began with a strategic alliance with Cuba, under which Venezuela supplied the island with 90,000 barrels per day (b/d) of oil at subsidised prices and agreed to invest up to $1 billion to revamp and supply an unfinished Soviet-era oil refinery at Cienfuegos in Cuba. When complete, this would bring total Venezuelan oil shipments to Cuba to 160,000 b/d.[31] This alliance was formalised as the 'Bolivarian Alternative for Latin America and the Caribbean' (or ALBA, meaning 'dawn' in Spanish). Chávez presented this as a rival continental project to the FTAA (whose initials are ALCA in Spanish). The goals of ALBA were to fight poverty and social exclusion through government-managed trade, Venezuelan oil wealth and Cuban know-how in public health and political organisation. But above all it was conceived by Chávez to be a political alliance against the United States. Bolivia joined ALBA in 2006; Nicaragua under Daniel Ortega followed suit in 2007, as did Haiti under Rene Préval. Chávez's promises of aid were more lavish than those of the United States. Venezuela offered a dozen Caribbean countries cheap credit for oil imports in a scheme known as Petrocaribe. Chávez also did his best to replace the IMF in Latin America: in 2005 and early 2006 Venezuela bought some $3.2 billion of Argentine government bonds, and an unspecified amount of Ecuador's debt.[32] Chávez was also a rather more active meddler in the region than Bush. His opponents argued, though without incontrovertible proof, that he financed the election campaigns of those sympathetic to him elsewhere in the region.

Despite his constant verbal attacks on the United States, Chávez continued to supply what he called 'the empire' with some 12 to 14 per cent of its oil imports, worth more than $30 billion in 2006.[33] The ties between Venezuela's oil industry and its main foreign market were close. Refineries in the US, some of them owned by Citgo, an affiliate of PdVSA, were configured for dealing with Venezuela's heavy crude. While Venezuela's oil exports to China grew more than tenfold between 2004 and 2006, they remained a small fraction of the total. Higher transport costs made them less profitable for Venezuela. Nevertheless, some in Washington took seriously Chávez's occasional threats to cut off exports to the US and re-route them to China. They were also worried by Chávez's dalliance with Iran's president, Mahmoud Ahmadi-Nejad. Venezuela and Cuba, along with Syria, were the only countries on the board of the UN International Atomic Energy Agency to vote against reporting Iran's nuclear activities to the UN Security Council.[34]

Yet more than for the United States, Chávez was a problem for his neighbours. For all his talk of regional unity, he was a factor of discord. Partly under his influence, Latin America looked more divided than it had been for a generation. That was symbolised at the fourth Summit of the Americas held at Mar del Plata in Argentina in November 2005.[35] There 29 countries – including Mexico, Colombia, Peru and Chile as well as the United States and Canada – affirmed their commitment to 'reactivate' negotiations for the FTAA. The Mercosur four and Venezuela said that 'the necessary conditions' for this were lacking. Outside the conference hall, Chávez spoke for two and a half hours to a rally of some 25,000 people organised by aides of Kirchner, and attended by Diego Maradona, a footballer made rich by globalisation. The Venezuelan president said he had come 'to bury' the FTAA and 'to take part in a birth, that of ALBA'. Back at the conference, Vicente Fox gave Chávez a public dressing down. George Bush flew on from Mar del Plata to Brasília, where Lula entertained him with a barbecue. Brazil 'doesn't want to bury the FTAA but to build it on a realistic basis', Celso Amorim, the foreign minister, felt obliged to make clear.[36] This disunity was repeated in Vienna six months later, at the fourth EU–Latin American summit. There the Mercosur presidents cancelled a scheduled meeting because of the dispute between Argentina and Uruguay over the paper mills. Chávez's attempt to secure one of the two rotating seats at the UN Security Council revealed similar divisions. Mercosur, Bolivia and Ecuador backed Venezuela; Chile and Peru abstained; and the rest of Latin America backed Guatemala, which originally was the consensus candidate but also had the support of the United States. Guatemala received more votes in the General Assembly than Venezuela but neither gained the needed two-thirds majority; Panama was eventually chosen as a compromise candidate.

Chávez posed a particular problem for Brazil. Under Lula, Brazil became less discreet in proclaiming its ambition to be seen as a regional leader and a global player. Its role was particularly important in trade diplomacy. It was instrumental in the formation of the G-20 group of developing countries at the WTO ministerial meeting at Cancún in 2003. It played a central role in the Doha round negotiations, and campaigned for a permanent seat on the

UN Security Council. Rather than the Free Trade Area of the Americas, many of Brazil's diplomats favoured a South American block in which their country would be the natural leader. But Brazil was not interested in joining Chávez's anti-American front, and it tried to maintain good relations with both the United States and Venezuela. Lula's friendly relations with Chávez went down well with his Workers' Party, many of whose members were less than enthusiastic about Lula's economic policy. And they helped to guarantee lucrative contracts in Venezuela for Brazilian construction firms, including a $1.2 billion bridge across the Orinoco. This stance also brought some embarrassments: Evo Morales's nationalisation of Petrobras's natural-gas assets in Bolivia, with Chávez's support, was a humiliation for Lula. Brazilian diplomats claimed that their quiet diplomacy was a moderating influence on Chávez. But it was hard to see much evidence of that.

For the purposes of trade, Latin America seemed to have settled into two blocks by 2006. Mexico, Central America, the Dominican Republic, Chile and (provided the US Congress ratified their FTAs) Colombia and Peru were committed to open trade and investment with the United States and the world in general. The other group comprised an expanded Mercosur (Bolivia and Ecuador were applying for full membership, though they hoped also to maintain preferential access to the US market). Yet Mercosur itself had become a fragile hostage to political change. Uruguay's left-wing president, Tabaré Vázquez, expressed his desire to seek a bilateral FTA with the United States. And although Brazil and Argentina had good reasons of national interest to be wary of an FTAA on the terms on which it was offered, there were powerful economic groups in both countries in favour of greater openness. That suggested that Mercosur might sooner or later return to its original vision, of promoting economies of scale for both local and foreign investors, of providing a support-club for democracy and for practical co-operation in transport and energy. But it might take a while.

The battle for Latin America's soul

Latin America did well in the previous era of globalisation, from 1870 to 1930. What ultimately undermined the region's progress then was turmoil in the world economy and the failure of its governments to allow more of their peoples to share in the benefits of growth; extreme inequalities underlay the half-century of political instability that followed. This time it can be different. Ever since the days of Rivadavia and Rosas, Latin American rulers have been divided between those who looked abroad in search of modernity and those who sought inspiration within, in the interior of their own countries and their traditions. A synthesis is surely within reach: the benefits of economic openness are clear, but the politicians must ensure that they reach the hinterland. While democracy can only thrive in Latin America if it goes hand in hand with faster economic growth, development is in part a political task, involving policies, institutions and choices of the kind that democracies are best equipped to mould.

Democracy has not been imposed on Latin America by a conquering army. Its arrival in plenitude, if not in perfection, draws on two centuries of liberal constitutionalism and democratic experiment. Over the past quarter of a century, democratic governments in Latin America have solved several big problems. They have conquered inflation, though that battle was long and costly. They have ended the self-imposed economic isolation of the region. In most places they have cut the armed forces down to size and trained them in a new democratic role. And they have started to tackle the region's historical legacy of extreme inequality, widespread poverty, chaotic urbanisation and educational neglect. They have had to do this while grappling with the rise of organised crime, partly fuelled from outside the region. These achievements have allowed other long-neglected problems, such as the poor quality of education in the region, to move to the forefront of public debate. The tasks ahead are less onerous but more complex. They can be summed up as further improving the region's economic performance, eliminating the extreme poverty that still afflicts 80 million Latin Americans, and ensuring that all in the region have access to economic opportunities, and that they can enjoy the rule of law and the rights and responsibilities of democratic citizens.

The return of economic growth in the years after 2004 provided a valuable breathing space for the region's democracies. Though the growth was partly due to high commodity prices, it was also in part the consequence of the attainment of financial stability. It made the record of economic reform look more effective. But it also blunted the impetus for further reform. That was understandable, but unfortunate. Over the past two centuries, Latin America's capacity to be knocked off course by outside events and its own shortcomings and mistakes is legendary. The sickening economic collapses of the 1980s and 1990s caused great hardship. Preventing their recurrence was vital. Fortunately, there are reasons to believe that Latin America is much better placed to ride out a slowdown in the world economy when it comes. Most governments no longer have large fiscal deficits, most have reduced their external debt and developed local-currency debt markets.

Raising the rate of economic growth in a sustainable way means increasing investment from its average level of 21 per cent of GDP in 2006, by a few percentage points. That is perfectly feasible. But it requires offering investors, both local and foreign, a stable and predictable environment, free of the risk of expropriation or abrupt reversals of macroeconomic policy. This in turn requires the construction of political consensuses – a new social contract. At its heart lies the need for governments to provide an effective safety-net for the poor, the unskilled and unemployed, while investing more in education, training, infrastructure and healthcare. Governments also need to do more to promote innovation, research and development and to let their companies compete without bureaucratic hindrance and oppressive regulation. And further reform of legal systems and policing is essential, to protect citizens and contracts alike.

Most Latin American countries were better placed in 2007 than they had been at any time in the previous quarter of a century. Incomplete though they were, and despite some costly mistakes of implementation, the economic reforms have provided the region with a platform from which to seek its fortune in the world. As we have seen, while they went under the unfortunate name of the 'Washington Consensus', the reforms were more a local creation than a foreign imposition. In many countries, increasingly self-confident and inclusive democracies are slowly filling in the gaps in the reformers' original list with imaginative social polices, institutional improvements and better governance. Radical social movements of sometimes questionable representa-tiveness might grab the headlines with street demonstrations, but the power of public opinion, expressed through the media, through local government or in civic groups is often more significant in quietly achieving change. In this everyday manner, Latin Americans are creating 'citizens' democracies'. Racial discrimination lingers, but is much diminished. Latin America's democratic societies are overwhelmingly *mestizo* and *mulato* in character. At the same time Latin America faces a favourable demographic moment, with fewer school-age children but not yet a large number of old people. This provides the opportunity to complete the reforms the region needs; it also makes it urgent to seize it.

With the rise of Hugo Chávez and his recruitment of a handful of countries for the 'Bolivarian alternative', for the first time since the end of the Cold War liberal democracy seemed to face a rival in Latin America. An accident of history – the surge in the oil price from 2001 onwards – has given spurious plausibility to an alternative course that Latin Americans seemed not so long ago to have turned their backs on. It is hard to overstate what is at stake in this ideological rivalry, this battle for Latin America's soul. The 'Bolivarian alternative' is based on flawed premises. Its diagnosis of the region's problems is based on a mistaken reading of history. It has given new life to dependency theory, when Latin Americans ought to be focussing on what they have to do for themselves in the fields of competitiveness, education and equal opportunity. Its penchant for constitution-writing is a dangerous distraction, not least because it adds another element of uncertainty for businesses to grapple with. If a new constitution were the most important tool for achieving democracy and development, Latin America would already be the world's leader on both counts.

Because of its dependence on oil wealth, *chavismo* was not easily exportable to other countries in any lasting manner. And politics in places like Bolivia and Ecuador had its own logic, or lack of it, and was not a simple copy of those of Venezuela. Even so, the rise of the 'Bolivarian alternative' was a cautionary tale for liberal democrats in Latin America. It was another reminder that extreme inequality provides fertile ground for populism. The populists have won power where inequality and economic setbacks have been combined with political systems or governments that have appeared to benefit narrow elites. One lesson was that if capitalism is to thrive it needs to be underpinned by an effective state and social policies, which have to be paid for with an adequate level of tax revenues. Another lesson for the privileged was that in a democracy the rule of law applies to everyone – even to them. If the government bails out delinquent or even unfortunate bankers when ordinary people are losing their jobs because of austerity, as happened in Ecuador, Mexico and Venezuela, it is hardly surprising if popular resentment with the political system grows. In his inaugural address as Guatemala's president in 1944, Juan José Arevalo promised 'to give civic and legal value to all people who live in the republic'.[37] As long as that remains an unfinished task in the region, populist would-be saviours will thrive.

There were lessons, too, for the Latin American left. Even as Venezuela's democracy was being hollowed out, there was no appetite in the region for criticising Chávez, at the Organisation of American States or in other purely Latin American forums. That risked establishing a dangerous tolerance for autocracy of any stripe, provided it was elected. In refusing to criticise Chávez, the left is forgetting its own strictures to the effect that democracy is more than just elections. It needs to recognise that the rule of law and democracy offer a far stronger guarantee of citizenship to the poor than the paternalist largesse of *caudillos*. In its enchantment with 'Bolivarianism', and renewed respect for Cuba, much of the left has forgotten the abiding lessons of the end of the Cold War, that central-planning failed and that communism was tyranny not liberation. If it is to offer a sustainable economic alternative for Latin Americans, the left will have to reconcile itself to capitalism.

After more or less synchronised democratisation and economic reform in the 1980s and 1990s, Latin America looks to be moving once again into a period of greater heterogeneity. Of the larger countries, Mexico, Brazil, Chile and perhaps Colombia and Peru seem set on a path of democratic development that looks likely to become increasingly successful in the coming years. Venezuela, Bolivia and Ecuador are setting their store by resource nationalism, their leaders appealing to the tenets of dependency theory and seeking to remake institutions in their own image. In the long term, this formula is unlikely to provide a path to development. As always, Argentina could go either way, but it is more likely to end up in the first camp. But these distinctions are not necessarily set in stone. Politics in each country in the region is driven as much by national histories, conflicts and imperatives as by continental fashion. Where political systems and the economy were reasonably strong, the underlying democratisation of Latin American societies gave rise to a demand for reform. Where such conditions were absent, the same process could lead to populism, though not necessarily of a uniform kind.

That this underlying democratisation is not better understood owes much to Latin America's status as the 'forgotten continent' to which, it is assumed, anachronistic stereotypes and generalisations can safely be applied. Neglect may indeed be mainly benign but it is also risky. Most of Latin America has bet on economic openness and democracy. This book has argued that the reasons for that are mainly internal to the region. Even so, external influences matter. If the United States and the European Union continue to turn their backs on the region, some Latin Americans may reconsider, especially if China starts to offer a serious alternative.

Largely overlooked by the outside world, Latin America has made much progress in the past few decades. A sense of perspective is important: two generations ago a majority of Latin Americans lived in semi-feudal conditions in the countryside; little more than a generation ago, many were being murdered because of their political beliefs. Not all of the improvement has been captured in the cold economic numbers. Indeed, one of the problems Latin America's democracies face is the persistent denial of progress by many academics, journalists and politicians, both within the region and among those who observe it from the United States and Europe.[38] This habit, which serves to undermine the legitimacy of democratic institutions, is not new. In Brazil, for example, scorn for representative democracy was widespread among such figures in the nineteenth century. It 'still permeates today both intellectual and popular language, and can without doubt be considered one of the most important outlines of our political culture', according to a leading Brazilian political scientist.[39] The same goes for Colombia, as a senior government official recently noted. 'To emphasise positive characteristics in Colombia is particularly daring in a place where part of the intellectual elite, for years if not decades, has dedicated itself to pointing out its failures, its physical and human misery [and] to ridicule its achievements.'[40]

This is not an argument for complacency in the face of Latin America's relative failures of development and the flaws of its democracies. Rather, it is to argue that it is time to liberate Latin America from some of the more defeatist and whimsical readings of its own history, time to look more to the future with at least cautious optimism. The relatively disappointing record of many of Latin America's democratic governments should be judged realistically against the scale of the problems that they have had to face. The problems may be more obviously visible, but progress has started to get the upper hand. Consolidating it requires incremental reform, not regressive revolution. It also requires patience, hard though that is to muster in the face of poverty. As Juan Bautista Alberdí, the Argentine liberal and constitutionalist, noted in 1837: *Las naciones, como los hombres, no tienen alas; hacen sus viajes a pie, paso por paso.* 'Nations, like men, do not have wings; they make their journeys on foot, step by step.'

GLOSSARY

AD (Acción Democrática)	social-democratic party in Venezuela
ALBA (Alternativa Boliviariana para América Latina y el Caribe)	Bolivarian Alternative for Latin America and the Caribbean, an anti-US regional alliance promoted by Hugo Chávez
antropofagia	term used by Oswald de Andrade, a Brazilian modernist writer, to denote the practice of 'cultural cannibalism', of devouring foreign cultural influences and regurgitating them in uniquely Brazilian ways
APRA (Alianza Popular Revolucionaria Américana)	populist movement founded by Victor Raúl Haya de la Torre; became a Peruvian political party
AUC (Auto-Defensas Unidas de Colombia)	United Self-Defence Forces of Colombia, the umbrella group of Colombia's right-wing paramilitaries
audiencia	the supreme judicial and administrative body in Spain's American colonies
ayllu	indigenous peasant community in the central Andes
Aymara	indigenous language spoken in north-western Bolivia and in Peru around Lake Titicaca
Barrio Adentro	'Inside the Neighbourhood', community health programmes organised by Venezuela's government under Hugo Chávez and mainly staffed by Cuban doctors
Bolsa Família	'Family Fund', large-scale anti-poverty programme in Brazil
cabildo	town council or town meeting
cacique	local political boss
campamentos	Chilean term for shantytowns
campesinos	peasant farmers

candomblé	religion of African origin in Brazil
Caracazo	rioting in Venezuela in protest at higher petrol prices and bus fares in 1989
caudillo	originally a regional warlord; by extension a political strongman, often of military background
CCTs	conditional cash transfer programmes, such as *Bolsa Família* and *Progresa/Oportunidades*
CEPAL (Comisión Económica para América Latina y el Caribe)	United Nations Economic Commission for Latin America and the Caribbean (ECLAC)
cepalista(s)	policies of state-led industrial protectionism promoted by CEPAL; those who supported these policies
cerrado	inland savannah (Brazil)
chavistas	supporters of Hugo Chávez, Venezuela's president
Chile Solidario	'Solidaristic Chile', a government programme aimed at eliminating extreme poverty
churrasco	barbecue (Brazil)
CIA	United States Central Intelligence Agency
colonia	neighbourhood (Mexico)
conos	cones; shantytown suburbs stretching to the north, east and south of Lima
contras	counter-revolutionary guerrilla force organised by the Reagan administration in the 1980s to fight the Sandinista regime in Nicaragua
convertibilidad	the name given locally to Argentina's currency board of 1991–2002 under which the peso was fixed by law at par to the dollar
COPEI	Christian democratic party in Venezuela
CORFO (Corporación de Fomento)	state development corporation in Chile
Cortes	parliament
criollo	in the colonial and independence periods, a person of European descent born in the Americas
CTM (Confederación de Trabajadores de México)	Mexican Workers' Confederation, the main trade union organisation under the PRI
cumbia	Colombian dance music
curacas	local Indian leaders in Peru
CVRD (Companhia Vale do Rio Doce)	Brazilian mining company
desarrollo para adentro	inward-looking development, the economic policies championed by CEPAL after the Second World War

descamisados	'shirtless ones', the urban poor in Argentina
ejido	communal landholding in Mexico; after the Mexican revolution, state-sponsored peasant community
ELN (Ejercito de Liberación Nacional)	National Liberation Army, the smaller of the two main Colombian guerrilla groups
Estado Novo	'New State'; Getúlio Vargas's quasi-fascist dictatorship in Brazil of 1937–45
estera	sheet of rush-matting used to build huts by squatters in Peru
EU	European Union
FARC (Fuerzas Armadas Revolucionarias de Colombia)	Revolutionary Armed Forces of Colombia, the larger of the country's two main guerrilla groups
favela	shantytown (Brazil)
fazenda	large agricultural estate (Brazil)
Fedecámaras (Federación de Cámaras y Asociaciones de Comercio y Producción de Venezuela)	Federation of Chambers of Commerce and Production of Venezuela, the country's main private-sector lobby
FMLN (Frente Farabundo Martí para la Liberación Nacional)	Farabundo Martí National Liberation Front, guerrilla coalition in El Salvador's civil war
foco	focus; rural guerrilla group
FONDEN (Fondo de Desarrollo Nacional)	National Development Fund (Venezuela)
FTAA	proposed Free Trade Area of the Americas
fuero	group or corporate rights under the Spanish colonial system
gaúcho	in Portuguese, an inhabitant of the Brazilian state of Rio Grande do Sul
GDP	Gross Domestic Product
gendarmerie	militarised police force (French)
generalísimo	supreme military commander and dictator
glasnost	the Russian term for openness, used to describe the civil and political reforms of Mikhail Gorbachev in the Soviet Union
grupúsculos	small radical left-wing factions
Guaraní	indigenous language widely spoken in Paraguay and in parts of Bolivia and Brazil
guevarista	guerrilla movements inspired by the example of Che Guevara

hacienda	large agricultural estates established by the Spanish *conquistadores*
hacendado(s)	owner(s) of large estates
IFE (Instituto Federal Electoral)	Federal Electoral Institute (Mexico)
ILD (Instituto Libertad y Democrácia)	Institute for Liberty and Democracy, a Lima think-tank
IMF	International Monetary Fund
indigenismo	current of thought, especially in Mexico and Peru, that promoted the importance of indigenous cultures and the integration of the Indian into the mainstream of society
INSS (Instituto Nacional do Seguro Social)	National Social Security Institute (Brazil)
junta	board or committee
junta militar	ruling military directorate
KGB	Soviet security and intelligence service
latifundio (plural: *latifundia*)	large landed estates
llaneros	cowboys or plainsmen from the Venezuelan and Colombian plains
llanos	tropical plains in southern Venezuela and south-eastern Colombia
lucha armada	armed struggle, i.e. guerrilla action
maquiladoras	export assembly plants
MAS (Movimiento al Socialismo)	Movement to Socialism; in Venezuela, a moderate social-democratic party; in Bolivia, a more radical socialist party led by Evo Morales
MBR-200 (Movimiento Bolivariano Revolucionario-200)	conspiratorial movement founded by Hugo Chávez and other military officers
mensalão	big monthly payment, as a political corruption scandal in Brazil was dubbed
mestizaje	the process of racial mixing
mestizo(a)	person of mixed Amerindian and Caucasian descent
milpa	maize field (Mexico and Central America)
mineiros	miners; inhabitants of the Brazilian state of Minas Gerais
minifundio	small plot worked by peasant farmer (*minifundista*)
MIR (Movimiento de la Izquierda Revolucionaria)	far-left group in Chile

misiones	missions; Chávez's Cuban-designed social programmes
MNR (Movimiento Nacional Revolucionario)	corporatist-nationalist party that led Bolivia's 1952 revolution
MST (Movimento Sem Terra)	Landless Workers' Movement (Brazil)
mulato(a)	mulatto; person of mixed African and Caucasian descent
MVR (Movimiento V República)	Fifth Republic Movement, a party formed by Hugo Chávez to contest Venezuela's 1998 presidential election
NAFTA	North American Free Trade Agreement
Nahuatl	an indigenous language spoken in central Mexico and used by the Aztecs
NGO	Non-governmental organisation
OAS	Organisation of American States
OECD	Organisation for Economic Co-operation and Development, a research and co-ordination body whose members are mainly developed countries
OPEC	Organisation of Petroleum Exporting Countries
Oportunidades	name assigned to *Progresa* anti-poverty programme by Vicente Fox's government in Mexico
PAN (Partido de Acción Nacional)	National Action Party, centre-right party in Mexico
pardo	mulatto; person of mixed African and Caucasian descent
PdVSA (Petróleos de Venezuela SA)	Venezuela's state-owned oil company
peninsulares	during the colonial period, Spanish-born residents of the Americas
perestroika	the Russian term for economic restructuring, used of Mikhail Gorbachev's reforms in the Soviet Union
PMDB (Partido do Movimento Democrático Brasileiro)	Party of the Brazilian Democratic Movement, centrist party created from the official opposition to the military regime of 1964–85
poderes facticos	de facto, rather than de jure, powers-that-be
PRC	Cuban Revolutionary Party
PRD (Partido de la Revolución Democrática)	Party of the Democratic Revolution, left-of-centre party in Mexico
PRI (Partido Revolucionario Institucional)	Institutional Revolutionary Party (Mexico)

Progresa	pioneering anti-poverty programme in Mexico involving cash payments to mothers whose children attend school and health checks
pronunciamiento	declaration of military rebellion against the government
PSDB (Partido da Social Democracia Brasileiro)	Party of Brazilian Social Democracy, a moderate centre-left grouping
PT (Partido dos Trabalhadores)	Workers' Party (Brazil)
puntofijismo	the pacted democracy adopted in Venezuela in 1958
Quechua (in Ecuador, Quichua)	most widely spoken indigenous language in the Andes
rancheras	Mexican popular songs that exalt rural traditions, somewhat akin to country music in the United States
ranchos	Venezuelan term for shantytowns or self-built urban slums
reconquista	the wars waged by the Christian kingdoms of Spain against the Moors
República de Indios	the legislation under which Indians in Peru and elsewhere retained considerable autonomy within their subordinate status during the Spanish colony
riesgo país	country risk, or the premium attached to emerging-market bonds
telenovelas	television soap operas
tlatoani	Aztec term for ruler or king (literally, 'he who speaks' in Nahuatl)
UDN (União Democrática Nacional)	National Democratic Union, the main conservative party in Brazil from 1945 to 1964
umbanda	Brazilian religious sect drawing on African elements but more recent origin than *candomblé*
la violencia	a civil war mainly between supporters of the Liberal and Conservative parties in Colombia lasting from 1948 to 1958
Yanqui	Yankee; more broadly, pertaining to the US
YPF (Yacimientos Petrolíferos Fiscales)	Argentina's state oil company, privatised in 1991
YPFB (Yacimientos Petrolíferos Fiscales Bolivianos)	Bolivia's state oil company
zambo(s)	of mixed African and Amerindian descent

NOTES

Preface

1. This was the title of an *Economist* cover (18 May 2006).

Chapter 1

1. Quoted in 'Out of Fear' by Ariel Dorfman, *Guardian*, 18 March 2006.
2. Graddol, David, *English Next* (2006), British Council.
3. *Guardian*, 19 July 2006.
4. 'Romancing the Globe' by Ibsen Martínez, *Foreign Policy*, November/December 2005.
5. World Bank (2006e), pp. 101–2.
6. 'Bush misfires in drive to end oil addiction', *Financial Times*, 2 February 2006 and 'Chávez quickens drive to wrest oil revenues', *Financial Times*, 28 April 2006.
7. Wilson, Dominic and Purushothaman, Roopa, 'Dealing with BRICS', Goldman Sachs Global Economics Paper No. 99, 1 October 2003.
8. World Bank (2004), Table 1, p. 2.
9. United Nations Economic Commission for Latin America (ECLAC/CEPAL), Social Panorama of Latin America, 2006. According to the World Bank's standard international measure of poverty (an income below $2 per day), 20.6 per cent of Latin Americans were poor in 2006. The Bank classes Bolivia, Haiti, Honduras and Nicaragua as 'poor' rather than 'middle-income' countries.
10. Mexico was something of a special case. Since 1928 it had been governed by a single party that later took the name of the Institutional Revolutionary Party (PRI). Under the PRI, Mexico enjoyed the outward trappings of liberal democracy but not its content. In 1994, the country was still engaged in a gradual transition to genuine democracy that culminated in the defeat of the PRI in the presidential election of 2000.
11. The others were Raúl Cubas in Paraguay (1999); Jamil Mahuad in Ecuador (2000); Alberto Fujimori in Peru (2000); Fernando de la Rua in Argentina (2001); Gonzalo Sánchez de Lozada in Bolivia (2003); Jean Bertrand Aristide in Haiti (2004); and Lucio Gutiérrez in Ecuador (2005). Fujimori resigned after he had unconstitutionally and fraudulently won a third consecutive term. Aristide's re-election was

denounced as fraudulent by Haiti's opposition. The other five on this list were democratically elected; Mesa was Sánchez de Lozada's vice-president.

12. *See* Chapter 11 for an explanation of 'democratic consolidation'.

13. *See* Chapter 6 for a discussion of the 'Washington Consensus'. 'Neoliberalism' has become a term of abuse in the region and beyond. If it means anything, it refers to revived conservatism.

14. The term harked back to Latin America's 'lost decade' of the 1980s, triggered by Mexico's debt default of 1982. *See* Chapter 5.

15. UNDP (2004), *La Democracia en América Latina: hacia una democracia de ciudadanas y cuidadanos*, UNDP, New York.

16. 'El Incierto Futuro de América Latina', *El País* (Madrid) 18 October 2004.

17. Inter-American Development Bank (2006a), 'Remittances 2005: Promoting financial democracy'; and press release, 18 March 2007.

18. Inter-American Development Bank (2000), 'Development Beyond Economics'.

19. 'São Paulo Growth and Poverty' (1978), A report from the São Paulo Justice and Peace Commission, The Bowerdean Press in association with the Catholic Institute for International Relations; National Research Council (2003), *Cities Transformed: Demographic Change and Its Implications in the Developing World*, The National Academies Press, Washington DC; de Soto, Hernando (1986), *El Otro Sendero*, Editorial El Barranco, Lima, p. 8.

20. de Soto, Hernando (2001), *The Mystery of Capital*, Black Swan Books, London, p. 30.

21. Santiso, Javier (2006), *Latin America's Political Economy of the Possible: Beyond Good Revolutionaries and Free Marketeers*, MIT Press.

22. 'Latin America's Shift to the Center', Oscar Arias, *Washington Post*, 15 March 2006.

23. Quoted in *El País*, 18 March 2006.

24. Interview with the author, London, September 2001.

25. For full transcript, *see* www.economist.com. Because of fully booked flights over the Carnival period, the author was unable to attend the interview in Brasília in February 2006. It was conducted by Brooke Unger, *The Economist*'s São Paulo bureau chief.

26. Quoted in the *Observer*, 14 May 2006.

27. *See* Chapter 7.

28. Populism first surfaced as a political term in nineteenth-century Russia, denoting middle-class intellectuals who embraced peasant communalism as an antidote to Western liberalism. In the United States, too, populism was a rural movement, reaching its zenith in the 1896 presidential campaign of William Jennings Bryan against the gold standard. The term would later be applied to Huey Long, the governor of Louisiana from 1928–32, who in a style similar to many Latin American populists campaigned against Standard Oil and built a ruthless political machine. In France, Pierre Poujade in the 1950s and Jean Marie Le Pen in recent times championed the 'little man', especially farmers and small shopkeepers, against big corporations, unions and foreigners. But it is in Latin America where populism has had the most enduring influence. *See* Conniff, Michael L (ed.) (1982), *Latin American Populism in Comparative Perspective*, University of New

Mexico Press, Albuquerque. Coniff in this work and another edited collection of essays (*Populism in Latin America* (1999), University of Alabama Press, Tuscaloosa and London) holds to the view, common among many political scientists, that populism is merely a style of political leadership with no bearings upon economic policy. Thus, he and his collaborators apply the term to leaders such as Peru's Alberto Fujimori and Carlos Menem whom, confusingly in my view, they see as 'neo-populist, neoliberals' rather than as mere conservatives. In contrast, Rudiger Dornbusch and Sebastian Edwards and their collaborators (*The Macroeconomics of Populism in Latin America* (1991), University of Chicago Press) link populism to unsustainable redistribution. There is indeed nothing inherently left wing about populism – some of its exponents were closer to fascism than socialism. Rather, it is at heart corporatist and anti-liberal. This passage in the text also draws on 'Latin America: The Return of Populism', *The Economist*, 15 April 2006.

29. Interview with the author, Mexico City, May 2005.

30. Gillespie, Richard (1982), *Soldiers of Perón: Argentina's Montoneros*, Oxford University Press, p. 44.

31. 'The Latinobarómetro Poll: The Democracy Dividend,' *The Economist*, 9 December 2006.

32. World Bank (2006a).

33. Interview with the author, Lima, February 2002.

34. ECLAC/CEPAL, Economic Survey of Latin America and the Caribbean 2005–6, Santiago, July 2006, p. 15.

35. Zweig, and his wife, committed suicide not long after he coined his famous phrase about Brazil.

36. Bushnell, David and Macaulay, Neill (1994), *The Emergence of Latin America in the Nineteenth Century*, 2nd edition, Oxford University Press, p. 3. The first known use of the term was by Michel Chevalier in the introduction to a book entitled *Lettres sur l'Amérique du Nord* published in 1836. Chevalier's essay was translated into Spanish in 1856. *See* Dunkerley, James (2004), *Dreaming of Freedom in the Americas: Four Minds and a Name*, Institute for the Study of the Americas, London, p. 37.

37. Marx, Anthony W (1998), *Making Race and Nation: A Comparison of the United States, South Africa and Brazil*, Cambridge University Press, p. 49.

38. Buarque de Holanda, Sergio (1996), *Raízes do Brasil*, 26th edition, Companhia das Letras, São Paulo, p. 53.

39. *Financial Times Magazine*, 7 June 2003.

40. *See* Chapter 12.

41. Paz, Octavio (1985), *The Labyrinth of Solitude and Other Writings*, Grove Press, p. 29.

42. Krauze, Enrique (1997), *Mexico: Biography of Power: A History of Modern Mexico, 1810–1996*, Harper Collins, p. 244.

43. della Paolera, Gerardo and Taylor, Alan M (2003), *A New Economic History of Argentina*, Cambridge University Press, p. 1.

44. Maddison, Angus (1998), *The World Economy: A Millenial Perspective*, OECD; della Paolera and Taylor, *A New Economic History of Argentina*, pp. 2–3.

45. In his 'Jamaica Letter' of 1815. *El Libertador: Writings of Simón Bolívar* (2003),

Oxford University Press, p. 27.

46. Author's conversation with an adviser to President Ricardo Lagos in 2002.

47. Montenegro, Santiago, 'Territorio, gobernabilidad y competitividad', Departamento Nacional de Planeación, Bogotá, May 2003. Paper available at www.dnp.gov.co

48. Figures taken from Rafael Fernández de Castro, *Reforma*, 8 May 2005.

49. Calvo, José Manuel, 'Crece la ola hispana', *El País*, 10 June 2005.

50. Ramírez, Sergio, 'El Caribe Somos Todos'. This article, which appeared in *El País* (Madrid) in 2001, can be found at www.sergioramirez.org.ni

51. Paz, *The Labyrinth of Solitude*, Chapter 2.

52. *See* Wiarda, Howard (2001), *The Soul of Latin America: The Cultural and Political Tradition*, Yale University Press.

53. Bushnell/Macaulay, *The Emergence of Latin America*, pp. 190–1.

54. Huntington, Samuel P (1998), *The Clash of Civilizations and the Remaking of World Order*, Touchstone Books, p. 46.

55. Rouquié, Alain (1997), *América Latina: Introducción al Extremo Occidente*, 4th edition, Siglo XXI Editores, Mexico.

Chapter 2

1. *See* Fernández-Armesto, Felipe (2003), *The Americas: A Hemispheric History*, Random House Modern Library, New York, Chapter 3.

2. Bulmer-Thomas, Victor (1994), *The Economic History of Latin America Since Independence*, Cambridge University Press, p. 27.

3. Quoted in Platt, DCM (1972), *Latin America and British Trade 1806–1914*, A & C Black, London, p. 4.

4. Maddison, Angus, *The World Economy*, p. 126.

5. Cárdenas, Enrique, Ocampo, José Antonio and Thorp, Rosemary (eds) (2000), *An Economic History of Twentieth-Century Latin America. Vol. 1: The Export Age*, Palgrave, Chapter 1.

6. Bulmer-Thomas, *The Economic History of Latin America*, pp. 61–6.

7. Ibid., p. 417.

8. *Financial Times* Special Report on the World Economy, 13 September 2006.

9. Hartlyn, Jonathan and Valenzuela, Arturo (1994), 'Democracy in Latin America Since 1930', in Bethell, Leslie (ed.), *The Cambridge History of Latin America*, Vol. VI, Part 2, pp. 99–100.

10. Thorp, Rosemary (1998), *Progress, Poverty and Exclusion: An Economic History of Latin America in the 20th Century*, Inter-American Development Bank, pp. 122–3.

11. Cardoso, Fernando Henrique and Faletto, Enzo (2003), *Dependencia y Desarrollo en América Latina*, Siglo XXI, Argentina, p. 23.

12. Ibid., p. 151.

13. Cardoso, Fernando Henrique with Winter, Brian (2006), *The Accidental President of Brazil: A Memoir*, PublicAffairs, pp. 96–8.

14. *See*, for example, Gunder Frank, Andre (1969), *Capitalism and Underdevelopment in Latin America*, Penguin Books.

15. Skidmore, Thomas E and Smith, Peter H (1997), *Modern Latin America*, 4th

edition, Oxford University Press, p. 7.

16. Galeano, Eduardo (1997), *Open Veins of Latin America*, Monthly Review Press, New York, p. 2.

17. Ibid., p. 267.

18. Ibid., p. 8.

19. To take just two of many possible examples of Galeano's questionable historical interpretations, contrast his view of the defeat in a civil war in 1891 of José Manuel Balmaceda, a Chilean president whom he portrays as an economic nationalist toppled by British intrigue, with the very different view in *The Cambridge History of Latin America*. (Blakemore, Harold, 'From the War of the Pacific to 1930', in Leslie Bethell (ed.) (1993b), *Chile Since Independence*, Cambridge University Press, pp. 33–85.) This concludes that 'Balmaceda had nothing like the clearly constructed policy on state intervention in the economy – including nitrates – ascribed to him.' (p. 55) Similarly, Galeano champions the Paraguay of Dr Gaspar Rodríguez de Francia (1814–40), a sinister dictator, and his successors as 'Latin America's most progressive country'. As Paul Gootenberg, a historian of leftish sympathy, has remarked: 'The dependency rehabilitation of such freakish characters as Dr Francia of Paraguay – who are now held to offer nineteenth-century Latin America its most viable and progressive path to development – should alert us that revisionism has gone astray.' (Gootenberg, Paul (1989), *Between Silver and Guano: Commercial Policy and the State in Postindependence Peru*, Princeton University Press, p. 10)

20. Bushnell, David (2000), *Colombia: Una Nación a Pesar de sí Misma*, 5th edition, Planeta, Bogotá, p. 246.

21. *See* Bucheli, Marcelo (2005), *Bananas and Business: The United Fruit Company in Colombia, 1899–2000*, New York University Press, Chapter 5.

22. *See* Chapter 4 for its record in Guatemala.

23. Posada Carbó, Eduardo, 'La historia y los falsos recuerdos', *Revista de Occidente*, Madrid, December 2003. My translation.

24. García Márquez, Gabriel (2002), *Vivir para contarla*, Knopf, New York, p. 74. García Márquez is an incorrigible hyperbolist. In this work, the first volume of his memoirs, he narrates his experience of the riots in Bogotá in 1948 known as the *Bogotazo*. 'The deaths in the streets of Bogotá, and at the hands of the official repression in subsequent years, must have been more than a million.' (p. 348) In fact, even the most pessimistic of historians put the figure at no higher than 200,000 over ten years – again, appalling enough, but not on the same scale.

25. Skidmore/Smith, *Modern Latin America*, p. 10.

26. Haber, Stephen, 'Introduction: Economic Growth and Latin American Economic Historiography', in Haber, Stephen (ed.) (1997), *How Latin America Fell Behind: Essays in the Economic Histories of Brazil and Mexico, 1800–1914*, Stanford University Press, pp. 1–33.

27. *See*, for example, Marichal, Carlos (coordinador) (1995), *Las inversiones extranjeras en América Latina, 1850–1930*, Fondo de Cultura Economica, Mexico; or Yarrington, Doug, 'The Vestey Cattle Enterprise and the Regime of Juan Vicente Gómez 1908–1935', *Journal of Latin American Studies*, Vol. 35, Part 1, February 2003, pp. 89–115.

28. Marichal, *Las inversiones extrarigeras en América Latina*, p. 23.

29. Thorp, Rosemary and Bertram, Geoffrey (1978), *Peru 1890–1977: Growth and Policy in an Open Economy*, Macmillan, p. 104 (table).

30. Coatsworth, John H and Williamson, Jeffrey G, 'Always Protectionist? Latin American Tariffs from Independence to Great Depression', *Journal of Latin American Studies*, Vol. 36, Part 2, May 2004.

31. Haber, *How Latin America Fell Behind*, p. 12.

32. *See* Chapter 5. The coup in Guatemala in 1954 was an exception in being wholly generated by the CIA. See Chapter 4.

33. Landes, David (1998), *The Wealth and Poverty of Nations*, Little, Brown, New York, p. 328. Italics in original.

34. Véliz, Claudio (1994), *The New World of the Gothic Fox: Culture and Economy in English and Spanish America*, University of California Press, p. 12. Other works in this vein include Wiarda, Howard, *The Soul of Latin America*; Harrison, Lawrence E (2000), *Underdevelopment Is a State of Mind: The Latin American Case*, Madison Books, Lanham; and Harrison, Lawrence E (1997), *The Pan-American Dream: Do Latin America's Cultural Values Discourage True Partnership with the United States and Canada?* Basic Books, New York. *See also* Vargas Llosa, Álvaro (2005), *Liberty for Latin America*, Farrar, Strauss and Giroux, New York, which mixes cultural and institutional explanations.

35. Véliz, *The New World of the Gothic Fox*, p. 53.

36. Wiarda, *The Soul of Latin America*, Chapters 4 and 5.

37. Véliz, *The New World of the Gothic Fox*, p. 53.

38. Rodó, José Enrique (1994), *Ariel*, Kapelusz Editora, Buenos Aires.

39. Wiarda, *The Soul of Latin America*, Chapter 5.

40. Foweraker, Joe, Landman, Todd and Harvey, Neil (2003), *Governing Latin America*, Polity Press, Chapter 3.

41. 'El Amor a Francia', *El País*, 19 March 2005

42. Rouquié, Alain (1987), *The Military and the State in Latin America*, University of California Press, p. 4.

43. Gunther, Richard, Montero, José Ramón and Botella, Joan (2004), *Democracy in Modern Spain*, Yale University Press, p. 2.

44. World Bank (1998).

45. Rodrik, Dani, Subramanian, Arvind and Trebbi, Francesco, 'Institutions Rule: The Primacy of Institutions over Geography and Integration in Economic Development', revised October 2002. Available at http://ksghome.harvard.edu/drodrik, p. 20.

46. Harriss, John, Hunter, Janet and Lewis, Colin M (1995), *The New Institutional Economics and Third World Development*, Routledge, London. *See* 'Introduction: Development and Significance of NIE', pp. 1–13.

47. de Soto, *El Otro Sendero*, pp. 13–14.

48. *See*, for example, Matos Mar, José (2004), *Desborde Popular y Crisis del Estado: Veinte Años Después*, Fondo Editorial del Congreso del Perú, Lima.

49. de Soto, *El Otro Sendero*, p. 288.

50. Ibid., p. 296.

51. de Soto, *The Mystery of Capital*.

52. Interview with the author, El Alto, January 2004.

53. Galiani, Sebastian and Schargrodsky, Ernesto, 'Property Rights for the Poor: Effects of Land Titling', Centro de Investigación en Finanzas, Universidad Torcuato di Tella, Buenos Aires, Documento de Trabajo June 2005.

54. Field, Erica and Torero, Maximo, 'Do Property Titles Increase Credit Access Among the Urban Poor: Evidence from a Nationwide Titling Program', March 2006. Available at www.economics.harvard.edu/faculty/field/papers. This study finds evidence that those with titles were somewhat more likely to gain a loan for construction material from the government-run Materials Bank.

55. Field, Erica, 'Entitled to Work: Urban Property Rights and Labor Supply in Peru', March 2006, unpublished paper available at website cited above.

56. Rodrik et al, 'Institutions Rule'.

57. La Porta, Rafael, López de Silanes, Florencio, Schleifer, Andrei and Vishny, Robert W, 'Law and Finance', National Bureau of Economic Research Working Paper 5661 and 'Legal Determinants of External Finance', NBER Working Paper 5879.

58. Cárdenas/Ocampo/Thorp, *An Economic History of Twentieth-Century Latin America*, Chapter 1.

59. Engerman, Stanley L and Sokoloff, Kenneth L, 'Factor Endowments, Institutions and Differential Paths of Growth Among New World Economies' in Haber, *How Latin America Fell Behind*, pp. 260–304.

60. Ibid., p. 275.

61. Coatsworth, John H, 'Structures, Endowments, and Institutions in the Economic History of Latin America', *Latin American Research Review*, Vol. 40, No. 3, October 2005.

62. Bulmer-Thomas, *The Economic History of Latin America*, p. 88.

63. Przeworski, Adam with Curvale, Carolina, 'Does politics explain the economic gap between the United States and Latin America?', available at www.nyu.edu/gsas/dept/politics/faculty/przeworski/papers

64. Cárdenas/Ocampo/Thorp, *An Economic History of Twentieth-Century Latin America*, p. 72.

Chapter 3

1. Many believe that the army overreacted. Debate still rages as to whether the M-19 was acting at the behest of drug traffickers. The files of many drug cases were among those consumed by fire during the assault.

2. Krauze, *Mexico: Biography of Power*, p. xiii.

3. These estimates are from Alexander Von Humboldt, the great German scientist-explorer who travelled widely in Spanish America in 1799–1804. They are quoted in Lynch, John (1986), *The Spanish American Revolutions 1808–1826*, 2nd edition, WW Norton & Company, New York, p. 19.

4. Ibid., p. 2.

5. Ibid., p. 18.

6. Carr, Raymond (ed.) (2000), *Spain: A History*, Oxford, p. 198.

7. Parry, J H, Sherlock, Philip and Maingot, Anthony (1987), *A Short History of the West Indies*, 4th edition, Macmillan, p. 140.

8. France did not recognise Haiti's independence until 1825, and then only after the new state agreed to pay reparations of 150 million francs (later reduced to 60 million); Haiti did not repay the resulting debt until 1922. In January 2004, Haiti's government commemorated the bi-centenary of independence. Jean-Bertrand Aristide, who was to be overthrown shortly afterwards, used the occasion to demand that France repay the reparations which, with interest, he said, amounted to $21.7 billion.

9. Walker, Charles F (1999), *Smoldering Ashes: Cuzco and the Creation of Republican Peru, 1780–1840*, Duke University Press, p. 13.

10. Lynch, *The Spanish American Revolutions*, p. 24.

11. Maxwell, Kenneth (2003), 'Why Was Brazil Different?', in *Naked Tropics: Essays on Empire and Other Rogues*, Routledge, p. 156. See also Wilcken, Patrick (2004), *Empire Adrift*, Bloomsbury.

12. Harvey, Robert (2000), *Liberators: Latin America's Struggle for Independence 1810–1930*, John Murray, Part 4.

13. Bushnell/Macaulay, *The Emergence of Latin America*, p. 59.

14. Fernández-Armesto, *The Americas: A Hemispheric History*, pp. 126–7.

15. Thomas, Hugh (1971), *Cuba or The Pursuit of Freedom*, Eyre & Spotiswoode, pp. 45–56.

16. Ibid., p. 46.

17. *See* Vargas Llosa, *Liberty for Latin America*, pp. 28–9.

18. Quoted in Galeano, *Open Veins of Latin America*, p. 37.

19. Basadre, Jorge (1987), *Peru: Problema y Posibilidad*, 5th edition, Libreria Studium, Lima, p. 281.

20. Panama was a province of Colombia until 1903, when it declared independence in a rebellion inspired by the United States.

21. The author of the phrase was John L O'Sullivan, the young editor of the New York *Morning News*. In 1845 he wrote that the US claim to the Oregon Territory was justified 'by the right of our manifest destiny to overspread and to possess the whole of the continent which Providence has given us for the development of the great experiment of liberty and federated self-government entrusted to us.'

22. Some Latin Americans had long seen the potential for river transport. 'The Mississippi is not more available for commerce than the Paraná; nor do the Ohio, Illinois or Arkansas water a larger or richer territory than the Pilcomayo, Bermejo, Paraguay and so many other great rivers,' noted Domingo Faustino Sarmiento, an Argentine writer and later president, in 1845.

23. 'In the Central Andes, the majority of people traditionally resided above 2,500 metres, where adverse corollaries of altitude include rugged terrain, fragile topography, steep slopes, poor soils, limited farmland, short growing seasons, high winds, aridity, elevated solar radiation, erratic rainfall, precarious nutrition, cold and hypoxia. Hypoxia is the technical term for low oxygen tension due to elevational decrease in barometric pressure. It is a pervasive source of chronic stress on all life ... cold and anoxia oblige people to eat more ... Consequently, it costs measurably more to support life and civilisation in mountains than in lowlands.' Moseley, Michael E (2001), *The Incas and Their Ancestors*, Thames and Hudson, London, p. 27. The author is referring to pre-conquest life, but many of

these factors apply today. Tourists to Cusco or to Lake Titicaca get a brief taste of some of these deprivations.

24. Lewis, Colin M, 'Public Policy and Private Initative: Railway Building in São Paulo 1860–89', University of London, Institute of Latin American Studies Research Papers No. 26, 1991.

25. Sarmiento, Domingo F (1998), *Facundo: or, Civilization and Barbarism*, Penguin Classics, London, p. 9.

26. Bushnell/Macaulay, *The Emergence of Latin America*, p. 53.

27. Lamounier, Bolívar (2005), *Da Independência a Lula: dois séculos de política brasileira*, Augurium Editora, São Paulo, p. 80.

28. Ibid., pp. 43–68.

29. Skidmore, Thomas E (1999), *Brazil: Five Centuries of Change*, Oxford University Press, p. 48.

30. Lynch, John (2006), *Simón Bolívar: A Life*, Yale University Press, p. xi.

31. Bolívar, Simón, *El Libertador*, p. xxx.

32. Bolívar, Simón, 'The Jamaica Letter', in *El Libertador*, p. 23.

33. Lynch, *Simón Bolívar*, p. 77.

34. Colombia's FARC guerrillas and Cuba's communist regime also pay rhetorical obeisance to Bolívar.

35. Lynch, *Simón Bolívar*, p. 304.

36. Lynch, John (2001), *Argentine Caudillo: Juan Manuel de Rosas*, Scholarly Resources, Wilmington, Delaware, p. 72.

37. There were occasional exceptions. In Colombia, a Liberal constitution in 1853 included universal male suffrage and popular election of the Supreme Court. In one province, the Liberals enacted female suffrage, but this was struck down by the Court before it could be implemented. Bushnell/Macaulay, *The Emergence of Latin America*, p. 212. Chile abolished the property qualification (though not the literacy requirement) for voting in 1874 (ibid., p. 237).

38. Shumway, Nicolas (1993), *The Invention of Argentina*, University of California Press, p. 183.

39. Thorp, *Progress, Poverty and Exclusion*, pp. 1–2.

40. *See* Wiarda, *The Soul of Latin America*, Chapter 6.

41. Klein, Herbert S, 'Migração Internacional na História das Américas', in Fausto, Boris (ed.) (1999), *Fazer a América: A Imigração em Massa para a América Latina*, Editora da Universidade de São Paulo, pp. 13–31.

42. Quoted in Krauze, *Mexico: Biography of Power*, pp. 217 and 231.

43. Ibid., p. 219.

44. Not to be confused with Benjamin Constant, a liberal politician of the French revolution after whom the Brazilian was named.

45. For an extraordinary account by an observer of this campaign, *see* da Cunha, Euclides, *Os Sertões*, translated as *Rebellion in the Backlands*, Picador, 1995. Mario Vargas Llosa drew heavily on da Cunha's book in his novel *War of the End of the World*. During the Canudos campaign, the army set up a camp on Monte Favela, a hill overlooking the settlement. As a result, the word *favela* entered the Portuguese language to describe a shantytown.

46. Rock, David (1987), *Argentina 1516–1987: From Spanish Colonization to Alfonsín*,

University of California Press, p. 125.

47. Rock, David (1993), 'Argentina in 1914' in Bethell, Leslie (ed.), *Argentina Since Independence*, Cambridge University Press, p. 117.

48. Data from Carlos Díaz Alejandro, quoted in Rock, 'Argentina in 1914', p. 120.

49. Spiritualism is a long-forgotten doctrine identified with Victor Cousin, a French philosopher. It attempted to reconcile idealism and materialism, Catholicism and rationalist philosophy. It was highly influential both in France and among Latin America's liberal intellectual elite in the late nineteenth century, as freemasonry was to be somewhat later. *See* Wiarda, *The Soul of Latin America*, p. 149.

50. Krauze, *Mexico: Biography of Power*, p. 359.

51. The point is made in Riding, Alan (1985), *Distant Neighbors: A Portrait of the Mexicans*, Knopf, Chapter 9.

52. Knight, Alan (1990), *The Mexican Revolution, Vol. 1: Porfirians, Liberals and Peasants*, University of Nebraska Press, p. 184.

53. Krauze, *Mexico: Biography of Power*, Chapters 14 and 15.

54. Maddison, Angus *et al.* (1992), *The Political Economy of Poverty, Equity and Growth: Brazil and Mexico*, The World Bank and Oxford University Press, p. 6.

55. Haya de la Torre, V R (1985), *El Antiimperialismo y el APRA*, 6th edition, APRA, Lima, p. 1.

56. Cotler, Julio (1995), 'Political Parties and the Problems of Democratic Consolidation in Peru', in Mainwaring, Scott and Scully, Timothy R, *Building Democratic Institutions: Party Systems in Latin America*, Stanford, p. 328.

57. Pike, Frederick B (1969), *The Modern History of Peru*, Praeger, p. 239.

58. Dunkerley, James (1988), *Power in the Isthmus: A Political History of Modern Central America*, Verso, p. 71.

59. Bulmer-Thomas, *The Economic History of Latin America*, p. 201.

60. Skidmore/Smith, *Modern Latin America*, p. 52.

61. I owe this point to Roberto Saba of the Asociación para los Derechos Civiles in Buenos Aires.

62. *See* Dunkerley, James (1984), *Rebellion in the Veins*, Verso, Chapters 1 and 2.

63. The figure comes from a commission of inquiry appointed by the government of Carlos Menem. Reuters, 28 September 1999.

64. In the United States and Russia in the late nineteenth century, rural populist movements arose which challenged some aspects of capitalist development. *See* Conniff, Michael L, 'Introduction: Towards a Comparative Definition of Populism', in Conniff, *Latin American Populism*; see also Chapter 1, note 28.

65. Castañeda, Jorge (1994), *Utopia Unarmed: The Latin American Left After the Cold War*, Vintage Books, p. 43.

66. Drake, Paul W, 'Requiem for Populism', in Conniff, *Latin American Populism*, p. 224.

67. Ibid.

68. Conniff in Conniff, *Latin American Populism*, p. 21.

Chapter 4

1. This was the finding both of the Truth Commission set up under the peace accord and of the Human Rights Office of the Archbishopric of Guatemala. *See* Jonas, Susanne (2000), *Of Centaurs and Doves: Guatemala's Peace Process*, Westview Press, Chapter 1.

2. Schlesinger, Stephen, and Kinzer, Stephen (1982), *Bitter Fruit: The Untold Story of the American Coup in Guatemala*, Sinclair Browne, London, p. 11.

3. Ronald Schneider quoted in ibid., p. 227.

4. Costa Rica had few Indians and, as a result, land was distributed more evenly, rural wages were higher and there were few *haciendas*. Although the franchise was limited, Costa Rica's coffee-growing elite laid the basis of a civilian political system in the late nineteenth century.

5. Bethell, Leslie and Roxborough, Ian, 'Introduction: The postwar conjuncture in Latin America: democracy, labor and the Left', p. 10, in Bethell and Roxborough (eds) (1992), *Latin America Between the Second World War and the Cold War 1944–48*, Cambridge University Press.

6. This paragraph draws on Bethell/Roxborough, *Latin America Between the Second World War and the Cold War*, Introduction, pp. 1–32, and Conclusion, pp. 327–34.

7. Dunkerley, *Power in the Isthmus*, p. 52.

8. Ubico granted United Fruit a second tract of land on the Pacific coast on similar terms.

9. Quoted in Streeter, Stephen M, 'Interpreting the 1954 US Intervention in Guatemala: Realist, Revisionist and Postrevisionist Perspectives', *The History Teacher*, Vol. 34, No. 1, November 2000.

10. Andrew, Christopher and Mitrokhin, Vasili (2006), *The Mitrokhin Archive II: The KGB and the World*, Penguin Books, p. 27.

11. The nickname derived from the Argentine usage of *che* as a frequent interjection.

12. Castañeda, Jorge (1997), *Compañero: The Life and Death of Che Guevara*, Bloomsbury, pp. 64 and 71.

13. Quoted in Schlesinger/Kinzer, *Bitter Fruit*, p. 184.

14. Quoted in Smith, Peter H (1996), *Talons of the Eagle: Dynamics of US-Latin American Relations*, Oxford University Press, p. 20.

15. Smith, Robert Freeman (1986), 'Latin America, the United States and the European Powers 1830–1930', p. 85, in Bethell, Leslie (ed.), *Cambridge History of Latin America*, Vol. IV, c. 1870–1930.

16. Bethell/Roxborough, *Latin America Between the Second World War and the Cold War*, p. 22, footnote.

17. See Chapter 3, note 20.

18. Quoted in Smith, Joseph (1994), *The Spanish–American War*, Longman, p. 28.

19. Smith, R F, 'Latin America, the United States and the European Powers', pp. 95–8.

20. Quoted in ibid., pp. 101–2.

21. McCullough, David (1977), *The Path Between the Seas: The Creation of the Panama Canal, 1870–1914*, Simon & Schuster, p. 384.

22. Quoted in Smith, P H, *Talons of the Eagle*, p. 53.

23. Ibid., p. 63.
24. Smith, R F, 'Latin America, the United States and the European Powers', p. 96.
25. Smith, P H, *Talons of the Eagle*, p. 73.
26. Ibid., p. 100.
27. Smith, R F, 'Latin America, the United States and the European Powers', p. 103.
28. Thomas, *Cuba or The Pursuit of Freedom*, p. 169.
29. Ibid., p. 74.
30. Laviana Cuetos, María Luisa (ed.) (1988), *José Martí*, Ediciones de Cultura Hispanica, Madrid, p. 91.
31. Quoted in Pérez, Louis A (1988), *Cuba Between Reform and Revolution*, Oxford University Press, p. 186.
32. Gott, Richard (2004), *Cuba: A New History*, Yale University Press, Chapter 4.
33. Ibid., p. 134.
34. Szulc, Tad (1986), *Fidel: A Critical Portrait*, Avon Books, New York, p. 203.
35. Ibid., p. 38.
36. For a powerful account of the effectiveness of this police state a dozen years after the revolution *see* Edwards, Jorge (1993), *Persona Non Grata*, Nation Books, New York. Edwards, a writer/diplomat, had been sent to Havana as chargé d'affaires by the Allende government in Chile, and was broadly sympathetic to the revolution.
37. Szulc, *Fidel*, p. 39.
38. Gott, *Cuba*, pp. 195–209.
39. Domínguez, Jorge I, 'US-Latin American Relations During the Cold War and its Aftermath', p. 40, in Bulmer-Thomas, Victor and Dunkerley, James (eds) (1999), *The United States and Latin America: The New Agenda*, Institute of Latin American Studies, University of London and David Rockefeller Center for Latin American Studies, Harvard University.
40. Like Martí, Castro rightly saw the United States as the chief threat to the revolution. But his anti-Americanism may have been given an edge by the Eisenhower administration's support for Batista. Szulc cites a letter from Fidel to Celia Sánchez, his companion, written on 5 June 1958 shortly after a rebel position had been bombed by Batista's air force using US-supplied bombs: 'I have sworn that the Americans will pay very dearly for what they are doing. When this war has ended, a much bigger and greater war will start for me, a war I shall launch against them. I realize that this will be my true destiny.' Szulc, *Fidel*, p. 39.
41. Ibid., p. 150.
42. Skidmore, *Brazil: Five Centuries of Change*, p. 112.
43. Vargas Llosa, Mario (1996), *La Utopía Arcaica: José María Arguedas y Las Ficciones del Indigenismo*, Fondo de Cultura Económica, Mexico, pp. 63–6.
44. Mariátegui, José Carlos (1968), *Siete Ensayos de Interpretación de la Realidad Peruana*, 13th edition, Amauta, Lima, pp. 44–5.
45. *See* Flores Galindo, Alberto (1991), *La Agonía de Mariátegui*, Editorial Revolución, Madrid.
46. Ibid., p. 229.
47. Guevara, Che (1969), *Guerrilla Warfare*, Penguin Books, p. 13.
48. Gillespie, *Soldiers of Perón*, p. 54.

49. 'John Paul's People: A Journey Through the Catholic World', by Stephen Moss, *Guardian*, 5 April 2005.

50. Julia Sweig, an American researcher who had access to the Castro government's archives, provides convincing evidence of this. *See* Sweig, Julia E (2002), *Inside the Cuban Revolution: Fidel Castro and the Urban Underground*, Harvard University Press.

51. Guevara, *Guerrilla Warfare*, p. 14.

52. Gerrasi, John (ed.) (1968), *Venceremos: The Speeches and Writings of Ernesto Che Guevara*, Weidenfeld and Nicholson, p. 137.

53. Andrew/Mitrokhin, *The Mitrokhin Archive II*, p. 31.

54. This paragraph draws on Kryzanek, Michael J (1996), *US–Latin American Relations*, Praeger, pp. 72–6, and Smith, P H, *Talons of the Eagle*, pp. 168–71.

55. Quoted in Andrew/Mitrokhin, *The Mitrokhin Archive II*, p. 28.

56. Ibid., pp. 40–1.

57. The Mitrokhin Archive, cited in this chapter and Chapter 5, is a trove of KGB documents secretly copied over twenty years by Vasili Mitrokhin, a senior KGB archivist, and smuggled out to Britain by the Secret Intelligence Service (MI6) in 1992. Since the original documents have not been released, its contents cannot be independently verified but they are highly plausible.

58. Castañeda, *Compañero*, pp. 58–61.

59. *Observer*, 6 November 2005.

60. Castañeda, *Compañero*, p. xiii.

61. Castañeda, *Utopia Unarmed*, p. 109.

62. Andrew/Mitrokhin, *The Mitrokhin Archive II*, pp. 134–5.

63. *See* Bonner, Raymond (1985), *Weakness and Deceit: US Policy and El Salvador*, Hamish Hamilton, Chapter 3; White, Alastair (1973), *El Salvador: Nation of the Modern World*, Ernest Benn Ltd, Chapter 9.

64. Dinges, John (1990), *Our Man in Panama*, Random House, pp. 299–319.

65. Kempe, Frederick (1990), *Divorcing the Dictator: America's Bungled Affair with Noriega*, G P Putnam's Sons, pp. 418–25.

66. Castañeda, *Utopia Unarmed*, p. 193.

67. Pérez-Stabile, Marifeli (1993), *The Cuban Revolution: Origins, Course and Legacy*, Oxford University Press, Chapter 1.

68. For example, in 1992, Andres Oppenheimer, a journalist for the *Miami Herald*, concluded in a well-reported book on Cuba's travails in this period that Castro's 'final hour may stretch [for] a matter of weeks or … a few years'. At the time, this view was widely shared. Oppenheimer, Andres (1992), *Castro's Final Hour: The Secret Story Behind the Coming Downfall of Communist Cuba*, Simon & Schuster, p. 9.

69. 'Cuba's Economy: Unappetising', *The Economist*, 23 June 2005.

70. Gott, *Cuba: A New History*, p. 322.

71. Telephone interview with the author, December 2005.

Chapter 5

1. There is some doubt as to whether Vargas himself wrote the letter, but it was released to the press immediately after his death and accepted by the public as authentic. *See* Skidmore, Thomas E (1967), *Politics in Brazil 1930–1964*, Oxford University Press, p. 142.
2. Skidmore, *Brazil: Five Centuries of Change*, p. 14.
3. Gaspari, Elio (2002), *A Ditadura Envergonhada*, Companhia das Letras, São Paulo, p. 53.
4. Ibid., p. 92; Gordon, Lincoln (2001), *Brazil's Second Chance: En Route Toward the First World*, Brookings Institution Press, p. 60.
5. Gordon, *Brazil's Second Chance*, p. 52.
6. Gaspari, *A Ditadura Envergonhada*, p. 102.
7. Rouquié (1987), p. 139.
8. Ibid., p. 235.
9. Whitehead, Laurence (1994), 'State Organisations in Latin America Since 1930', p. 37, in Bethell, Leslie (ed.), *The Cambridge History of Latin America*, Vol. VI, Part 2, Cambridge University Press.
10. Rouquié (1987), p. 248.
11. Angell, Alan, 'Chile Since 1958', p. 156, in Bethell, *Chile Since Independence*.
12. Ibid., p. 158.
13. Larraín, Felipe and Meller, Patricio (1991), 'The Socialist-Populist Chilean Experience', pp. 188–9, in Dornbusch/Edwards (eds), *The Macroeconomics of Populism in Latin America*.
14. Ibid., pp. 186–7.
15. Whitehead, 'State Organisations', p. 38.
16. Larraín/Meller, 'The Socialist-Populist Chilean Experience'.
17. Andrew/Mitrokhin, *The Mitrokhin Archive II*, pp. 71–2.
18. Dinges, John and Landau, Saul (1980), *Assassination on Embassy Row*, Writers and Readers, London, pp. 38–41.
19. Andrew/Mitrokhin, *The Mitrokhin Archive II*, Chapter 4.
20. Angell, 'Chile Since 1958', p. 168.
21. Rouquié (1987), p. 240.
22. Prats González, Carlos (1985), *Memorias: Testimonio de un Soldado*, Pehuén Editores, pp. 485–6.
23. Ibid., p. 509.
24. 'The Legacy of a Crushed Dream: Never Again', Ricardo Lagos, *International Herald Tribune*, 11 September 2003.
25. McGuire, James W (1997), *Peronism Without Perón: Unions, Parties and Democracy in Argentina*, Stanford University Press, p. 19.
26. Gillespie, *Soldiers of Perón*, Chapters 1 and 2.
27. Ibid., p. 71.
28. 'El Ultimo Perón', Tomás Eloy Martínez, *El País*, 1 August 2004.
29. Torre, Juan Carlos and de Riz, Liliana (1993), 'Argentina Since 1946', p. 327, in Bethell, *Argentina Since Independence*.
30. Gillespie, *Soldiers of Perón*, p. 223.

31. Torre/de Riz, 'Argentina Since 1946', p. 328.
32. *See* the Commission's Report at www.nuncamas.org
33. Quoted in 'Obituary: Augusto Pinochet', *The Economist*, 16 December 2006.
34. Cited in Rouquié (1987), p. 142.
35. *See* Smith, P H, *Talons of the Eagle*, pp. 199–203.
36. O'Donnell, Guillermo (1997), *Contrapuntos: Ensayos escogidos sobre autoritarismo y democratización*, Paidós, Buenos Aires, pp. 75–6.
37. *See* Lowenthal, Abraham F (ed.) (1975), *The Peruvian Experiment: Continuity and Change Under Military Rule*, Princeton University Press; Matos Mar, José and Mejía, José Manuel (1980), *La Reforma Agraria en el Perú*, Instituto de Estudios Peruanos.
38. Bulmer-Thomas, *The Economic History of Latin America*, p. 283.
39. Ibid., p. 356.
40. Ibid., p. 271.
41. Ibid., p. 364.
42. *See* Kuczynski, Pedro-Pablo (1988), *Latin American Debt*, Johns Hopkins University Press, pp. 45–50; Edwards, Sebastian (1995), *Crisis and Reform in Latin America: From Despair to Hope*, World Bank and Oxford University Press, p. 23.
43. Biglaiser, Glen (2002), *Guardians of the Nation? Economists, Generals and Economic Reform in Latin America*, University of Notre Dame Press, p. 13.
44. Ibid., p. 11.
45. Ibid., p. 10.
46. And to a lesser extent Uruguay's military regime.
47. Biglaiser, *Guardians of the Nation?*, Chapters 3 and 4.

Chapter 6

1. Interview with the author, Buenos Aires, October 2001.
2. Ibid.
3. Interview with the author, reported in 'Argentina's Economy: Down, and Almost Out, in Buenos Aires', *The Economist*, 1 November 2001.
4. 'Argentina: Between the Creditors and the Streets', *The Economist*, 3 January 2002.
5. Interview with Rosendo Fraga, Argentine political analyst, Buenos Aires, March 2004.
6. *Guardian*, 14 January 2004.
7. Green, Duncan (2003), *Silent Revolution: The Rise and Crisis of Market Economics in Latin America*, Monthly Review Press, New York, and Latin American Bureau, London, p. 171.
8. 'Free Trade in the Americas', *International Herald Tribune*, 7 November 2005.
9. 'The Washington Consensus: A Damaged Brand', Moisés Naím, *Financial Times*, 28 October 2002.
10. Véganzones, Marie-Ange with Winograd, Carlos (1997), *Argentina in the 20th Century: An Account of Long-Awaited Growth*, OECD, Chapter 4.
11. According to a study by Andrea Goldstein of the OECD quoted in 'Back on the Pitch: A Survey of Business in Latin America', Reid, Michael, *The Economist*, 6

December 1997, p. 10.

12. World Bank, 'Public Policy for the Private Sector', Note No. 88, September 1996. I am grateful to Andrea Goldstein for this reference.

13. Reid, 'Back on the Pitch', p. 11.

14. Edwards, S, *Crisis and Reform in Latin America*, pp. 97–8.

15. Tountoundjian, Beatriz (1990), 'La Lucha por la Sobrevivencia en la Hiperinflación Argentina', Mimeo, Instituto Fernando Braudel de Economia Mundial, São Paulo.

16. della Paolera, Gerardo and Taylor, Alan M (2001), *Straining at the Anchor: The Argentine Currency Board and the Search for Macroeconomic Stability, 1880–1935*, University of Chicago Press, p. 17.

17. Blustein, Paul (2005), *And the Money Kept Rolling In (and Out): Wall Street, the IMF and the Bankrupting of Argentina*, PublicAffairs, pp. 26 and 35.

18. Ibid., Chapter 3.

19. Mussa, Michael (2002), *Argentina and the Fund: From Triumph to Tragedy*, Institute for International Economics, Washington DC, p. 12.

20. Blustein, *And the Money Kept Rolling In (and Out)*, pp. 131–2.

21. Ibid., pp. 82–6 and 122–3.

22. Statement by President Kirchner on 15 December 2005 announcing early repayment of Argentina's debts to the IMF, at www.presidencia.gov.ar

23. Mussa, *Argentina and the Fund*, p. 7; on the home-grown origins of the currency board *see also* Blustein, *And the Money Kept Rolling In (and Out)*, Chapter 2.

24. Interview with the author, Buenos Aires, March 2004.

25. Interview with the author, Buenos Aires, March 2004.

26. Interview with the author at Inter-American Development Bank annual meeting, Lima, March 2004.

27. Interviews with the author, Buenos Aires, February 2003 and March 2004.

28. 'Argentina: Tucking in to the Good Times', *The Economist*, 23 December 2006.

29. Williamson, John (2004), 'A Short History of the Washington Consensus', paper at www.iie.com/jwilliamson.htm, p. 3.

30. Edwards, S, *Crisis and Reform in Latin America*, p. 24.

31. Thorp, *Progress, Poverty and Exclusion*, p. 332.

32. Carbonetto, Daniel et al. (1987), *El Perú Heterodoxo: un modelo economico*, Instituto Nacional de Planificación, Lima, p. 81.

33. Cited in Edwards, S, *Crisis and Reform in Latin America*, p. 48.

34. Williamson, 'A Short History of the Washington Consensus', p. 6.

35. The list was originally published by Williamson in 'Latin American Adjustment: How Much Has Happened' published by the IIE in 1990.

36. Williamson, 'A Short History of the Washington Consensus', p. 2.

37. Brazil did not conquer inflation until the mid-1990s (*see* Chapter 8).

38. 'Managing International Debt: How One Big Battle Was Won', by invitation by William Cline, *The Economist*, 18 February 1995.

39. Cited in Rajapatirana, Sarath (1997), *Trade Policies in Latin America and the Caribbean: Priorities, Progress and Prospects*, International Center for Economic Growth, Santiago and San Francisco, p. 8.

40. Bouzas, Roberto and Keifman, Saúl, 'Making Trade Liberalisation Work', in

Kuczynski, Pedro-Pablo and Williamson, John (eds) (2003), *After the Washington Consensus: Restarting Growth and Reform in Latin America*, Institute for International Economics, Washington DC, p. 160.

41. Devlin, Robert and Giordano, Paolo, 'The Old and New Regionalism: Benefits, Costs and Implications for the FTAA', in Estevadeordal, Antoni, Rodrik, Dani, Taylor, Alan M and Velasco, Andrés (2004), *Integrating the Americas: The FTAA and Beyond*, Harvard University Press, p. 145.

42. Wise, Carol and Roett, Riordan (eds) (2000), *Exchange Rate Politics in Latin America*, Brookings Institution, p. 1.

43. Aspe Armilla, Pedro (1993), *El camino mexicano de la transformación económica*, Fondo de Cultura Económica, Mexico City, Chapter 5.

44. For details *see* Chapter 8.

45. The term 'sudden stop' was coined by Guillermo Calvo, then the chief economist at the Inter-American Development Bank, with reference to the drying up of capital inflows to Latin America in 1998.

46. Blustein, *And the Money Kept Rolling In (and Out)*, p. 78.

47. José Antonio Ocampo, CEPAL's secretary general at the time, points out that low growth lasted for six years, from 1998 to 2003 inclusive. *See* Ocampo, José Antonio (2004), *Reconstruir el futuro: Globalización, desarrollo y democracia en América Latina*, Editorial Norma, Bogotá, p. 18, footnote.

48. Edwards, S, *Crisis and Reform in Latin America*, p. 205.

49. Ibid., pp. 203–4.

50. Like Argentina under its currency board, Ecuador has renounced an independent monetary and exchange-rate policy. Its non-oil exporters risk becoming uncompetitive in relation to rivals in neighbouring countries if those countries devalue their currencies.

51. 'Oversold: The World Bank Changes Its Tune on Latin America's Privatised Pensions', *The Economist*, 23 September 2004.

52. Visit by the author, April 1980.

53. Nellis, John, Menezes, Rachel and Lucas, Sarah, 'Privatization in Latin America', Center for Global Development and Inter-American Dialogue Policy Brief, Washington DC, January 2004, Vol. 3, Issue 1.

54. 'Bolivia: Water, Oil and the Mob', *The Economist*, 20 January 2005.

55. 'Bolivians Find that Post-multinational Life Has Its Problems', Juan Forero *International Herald Tribune*, 15 December 2005.

56. Peet, John, 'Priceless: A Survey of Water', *The Economist*, 19 July 2003.

57. Galiani, Sebastián *et al.*, 'The Benefits and Costs of Privatization in Argentina: A Microeconomic Analysis', in Chong, Alberto and López-de-Silanes, Florencio (2005), *Privatization in Latin America: Myths and Reality*, World Bank and Stanford University Press, Chapter 2.

58. Chong/López-de-Silanes, *Privatization in Latin America*, p. 5.

59. Interview with the author, Mexico City, October 1997.

60. Chong/López-de-Silanes, *Privatization in Latin America*, Chapter 1.

61. Ibid.

62. *Veja*, 1 November 2006.

63. Edwards, S, *Crisis and Reform in Latin America*, p. 199.

64. Galiani, S et al., 'The Benefits and Costs of Privatisation in Argentina', pp. 97–8.
65. Chong/López-de-Silanes, *Privatization in Latin America*, p. 27.
66. In addition to its telecoms interests, Slim's family controlled industrial, retailing and infrastructure businesses and a bank. *See* 'Time to Wake Up: A Survey of Mexico', Reid, Michael, *The Economist*, 18 November 2006.
67. *Veja*, 13 September 2000.
68. Inter-American Development Bank (2001), 'Competitiveness: The Business of Growth', p. 179.
69. Quoted in Chong/López-de-Silanes, *Privatization in Latin America*, p. 51.
70. Nellis et al., 'Privatization in Latin America'.
71. Nellis, John and Birdsall, Nancy (eds) (2005), *Reality Check: The Distributional Impact of Privatization in Developing Countries*, Center for Global Development, Washington DC, p. 26.
72. *See* 'The Latinobarómetro Poll: Democracy's Ten-Year Rut', *The Economist*, 27 October 2005; 'The Latinobarómetro Poll: The Democracy Dividend', *The Economist*, 9 December 2006.
73. Lora, Eduardo and Panizza, Ugo, 'Structural Reform in Latin America Under Scrutiny', Inter-American Development Bank Research Department paper, March 2002, p. 7.
74. Edwards, S, *Crisis and Reform in Latin America*, p. 194.
75. International Finance Corporation, 'Doing Business in 2005', available at www.doingbusiness.org
76. Ocampo, *Reconstruir el futuro*, pp. 29–31.
77. Ibid., p. 24.
78. Lora/Panizza, 'Structural Reform in Latin America Under Scrutiny', Section 3.
79. Ocampo, *Reconstruir el futuro*, p. 43.
80. *El País*, 6 November 2005.
81. Interview with the author, Milan, March 2003.
82. Williamson, John (2003), 'Overview: An Agenda for Restarting Growth and Reform', in Kuczynski/Williamson (eds), *After the Washington Consensus*.
83. ECLAC, Economic Survey of Latin America and the Caribbean, various years; Thorp, *Progress, Poverty and Exclusion*, p. 332.
84. Lora/Panizza, 'Structural Reform in Latin America Under Scrutiny'; ECLAC, Preliminary Balance of the Economies of Latin America and the Caribbean, 2005, Santiago. Average weighted by size of economies.
85. *Financial Times*, 22 June 2005.
86. *See* Eichengreen, Barry and Hausmann, Ricardo (2003), 'Original Sin and the Road to Redemption', paper available at http://ksghome.harvard.edu
87. Williamson, 'A Short History of the Washington Consensus', p. 5.
88. Stiglitz, Joseph E (2002), *Globalization and Its Discontents*, W W Norton, New York and London, Chapter 3.
89. Naím, Moisés (1993), *Paper Tigers and Minotaurs: The Politics of Venezuela's Economic Reforms*, Carnegie Endowment for International Peace, Washington DC, p. 141.
90. *See*, for example, Santiso, *Latin America's Political Economy of the Possible*.
91. Stiglitz, *Globalization and Its Discontents*, p. 53.

92. Equity was not seen as particularly important in Washington in 1989, Williamson wrote later. Williamson, 'A Short History of the Washington Consensus', p. 8, footnote.

93. *See* Birdsall, Nancy and de la Torre, Augusto with Menezes, Rachel (2001), 'Washington Contentious: Economic Policies for Social Equity in Latin America', Carnegie Endowment for International Peace and Inter-American Dialogue.

94. ECLAC/CEPAL, Social Panorama of Latin America, 2006.

95. Data at www.worldbank.org/lacpoverty

96. World Bank (2004).

97. World Bank (2006a), pp. 26–7.

98. Birdsall *et al.*, 'Washington Contentious'.

99. World Bank (2006a), p. xi.

100. ECLAC/CEPAL, Social Panorama of Latin America, 2005, p. 117.

101. World Bank (2006a), p. 5. The GINI coefficient is a measure of the inequality of a statistical distribution; when applied to income distribution, 1 indicates absolute inequality (i.e. one person would hold all the income) and zero would indicate absolute equality (everyone would have the same income).

102. Interview with Luis Alberto Moreno, president of the Inter-American Development Bank, Paris, January 2006.

103. Fundação Getúlio Vargas, Centro de Politicas Sociais and UNDP International Poverty Centre, 'Crescimento Pró-Pobre: O Paradoxo Brasileiro', paper available at www.fgv.br/cps/pesquisas/propobre

104. Data collected for the World Bank. The author thanks Michael Walton for sharing this with him.

Chapter 7

1. Marcano, Cristina and Barrera Tyszka, Alberto (2005), *Hugo Chávez Sin Uniforme: Una Historia Personal*, Debate, Caracas.

2. This point was first made to me by the late Janet Kelly, a political economist at the IESA business school, interview in Caracas, October 1999. The comparison is also made by Marcano and Barrera.

3. In a speech to several hundred officials and political cadres in November 2004, Chávez said: 'I want you to know that in this new stage, he who is with me is with me, he who is is not with me is against me. I don't accept half-tones.' 'El Nuevo Mapa Estratégico: Intervenciones de Hugo Chávez Frias, 12 y 13 de Noviembre, 2004', available at www.emancipacion.org

4. García Márquez, Gabriel, 'El Enigma de los dos Chávez', *Revista Cambio*, February 1999, available at www.voltairenet.org

5. Petkoff, Teodoro, 'Prólogo' to Marcano/Barrera, *Hugo Chávez Sin Uniforme*, p. 10.

6. Gott, Richard (2005), *Hugo Chávez and the Bolivarian Revolution*, Verso, p. 3.

7. 'Nueva Izquierda?', Carlos Fuentes, *Reforma* (Mexico), 1 February 2006.

8. Interview with the author, Caracas, April 2005.

9. McCoy, Jennifer L and Myers, David J (eds) (2004), *The Unraveling of Representative Democracy in Venezuela*, Johns Hopkins University Press, Introduction, p. 3.

10. Gall, Norman, 'Desordem venezuelana afeta petróleo', *O Estado de São Paulo*, 5 February 2006.
11. Maddison, *The World Economy*; Naím, *Paper Tigers and Minotaurs*, p. 19.
12. Thorp, *Progress, Poverty and Exclusion*, p. 317.
13. The term was coined after the discovery of natural-gas deposits in the North Sea prompted the Dutch guilder to revalue in the 1970s.
14. In the two decades after 1982, Venezuela recorded an aggregate current-account surplus of more than $50 billion. In normal circumstances, that should have strengthened the currency. In fact, by 2002 the bolívar was worth just 1 per cent of its value of January 1983. *See* Ortíz, Nelson, 'Entrepreneurs: Profits Without Power?', in McCoy/Myers, *The Unraveling of Representative Democracy*, p. 79.
15. Little, Walter and Herrera, Antonio, 'Political Corruption in Venezuela', p. 270, in Little, Walter and Posada-Carbó, Eduardo (eds) (1996), *Political Corruption in Europe and Latin America*, Macmillan.
16. For the strengths and weaknesses of the Punto Fijo system, *see* McCoy/Myers, *The Unraveling of Representative Democracy*, and Philip, George (2003), *Democracy in Latin America*, Polity Press, Chapter 8.
17. Torres, Gerver (2001), *Un Sueño para Venezuela*, Banco Venezolano de Credito, p. 36; Naím, *Paper Tigers and Minotaurs*, p. 37. The fall in government oil revenues per head was partly the consequence of a growing population, as migrants flooded in, especially from Colombia and Peru, but it was also because of the government policy of pursuing a higher oil price rather than increased production.
18. Naím, *Paper Tigers and Minotaurs*, Chapter 2.
19. Inauguration covered by the author.
20. Philip, *Democracy in Latin America*, p. 142.
21. 'Ex-President Perez Set to Return in Caracas Poll', report by the author in the *Guardian*, 3 December 1988.
22. Naim, *Paper Tigers and Minotaurs*, p. 28.
23. Ibid., p. 39.
24. *See* López Maya, Margarita, 'The Venezuelan Caracazo of 1989: Popular Protest and Institutional Weakness', *Journal of Latin American Studies*, Vol. 35, Part 1, February 2003.
25. Ibid., p. 130. Others have cited figures of over a thousand dead, but without any hard evidence.
26. Quoted in García Márquez, Gabriel, 'El Engima de los dos Chávez'.
27. For Chávez's early life, *see* Marcano/Barrera, *Hugo Chávez Sin Uniforme*.
28. Ibid., p. 153.
29. Ibid., p. 118.
30. Ibid., pp. 125–6.
31. Naím, *Paper Tigers and Minotaurs*, p. 118.
32. Marcano/Barrera, *Hugo Chávez Sin Uniforme*, p. 151.
33. Palma, Pedro A, 'La Economía Venezolana en el Quinquenio 1994–1998: de una crisis a otra', *Nueva Economía*, Año VIII, No. 12, April 1999, Caracas, pp. 99–104.
34. Venezuela had had three short-lived republics during the independence struggle. The fourth dated from 1830. Richard Gott suggests that the notion of a 'Fifth

Republic' may have echoed the millenarian idea of a 'Fifth Monarchy' led by saints after those of Babylon, Persia, Greece and Rome. Gott, *Hugo Chávez and the Bolivarian Revolution*, p. 136.

35. Ibid., p. 13.
36. 'Venezuela: On Troubled Waters', *The Economist*, 7 March 2002.
37. 'Venezuela's Crisis: Towards the Endgame', *The Economist*, 11 April 2002.
38. Marcano/Barrera, *Hugo Chávez Sin Uniforme*, pp. 245–6. The opposition blamed the attack on the demonstration on members of the Bolivarian Circles. The government claimed that the killings were the work of opposition agents provocateurs but it used its majority in the National Assembly to block the appointment of a truth commission on the events of 11 April 2002.
39. Marcano/Barrera, *Hugo Chávez Sin Uniforme*, p. 248; Gott, *Hugo Chávez and the Bolivarian Revolution*, p. 227.
40. Marcano/Barrera, *Hugo Chávez Sin Uniforme*, p. 259.
41. Interview with Hugo Chávez, *Newsweek*, 10 October 2005.
42. 'U.S. Strongly Opposes Venezuelan Coup', *Associated Press*, 27 February 2002.
43. 'El Nuevo Mapa Estratégico'. Chávez went on: 'So that's when we decided to work on the missions, we designed the first one here and I began to ask for help from Fidel.'
44. 'Venezuela: Mission Impossible', *The Economist*, 16 February 2006.
45. Ibid.
46. 'By Invitation: What Really Happened in Venezuela?', Jennifer McCoy, *The Economist*, 2 September 2004.
47. Interview with the author, Caracas, April 2005.
48. Visit by the author, April 2005.
49. Lapper, Richard (2006), 'Living with Hugo: U.S. Policy Towards Hugo Chávez's Venezuela', Council on Foreign Relations, New York, November 2006, p. 12.
50. ECLAC/CEPAL, Economic Survey of Latin America and the Caribbean, 2005–6.
51. Economist Intelligence Unit (2006), Venezuela Country Report, December 2006, London.
52. *New York Times*, 30 October 2005.
53. 'Vuelvan Caras Mission: 2 Years of Achievements', *Ven-Global News*, 20 March 2006, Ministry of Information's website, www.mci.gob.ve
54. Quoted in Lapper, 'Living with Hugo', p. 15.
55. 'Hugo Boss', Javier Corrales, *Foreign Policy*, January–February 2006, p. 38.
56. Gall, Norman, 'Chávez sobreviverá à desordem?', *O Estado de São Paulo*, 22 January 2006.
57. 'Venezuela: Crimes and Misdemeanours', *The Economist*, 20 April 2006.
58. 'Venezuela: The Sickly Stench of Corruption', *The Economist*, 30 March 2006; Gall, 'Chávez sobreviverá à desordem?'.
59. Lapper, 'Living with Hugo', p. 27. Because much of it is heavy and sulphurous, Venezuela's oil sells for around $10 less per barrel than Brent or West Texas Intermediate.
60. Economist Intelligence Unit (2006).
61. 'El Nuevo Mapa Estratégico'.
62. Interview with the author.

63. 'Hugo Chávez's Venezuela: Oil, Missions and a Chat Show', *The Economist*, 21 May 2005.
64. 'The Latinobarómetro Poll: The Democracy Dividend', *The Economist*, 9 December 2006.
65. Corrales, 'Hugo Boss'.
66. This point is made in different ways by both Yepes and Gall.

Chapter 8

1. Visits by the author, January 1986 and January 2005.
2. Interview with Nicolás Eyzaguirre, finance minister, Santiago, January 2005.
3. Bosworth, Barry P, Dornbusch, Rudiger and Labán, Raúl (eds) (1994), *The Chilean Economy: Policy Lessons and Challenges*, The Brookings Institution, Washington DC, p. 23.
4. Dornbusch, Rudiger and Edwards, Sebastian, 'Exchange Rate Policy and Trade Strategy', in ibid., p. 81.
5. Solimano, Andrés, 'The Chilean Economy in the 1990s: On a "Golden Age" and Beyond', in Taylor, Lance (ed.) (1999), *After Neoliberalism: What Next for Latin America?*, University of Michigan Press, p. 115.
6. Interview with the author, Santiago, January 2005.
7. Lagos, Ricardo (2003), *Conversaciones en el Camino*, Ediciones B, Santiago, pp. 48–9.
8. Speech to the Third Ministerial Conference of the Community of Democracies, Santiago, April 2005, reproduced in Lagos, Ricardo (2005), *The 21st Century: A View from the South*, First, London, p. 55.
9. Interview with Vittorio Corbo, Central Bank president, Santiago, January 2005.
10. *Financial Times*, 6 May 2006.
11. Angell, Alan, 'Democratic Governability in Chile', unpublished paper supplied to the author.
12. Solimano, 'The Chilean Economy in the 1990s', p. 123; SalmonChile (undated), *La Acuicultura en Chile*, TechnoPress SA, Santiago, Chapter 1.
13. Interview with the author, Santiago, January 2005.
14. World Economic Forum, press release, 28 September 2005, Geneva.
15. According to Ricardo Lagos, interview with the author, Santiago, January 2005.
16. Ibid.
17. Interview with the author, Santiago, January 2005.
18. 'Chile: Testing times for Michelle Bachelet', *The Economist*, 24 June 2006.
19. Speech to the Community of Democracies in Lagos, *The 21st Century*, p. 54.
20. *See* Sola, Lourdes and Whitehead, Laurence (2006), *Statecrafting Monetary Authority: Democracy and Financial Order in Brazil*, Centre for Brazilian Studies, University of Oxford, Introduction pp. 1–11.
21. Cardoso, Fernando Henrique (2006), *A Arte da Política: A História que Vivi*, Civilização Brasileira, Rio de Janeiro, p. 140.
22. The term was coined by Guillermo O'Donnell. *See* Chapter 11, p. 283.
23. Weyland, Kirk, 'The Brazilian State in the New Democracy', in Kingstone, Peter R and Power, Timothy J (eds) (2000), *Democratic Brazil: Actors, Institutions and*

Processes, University of Pittsburgh Press, p. 40.

24. Cardoso, *A Arte da Política*, p. 108.
25. Lamounier, *Da Independência a Lula*, p. 258.
26. Power, Timothy, 'Political Institutions in Democratic Brazil: Politics as a Permanent Constitutional Convention', in Kingstone/Power, *Democratic Brazil*, p. 21.
27. Much of the political science literature on Brazil published in the second half of the 1990s was deeply pessimistic even as the country's prospects were being transformed. That was because it was based on fieldwork conducted during the 1980s or early 1990s.
28. Cardoso/Winter, *The Accidental President*, pp. 175–7.
29. Ibid., p. 180.
30. Cardoso, *A Arte da Política*, p. 141.
31. Ibid., p. 208.
32. World Bank (2006e), p. 140.
33. Cardoso/Winter, *The Accidental President*, p. 167; Cardoso, *A Arte da Política*, pp. 130–5.
34. Lamounier, *Da Independência a Lula*, p. 205.
35. Ibid., p. 213.
36. 'Brazil: Inactive Workers, Inactive Congress', *The Economist*, 27 June 1997; 'Reforming Brazil: Is it for Real', *The Economist*, 17 May 1997.
37. Study by IPEA, a government-backed think-tank, cited in Cardoso, Eliana, 'Brazil's Currency Crisis: The Shift from an Exchange Rate Anchor to a Flexible Regime', in Wise/Roett, *Exchange Rate Politics in Latin America*, p. 72.
38. ECLAC/CEPAL, Panorama Social de América Latina, 2005, p. 130. Some of this increase was gobbled up by pensions.
39. Interview with the author, Brasília, March 1999.
40. Cardoso, Eliana, *Brazil's Currency Crisis*, p. 76.
41. Cardoso, *A Arte da Política*, pp. 388 and 415.
42. Cardoso, Eliana, *Brazil's Currency Crisis*, pp. 70 and 82.
43. Cardoso, *A Arte da Política*, pp. 363–6.
44. 'Brazil 2015: A Reform Agenda', presentation by Armando Castelar Pinheiro, IDB, Washington DC, 4 October 2005.
45. Cardoso, *A Arte da Política*, pp. 12–13.
46. 'Brazil's Presidential Election: The Meaning of Lula', *The Economist*, 3 October 2002.
47. This anecdote was told to the author by Julio María Sanguinetti, a former president of Uruguay.
48. 'Poor Man's Burden', Barry Bearak, *New York Times Magazine*, 27 June 2004.
49. Having governed it for the best part of two decades, in 2004 the PT lost an election for mayor of Porto Alegre to José Fogaça, a PMDB member and supporter of Cardoso.
50. 'Brazil's Presidential Election: From Pauper to President', *The Economist*, 31 January 2002.
51. Meeting attended by the author, London, September 2003.
52. 'Brazil: Love Lula if You're Poor, Worry if You're Not', *The Economist*, 30 September 2006.

53. Interview with *The Economist*, 24 February 2006.

54. Ibid.

55. Palocci resigned after an aide admitted leaking details of the bank account of the caretaker at a house in Brasília rented by several of the minister's former associates from Ribeirão Preto. The leak was an attempt to smear the caretaker, who had contradicted the minister's testimony to a Congressional committee that he had not visited the house. *See* 'Corruption in Brazil: House Calls', *The Economist*, 23 March 2006.

56. *See* Hunter, Wendy and Power, Timothy J (forthcoming), 'Rewarding Lula: Executive Power, Social Policy, and the Brazilian Elections of 2006', *Latin American Politics and Society*.

57. Data from Instituto de Pesquisa Econômica Aplicada (IPEA), available at www.ipeadata.gov.br

58. In March 2007 Brazil's statistics institute issued a new set of national accounts that measure the contribution of services to GDP more accurately. Under the old methodology, annual average growth during Lula's first term was 2.6 per cent, only slightly higher than in the Cardosa period. Where possible, this chapter uses the new GDP figures.

59. World Bank (2006e), p. 74.

60. Cardoso, *A Arte da Política*, p. 168.

61. Thomas, Hugh (1993), *The Conquest of Mexico*, Pimlico, pp. 296–8.

62. Krauze, *Mexico: Biography of Power*, p. 697.

63. Poniatowska, Elena (1992), *La noche de Tlatelolco*, Ediciones Era, Mexico City, p. 170.

64. Author's translation. The poem was written especially for a book of interviews with survivors prepared by Elena Poniatowska, a young journalist who would later become one of Mexico's best-known writers, and which when it was published in 1971 made the first dent in the regime's wall of silence concerning the massacre. Poniatowska, *La noche de Tlatelolco*, p. 163.

65. Krauze, *Mexico: Biography of Power*, pp. 736–7.

66. Ibid., p. 681.

67. Ibid., p. 743.

68. Preston, Julia and Dillon, Samuel (2005), *Opening Mexico: The Making of a Democracy*, Farrar, Strauss and Giroux, Chapter 4; Aguilar Camín, Héctor (2004), *Después del milagro*, 16th edition, Ediciones Cal y Arena, Mexico City, Chapter 1.

69. Preston/Dillon, *Opening Mexico*, Chapter 6. In 1994, Arturo Nuñez, the head of the IFE, admitted that the computer system had been forced to fail. *See* Domínguez, Jorge I and McCann, James A (1996), *Democratizing Mexico: Public Opinion and Electoral Choices*, Johns Hopkins University Press, pp. 151–2.

70. Interview with the author, Mexico City, July 1992.

71. Preston/Dillon, *Opening Mexico*, p. 481.

72. Congress covered by author. *See* 'Mexico: Ring In the Old', *The Economist*, 14March 1993.

73. Preston/Dillon, *Opening Mexico*, p. 219.

74. Gómez Tagle, Silvia, 'Public Institutions and Electoral Transparency', p. 89, in

Middlebrook, Kevin J (2004), *Dilemmas of Political Change in Mexico*, Institute of Latin American Studies, London, and Center for US–Mexican Studies, San Diego.

75. Interview with the author, Mexico City, July 1991.
76. Interview with the author, Mexico City, July 1991.
77. 'Mexico: Salt of the Earth', *The Economist*, 19 October 1991.
78. 'The Clash in Mexico' and 'Mexico: The Revolution Continues', *The Economist*, 22 January 1994.
79. Preston/Dillon, *Opening Mexico*, pp. 245–50.
80. Haber, Stephen, 'Why Institutions Matter: Banking and Economic Growth in Mexico', paper available at www.stanford.edu/~haber/papers; World Bank (2001), p. 242.
81. Interview with the author, Mexico City, September 2006.
82. Preston/Dillon, *Opening Mexico*, p. 261.
83. Rubio, Luis and Kaufman Purcell, Susan (1998), *Mexico Under Zedillo*, Lynne Rienner, Boulder, Colorado, p. 14.
84. Preston/Dillon, *Opening Mexico*, p. 305.
85. *Financial Times*, 15 June 2005; *El País*, 26 June 2005. Raúl Salinas claimed in an interview with the *Financial Times* in 2005 that the money was an 'investment fund' that he was managing for a group of Mexican businessmen, but he gave no explanation as to why it was held in private Swiss accounts.
86. The following paragraphs draw on Reid, 'Time to Wake Up'.
87. Press conference attended by the author, Mexico City, May 2005; 'Mexico: Will the Real Andrés Manuel López Obrador Please Stand Up?', *The Economist*, 28 May 2006.
88. 'Triunfo ciudadano', Manuel Camacho Solís, *El Universal*, Mexico City, 3 July 2006.
89. The tribunal criticised Fox and the businessmen for their campaign interventions, though it is hard to imagine these would have provoked comment in many other countries.
90. Interview with the author, Mexico City, September 2006.
91. Interview with the author, Mexico City, September 2006.

Chapter 9

1. Raffo, Emma (1985), *Vivir en Huáscar: Mujer y Estrategias de Sobrevivencia*, Fundación Friedrich Ebert, Lima.
2. 'Peru: The Problems of Staying Alive', *Sunday Times Magazine*, 12 November 1972.
3. Raffo, *Vivir en Huáscar*.
4. World Bank (2006b), p. 51.
5. Data from Pan-American Health Organisation.
6. Visits by the author in the 1980s, December 2004 and March 2006.
7. 'Peru: Go North, Limeño', *The Economist*, 13 May 2004.
8. Interview with Carlos Neuhaus, director of Megaplaza, November 2006.
9. Interview, San Juan de Lurigancho, March 2006.
10. Raffo, Emma and Alva, Maritza (2006), 'Re-encuentro con muejeres y families

pobres en un pueblo joven de Lima', unpublished manuscript.

11. *Financial Times*, 15 April 2006.
12. ECLAC Notes, No. 47, August 2006.
13. World Bank (2006b), Chapter 23.
14. Interview, San Juan de Lurigancho, March 2006.
15. Interview with Ana María and Sonia Chuquimango, teachers, San Juan de Lurigancho, March 2006.
16. Matos Mar, *Desborde Popular y Crisis del Estado*, p. 78.
17. de Soto, *El Otro Sendero*.
18. Interview with the author, San Juan de Lurigancho, December 2004.
19. Information from Sir Peter Heap, then the British ambassador to Brazil.
20. *O Estado de São Paulo*, 22 December 2006.
21. Guedes, Patricia Mota and Oliveira, Nilson Vieira (2006), 'Democratization of consumption', Braudel Papers No. 38, Fernand Braudel Institute of World Economics, São Paulo.
22. Perlman, Janice E, 'The Metamorphosis of Marginality: The Favelas of Rio de Janeiro 1969–2002', summary available at http://www.worldbank.org/urban/upgrading/meta.html
23. ECLAC, Statistical Year Book 2005.
24. Interview with the author, Rio de Janeiro, January 1999.
25. Cardoso, *A Arte da Política*, p. 510.
26. Unpublished data supplied to the author by the World Bank.
27. Quoted in 'Nation Set to Earn Its Way Out of Shadows', *Financial Times*, 9 May 2007.
28. Guedes/Oliveira, 'Democratization of consumption'.
29. Galeano, *Open Veins of Latin America*, p. 251.
30. *See* Chapter 2.
31. Interview with the author, El Alto, January 2004.
32. This paragraph draws on Inter-American Development Bank, 'Development Bryond Economics'.
33. Inter-American Development Bank (2006c), 'Remittances as a Development Tool'.
34. World Bank (2006d).
35. Reid, 'Time to Wake Up'.
36. International Labour Organization, *Panorama Laboral 2006*, America Latina y el Caribe, Oficina Regional, Lima.
37. Maloney, William, 'Informality Revisited', *World Development*, Vol. 32, Issue 7, 2004.
38. World Bank (2003), p. 28.
39. Interview with the author, Quito, January 2004.
40. World Bank (1994).
41. Sieder, Rachel (ed.) (2002), *Multiculturalism in Latin America: Indigenous Rights, Diversity and Democracy*, Palgrave, Introduction.
42. Yashar, Deborah J (2005), *Contesting Citizenship: The Rise of Indigenous Movements and the Postliberal Challenge*, Cambridge University Press, Chapters 2 and 3.
43. ECLAC, Current Situation of Indigenous and Afro-American Peoples in Latin

America, July 2000.
44. Marx, *Making Race and Nation*, pp. 164–77.
45. *Gazeta Mercantil*, 28 April 1998.
46. *Newsweek*, 9 March 1998.
47. Marx, *Making Race and Nation*, Chapter 10.
48. Cardoso/Winter, *The Accidental President*, pp. 252–3.
49. *Veja*, 14 May 2003.
50. World Bank (2005a).
51. In the early 2000s, the prosperity of the coffee belt was threatened by a plunge in coffee prices, partly because of large-scale planting in Vietnam; prices have since recovered.
52. 'Brazil's Landless Movement: A Thin Red Line', *The Economist*, 19 May 2005.
53. Cardoso, *A Arte da Política*, pp. 529–41.
54. Visit by the author, July 1997.
55. *See* Chapter 4.
56. Lehmann, David (1996), *The Struggle for the Spirit: Religious Transformation and Popular Culture in Brazil and Latin America*, Polity Press, Introduction.
57. Ibid., pp. 17 and 11.
58. 'Pentecostals: Christianity Reborn', *The Economist*, 23 December 2006.
59. Véliz, *The New World of the Gothic Fox*, p. 53.
60. Figures from www.internetworldstats.com
61. *See* Chapter 7.
62. 'The Latinobarómetro Poll: The Democracy Dividend', *The Economist*, 9 December 2006.

Chapter 10

1. Interview with the author, Mexico City, September 2006.
2. Concejo Nacional de Evaluación de la Politica de Desarrollo Social, bulletin, 1 October 2006.
3. *See* Parker, Susan W, Behrman, Jere R and Todd, Petra E, 'The Longer-Term Impacts of Mexico's Oportunidades School Subsidy Programme on Educational Attainment, Cognitive Achievement and Work', April 2005, unpublished paper.
4. Santiago Levy, interview with the author, Mexico City, September 2006.
5. For more on *Bolsa Família*, *see* Chapter 8.
6. 'The Long Road Back: A Survey of Argentina', Reid, Michael, *The Economist*, 5 June 2004, p. 7.
7. Interview with the author, Santiago, January 2005.
8. Interview with the author, Santiago, January 2005.
9. Whitehead, 'State Organisations in Latin America Since 1930', p. 77.
10. Interview with the author, Mexico City, September 2006.
11. Reid, 'Time to Wake Up'.
12. Speech to the Permanent Council of the Organisation of American States, 14 June 2000.
13. Whitehead, 'State Organisations in Latin America Since 1930', p. 17.
14. The concept of 'patrimonialism' was used by Max Weber to refer to a form of

traditional authority in which an administration and a military force are 'purely personal instruments' of a ruler or, by extension, of powerful individuals. *See* Weber, Max (1978), *Economy and Society*, Vol. 1, University of California Press, p. 231.

15. Paz, Octavio, 'The Philanthropic Ogre', in Paz, *The Labyrinth of Solitude*, p. 397.
16. This point was made by Guillermo O'Donnell in a talk at the London School of Economics, April 2004.
17. Whitehead, 'State Organisations in Latin America Since 1930', p. 36.
18. Ibid., p. 12.
19. Lora, Eduardo (2006), 'State Reform in Latin America: A Silent Revolution' in Lora, Eduardo (ed.), *The State of State Reform in Latin America*, Inter-American Development Bank and Stanford University Press, p. 5.
20. This paragraph draws on Lora, 'State Reform in Latin America'.
21. World Bank (2004), pp. 251–5.
22. Ibid., p. 252.
23. OECD: Mexico, OECD Economic Surveys, Vol. 2005/18, November 2005.
24. Lora, Eduardo, 'Trends and Outcomes of Tax Reform', in Lora, *The State of State Reform in Latin America*, p. 197 (table).
25. Inter-American Development Bank (2006), pp. 65–73.
26. Lora, *The State of State Reform in Latin America*, p. 17.
27. *Veja*, 7 February 2007; similar criticisms were made in the Brazilian and foreign press by several other retired diplomats.
28. The Ceará reforms are the subject of Tendler, Judith (1997), *Good Government in the Tropics*, Johns Hopkins University Press, Baltimore and London.
29. Ibid., p. 9.
30. Author's interview with Sylvia Montenegro, director of the Ceará Public Health School, Fortaleza, December 1996. Information in this paragraph from interviews in Fortaleza in December 1996, Tendler, *Good Government in the Tropics* and World Bank (2006e), pp. 52–5.
31. Information in this paragraph from interviews in Fortaleza in December 1996, Tendler, *Good Government in the Tropics*, and World Bank (2006e), pp. 52–5.
32. ECLAC/CEPAL, Social Panorama of Latin America, 2002–3, pp. 174–9; ibid., 2005, pp. 117–19.
33. World Bank (2004), p. 271.
34. Visit by the author, January 2004.
35. PREAL (2005), 'Quantity without Quality: A Report Card on Education in Latin America', Partnership for Educational Revitalisation in Latin America, Washington DC, 2005, p. 11.
36. UNESCO (2006), Regional Overview: Latin America and the Caribbean, Education for All, Global Monitoring Report, p. 7.
37. Interview with the author, Mexico City, September 2006.
38. Wolff, Laurence and de Mora Castro, Claudio, 'Education and Training: The Task Ahead', in Kuczynski/Williamson, *After the Washington Consensus*, p. 193.
39. World Bank (2003), p. 28.
40. PREAL, 'Quantity without Quality'.
41. This paragraph draws on Wolff/de Mora Castro, 'Education and Training'; PREAL,

'Quantity without Quality', p. 6; and 'Education in Latin America: Cramming Them In', *The Economist*, 9 May 2002.

42. Interview with the author, San Juan de Lurigancho, March 2006.
43. Author's interview with Richard Webb, Lima, March 2006.
44. Interview with the author, Oaxaca, September 2006.
45. Wolff/de Mora Castro, 'Education and Training', pp. 191–2.
46. Author's interview with José Joaquín Brunner, Chilean educationalist, Santiago, January 2005;Wolff/de Mora Castro, 'Education and Training', p. 202.
47. Interview with the author, Santiago Tlazoyaltepec, September 2006.
48. 'Violence Against Women in Ciudad Juárez', Washington Office on Latin America, www.wola.org, updated 22 December 2006.
49. Interview with the author, Ciudad Juárez, May 2005.
50. Morrison, Andrew, Buvinic, Mayra and Shifter, Michael, 'The Violent Americas: Risk Factors, Consequences, and Policy Implications of Social and Domestic Violence', in Fruhling, Hugo, and Tulchin, Joseph S (2003), *Crime and Violence in Latin America: Citizen Security, Democracy and the State*, Johns Hopkins University Press, Baltimore and London, p. 93; Pan-American Health Organisation, Mortality Indicators, available at www.paho.org; World Health Organization (2002), World Report on Violence and Health, summary, p. 7.
51. 'Crime and Policing in Latin America: The Battle for Safer Streets', *The Economist*, 30 September 2004.
52. Amnesty International press release, 9 June 2005.
53. 'The Latinobarómetro Poll: The Democracy Divided', *The Economist*, 9 December 2006.
54. Author's interview with Javed Burki, World Bank, Rio de Janeiro, 1997.
55. Comments by Mauricio Rubio, seminar on crime and violence organised by Inter-American Development Bank, Rio de Janeiro, March 1997.
56. This paragraph draws on a report by WOLA, an NGO based in Washington DC. 'Youth Gangs in Central America', Washington Office on Latin America, November 2006.
57. Paes Mano, Bruno, de Araújo Faria, Maryluci and Gall, Norman (2005), 'Diadema', Braudel Papers No. 26, Fernand Braudel Institute of World Economics, São Paulo.
58. *See* Fruhling, Hugo, 'Police Reform and the Process of Demcoratization', in Fruhling/Tulchin, *Crime and Violence in Latin America*, pp. 15–21.
59. Pinheiro, Paulo Sérgio, 'O passado não está morto: nem passado é ainda', in Dimenstein, Gilberto (1996), *Democracia em pedaços*, Companhia das Letras, São Paulo, pp. 27–30.
60. Author's interview with Bernardo León, former presidential adviser on police and judicial reform, Mexico City, September 2006.
61. *The Economist*, 9 December 2006.
62. 'Crime and Policing in Latin America: The Battle for Safer Streets', *The Economist*, 30 September 2004.
63. 'Drugs, War and Democracy: A Survey of Colombia', Reid, Michael, *The Economist*, 19 April 2001.
64. 'Brazil: Policing the Police', *The Economist*, 10 April 1997.

65. An Argentine judge subsequently indicted senior Iranian officials for the bombing which was widely attributed to Hizbullah.

66. 'Brazil: Protecting Citizens from Themselves', *The Economist*, 20 October 2005.

67. *Financial Times*, 17 February 2007.

68. WHO (2002), World Report on Violence and Health, p. 4.

69. This paragraph draws on Fruhling, 'Police Reform and the Process of Democratization', pp. 33–6; Braudel Institute, 'Diadema' and *The Economist*, 'Protecting Citizens from Themselves'.

70. Costa, Gino and Basombrío, Carlos (2004), *Liderazgo civil en el Ministerio del Interior*, Instituto de Estudios Peruanos, Lima.

71. Telephone interview, September 2004.

72. Sousa, Mariana, 'A Brief Overview of Judicial Reform in Latin America: Objectives, Challenges and Accomplishments', in Lora, *The State of State Reform in Latin America*, p. 95.

73. 'Brazil: The Mob Takes On the State', *The Economist*, 18 May 2006.

74. Interview with the author, Bogotá, March 1988.

75. The term 'Medellín cartel' was coined by officials at the US Drug Enforcement Administration. But it is a misnomer. A cartel is a coalition of producers acting together to restrict supply and thus drive up the price of a product (such as OPEC with oil). But the 'Medellín cartel' presided over a massive increase in the supply of cocaine to the US and a steep fall in its price.

76. Duzán, María Jimena (1994), *Death Beat: A Colombian Journalist's Life Inside the Cocaine Wars*, Harper Collins, p. 91.

77. Strong, Simon (1995), *Whitewash: Pablo Escobar and the Cocaine Wars*, Macmillan, Chapter 3.

78. Bowden, Mark (2001), *Killing Pablo*, Atlantic Books, pp. 232–65.

79. 'Legacy of Defeat in the Fight Against a Deadly Trade', Michael Reid, *The Guardian*, 14 August 1993; 'Colombia's Drugs Business: The wages of prohibition', *The Economist*, 24 December 1994.

80. Youngers, Coletta A and Rosin, Eileen (eds) (2005), *Drugs and Democracy in Latin America: The Impact of U.S. Policy*, Lynne Rienner, Boulder, Colorado, Chapter 1.

81. Interview with the author, Washington DC, September 1994.

82. Visit by the author, February 2001.

83. Interview with the author, San Vicente del Caguán, February 2001.

84. Rangel Suárez, Alfredo, 'Las FARC-EP: una mirada actual', in Deas, Malcolm and Llorente, María Victoria (eds) (1999), *Reconocer la Guerra para Construrir La Paz*, Grupo Editorial Norma, Bogotá, pp. 23–51; *see also* Pécaut, Daniel (2001), *Guerra Contra La Sociedad*, Espasa Hoy, Bogotá, pp. 39–42; and Dudley, Stephen (2004), *Walking Ghosts: Murder and Guerrilla Politics in Colombia*, Routledge, New York and London.

85. Reid, 'Drugs, War and Democracy'.

86. Interview with the author, February 2001.

87. Quoted in Reid, 'Drugs, War and Democracy'.

88. Pécaut, *Guerra Contra La Sociedad*, p. 37.

89. Interview with the author, February 2001.

90. Interview with the author, Bogotá, February 2001.

91. Interview with the author, Bogotá, May 2003.
92. Author's interview with Juan Manuel Santos, defence minister, London, February 2007.
93. Interview with the author, London, July 2005.
94. Interview with the author, Bogotá, February 2007.
95. See Ministry of Defence website, www.mindefensa.gov.co

Chapter 11

1. Visit by the author.
2. *See* Sachs, Jeffrey (2005), *The End of Poverty*, Penguin, Chapter 5.
3. Interview with the author, La Paz, July 1997.
4. 'The Andean Coca Wars: A Crop that Refuses to Die', *The Economist*, 4 March 2000.
5. Conversation with *Economist* editors, London, January 2004. I am grateful to Gonzalo Sánchez de Lozada for permission to quote from this off-the-record conversation.
6. This observation was made by Olivia Harris in a talk at Canning House, London, in February 2006.
7. Interview with the author, Cochabamba, January 2004.
8. Quoted in Huntington, Samuel P (1991), *The Third Wave: Democratization in the Late Twentieth Century*, University of Oklahoma Press, p. 6.
9. *See*, for example, Foweraker *et al.*, *Governing Latin America*, Chapter 2.
10. Dahl, Robert A (2000), *On Democracy*, Yale University Press, p. 85.
11. *See* Linz, Juan J and Stepan, Alfred (1996), *Problems of Democratic Transition and Consolidation: Southern Europe, South America and Post-Communist Europe*, Johns Hopkins University Press, Chapter 1; Philip, *Democracy in Latin America*, Chapter 1. On the importance of the state in supplying public goods, Linz and Stepan (p. 12) cite Adam Smith, who wrote of 'the [state's] duty of erecting and maintaining certain public works and certain public institutions which it can never be for the interest of any individual, or small number of individuals, to erect and maintain; because the profit could never repay the expense to any individual or small number of individuals, though it may frequently do much more than repay it to a great society.'
12. *See* Wolf, Martin (2004), *Why Globalization Works: The Case for the Global Market Economy*, Yale University Press, Chapter 3; Dahl, *On Democracy*, pp. 58–9.
13. Dahl, *On Democracy*, Chapter 14.
14. According to Huntington, the third wave began on 25 April 1974, with a coup against Portugal's dictatorship, and extended across southern Europe, Latin America, Asia and the former Soviet bloc, involving democratic transitions in 35 countries in all. Huntington sees the 'first wave' of democratisation as lasting from 1828 to 1926, and involving 33 countries, including Chile, Colombia, Argentina and Uruguay, although there were reversals to authoritarian rule in 22 of these countries in 1922–42. A second, short, wave of democratisation saw 42 countries, including Argentina, Uruguay, Bolivia, Brazil, Peru and Ecuador undergo democratic transitions in 1943–62, with reversals in 22 countries, including much

of Latin America, from 1958 to 1975. Huntington, *The Third Wave*, Chapter 1.

15. 'The Latinobarómetro Poll: Democracy's Low-level Equilibrium', *The Economist*, 12 August 2004.

16. 'The Latinobarómetro Poll: The Democracy Dividend', *The Economist*, 9 December 2006.

17. 'The Latinobarómetro Poll: Democracy's Ten-year Rut', *The Economist*, 27 October 2005. Full data is available at www.latinobarometro.org

18. Adam Przeworski defined consolidated democracy as 'when a particular set of institutions becomes the only game in town' or when 'it becomes self-reinforcing', cited in Philip, *Democracy in Latin America*, p. 7.

19. Hartlyn/Valenzuela, 'Democracy in Latin America Since 1930', p. 104.

20. Dahl, *On Democracy*, p. 119.

21. McCoy/Myers, *The Unraveling of Representative Democracy in Venezuela*.

22. Foweraker *et al.*, *Governing Latin America*, pp. 43–4.

23. Whitehead, Laurence, 'The Viability of Democracy', p. 7, in Crabtree, John and Whitehead, Laurence (eds) (2001), *Towards Democratic Viability: The Bolivian Experience*, Palgrave.

24. O'Donnell, *Contrapuntos*, p. 293.

25. The term was coined by Huntington.

26. Cardoso, Fernando Henrique, 'Una Visión del Desarrollo de America Latina y el Caribe: Avances, Retos e Instituciones', lecture at the Inter-American Development Bank, 27 February 2003, p. 4.

27. In Guatemala, the following year, Jorge Serrano tried the same tactic, but failed and was dismissed from office by Congress.

28. Two other presidents were removed from office on grounds of corruption. Fernando Collor was impeached in Brazil in 1993, and Abdalá Bucaram in Ecuador in 1997. In Collor's case, the impeachment appeared justified, while that of Pérez was more debatable. Ecuador's Congress did not bother with impeachment, simply declaring the volatile Bucaram – whose nickname was *el loco*, or the madman – 'mentally unfit'.

29. *See* Chapter 7.

30. *See* 'The United States and Venezuela: Tales from a Failed Coup', *The Economist*, 25 April 2002. A State Department spokesman denied the allegations of American involvement in the coup in a letter ('Events in Venezuela') published in *The Economist*, 16 May 2002. Otto Reich, the Assistant Secretary of State for Western Hemisphere Affairs, was reported by the *New York Times* as having summoned several Latin American ambassadors to his office to urge them to support the change of government. 'Castro's Shadow: America's man in Latin America and His Obsession', William Finnegan, *New Yorker*, 14 and 21 October 2002.

31. Foweraker *et al.*, *Governing Latin America*, pp. 47–50.

32. International Institute for Strategic Studies, *The Military Balance 2006*, London, p. 306.

33. Hartlyn/Valenzuela, 'Democracy in Latin America Since 1930', pp. 129–35.

34. Foweraker *et al.*, *Governing Latin America*, p. 127.

35. Zovatto, Daniel (2006), 'Elecciones y democracia en America Latina: Balance electoral Latinoamericano, Noviembre 2005–Diciembre 2006', draft paper, IDEA

Internacional, San José, Costa Rica.

36. *See* Chapter 8.

37. Bowen, Sally and Holligan, Jane (2003), *The Imperfect Spy: The Many Lives of Vladimiro Montesinos*, Peisa, Lima, Chapter 15.

38. 'By invitation: What Really Happened in Venezuela?', McCoy, Jennifer, *The Economist*, 4 September 2004.

39. See Castañeda, Jorge G, 'Latin America's Left Turn', *Foreign Affairs*, May–June 2006.

40. Payne, Mark J, Zovatto, Daniel, Carillo Flores, Fernando and Allamand Zavala, Andres (2003), *La Política Importa: Democracia y desarrollo en América Latina*, Banco Interamericano de Desarrollo y el Instituto Internacional para la Democracia y la Asistencia Electoral, *see* table, p. 91; 2007 figure from http://www.idea.int/americas/gender.cfm. In countries with two-chamber legislatures, the figures refer to percentages in the lower-house.

41. Programa de las Naciones Unidas para el Desarrollo (PNUD) (2004), *La Democracia en América Latina: Hacia una democracia de ciudadanas y ciudadanos*, p. 81.

42. Sabatini, Christopher, 'Latin America's Lost Illusions: Decentralisation and Political Parties, *Journal of Democracy*, Vol. 14, No. 2, April 2003, p. 139.

43. Quoted in Dahl, *On Democracy*, p. 95.

44. Mainwaring, Scott and Shugart, Matthew Soberg (eds) (1997), *Presidentialism and Democracy in Latin America*, Cambridge University Press, p. 2.

45. Power, Timothy J, 'Political Institutions in Democratic Brazil', in Kingstone/Power, *Democratic Brazil*, p. 12.

46. Author's interview with Santiago Creel, interior minister, Mexico City, May 2005.

47. Interview with the author, Lima, July 1995. *See* 'Peru: The Dark Side of the Boom', *The Economist*, 5 August 1995.

48. Hartlyn/Valenzuela, 'Democracy in Latin America Since 1930', p. 114.

49. Inter-American Development Bank, 'The Politics of Policies, Economic and Social Progress in Latin America', 2006 report, p. 37.

50. Ibid, pp. 45–56.

51. Ibid., p. 51.

52. The view comes from Sartori, quoted in Mainwaring, Scott and Scully, Timothy R (eds) (1995), *Building Democratic Institutions: Party Systems in Latin America*, Stanford University Press, p. 3.

53. Mainwaring/Scully, *Building Democratic Institutions*, p. 5.

54. Mainwaring, Scott P (1999), *Rethinking Party Systems in the Third Wave of Democratization*, Stanford University Press, p. 5.

55. 'The Disorders of Progress: A Survey of Brazil', Reid, Michael, *The Economist*, 27 March 1999, p. 8.

56. *See* Chapter 8.

57. Lamounier, *Da Independência a Lula*, p. 231.

58. Ibid., p. 242.

59. Sabatini, 'Latin America's Lost Illusions'.

60. *Veja*, 20 June 2004.

61. Di Tella, Torcuato (1998), *Los Partidos Politicos*, A–Z Editora, Buenos Aires, p. 10.

62. Van Cott, Donna Lee, 'From Exclusion to Inclusion: Bolivia's 2002 Elections', *Journal of Latin American Studies*, Vol. 35, Part 4, November 2003, pp. 752–3.
63. The comment was by Jorge Rueda, an engineer at a sugar mill, interviewed by the author at a Gaviria rally in Palmira, southern Colombia, November 1989.
64. Reid, Michael, 'The Disorders of Progress', p. 9.

Chapter 12

1. 'Nervous Mexico Prepares to Wed a Superpower', Reid, Michael, *The Guardian*, 3 July 1992.
2. Interview with the author, Tlaxcala, May 2005.
3. World Bank (2005b), p. 2.
4. Interview with the author, Monterrey, September 2006.
5. Reid, 'Time to Wake Up'.
6. *El País*, 18 April 2005.
7. Robert Cooper, chef de cabinet of Javier Solana, the EU's high representative for foreign affairs, quoted in the *Financial Times Magazine*, 1 February 2003.
8. Quoted in Bushnell/Macaulay, *The Emergence of Latin America in the Nineteenth Century*, p. 25.
9. *See* Davidow, Jeffrey (2004), *The US and Mexico: The Bear and the Porcupine*, Princeton, New Jersey, Chapter 2. Davidow was the American ambassador to Mexico from 1998 to 2001 and prior to that the Assistant Secretary of State for Western Hemisphere Affairs.
10. United Nations Office on Drugs and Crime, World Drug Report 2006, p. 95.
11. Interview with the author, Washington DC, September 2006.
12. 'South America: China to Cushion Vulnerability to US Slowdown', J P Morgan Chase Bank, Economic Research Note, 11 August 2006.
13. World Bank (2006c).
14. Figures from UNIDO quoted in World Bank (2006c), p. 6.
15. Devlin, Robert, Estevadeordal, Antoni and Rodríguez Clare, Andrés, *The Emergence of China: Opportunities and Challenges for Latin America and the Caribbean*, Inter-American Development Bank, 2006, p. xxiv.
16. Alfredo Thorne, 'Mexico's Manufacturing Comeback Since 2001 Shock', J P Morgan Research Note, 31 March 2006.
17. Aykut, Dilek and Goldstein, Andrea, 'Developing Country Multinationals: South-South Investment Comes of Age', OECD Development Centre, Working Paper No. 257, December 2006.
18. Montenegro, Santiago, 'Más allá de la violencia: fortalezas de Colombia', Departamento Nacional de Planificación, 2003.
19. World Bank (2002).
20. 'Brazilian Agriculture: The Harvesting of Nature's Bounty', *The Economist*, 3 November 2005.
21. *International Herald Tribune*, 11 April 2006.
22. World Bank (2006c), p. 6.
23. Bolívar, letter to General Juan José Flores: 'Ploughing the Sea', in *El Libertador*, pp. 145–9.

24. Alfredo Valladão, talk at Canning House, London, 2005.

25. 'Remapping South America: A Survey of Mercosur', Reid, Michael, *The Economist*, 12 October 1996.

26. Data from Argentina's foreign ministry, available at www.cei.gov.ar

27. *See*, for example, 'A Politização do Mercosul', Rubens Barbosa, *O Estado de São Paulo*, 25 July 2006; Felix Peña, an Argentine former diplomat and a leading promoter of Mercosur, noted in 2006 that the group had come to be 'viewed with scepticism' by outsiders. 'Mercosur is in a very bad state ... We can't continue like this.' (Felix Peña, Newsletter, December 2006.)

28. 'Argentina's Energy Shortages: The Laws of Economics Bite Back', *The Economist*, 22 April 2004.

29. 'Energy in South America: The Explosive Nature of Gas', *The Economist*, 9 February 2006.

30. Malamud, Carlos, 'The Obstacles to Regional Integration in Latin America', newsletter of Real Instituto Elcano, Madrid, December 2005.

31. Reuters, 12 April 2006.

32. 'Latin Allies Forge a Political Bond', *Financial Times*, 12 July 2006.

33. Shifter, Michael, 'Hugo Chávez: A Test for US Policy', Inter-American Dialogue, March 2007.

34. Ibid.

35. An extraordinary summit was held in Monterrey, Mexico, in 2003.

36. *El País*; *New York Times*; *Washington Post*; 5 November 2005.

37. Schlesinger/Kinzer, *Bitter Fruit*, p. 34.

38. Gall, Norman (2004), 'Latin America's Struggling Institutions: Is Democracy Threatened?' Braudel Papers No. 34, Fernand Braudel Institute of World Economics, São Paulo.

39. Lamounier, *Da Independência a Lula*, p. 15.

40. Montenegro, 'Más allá de la violencia'.

BIBLIOGRAPHY

Aguilar Camín, Héctor, *Después del milagro*, 16th edition, Ediciones Cal y Arena, Mexico City, 2004

Andrew, Christopher and Mitrokhin, Vasili, *The Mitrokhin Archive II: The KGB and the World*, Penguin Books, 2006

Aspe Armilla, Pedro, *El camino mexicano de la transformación económica*, Fondo de Cultura Económica, Mexico City, 1993

Basadre, Jorge, *Perú: Problema y Posibilidad*, 5th edition, Libreria Studium, Lima, 1987

Bethell, Leslie (ed.):

—— (1993a) *Argentina Since Independence*, Cambridge University Press

—— (1993b) *Chile Since Independence*, Cambridge University Press

Bethell, Leslie and Roxborough, Ian (eds), *Latin America Between the Second World War and the Cold War 1944–48*, Cambridge University Press, 1992

Biglaiser, Glen, *Guardians of the Nation? Economists, Generals and Economic Reform in Latin America*, University of Notre Dame Press, 2002

Birdsall, Nancy and de la Torre, Augusto with Menezes, Rachel, 'Washington Contentious: Economic Policies for Social Equity in Latin America', Carnegie Endowment for International Peace and Inter-American Dialogue, 2001

Blustein, Paul, *And the Money Kept Rolling In (and Out): Wall Street, the IMF and the Bankrupting of Argentina*, PublicAffairs, 2005

Bolívar, Simón, *El Libertador: Writings of Simón Bolívar*, Oxford University Press, 2003

Bonner, Raymond, *Weakness and Deceit: US Policy and El Salvador*, Hamish Hamilton, 1985

Bosworth, Barry P, Dornbusch, Rudiger and Labán, Raúl (eds), *The Chilean Economy: Policy Lessons and Challenges*, The Brookings Institution, Washington DC, 1994

Bowden, Mark, *Killing Pablo*, Atlantic Books, 2001

Bowen, Sally and Holligan, Jane, *The Imperfect Spy: The Many Lives of Vladimiro Montesinos*, Peisa, Lima, 2003

Buarque de Holanda, Sergio, *Raízes do Brasil*, 26th edition, Companhia das Letras, São Paulo, 1996

Bucheli, Marcelo, *Bananas and Business: The United Fruit Company in Colombia, 1899–2000*, New York University Press, 2005

Bulmer-Thomas, Victor, *The Economic History of Latin America Since Independence*, Cambridge University Press, 1994

Bushnell, David and Macaulay, Neill, *The Emergence of Latin America in the Nineteenth Century*, 2nd edition, Oxford University Press, 1994

Bushnell, David, *Colombia: Una Nación a Pesar de sí Misma*, 5th edition, Planeta, Bogotá, 2000

Carbonetto, Daniel *et al.*, *El Perú Heterodoxo: un modelo económico*, Instituto Nacional de Planificación, Lima, 1987

Cárdenas, Enrique, Ocampo, José Antonio and Thorp, Rosemary (eds), *An Economic History of Twentieth-Century Latin America. Vol 1: The Export Age*, Palgrave, 2000

Cardoso, Fernando Henrique and Faletto, Enzo, *Dependencia y Desarrollo en América Latina*, Siglo XXI, Argentina, 2003

Cardoso, Fernando Henrique, *A Arte da Política: A História que Vivi*, Civilização Brasileira, Rio de Janeiro, 2006

Cardoso, Fernando Henrique with Winter, Brian, *The Accidental President of Brazil: A Memoir*, PublicAffairs, 2006

Carr, Raymond (ed.), *Spain: A History*, Oxford, 2000

Castañeda, Jorge:
—— (1994) *Utopia Unarmed: The Latin American Left After the Cold War*, Vintage Books
—— (1997) *Compañero: The Life and Death of Che Guevara*, Bloomsbury

Chong, Alberto and López-de-Silanes, Florencio, *Privatization in Latin America: Myths and Reality*, World Bank and Stanford University Press, 2005

Coatsworth, John H and Williamson, Jeffrey G, 'Always Protectionist? Latin American Tariffs from Independence to Great Depression', *Journal of Latin American Studies*, Vol. 36, Part 2, May 2004

Coatsworth, John H, 'Structures, Endowments, and Institutions in the Economic History of Latin America', *Latin American Research Review*, Vol. 40, No. 3, October 2005

Conniff, Michael L (ed.):
—— (1982) *Latin American Populism in Comparative Perspective*, University of New Mexico Press, Albuquerque
—— (1999) *Populism in Latin America*, University of Alabama Press, Tuscaloosa and London

Costa, Gino and Basombrío, Carlos, *Liderazgo civil en el Ministerio del Interior*, Instituto de Estudios Peruanos, Lima, 2004

Cotler, Julio, 'Political Parties and the Problems of Democratic Consolidation in Peru', in Mainwaring, Scott and Scully, Timothy R, *Building Democratic Institutions: Party Systems in Latin America*, Stanford, 1995

Dahl, Robert A, *On Democracy*, Yale University Press, 1998

Davidow, Jeffrey, *The US and Mexico: The Bear and the Porcupine*, Princeton, New Jersey, 2004

Devlin, Robert and Giordano, Paolo, 'The Old and New Regionalism: Benefits, Costs and Implications for the FTAA', in Estevadeordal, Antoni, Rodrik, Dani, Taylor, Alan M and Velasco, Andrés, *Integrating the Americas: The FTAA and Beyond*, Harvard University Press, 2004

Dinges, John, *Our Man in Panama*, Random House, 1990

Dinges, John and Landau, Saul, *Assassination on Embassy Row*, Writers and Readers, London, 1980

Domínguez, Jorge I and McCann, James A, *Democratizing Mexico: Public Opinion and Electoral Choices*, Johns Hopkins University Press, 1996

Domínguez, Jorge I, 'US–Latin American Relations During the Cold War and Its Aftermath', in Bulmer-Thomas, Victor and Dunkerley, James (eds), *The United States and Latin America: The New Agenda*, Institute of Latin American Studies, University of London and David Rockefeller Center for Latin American Studies, Harvard University, 1999

Dornbusch, Rudiger and Edwards, Sebastian (eds), *The Macroeconomics of Populism in Latin America*, University of Chicago Press, 1991

Dudley, Stephen, *Walking Ghosts: Murder and Guerrilla Politics in Colombia*, Routledge, New York and London, 2004

Dunkerley, James:
—— (1984) *Rebellion in the Veins*, Verso
—— (1988) *Power in the Isthmus: A Political History of Modern Central America*, Verso
—— (2004) *Dreaming of Freedom in the Americas: Four Minds and a Name*, Institute for the Study of the Americas, London

Duzán, María Jimena, *Death Beat: A Colombian Journalist's Life Inside the Cocaine Wars*, Harper Collins, 1994

Edwards, Jorge, *Persona Non Grata*, Nation Books, New York, 1993

Edwards, Sebastian, *Crisis and Reform in Latin America: From Despair to Hope*, World Bank and Oxford University Press, 1995

Engerman, Stanley L and Sokoloff, Kenneth L, 'Factor Endowments, Institutions and
　　Differential Paths of Growth Among New World Economies', in Haber, Stephen (ed.),
　　How Latin America Fell Behind: Essays on the Economic Histories of Brazil and Mexico,
　　1800–1914, Stanford University Press, 1997
Fernand Braudel Institute of World Economics, São Paulo:
—— (1990) Tountoundjian, Beatriz, 'La Lucha por la Sobrevivencia en la Hiperinflación
　　Argentina', Mimeo
—— (2004) Gall, Norman, 'Latin America's Struggling Institutions: Is Democracy Threatened?',
　　Braudel Papers No. 34
—— (2005) Paes Mano, Bruno, de Araújo Faria, Maryluci and Gall, Norman, 'Diadema',
　　Braudel Papers No. 26
—— (2006) Guedes, Patricia Mota and Oliveira, Nilson Vieira, 'Democratization of
　　Consumption', Braudel Papers No. 38
Fernández-Armesto, Felipe, *The Americas: A Hemispheric History*, Random House Modern
　　Library, New York, 2003
Field, Erica and Torero, Maximo, 'Do Property Titles Increase Credit Access Among the Urban
　　Poor: Evidence from a Nationwide Titling Program', March 2006. Available at www.
　　economics.harvard.edu/faculty/field/papers
Field, Erica, 'Entitled to Work: Urban Property Rights and Labor Supply in Peru', March 2006,
　　unpublished paper
Flores Galindo, Alberto, *La Agonia de Mariátegui*, Editorial Revolución, Madrid, 1991
Foweraker, Joe, Landman, Todd and Harvey, Neil, *Governing Latin America*, Polity Press, 2003
Fruhling, Hugo, 'Police Reform and the Process of Democratization', in Fruhling, Hugo and
　　Tulchin, Joseph S (eds), *Crime and Violence in Latin America: Citizen Security, Democracy*
　　and the State, Johns Hopkins University Press, Baltimore and London, 2003
Galeano, Eduardo, *Open Veins of Latin America: Five Centuries of the Pillage of a Continent*,
　　Monthly Review Press, New York, 1997
Galiani, Sebastian and Schargrodsky, Ernesto, 'Property Rights for the Poor: Effects of Land
　　Titling', Centro de Investigación en Finanzas, Universidad Torcuato di Tella, Buenos Aires,
　　Documento de Trabajo June 2005
García Márquez, Gabriel, *Vivir para contarla*, Knopf, New York, 2002
Gaspari, Elio, *A Ditadura Envergonhada*, Companhia das Letras, São Paulo, 2002
Gerrasi, John (ed.), *Venceremos: The Speeches and Writings of Ernesto Che Guevara*, Weidenfeld
　　and Nicholson, 1968
Gillespie, Richard, *Soldiers of Perón: Argentina's Montoneros*, Oxford University Press, 1982
Gootenberg, Paul, *Between Silver and Guano: Commercial Policy and the State in*
　　Postindependence Peru, Princeton University Press, 1989
Gordon, Lincoln, *Brazil's Second Chance: En Route Toward the First World*, Brookings
　　Institution Press, 2001
Gott, Richard:
—— (2004) *Cuba: A New History*, Yale University Press
—— (2005) *Hugo Chávez and the Bolivarian Revolution*, Verso
Green, Duncan, *Silent Revolution: The Rise and Crisis of Market Economics in Latin America*,
　　Monthly Review Press, New York, and Latin American Bureau, London, 2003
Guevara, Che, *Guerrilla Warfare*, Penguin Books, 1969
Gunther, Richard, Montero, José Ramón and Botella, Joan, *Democracy in Modern Spain*, Yale
　　University Press, 2004
Haber, Stephen, 'Introduction: Economic Growth and Latin American Economic
　　Historiography', in Haber, Stephen (ed.), *How Latin America Fell Behind: Essays in the*
　　Economic Histories of Brazil and Mexico, 1800–1914, Stanford University Press, 1997
Harriss, John, Hunter, Janet and Lewis, Colin M, *The New Institutional Economics and Third*
　　World Development, Routledge, London, 1995
Hartlyn, Jonathan and Valenzuela, Arturo, 'Democracy in Latin America Since 1930', in Bethell,
　　Leslie (ed.), *The Cambridge History of Latin America*, Vol. VI, Part 2, 1994
Harvey, Robert, *Liberators: Latin America's Struggle for Independence 1810–1930*, John Murray,
　　2000

Haya de la Torre, VR, *El Antiimperialismo y el APRA*, 6th edition, APRA, Lima, 1985

Huntington, Samuel P:

—— (1991) *The Third Wave: Democratization in the Late Twentieth Century*, University of Oklahoma Press

—— (1998) *The Clash of Civilizations and the Remaking of World Order*, Touchstone Books

Inter-American Development Bank Reports on Economic and Social Progress in Latin America, Washington DC:

—— (2000) 'Development Beyond Economics'

—— (2001) 'Competitiveness: The Business of Growth'

—— (2006) 'The Politics of Policies, 2006'

Inter-American Development Bank, other publications:

—— (2006a) 'Remittances 2005: Promoting Financial Democracy'

—— (2006b) Devlin, Robert, Estevadeordal, Antoni and Rodríguez Clare, Andrés, *The Emergence of China: Opportunities and Challenges for Latin America and the Caribbean*

—— (2006c) 'Remittances as a Development Tool'

International Labour Organization, *Panorama Laboral 2006*, America Latina y el Caribe, Oficina Regional, Lima, December 2006

Jonas, Susanne, *Of Centaurs and Doves: Guatemala's Peace Process*, Westview Press, 2000

Kempe, Frederick, *Divorcing the Dictator: America's Bungled Affair with Noriega*, G P Putnam's Sons, 1990

Kingstone, Peter R and Power, Timothy J (eds), *Democratic Brazil: Actors, Institutions and Processes*, University of Pittsburgh Press, 2000

Klein, Herbert S, 'Migração Internacional na História das Americas', in Fausto, Boris (ed.), *Fazer a América: A Imigração em Massa para a América Latina*, Editora da Universidade de São Paulo, 1999

Knight, Alan, *The Mexican Revolution, Vol. 1: Porfirians, Liberals and Peasants*, University of Nebraska Press, 1990

Krauze, Enrique, *Mexico: Biography of Power: A History of Modern Mexico, 1810–1996*, Harper Collins, 1997

Kryzanek, Michael J, *US–Latin American Relations*, Praeger, 1996

Kuczynski, Pedro Pablo, *Latin American Debt*, Johns Hopkins University Press, 1988

Kuczynski, Pedro Pablo and Williamson, John (eds), *After the Washington Consensus: Restarting Growth and Reform in Latin America*, Institute for International Economics, Washington DC, 2003

La Porta, Rafael, López de Silanes, Florencio, Schleifer, Andrei and Vishny, Robert W, 'Law and Finance', National Bureau of Economic Research Working Paper 5661 and 'Legal Determinants of External Finance', NBER Working Paper 5879

Lagos, Ricardo:

—— (2003) *Conversaciones en el Camino*, Ediciones B, Santiago

—— (2005) *The 21st Century: A View from the South*, First, London

Lamounier, Bolívar, *Da Independência a Lula: dois séculos de política brasileira*, Augurium Editora, São Paulo, 2005

Landes, David, *The Wealth and Poverty of Nations*, Little, Brown, New York, 1998

Lapper, Richard, 'Living with Hugo: U.S. Policy Towards Hugo Chávez's Venezuela', Council on Foreign Relations, CSR No. 20, New York, November 2006

Larraín, Felipe and Meller, Patricio, 'The Socialist-Populist Chilean Experience', in Dornbusch, Rudiger and Edwards, Sebastian (eds), *The Macroeconomics of Populism in Latin America*, University of Chicago Press, 1991, pp. 188–9

Laviana Cuetos, María Luisa (ed.), *José Martí*, Ediciones de Cultura Hispanica, Madrid, 1988

Lehmann, David, *The Struggle for the Spirit: Religious Transformation and Popular Culture in Brazil and Latin America*, Polity Press, 1996

Lewis, Colin M, 'Public Policy and Private Initiative: Railway Building in São Paulo 1860–89', University of London, Institute of Latin American Studies Research Papers No. 26, 1991

Linz, Juan J and Stepan, Alfred, *Problems of Democratic Transition and Consolidation: Southern Europe, South America and Post-Communist Europe*, Johns Hopkins University Press, 1996

Little, Walter and Herrera, Antonio, 'Political Corruption in Venezuela', in Little, Walter and Posada-Carbó, Eduardo (eds), *Political Corruption in Europe and Latin America*, Macmillan, 1996, p. 270

López Maya, Margarita, 'The Venezuelan Caracazo of 1989: Popular Protest and Institutional Weakness', *Journal of Latin American Studies*, Vol. 35, Part 1, February 2003

Lora, Eduardo and Panizza, Ugo, 'Structural Reform in Latin American Under Scrutiny', Inter-American Development Bank Research Department paper, March 2002

Lora, Eduardo (ed.), *The State of State Reform in Latin America*, Inter-American Development Bank and Stanford University Press, 2006

Lowenthal, Abraham F (ed.), *The Peruvian Experiment: Continuity and Change Under Military Rule*, Princeton University Press, 1975

Lustig, Nora (ed.), *Coping with Austerity: Poverty and Inequality in Latin America*, Brookings Institution, 1995

Lynch, John:
—— (1986) *The Spanish American Revolutions 1808–1826*, 2nd edition, WW Norton & Company, New York
—— (2001) *Argentine Caudillo: Juan Manuel de Rosas*, Scholarly Resources, Wilmington, Delaware
—— (2006) *Simón Bolívar: A Life*, Yale University Press

McCoy, Jennifer L and Myers, David J (eds), *The Unraveling of Representative Democracy in Venezuela*, Johns Hopkins University Press, 2004

McCullough, David, *The Path Between the Seas: The Creation of the Panama Canal, 1870–1914*, Simon & Schuster, 1977

McGuire, James W, *Peronism Without Perón: Unions, Parties and Democracy in Argentina*, Stanford University Press, 1997

Maddison, Angus *et al.*, *The Political Economy of Poverty, Equity and Growth: Brazil and Mexico*, The World Bank and Oxford University Press, 1992

Maddison, Angus, *The World Economy: A Millennial Perspective*, OECD, 1998

Mainwaring, Scott and Scully, Timothy R (eds), *Building Democratic Institutions: Party Systems in Latin America*, Stanford University Press, 1995

Mainwaring, Scott and Shugart, Matthew Soberg (eds), *Presidentialism and Democracy in Latin America*, Cambridge University Press, 1997

Mainwaring, Scott P, *Rethinking Party Systems in the Third Wave of Democratization*, Stanford University Press, 1999

Marcano, Cristina and Barrera Tyszka, Alberto, *Hugo Chávez Sin Uniforme: Una Historia Personal*, Debate, Caracas, 2005

Mariátegui, José Carlos, *Siete Ensayos de Interpretación de la Realidad Peruana*, 13th edition, Amauta, Lima, 1968

Marichal, Carlos (coordinador), *Las inversiones extranjeras en América Latina, 1850–1930*, Fondo de Cultura Economica, Mexico, 1995

Marx, Anthony W, *Making Race and Nation: A Comparison of the United States, South Africa and Brazil*, Cambridge University Press, 1998

Matos Mar, José and Mejía, José Manuel, *La Reforma Agraria en el Perú*, Instituto de Estudios Peruanos, 1980

Matos Mar, José, *Desborde Popular y Crisis del Estado: Veinte Años Después*, Fondo Editorial del Congreso del Perú, Lima, 2004

Maxwell, Kenneth, 'Why Was Brazil Different?', in *Naked Tropics: Essays on Empire and Other Rogues*, Routledge, New York and London, 2003

Mesa-Lago, Carmelo, *Market, Socialist and Mixed Economies: Comparative Policy and Peformance – Chile, Cuba and Costa Rica*, Johns Hopkins University Press, 2000

Middlebrook, Kevin J, *Dilemmas of Political Change in Mexico*, Institute of Latin American Studies, London, and Center for US–Mexican Studies, San Diego, 2004

Morrison, Andrew, Buvinic, Mayra and Shifter, Michael, 'The Violent Americas: Risk Factors, Consequences, and Policy Implications of Social and Domestic Violence', in Fruhling, Hugo and Tulchin, Joseph S, *Crime and Violence in Latin America: Citizen Security, Democracy and the State*, Johns Hopkins University Press, Baltimore and London, 2003

Moseley, Michael E, *The Incas and Their Ancestors*, Thames and Hudson, London, 2001

Mussa, Michael, *Argentina and the Fund: From Triumph to Tragedy*, Institute for International Economics, Washington DC, 2002

Naím, Moisés, *Paper Tigers and Minotaurs: The Politics of Venezuela's Economic Reforms*, Carnegie Endowment for International Peace, 1993

National Research Council, *Cities Transformed: Demographic Change and Its Implications in the Developing World*, National Academies Press, Washington DC, 2003

Nellis, John, Menezes, Rachel and Lucas, Sarah, 'Privatization in Latin America', Center for Global Development and Inter-American Dialogue Policy Brief, Washington DC, January 2004, Vol. 3, Issue 1

Nellis, John and Birdsall, Nancy (eds), *Reality Check: The Distributional Impact of Privatization in Developing Countries*, Center for Global Development, Washington DC, 2005

Ocampo, José Antonio, *Reconstruir el futuro: Globalización, desarrollo y democracia en América Latina*, Editorial Norma, Bogotá, 2004

O'Donnell, Guillermo, *Contrapuntos: Ensayos escogidos sobre autoritarismo y democratización*, Paidós, Buenos Aires, 1997

OECD: Mexico, OECD Economic Surveys, Vol. 2005/18, November 2005

Oppenheimer, Andres, *Castro's Final Hour: The Secret Story Behind the Coming Downfall of Communist Cuba*, Simon & Schuster, 1992

Palma, Pedro A, 'La Economía Venezolana en el Quinquenio 1994–1998: de una crisis a otra', *Nueva Economía*, Año VIII, No. 12, April 1999, Caracas

Pan-American Health Organization, Mortality Indicators, available at www.paho.org

della Paolera, Gerardo and Taylor, Alan M:
—— (2001) *Straining at the Anchor: The Argentine Currency Board and the Search for Macroeconomic Stability, 1880–1935*, University of Chicago Press
—— (2003) *A New Economic History of Argentina*, Cambridge University Press, 2003

Parry, J H, Sherlock, Philip and Maingot, Anthony, *A Short History of the West Indies*, 4th edition, Macmillan, 1987

Payne, Mark J, Zovatto, Daniel, Carillo Flores, Fernando and Allamand Zavala, Andres, *La Política Importa: Democracia y desarrollo en América Latina*, Banco Interamericano de Desarrollo y el Instituto Internacional para la Democracia y la Asistencia Electoral, 2003, Chapter 3

Paz, Octavio, *The Labyrinth of Solitude and Other Writings*, Grove Press, 1985

Pécaut, Daniel, *Guerra Contra La Sociedad*, Espasa Hoy, Bogotá, 2001

Peet, John, 'Priceless: A Survey of Water', *The Economist*, 19 July 2003

Pérez, Louis A, *Cuba Between Reform and Revolution*, Oxford University Press, 1988

Pérez-Stabile, Marifeli, *The Cuban Revolution: Origins, Course and Legacy*, Oxford University Press, 1993

Philip, George, *Democracy in Latin America*, Polity, 2003

Pike, Frederick B, *The Modern History of Peru*, Praeger, 1969

Pinheiro, Paulo Sérgio, 'O passado não está morto: nem passado é ainda', in Dimenstein, Gilberto, *Democracia em pedaços*, Companhia das Letras, São Paulo, 1996

Platt, D C M, *Latin America and British Trade 1806–1914*, A & C Black, London, 1972

Poniatowska, Elena, *La noche de Tlatelolco*, Ediciones Era, Mexico City, 1992

Posada Carbó, Eduardo, 'La historia y los falsos recuerdos', *Revista de Occidente*, Madrid, December 2003

Prats González, Carlos, *Memorias: Testimonio de un Soldado*, Pehuén Editores, 1985

PREAL, 'Quantity Without Quality: A Report Card on Education in Latin America, Partnership for Educational Revitalisation in Latin America', Washington DC, 2005

Preston, Julia and Dillon, Samuel, *Opening Mexico: The Making of a Democracy*, Farrar, Strauss and Giroux, 2005

Przeworski, Adam with Curvale, Carolina, 'Does politics explain the economic gap between the United States and Latin America?', www.nyu.edu/gsas/dept/politics/faculty/przeworski/papers

Raffo, Emma, *Vivir en Huáscar: Mujer y Estrategias de Sobrevivencia*, Fundación Friedrich Ebert, Lima, 1985

Rajapatirana, Sarath, *Trade Policies in Latin America and the Caribbean: Priorities, Progress and Prospects*, International Center for Economic Growth, Santiago and San Francisco, 1997

Rangel Suárez, Alfredo, 'Las FARC-EP: una mirada actual', in Deas, Malcolm and Llorente, María Victoria (eds), *Reconocer la Guerra para Construir La Paz*, Grupo Editorial Norma, Bogotá, 1999

Reid, Michael:

—— 'Remapping South America: A Survey of Mercosur', *The Economist*, 12 October 1996

—— 'Back on the Pitch: A Survey of Business in Latin America', *The Economist*, 6 December 1997

—— 'The Disorders of Progress: A Survey of Brazil', *The Economist*, 27 March 1999

—— 'Drugs, War and Democracy: A Survey of Colombia', *The Economist*, 19 April 2001

—— 'The Long Road Back: A Survey of Argentina', *The Economist*, 5 June 2004

—— 'Time to Wake Up: A Survey of Mexico', *The Economist*, 18 November 2006

Riding, Alan, *Distant Neighbors: A Portrait of the Mexicans*, Knopf, 1985

Rock, David:

—— (1987) *Argentina 1516–1987: From Spanish Colonization to Alfonsín*, University of California Press

—— (1993), 'Argentina in 1914', in Bethell, Leslie (ed.), *Argentina Since Independence*, Cambridge University Press

Rodó, José Enrique, *Ariel*, Kapelusz Editora, Buenos Aires, 1994

Rodrik, Dani, Subramanian, Arvind and Trebbi, Francesco, 'Institutions Rule: The Primacy of Institutions over Geography and Integration in Economic Development', revised October 2002, http://ksghome.harvard.edu/drodrik

Rouquié, Alain:

—— (1987) *The Military and the State in Latin America*, University of California Press

—— (1997) *América Latina: Introducción al Extreme Occidente*, 4th edition (in Spanish), Siglo XXI Editores, Mexico

Rubio, Luis and Kaufman Purcell, Susan, *Mexico Under Zedillo*, Lynne Rienner, Boulder, Colorado, 1998

Sabatini, Christopher, 'Latin America's Lost Illusions: Decentralization and Political Parties', *Journal of Democracy*, Vol. 14, No. 2, April 2003

Sachs, Jeffrey, *The End of Poverty*, Penguin, 2005

SalmonChile, *La Acuicultura en Chile*, TechnoPress SA, Santiago, undated

Santiso, Javier, *Latin America's Political Economy of the Possible: Beyond Good Revolutionaries and Free Marketeers*, MIT Press, 2006

São Paulo Justice and Peace Commission, *São Paulo Growth and Poverty*, The Bowerdean Press in association with the Catholic Institute for International Relations, 1978

Sarmiento, Domingo F, *Facundo: or, Civilization and Barbarism*, Penguin Classics, London, 1998

Schlesinger, Stephen and Kinzer, Stephen, *Bitter Fruit: The Untold Story of the American Coup in Guatemala*, Sinclair Browne, London, 1982

Shifter, Michael, *Hugo Chávez: A Test for U.S. Policy*, Inter-American Dialogue, Washington DC, 2007

Shumway, Nicolas, *The Invention of Argentina*, University of California Press, 1993

Sieder, Rachel (ed.), *Multiculturalism in Latin America: Indigenous Rights, Diversity and Democracy*, Palgrave, 2002

Skidmore, Thomas E:

—— (1967) *Politics in Brazil 1930–1964*, Oxford University Press

—— (1999) *Brazil: Five Centuries of Change*, Oxford University Press

Skidmore, Thomas and Smith, Peter H, *Modern Latin America*, 4th edition, Oxford University Press, 1997

Smith, Joseph, *The Spanish-American War*, Longman, 1994

Smith, Peter H, *Talons of the Eagle: Dynamics of US-Latin American Relations*, Oxford University Press, 1996

Smith, Robert Freeman, 'Latin America, the United States and the European Powers 1830–1930', in Bethell, Leslie (ed.), *Cambridge History of Latin America, Vol. IV, c.1870–1930*, Cambridge University Press, 1986

Sola, Lourdes and Whitehead, Laurence, *Statecrafting Monetary Authority: Democracy and Financial Order in Brazil*, Centre for Brazilian Studies, University of Oxford, 2006

de Soto, Hernando:

—— (1986) *El Otro Sendero*, Editorial El Barranco, Lima

—— (2001) *The Mystery of Capital*, Black Swan Books, London

Stiglitz, Joseph E, *Globalization and Its Discontents*, W W Norton, New York and London, 2002

Streeter, Stephen M, 'Interpreting the 1954 US Intervention in Guatemala: Realist, Revisionist and Postrevisionist Perspectives', *The History Teacher*, Vol. 34, No. 1, November 2000

Strong, Simon, *Whitewash: Pablo Escobar and the Cocaine Wars*, Macmillan, 1995

Sweig, Julia E, *Inside the Cuban Revolution: Fidel Castro and the Urban Underground*, Harvard University Press, 2002

Szulc, Tad, *Fidel: A Critical Portrait*, Avon Books, 1986

Taylor, Lance (ed.), *After Neoliberalism: What Next for Latin America?*, University of Michigan Press, 1999

di Tella, Torcuato, *Los Partidos Politicos*, A–Z Editora, Buenos Aires, 1998

Tendler, Judith, *Good Government in the Tropics*, Johns Hopkins University Press, Baltimore and London, 1997

Thomas, Hugh:

—— (1971) *Cuba or The Pursuit of Freedom*, Eyre & Spotiswoode

—— (1993) *The Conquest of Mexico*, Pimlico

Thorp, Rosemary, *Progress, Poverty and Exclusion: An Economic History of Latin America in the 20th Century*, Inter-American Development Bank, 1998

Thorp, Rosemary and Bertram, Geoffrey, *Peru 1890–1977: Growth and Policy in an Open Economy*, Macmillan, 1978

Torre, Juan Carlos and de Riz, Liliana, 'Argentina Since 1946', in Bethell, Leslie (ed.), *Argentina Since Independence*, Cambridge University Press, 1993

Torres, Gerver, *Un Sueño para Venezuela*, Banco Venezolano de Credito, 2001

UNDP, *La Democracia en América Latina: hacia una democracia de ciudadanas y ciudadanos*, UNDP, New York, 2004

United Nations Economic Commission for Latin America (ECLAC/CEPAL), Santiago, Chile:

—— Economic Survey of Latin America and the Caribbean, various years

—— Social Panorama of Latin America, various years

—— Preliminary Balance of the Economies of Latin America and the Caribbean, various years

UNESCO, Regional Overview: Latin America and the Caribbean, Education for All, Global Monitoring Report, 2006

Van Cott, Donna Lee, 'From Exclusion to Inclusion: Bolivia's 2002 Elections', *Journal of Latin American Studies*, Vol. 35, Part 4, November 2003

Vargas Llosa, Álvaro, *Liberty for Latin America*, Farrar, Strauss and Giroux, New York, 2005

Vargas Llosa, Mario, *La Utopía Arcaica: José María Arguedas y Las Ficciones del Indigenismo*, Fondo de Cultura Económica, Mexico, 1996

Véganzones, Marie-Ange with Winograd, Carlos, *Argentina in the 20th Century: An Account of Long-Awaited Growth*, OECD, 1997

Véliz, Claudio, *The New World of the Gothic Fox: Culture and Economy in English and Spanish America*, University of California Press, 1994

Walker, Charles F, *Smoldering Ashes: Cuzco and the Creation of Republican Peru, 1780–1840*, Duke University Press, 1999

Washington Office on Latin America (WOLA), 'Youth Gangs in Central America', November 2006

Weber, Max, *Economy and Society*, Vol. 1, University of California Press, 1978

White, Alastair, *El Salvador: Nation of the Modern World*, Ernest Benn Ltd, 1973

Whitehead, Laurence:
—— (1994) 'State Organisations in Latin America Since 1930', in Bethell, Leslie (ed.), *The Cambridge History of Latin America*, Vol. VI, Part 2, Cambridge University Press
—— (2001) 'The Viability of Democracy', in Crabtree, John and Whitehead, Laurence (eds), *Towards Democratic Viability: The Bolivian Experience*, Palgrave
Wiarda, Howard, *The Soul of Latin America: The Cultural and Political Tradition*, Yale University Press, 2001
Wilcken, Patrick, *Empire Adrift: The Portuguese Court in Rio 1808–1821*, Bloomsbury, London, 2004
Williamson, John, 'A Short History of the Washington Consensus', 2004, www.iie.com/jwilliamson.html
Wilson, Dominic and Purushothaman, Roopa, 'Dealing with BRICS', Goldman Sachs Global Economics Paper No. 99, 1 October 2003
Wise, Carol and Roett, Riordan (eds), *Exchange Rate Politics in Latin America*, Brookings Institution, 2000
Wolf, Martin, *Why Globalization Works: The Case for the Global Market Economy*, Yale University Press, 2004
Wolff, Laurence and de Mora Castro, Claudio, 'Education and Training: The Task Ahead', in Kuczynski, Pedro-Pablo and Williamson, John, *After the Washington Consensus*, 2003
World Bank, Latin America and Caribbean Department, Washington DC:
—— (1994) Psacharopolous, George and Patrinos, Harry (eds), *Indigenous People in Latin America*,
—— (1998) Burki, Shahid Javed and Perry, Guillermo E, *Beyond the Washington Consensus: Institutions Matter*
—— (2001) Guigale, Marcelo M, Lafourcade, Olivier and Nguyen, Vinh H, *Mexico: A Comprehensive Development Agenda for the New Era*
—— (2002) de Ferranti, David, Perry, Guillermo E, Lederman, Daniel and Maloney, William F, *From Natural Resources to the Knowledge Economy: Trade and Job Quality*
—— (2003) de Ferranti, David, Perry, Guillermo E *et al.*, *Closing the Gap in Education and Technology*
—— (2004) de Ferranti, David, Perry, Guillermo E, Ferreira, Francisco H G and Walton, Michael, *Inequality in Latin America: Breaking with History?*
—— (2005a) de Ferranti, David, Perry, Guillermo E, Lederman, Daniel, Foster, William and Valdés, Alberto, *Beyond the City: The Rural Contribution to Development*
—— (2005b) Lederman, Daniel, Maloney, William F and Servén, Luis, *Lessons from NAFTA for Latin America and the Caribbean*
—— (2006a) Perry, Guillermo E, Arias, Omar S, López, J Humberto, Maloney, William F and Servén, Luis, *Poverty Reduction and Growth: Virtuous and Vicious Circles*
—— (2006b) *Perú: La Oportunidad de un País Diferente*
—— (2006c) *Latin America and the Caribbean Response to the growth of China and India: Overview of Research Findings and Policy Implications* (draft version), Office of the Chief Economist, Latin America and Caribbean Region
—— (2006d) Fajnzylber, Pablo and Lopez, J Humberto, *Close to Home: The Development Impact of Remittances in Latin America*
—— (2006e) Thomas, Vinod, *From Inside Brazil: Development in a Land of Contrasts*, Conference Edition
World Health Organization, World Report on Violence and Health, 2002, summary
Yashar, Deborah J, *Contesting Citizenship: The Rise of Indigenous Movements and the Postliberal Challenge*, Cambridge University Press, 2005
Youngers, Coletta A and Rosin, Eileen (eds), *Drugs and Democracy in Latin America: The Impact of U.S. Policy*, Lynne Rienner, Boulder, Colorado, 2005

INDEX